PRIME LIVING LOCATIONS IN JAPAN

D0367024

CHINA

RUSSIA

HOKKAIDO

Akon National Park

Obihiro

Kushiro

HOKKAIDŌ
北海道

Sapporo

Hakodate

Aomori

Hachinohe

Akita

Sea of Japan

Morioka

JAPAN
日本

Sendai

Fukushima

Niigata

THE CENTRAL MOUNTAINS

Nagano

Maebashi

Kanazawa

Matsumoto

Takasaki

TŌKYŌ

Chiba

Yokohama

Kamakura

KANSAI

Nagoya

SETO INLAND SEA

Kyōto

TOKYO

Kōbe

Hiroshima

Osaka

HONSHŪ
本州

Takamatsu

Fūkuoka

Matsuyama

Tokushima

Beppu

Kōchi

SHIKOKU
四国

Nagasaki

KYUSHU

PACIFIC

OCEAN

Kagoshima

KYŪSHŪ
九州

East China Sea

0   100 mi

0   100 km

© AVALON TRAVEL

Contents

At Home in Japan

It's easy to fall in love with the sheer beauty of Japan—rugged mountains and coast, subtle changing of seasons, carefully practiced ancient arts, intriguing cuisine, and, of course, the people. From the cold and snowy north to balmy southern islands, you're never far from volcanoes, hot springs, and the sea. An efficient transportation network makes traveling a pleasure by train, airplane, bus, ferry, or bicycle. You can ski the Japan Alps, stay in a temple in Kyoto, hike the 88 temple pilgrimage in Shikoku, visit pottery villages in Kyushu, and swim Okinawa's coral seas. During my 25 years in Japan, I have photographed wildflowers on northernmost Rebun Island in view of Russia's Sakhalin Island, watched salmon spawn in rushing rivers, cycled over steaming volcanoes, and climbed 12,388-foot Mount Fuji to watch the sun rise over the Pacific.

But Japan in the 21st century is also a modern consumer society with every convenience yen can buy. As a first-time visitor, judging by the fast food, fashions, and fads, you may think Japan completely Westernized. You might wonder, "Where are the kimonos, samurai, and geisha?" The fact is, contemporary Japanese culture is a comfortable, seamless blend of wa (Japanese), yo (Western), and other cultural influences. This is not surprising if you consider that Japanese have been eating pan (bread) and castella (sponge cake) since Portuguese ships landed in 1543, and playing baseball with a passion since it was introduced by an American teacher in 1871. Even their writing system combines Chinese kanji characters, Japanese kana symbols, and the Latin alphabet.

In Japan you can wear your hair black or bleached blond, wear jeans

LIVING ABROAD IN
JAPAN

RUTHY KANAGY

or *yukata* (cotton kimono), sip a latte or *matcha* (powdered green tea), eat French pastries, Chinese noodles, or squid pizza. You can play golf or practice *kendo* (fencing), go to the opera or Kabuki (traditional theater), and watch the Giants or *sumo* from your sofa or *tatami* mats. After a day of hiking or snowboarding, you can soak in a *rotenburo* (outdoor spa) and collapse onto your futon or bed.

Whether you plan to study, teach, seek a corporate job, or start your own business, unlike a passing tourist you will have time to delve deeply into your areas of interest. You can observe how Japanese traditions and history are reflected in daily life, how family and respect for others are cultivated, how teamwork is valued from preschool to adulthood, and how persistence and *gambaru* (trying hard) are often emphasized over innate ability.

With so many choices, how do you choose where to live? Urban or rural, mountains or coast, traditional or high-tech, north or south? In my case, eastern Hokkaido was where I formed my identity, in a small town among dairy farms, my missionary parents and siblings the only Americans around. In my teens, I moved to Sapporo, Hokkaido's capital, and then Tokyo, to attend American schools. As an adult I returned to Hokkaido to teach at a university and, more recently, went back to Tokyo for three years to research Japanese education. While I love Tokyo's fast pace and infinite choices for restaurants, shops, movies, museums, parks, and rivers, the mountains and plains of Hokkaido are still my *kokoro no furusato* (home of the heart).

▶ WHAT I LOVE ABOUT JAPAN

- Nadeshiko Japan, the women's national soccer team, winning the 2011 World Cup and galvanizing the country.
- That ramen noodle shops have distinctive flavors in each region.
- The *Astro Boy* melody from the '60s at Takada-no-baba station in Tokyo, which signals the closing train doors.
- Trains arriving on time—and during rush hour, conductors helping to push people on.
- Food carts on long-distance trains, which offer coffee, boxed lunches, and frozen *mikan* (mandarin oranges) in summer.
- That political campaigns last only two weeks—by law.
- *Omoiyari*—people who put the welfare of others before their own comfort.
- The hearty *"Irasshaimase"* and *"Arigatoo gozaimasu"* by the entire staff to welcome customers in banks, stores, restaurants, and hotels.
- Quiet gardens and parks, where grandparents walk with their grandchildren.
- Sinking into an outdoor *onsen* (hot springs) and gazing up at snow-covered mountains.
- Sipping *matcha* (powdered green tea) and nibbling on a sweet in a Japanese garden.
- That *konbini* (convenience stores) are truly convenient, with 10 kinds of salads, 20 kinds of *onigiri* (rice balls), and 30 kinds of entrées.
- Vending machines everywhere with hot and cold drinks, corn soup, sake, and beer.
- Half-off sushi, sashimi, and deli items, 30 minutes before closing at supermarkets.
- Temple bells ringing in the New Year with 108 gongs, along with sweet *amazake* to drink.

WELCOME TO JAPAN

INTRODUCTION

The appeal of living in a different country—as opposed to being a tourist—is that you can go beyond fascination with cultural differences and perceived mystique. Although some Japanese may befriend you only because of your exotic allure or to practice English, many have traveled or lived abroad and are internationally minded.

An American woman who spent a year in Japan says, "I went to Japan because I wanted to live abroad and was interested in the country. It seemed like an easy transition—from the West to the Westernized east—and in some ways it was. I also was attracted to Japan's safety, as I took my then-two-year-old with me. I taught in two international preschools. Unfortunately, I didn't have much time to study Japanese—plus I wasn't truly immersed, being surrounded by people who wanted me to speak English with them!"

Is there a down side to life in Japan? Certainly; this is true in every culture. If you've never known what it's like to be a minority member, you may go through a transitional period, even culture shock. You will be labeled *gaijin,* "outside person," one of two million in Japan. Like it or not, your face will lead the way; you can never be anonymous. Staring is not so overt in cities, but in outlying regions you may end up playing Pied Piper to a parade of giggling children. On the other hand, if you are Asian you may find yourself disappearing into the crowd for the first time.

© LUCIAN MILASAN/WWW.123RF.COM

aerial view of Japan's capital city, seen from the Tokyo Metropolitan Government Building

The language barrier should not be underestimated. Written Japanese utilizes about 2,000 *kanji* characters plus 46 *kana* syllables. Although signs in airports and train stations often display *romaji*, or alphabetic transcription, for the benefit of visitors, most signs, newspapers, magazines, menus, maps, and train schedules will be indecipherable if you can't read Japanese. Having to ask for help translating rental contracts, utility bills, doctor's prescriptions, job applications, and the like—indeed, being illiterate—can be demoralizing. And although English is taught in schools, Japanese people are often hesitant to try out their English with you. You may miss not having anyone to chat with.

The housing search will also take a bit of patience. Unfortunately, there are landlords who specify "no foreigners." Help Wanted ads frequently specify age, gender, nationality, and language ability, and require a photo.

But there are benefits to being from another planet—uh, country. You may be excused for not knowing the proper way to bow or remove your shoes. And spoken Japanese is not so difficult if you have a good ear and good materials. Japan is one of the safest countries in the world, and people are helpful if you get lost. If you encounter roadblocks, learn to laugh at yourself and laugh with others.

The Lay of the Land

According to legend, the islands of Japan were created by the sun goddess millennia ago—a string of volcanoes rose from the sea like jewels, ringed by myriad droplets. In Japanese world maps, Japan is naturally positioned at the center, with the Pacific Ocean and the Americas to the east and Asia, Africa, and Europe to the west. Japanese call their country "Nihon" or "Nippon" and write it with these two characters, 日本, meaning "sun" and "source," respectively. Koreans call their neighbor "Il-bon," English-speakers say "Japan," and the French refer to it as "Japon." Many people are surprised to learn that Japan is slightly larger than New Zealand, the United Kingdom, Italy, Finland, and Malaysia.

Perched at the western edge of the Pacific Ocean, Japan's closest neighbors are Korea, China, and Russia. In just a couple of hours, you can be in Seoul, Beijing, Taipei, or Hong Kong; Singapore, Bangkok, Manila, and Jakarta are equally accessible. If your destination is down under to Australia or New Zealand, there's no jet lag, because you stay in a time zone similar to Japan's.

With land area roughly the size of California, Japan is home to 126 million people. Four main islands and 3,000 smaller islands stretch almost 3,000 kilometers (1,850 miles) from north to south, the distance from Maine to Florida. Almost 80 percent of the land is mountainous, with 15 percent agricultural land, 3 percent residential, and 0.4 percent industrial.

Hokkaido, the frontier island to the north, is strikingly similar to the United States' Pacific Northwest in geography and climate, with cool summers, snowy winters, open spaces, and unspoiled nature. The Tohoku (northeast) region of the main island of Honshu has cold and snowy winters and relatively hot summers.

The Pacific seaboard of central Honshu, from Tokyo to Osaka and Kobe, has the highest concentration of population and industry in all Japan. Nearly one out of four Japanese lives in the Kanto region, the great plain surrounding Tokyo. Tokyo, which means "eastern capital," is a megalopolis situated at the same latitude as Las Vegas and Atlanta, with equally hot (and humid) summers and cold winters. Tokyo is 8,740 kilometers (5,431 miles) from Los Angeles, 9,560 kilometers (5,941 miles) from London, and 1,770 kilometers (1,100 miles) from Shanghai.

Traveling northwest from Tokyo over the central mountains to the Sea of Japan, you will find a more traditional, rice-growing region less touched by urbanization—at least before the bullet train tunneled through the mountains. Shikoku and Kyushu, the islands south and west of Honshu, have major cities and industries, but still maintain an agricultural base. Okinawa is semitropical and has a distinct culture and language in addition to standard Japanese; it is also the site of the largest U.S. military installations in Japan. Ishigaki city has the same latitude as Honolulu.

COUNTRY DIVISIONS

Japan is divided into eight regions that represent historical boundaries and present administrative divisions. From north to south they are Hokkaido, Tohoku (northeast), Kanto (east), Chubu (central), Kinki (west-central), Chugoku (west), Shikoku, and Kyushu. There are 47 *ken,* or prefectures, including Metropolitan Tokyo-*to,* Osaka-*fu,*

COMPARING JAPAN TO THE UNITED STATES

Age Structure
- Japan: 0-14 years 13.1 percent; 15-64 years 64 percent; 65+ years 22.9 percent; median age 44.8 years
- United States: 0-14 years, 20.1 percent; 15-64 years, 66.8 percent; 65+ years, 13.1 percent; median age 36.9 years

Arable Land
- Japan: 11.6 percent
- United States: 20 percent

Birth Rate
- Japan: 8.4 births/1,000 population
- United States: 13.68 births/1,000 population

Climate
- Japan: Cool temperate north to tropical south
- United States: Mostly temperate, also tropical, arctic, and arid

Coastline
- Japan: 29,751 kilometers
- United States: 19,924 kilometers

Ethnic Groups
- Japan: Japanese 98.5 percent; Korean 0.5 percent; Chinese 0.4 percent; Other (Ainu, Brazilian, Filipino, etc.) 0.7 percent
- United States: Anglo 77 percent; African-American 13 percent; Asian 4.2 percent; Alaska native 1.5 percent; Hawaiian, Pacific Islander 0.3 percent; Other 4 percent

Fiscal Year
- Japan: April 1 to March 31
- United States: October 1 to September 31

Gross Domestic Product (GDP)
- Japan: $5.855 trillion
- United States: $15.06 trillion

GDP per Capita
- Japan: $42,800
- United States: $47,600

Government Type
- Japan: Parliamentary government with constitutional monarch
- United States: Constitution-based federal republic

Gun-Related Deaths/Year
- Japan: 94
- United States: 31,347*

Infant Mortality
- Japan: 2.2 deaths/1,000 live births
- United States: 5.98 deaths/1,000 live births

Landmass
- Japan: 377,835 square kilometers
- United States: 9.6 million square kilometers

Life Expectancy
- Japan: 84 years
- United States: 78.5 years

Literacy
- Japan: 99 percent
- United States: 97 percent

Natural Resources
- Japan: Negligible minerals, fish
- United States: Coal, copper, lead, molybdenum, phosphates, uranium, bauxite, gold, iron, mercury, nickel, etc.

Obesity
- Japan: 3.1 percent
- United States: 33.9 percent

Oil Consumption
- Japan: 4.452 million barrels/day
- United States: 19.15 million barrels/day

Population
- Japan: 127 million
- United States: 313 million

Religion
- Japan: Shinto 84 percent; Buddhist 71 percent; Other 15 percent (1 percent Christian)
- United States: Protestant 52 percent; Catholic 24 percent; Jewish 1.7 percent; Muslim 1 percent; Other 19 percent

School Year
- Japan: April to March
- United States: September to June

Unemployment Rate
- Japan: 4.6 percent
- United States: 8.3 percent

Source: *The World Fact Book* (www.cia.gov/library/publications/the-world-factbook/index.html)

*CDC National Center for Health Statistics mortality report online, 2010

TEMPERATURE AND PRECIPITATION

Naha

- Yearly Average Temperature: 22.3°C/72.1°F
- January Average: 14°C/57.2°F
- August Average: 30°C/86°F
- Annual Rainfall: 2,037 millimeters/80.2 inches

Niigata

- Yearly Average Temperature: 13.2°C/55.8°F
- January Average: 2°C/35.6°F
- August Average: 28°C/82.4°F
- Annual Rainfall: 1,778 millimeters/70 inches

Sapporo

- Yearly Average Temperature: 8.2°C/46.8°F
- January Average: -6°C/21.2°F
- August Average: 22°C/71.6°F
- Annual Rainfall: 1,130 millimeters/44.5 inches

Tokyo

- Yearly Average Temperature: 15.6°C/60.1°F
- January Average: 5°C/41°F
- August Average: 30°C/86°F
- Annual Rainfall: 1,490 millimeters/58.7 inches

Source: Tokyo Meteorological Agency

and Kyoto-*fu*. Each prefecture has a *chiji* (governor) and is divided into *gun* (counties), *shi* (cities), *cho* (towns), and *mura* (villages).

Tokyo is the geographic, political, economic, and educational center of Japan—imagine Los Angeles, Chicago, New York, and Washington, D.C., merged into a megalopolis. The central government has much more control over prefectures than in the United States, where states have considerable power with respect to the federal government. The highest concentration of people is in Tokyo (population 12.8 million), where almost 6,000 people squeeze into each square kilometer. If you want more breathing room, you might want to head north. Hokkaido has just 5.6 million residents in an area the size of the state of Indiana, which works out to 68 people per square kilometer.

CLIMATE

Japan's climate ranges from subarctic to subtropical. Hokkaido has cool summers and very cold winters, similar to Alaska. Honshu, Shikoku, and Kyushu have relatively cold winters and hot, muggy summers. Okinawa is subtropical, with an aqua sea, flowers, palm trees, and sugar cane year-round. Japan has four distinct seasons—a fact pointed out to me by many Japanese as being "unique." (In reply, I mention the changing seasons and spectacular fall colors in New England and other parts of the United States.)

Most areas of Japan south of Hokkaido have *tsuyu*, or rainy season, lasting from late May to July. The rains begin in Okinawa and reach Tokyo in mid-June. Hot and very humid weather follows the rains. From summer to late fall, typhoons formed in the Pacific head northward toward Korea and Japan. They may cause extensive flooding, landslides, and wind damage to ripening rice crops. *Taifu*, as they're called in Japanese,

EARTHQUAKE SAFETY

広域避難地
Large Refuge Area

大仙公園
Daisen Park

地震で最も恐ろしいのは火災です
地震がおこってもあわてず
まず火の始末に
心がけましょう

堺市 SAKAI CITY

© RUTHY KANAGY

WAYS TO PREPARE FOR AN EARTHQUAKE

- Secure furniture so it can't fall over or fall down.
- Confirm the strength of your house and walls.
- Always be ready to extinguish fires.
- Prepare emergency supplies in advance.
- Discuss emergency planning with your family.
- Know potential hazards in your area.

TIPS DURING AN EARTHQUAKE

- Check all fire sources. Put out fires quickly.
- Remain calm. Be careful of fallen furniture and broken glass.
- Make sure you have a way out: Open doors and windows.
- Don't rush out in a panic. Watch out for falling objects.
- Stay away from concrete walls and other objects that may fall.
- Get accurate information from radio, television, fire stations, local authorities, etc.
- Make sure your family and neighbors are safe.
- Make sure electricity and gas are shut off before evacuation.
- In case of tsunami warning, run to higher ground.

are given numbers rather than being personified with male or female names as in the United States. The day after a typhoon blows through is called *taifu-ikka,* and is usually exceedingly clear; you can easily see Mount Fuji from the center of Tokyo.

The mountain ranges forming the backbone of Japan divide the country into two distinct precipitation zones, east and west. In winter, areas bordering the Sea of Japan to the west are blanketed with deep snow, dumped by the northwesterly winds off the continent (China). Niigata prefecture has an annual snowfall of four to five meters (13–16 feet) and is known as Yukiguni, or Snow Country, the setting of Nobel Prize–winner Kawabata Yasunari's novel. East of the mountains, the Pacific seaboard experiences less precipitation in winter but humid summers from the seasonal Pacific winds. December is the driest month in Tokyo with the skies at their clearest; a light snowfall or two is not unusual.

Earthquakes and Volcanoes

Japanese children agree on the most fearful things in life: *jishin, kaminari, kaji,* and *oyaji,* or "earthquakes, thunder, fire, and Dad." The Pacific Ring of Fire encircles the coasts of South and North America, down the Japanese archipelago to Southeast Asia. Japanese throughout history have faced natural disasters, such as earthquakes, tsunami, volcanic eruptions, and landslides. In 1923 the Great Kanto Earthquake and its fiery aftermath killed 100,000 people in Tokyo. The Great Hanshin-Awaji Earthquake of 1995 devastated the regions of Kobe and Osaka with more than 6,000 people losing their lives. Most recently, in March 2011, a 9.0 magnitude earthquake off the Pacific coast northeast of Tokyo and massive tsunami resulted in several nuclear explosions at the Fukushima Dai-ichi Nuclear Power Plant, forcing hundreds of thousands of residents to evacuate. Dealing with radiation and rebuilding communities after the Great East Japan disaster will take many years.

There is always a danger of tsunami after a major earthquake, and schools and cities regularly hold evacuation drills. Most earthquakes are relatively minor, and newer buildings are constructed to be earthquake resistant—skyscrapers in Tokyo were mostly undamaged in the March 2011 earthquake. Every city and town in Japan has emergency evacuation procedures and designated safe locations. It is advisable to obtain this information from your local government when you arrive.

Japan has at least 60 active volcanoes. The tallest, at 3,776 meters (12,388 feet), is Mount Fuji. It last erupted in 1707 and is constantly monitored, as are all active mountains. On the plus side, all this seismic activity results in abundant natural hot springs. Anywhere you travel in Japan, you aren't far from *onsen* (hot spring) resorts and inns, where you can soak in rejuvenating minerals. Japan's rivers are short and fast flowing, and they form deep gorges in the mountains; most have been dammed for hydroelectric power. The longest river, Shinano-gawa, is 367 kilometers (228 miles) long; the largest lake, Biwa-ko, is 674 square kilometers (260 square miles); and the deepest lake, Tazawa-ko, is 423 meters (1,388 feet) deep. The sheer beauty of mountains, rivers, and sea in Japan is striking.

FLORA AND FAUNA

A wide range of temperatures and plentiful rain create a rich environment for abundant flora, with more than 4,500 native plant species. Subtropical plants grow in Okinawa

© RUTHY KANAGY

Shika (deer) inhabit Japan's temperate zone.

and the Ogasawara Islands below Tokyo; broadleaf evergreen forests and oaks thrive in warm, temperate regions (Honshu, Shikoku, and Kyushu); broadleaf deciduous forests and beeches are found in cool, temperate areas of northern Honshu and southern Hokkaido; and subalpine Sakhalin firs and Ezo spruces, as well as alpine plants like *komakusa* (scientific name *Dicentra peregrina*), flourish in central Honshu and Hokkaido.

Diverse climatic conditions also foster a variety of fauna, such as Southeast Asiatic tropical animals (coral fish, turtles, sea snakes, eagles, flying foxes, and lizards) and, in the temperate zone, sea lions, fur seals, and beaked whales off central Honshu. *Tanuki* (raccoon dog), *shika* (deer), and mandarin foxes also inhabit this zone. Hokkaido is home to subarctic Siberian animals, such as the brown bear, grouse, lizard, and sometimes the walrus. There are many types of Asian land salamanders, cicadas, dragonflies, and swallowtail butterflies. Though sensitivity to the environment is gradually increasing in Japan, many species have become extinct, endangered, or vulnerable— but take heart in knowing that on Yakushima Island (south of Kyushu), there lives a 7,200-year-old Jomon cedar with a circumference of 16 meters (52.5 feet) that is designated a World Heritage tree.

Social Climate

Family ties are strong in Japan and bind not only the living extended family but also generations of ancestors. You may notice that Japanese are not physically demonstrative in public and you won't see any kissing and hugging on the streets. You do see friends and parents and children holding hands. One of the ways families express warmth and affection is to snuggle around the *kotatsu* (heated table covered with a comforter) in the winter, eating *mikan* (mandarin oranges) and watching TV. Another way is to scrub each other's backs in the family bath. Parents and children sleep together on the family futon, often until the children are age 10 or so.

You will find that most people are very honest. If you forget something on the subway, you will most likely find it at the lost and found office. Once I left a silver tray, which was a gift for someone, on the train. I called the railway station and recovered it the same day. Another time I forgot my camera and got it back again. I feel safe riding the subway at midnight. If you get lost in the city, there is no need to panic; people are genuinely helpful. Don't be surprised if they even lead you to your final destination. And there's always a *kouban,* or police box, nearby with detailed maps to help you find your way.

SHARED VALUES

Every culture transmits values to its youth, first in the context of family, and then through the educational process. In Japan, some of the core values are thinking of others, doing your best, not giving up, respecting your elders, knowing your role, and working in a group. These concepts are taught explicitly and implicitly from nursery school into the working world. From a very young age, Japanese children are taught *omoiyari* (to notice and think of others). Students must pass difficult entrance examinations to move to the next level of education, and in the process, they learn that *ganbaru* (effort) and *gaman* (enduring) are more crucial in reaching their goals than innate ability.

In every social situation, identity and status are largely determined by age, gender, sibling rank, and your year of entry to the group—which are also cues for the appropriate thing to say (or not) to each other. Having clear social roles provides a sense of security and comfort, but it can also feel binding. For those coming from a Western culture with a strong sense of independence, work situations where interactions are based on age or seniority, rather than talent or ability, may feel confining and frustrating. Greater awareness of cultural differences and values is helpful in understanding such situations.

Japanese values are reflected in the phrases used in daily interactions, which smooth relationships and acknowledge the presence of others. Wherever you go in Japan, everyone knows the precise words to say before and after meals, when you leave home, when you arrive at school or work, when you part with someone and meet them again. When you enter a store, restaurant, bank, or post office, the entire staff welcomes you with *"Irasshai-mase"* and showers you with *"Arigatoo gozaimasu"* when you leave. Soon you absorb the rhythm of these expressions so thoroughly that you miss them when you leave Japan.

The most versatile phrase to learn before you go to Japan is *"Onegai shimasu,"* which

REWARDS OF JAPAN

© DAVID GRACON

I asked David Gracon, who lived in Kanazawa for two years, about his experience:

What were the biggest rewards of living in Japan?

The culture is very different, so being exposed to this can be very rewarding. You will no longer think of your culture as the one and only way of being or acting. It forces you to see your own culture in new ways and be open to cultural difference.

Were there any frustrations living in Japan?

Not knowing Japanese. The level of spoken English will probably be lower than you expect, especially in rural areas, where it will be next to nothing. So even mundane interactions like shopping or banking can be a problem. Plus not being able to express complicated thoughts, or having to use really simple English can become tiresome. Learning Japanese is vital, and the more you learn, the better the experience will be. You will often be the focus of attention, which can get tiresome. Sometimes I just wanted to blend in. You will be a social minority and will face discrimination, but this is a good learning experience, in my opinion, however painful it may be.

What would you tell other people to encourage or discourage them from moving to Japan?

If you are open to new cultures, flexible, and have the ability and patience to cope with cultural ambiguity, you can learn a lot about yourself and your culture. If you're close-minded and not interested in learning about different cultural practices, don't go. Likewise, don't go if you don't plan on learning Japanese. Read books on the culture before you go, and, once there, be prepared to deal with situations that may be completely outside your frame of reference.

© RUTHY KANAGY

Kimonos are worn for special occasions, such as this visit to the Asakusa district in old Tokyo.

means, roughly, "I wish for" or "I sincerely request." It's the perfect thing to say when you introduce yourself, when you buy something, when you ask a favor, when you order in a restaurant, and when you ask someone to dance.

ISLAND MENTALITY

Before going to Japan, you may expect that everyone will look the same, dress the same, live the same, and talk the same. To a certain extent, this is true. Japanese people may appear to be more or less uniform in dress or behavior. This reflects an underlying value of not calling attention to oneself in public, especially among the older generation. However, Japan is neither monocultural nor monolingual. In addition to Ainu, the indigenous people of Japan, a flow of people and ideas has entered the country from China, Korea, Portugal, Spain, Germany, France, the Netherlands, England, North America, Brazil, and elsewhere for at least 2,000 years. Buddhism and Christianity, the writing system, medicine, models of government, business, and education, as well as sports and cuisine have derived—in part—from the outside and become a part of Japanese culture. In turn, Japan has exerted an influence on many other cultures.

The fact that Japan is an island nation with no land bridge to other countries seems to have an effect on the Japanese psyche and identity. When I lived in Japan, people would say almost apologetically, "We're just a small island nation." Overlooked is the fact that plenty of other smaller island nations, like England, New Zealand, and Madagascar, don't apologize for their size. On the flip side, a long history of being isolated and battered by typhoons and earthquakes has fostered a sense of *shima-guni konjo,* or the island fighting spirit.

Being surrounded by a vast sea, Japanese children are naturally curious about what's on the other side and express it in a song called *Umi:* "The ocean is so wide and big, I wish I could go see other countries." Maybe it's this longing to see what's on the other side that fuels the stream of millions of travelers who take to the air at New Year's, Golden Week (early May), and Obon (mid-August), landing in Hong Kong, Hawaii, New York, and Paris. Needless to say, holiday periods are good times *not* to plan your trip to Japan!

HISTORY, GOVERNMENT, AND ECONOMY

From samurai with swords to salary men at Starbucks, from shoguns to CEOs and ukiyoe to anime—how did Japanese society transform itself to what it is today? To understand Japan in the 21st century, it's a good idea to become familiar with its history, both political and economic.

Japan's long history seems to alternate between periods of intense contact with the outside world followed by years of isolation. As far back as 2,000 years ago, China and Korea were major influences on Japan, as sources of learning, religion, and technology. From the mid-1500s until they were ousted in 1603, Portuguese and Spanish traders brought goods and ideas from China and the West. Despite attempts by the Mongols to invade Japan in the 13th century, the nation was never "conquered" by a foreign power—that is, until the end of World War II, when the United States and Allies occupied the country for seven years.

In the past 150 years, since 250 years of isolation under Tokugawa ended and Western ideas and institutions took hold, Japan has changed from a labor-intensive

© RUTHY KANAGY

agricultural economy with taxation by bales of rice into an industrialized, free-market economy. Today Japan has the third-highest gross domestic product (GDP) in the world, after the United States and China, and the largest auto manufacturer in the world (Toyota).

History

The question of where the people of Japan originated is still under debate. Japan is mentioned in Chinese historical texts as early as the first century A.D. Historical records going back almost 2,000 years document the flow of people from China and Korea and Southeast Asia. The indigenous Ainu came to these islands much earlier, perhaps migrating across the land bridge over the northern Pacific. Present-day Japanese exhibit a range of facial and physical features that reflect the long history of migration to and from the Asian continent.

EARLY HISTORY
Jomon Period
The exact origin of Nihon (or Nippon) and its inhabitants is shrouded in mystery, but archaeological evidence shows that human inhabitants were living on the land at least 30,000 years ago. The people of this Paleolithic period were hunters and gatherers who used stone blades. At that time, the islands were not separated, but were attached to the Chinese continent. Gradually, a shift in the earth's plates and the changing climate caused sea levels to rise until they became islands. Parallel to these scientific findings is the Japanese legend about the sun goddess, Amaterasu Omikami, who created the islands of Japan. Her descendant, Jimmu Tenno (Emperor Jimmu), founded an empire in 660 B.C. Each year on February 11, this mythical event from several thousand years back is marked by 126 million Japanese people as national Foundation Day—a welcome day off to go skiing, shop, or relax at home.

The prehistoric stretch from approximately 10,000 to 300 B.C. is known as the Jomon period, named for the "rope marks" decorating the pottery of that era. People were organized into clans and tribes that cultivated plants. It was during this time that rice cultivation was introduced to Japan from the Chinese continent. While the Jomon people were building simple houses with thatched roofs, the Egyptians (or rather, their slaves) were constructing pyramids on the other side of the globe.

Yayoi Period
Gradually, from around 300 B.C., a different kind of culture emerged—people with bronze and iron techniques, weapons, and less decorative ceramics. Known as the Yayoi period, this era saw the irrigated cultivation of rice and other grains spread widely. The agricultural base established more than 2,300 years ago continues to influence Japanese society today. By A.D. 300, the influence of the Yayoi culture extended over present-day Honshu, Shikoku, and Kyushu, the main islands, excluding Hokkaido to the far north.

Yamato Period
Over time, the organization of numerous tribes and clans became more hierarchical,

with the *uji* (local clans) ruling over *be* (peasants) and slaves. The powerful clans of the Yamato region centered in Nara (some scholars say northern Kyushu) were subject to rulers, including a queen, Himiko. They built huge, keyhole-shaped mounded tombs, or *kofun,* to bury their rulers, and surrounded them with life-sized clay sculptures of servants and animals known as *haniwa.* These years from 300 to 645 are called the Kofun or Yamato period and were the beginning of the first unified state. During the same period, statues of the Roman emperor were being erected throughout the Roman Empire.

This was also a time when Japan established closer contact with China and Korea. Many of the items excavated by archaeologists from large *kofun* have been shown to be nearly identical to pottery and other items from the same period found in Korea. Thus, based on evidence from the burial mounds, it is thought that the ruling classes of Yamato—who came to power during the imperial dynasty and have lasted through the present Japanese emperor—must have come from Korea centuries ago. The *kofun* were built until the seventh century, and some still remain intact for you to see. Gradually, due to influence from China, the clan-based Japanese society gave way to a centralized administration centered on the emperor.

Asuka and Nara Periods

At the start of the Asuka period (593–710), Empress Suiko held court in the Asuka region of Yamato, just south of the city of Nara. Her regent was Shotoku Taishi (Prince Shotoku, 574–622), who played an important role in shaping Japanese society and government on the Chinese model, with a centralized government, a bureaucracy based on merit, and a 17-article constitution. Buddhism had been brought into the region in the mid-6th century, also via China. Through Prince Shotoku's influence, the court sponsored Buddhist teachings and Confucian virtues and built Korean- (and later Chinese-) style temples and palaces. Up to this time, the language spoken in Japan had no written form. Chinese characters were slowly adopted to write Japanese. (If the American continents had been lined up next to China, we might write English in Chinese characters today.) In 645, a series of reforms—the Taika no Kaishin (Taika Reforms)—were enacted to strengthen imperial power.

In 710, the imperial court built a splendid new capital patterned after the Chinese capital city of Ch'ang-an, in Nara. The native Japanese religion up to this point had been Shinto, worshipping *kami* (the sacred in nature) and venerating the virtues of loyalty and wisdom. The emperors were also considered divine, having descended from the sun goddess in an unbroken chain. However, during the Nara period (710–794), they patronized Buddhism and its teachings as a means of protecting the state and fostering a peaceful society. During this period, the ancient tales passed down orally regarding the founding of Japan were written down for the first time as the *Kojiki (Record of Ancient Matters)* and *Nihon Shoki (Chronicles of Japan).* With the adoption of Buddhism, numerous temples were constructed in the capital and provinces, and Buddhist priests gradually gained political power and wealth. In Nara, a giant statue of Buddha was built inside Todai-ji temple, which is still the largest in the world and can be seen today. Around the same time, on the other side of the globe, Catholic monks were gaining influence in Europe.

Heian Period

In 784, Emperor Kanmu moved the capital to Heiankyo (Heian court), where Kyoto is now, to get away from rivalries among the nobles and Buddhist clerics. This was the start of the Heian period (794–1185), when imperial culture flourished in a city that remained the capital for the next 1,000 years. Chinese characters, borrowed earlier, were used by the elite to write Chinese-style texts. During the Heian period, the characters were modified, and a set of syllabic letters called *kana* were invented that better represented the syllable structure of Japanese. *Kanji* (Chinese characters) are composed of many strokes and stand for whole words, but the new *kana* represented Japanese sounds and were used to write Japanese literature and other texts. Both scripts are still used today.

Many women of the imperial court produced literature and wrote diaries in the new *kana*. The most famous of these writers was Murasaki Shikibu, a woman who wrote the world's first novel (the classic *Tale of Genji*, about the amorous adventures of Prince Genji) around 1002. Politically, the imperial court came under the domination of the Fujiwara nobles, who used the strategy of marrying into the emperor's family to gain control. The court gradually lost hold of the provinces where bands of *bushi* (warriors) were in ascendancy. One of these warrior groups was the Taira family, who took over power of the court and capital in the middle of the 12th century, but they did not last for long. In Europe, Romanesque cathedrals were being built, and the Crusaders began to flex their military might.

FEUDAL PERIOD
The First Shogun

Five years of fierce battles between the Taira clan and the rival warrior band of Minamoto no Yoritomo followed. In the famous battle of Dannoura at Ichi no Tani, on the western tip of Honshu, Minamoto (also called Genji) defeated Taira (also called Heike) and set up a military government in Kamakura, eastern Honshu, south of present-day Tokyo. The years 1185 to 1333 are known as the Kamakura period. The emperor, far away in Kyoto, was little more than a figurehead surrounded by the court aristocracy. In 1192, the emperor granted Yoritomo the title of shogun (generalissimo), and the *bushi* emerged as the new ruling class. In the late 13th century, the Mongols, led by Kublai Khan, twice attempted to invade Japan, but were pushed back with the help of *kamikaze* (divine winds).

A Century of Wars

The military government in Kamakura was overthrown in 1333. A new shogun, Ashikaga Takauji, moved his military government to a part of Kyoto known as Muromachi. Thus, the period between 1333 and 1568 came to be called the Muromachi period. Takauji and his successors become patrons of the Zen sect of Buddhism. *Chanoyu* (tea ceremony), Zen-style gardens of raked stones, and brush painting developed from Zen philosophy. From 1467 to 1568, rival imperial courts in Kyoto battled for legitimacy. This was followed by almost a century of wars (Sengoku Jidai) between *daimyo* (feudal lords) battling for control of their domains. It was also during this time, in 1543, that shipwrecked Portuguese soldiers brought firearms into Japan; and in 1549, missionary Francis Xavier was the first to introduce Christianity to the country.

© RUTHY KANAGY

the 16th-century *daimyo* (feudal lord)
Date Masamune

REUNIFICATION

From the warring feudal lords emerged two powerful military leaders—Oda Nobunaga and Toyotomi Hideyoshi—who began to reunify the country and reform its feudal institutions. This Azuchimomoya Momoyama era (1568–1600) saw the construction of splendid castles, gold, and glitter, and open contact with the outside world. Painting, decorative designs on screens, and the tea ceremony also flourished. Hideyoshi had visions of conquering Korea and China, but his invasions ended in failure, and he died in 1598.

Shogun of Edo

In 1600, after winning the Battle of Sekigahara, Tokugawa Ieyasu took the title of shogun and established his rule over the country from the city of Edo (now Tokyo). The two and a half centuries from 1600 to 1868 are called the Edo, or Tokugawa, period. The shogun controlled Edo, the core of Japan, and assigned the *daimyo* to *han* (domains) based on depth of loyalty. (The English expression "head honcho" is derived from *han*.) Status distinctions were strictly enforced through a four-class system of *shi* (samurai), *no* (peasants), *ko* (artisans), and *sho* (merchants). Swords were confiscated from everyone but the samurai, whose power depended on the peasants, who produced rice for the nation. Each peasant family was granted about a half acre of land and required to pay heavy taxes in the form of bales of rice.

Left out of the four official classes was a group treated as outcasts. They were despised for handling animal carcasses and leather, which made them unclean, according to Buddhism. Sadly, their contemporary descendants—known as *burakumin*—though legally in possession of every right of Japanese citizens, still face discrimination in education, jobs, and marriage.

The shogun kept tight control over the 250 or so regional *daimyo,* decreeing that they be in attendance in Edo every other year, leaving their wives and children behind as hostages. Christianity had spread rapidly in Japan 50 years after its introduction by European missionaries. Fearing cultural and political influence from the West, Tokugawa banned Christianity, severely persecuted Japanese Christians, and banned trade with the outside world, except for the Dutch, who were corralled on an island in the port of Nagasaki. The isolation would last 250 years.

Urban Culture

During a long isolation from the outside world, things were not static inside Japan. The cities of Osaka, Kyoto, Himeji, and other castle towns became commercial centers

NAKASENDO

© RUTHY KANAGY

Usui checkpoint, along the Nakasendo

During the Tokugawa era, the Nakasendo, or Central Mountain Highway, was one of three routes linking the old capital of Kyoto in the west to the new eastern capital of Edo (now Tokyo). Colorful processions of *daimyo* lords and their retainers, as well as merchants and other travelers, made the 520-kilometer journey on foot, stopping at 69 *shukuba* (post towns) for food and lodging. Itabashi (Wood Bridge) was one of the last stations on the journey, and rice shops, sake shops, and family-run inns flourished. In Itabashi samurai lords would bathe and refresh themselves before rising at 4 A.M. for the final leg into the capital. Two stone markers, or *ichiri-zuka*, erected in 1604, marked the remaining distance to Nihonbashi bridge, the final destination in Edo: three-*ri* (12 kilometers).

The Tokugawa shogun also traveled the Nakasendo to the area near Itabashi, taking pleasure in escaping the capital to the broad Musashino plain. Less than a day's journey from Edo and its one mil-

lion inhabitants, he hunted duck and wild boars using greyhounds imported before the doors to the West were shut in 1600. A 1905 photograph displayed in the Itabashi city museum depicts the last shogun hunting duck on the Maeda estate.

Today, grim concrete and asphalt have paved over the shogun's former hunting ground. Itabashi is a city of half a million, swallowed up by Metropolitan Tokyo. The old Nakasendo is called Route 17 and is lined with high-rise condos sprouting like giant mushrooms. Four lanes of trucks, buses, and cars clog the ancient route to Kyoto. Today remnants of a more verdant past survive in the names of subway stations on the Mita line: Field Door, Aspiring Village, Lily Swamp, Original Field, and Duck's Nest. The twin stone *ichiri-zuka* markers, moved when the highway was widened, are hidden under a steel pedestrian overpass, mute shadows of their important role for travelers on the Nakasendo.

© RUTHY KANAGY

Japan celebrates its feudal past during the Jidai Matsuri (Festival of the Ages) in Kyoto every October.

where citizens enjoyed urban cultural events, such as Kabuki and Bunraku (puppet) theater. Books were published and widely disseminated; colorful *ukiyo-e* (wood-block prints; literally, "pictures of a floating world") of courtesans in kimonos, Kabuki actors, and 47 views of Mount Fuji were widely circulated. In the 19th century, British, Russian, and American ships began to approach Japan and other parts of Asia seeking trade. The shogun failed to expel the "barbarians," and in 1853, after Commodore Perry's ships arrived in Japan, he relented. Around the same time, several powerful *daimyo* from Kyushu fought to restore the emperor to power, then challenged and overthrew the shogun's authority in 1868.

MODERN HISTORY
Meiji Era

The centuries of relative peace under samurai control gave way to a larger world, with new rulers and new rules. In an event known as the Meiji Restoration, the new Meiji emperor was transferred from the imperial court of Kyoto in the west to Edo, which was renamed Tokyo (Eastern Capital). The goal of the former samurai, now political leaders, was to reform the social, economic, and political institutions following Western models in order to shore up the country and the military. During this Meiji period (1868–1912), a constitution was adopted in 1889, and a parliamentary government developed. Observing the colonial practices of Western nations, the Japanese military fought wars with China (1894–1895) and Russia (1905) to assert their imperialistic aspirations. Japan colonized Korea in 1910, imposing Japanese names on Koreans and the adoption of Japanese language in schools; in addition, thousands of Koreans were forcibly brought to Japan as cheap labor in mining, construction, and shipping. This continued until the end of World War II. Today, third- and fourth-generation descendants of these Korean immigrants, born and raised in Japan, are still denied citizenship.

Taisho Era

The Meiji emperor died in 1912, and his son became the Taisho emperor. The Taisho period (1912–1926), ruled by a Liberal party government supported by wealthy businessmen, saw increased international diplomacy and Japan's economic expansion in Asia and the Pacific. Universal suffrage for men was instituted in 1925. (Women did not get the right to vote until two decades later.)

Showa Era

The beginning decades of Showa (1926–1989) were all about nationalism and military expansion. Japan dropped out of the League of Nations, and liberal politicians were replaced with ultra-nationalistic politicians. Spurred by the euphemistic slogan, "The Greater East Asia Co-Prosperity Sphere," Japan invaded and occupied Manchuria in 1931. This was followed by war in China and the invasion of all of Southeast Asia. The years 1937–1938 saw the Rape of Nanking, in which the Japanese military used civilians for scientific experiments, raping and slaughtering more than 300,000 Chinese—another holocaust, but this one mostly unknown to the world. The military also forced thousands of Korean, Filipino, and other Asian women into sexual slavery in the name of "serving" Japanese soldiers. (The stories of these "comfort women," now elderly or deceased, have only begun to emerge in recent years.)

In 1941, Japan attacked Pearl Harbor and brought the United States into battle in the Pacific. From 1937 to 1945, almost every Japanese citizen suffered hunger and severe deprivation. Families were separated and children and their teachers were sent to safety in the countryside, where there was some food. Household items, such as pots and pans, and anything else made of metal were sacrificed for the military cause. At this time, the Showa emperor was believed to be *kami* (divine), descended from Amaterasu Omikami. Any word of doubt or resistance to the national agenda could land a person in prison. Millions of young men were drafted into the war, ordered to fight to the death—and even to take their own lives, for capture was considered worse humiliation than death. Intense firebombing by the U.S. military day after day brought terror to cities all over Japan. In the spring of 1945, 100,000 Okinawans (one-third of the prefecture's population) were killed in battles between Japanese and U.S. forces for control of the islands.

On August 6, 1945, the United States dropped the world's first atomic bomb on the citizens of Hiroshima. As many as 80,000 people died instantaneously from the searing heat, fire, and radiation, and 60,000 more perished by the end of 1945 from related ailments. Many more people died from radiation sickness, the effects of which still exist today. Three days later, on August 9, the city of Nagasaki in Kyushu—the cradle of Christianity—was bombed, with casualties estimated at more than 100,000. Those who were able to get some kind of medical care from the government were fortunate; Korean *hibakusha* (atomic bomb victims) in Hiroshima and Nagasaki were not. All would surely testify to their conviction that nuclear weapons must never again be used against humankind. If you get a chance to visit Hiroshima and Nagasaki, by all means go. The pictures, artifacts, and words in the Peace Park and museums are moving. If only every world leader could listen to the message.

On August 15, 1945, another shock wave spread throughout Japan. For the first time, the emperor's voice was broadcast over radio waves, announcing Japan's unconditional surrender and stating that he was no longer *kami* (divine). From the 19th century to the end of World War II, Shinto had been the national religion of Japan. The emperor was worshiped as the chief *kami*. Schools and workplaces were required to display the Japanese flag—*hi no maru* (round sun)—and sing the national anthem, whose lyrics praised the emperor and were associated with the militaristic state. Trained to believe in victory and to pray to the Tenno (emperor), the entire nation was stunned. After the war, religion was officially separated from the state by law, but controversy still remains over whether yearly visits by the prime minister to Yasukuni Shrine in Tokyo, which enshrines the remains of high-ranked military leaders, are state visits or private.

From 1945 to 1952, the United States Allied Forces occupied Japan. The United States gave Japan a new constitution, restored a democratic form of government, and passed laws giving women the right to vote for the first time. They also broke up the monopoly of powerful *zaibatsu*—industrial and financial conglomerates that controlled the Japanese economy from 1868 to 1945. By the early 1950s, Japan's per capita consumption of goods was less than one-fifth that of the United States. Over the next 20 years, the economy grew at an average rate of 8 percent per year (10 percent during the 1960s). One factor contributing to economic growth was the high personal savings rate by citizens—much higher than in the United States.

The new constitution adopted after World War II was drafted and written in English by the Americans and translated into Japanese. Curiously, it contains several articles that are not in the U.S. Constitution: an equal rights clause for men and women, and a "peace clause" in which the Japanese government forever renounces war as a right of sovereignty. Article 9 states:

> Aspiring sincerely to an international peace based on justice and order, the Japanese people forever renounce war as a sovereign right of the nation and the threat or use of force as means of settling international disputes. (2) In order to accomplish the aim of the preceding paragraph, land, sea, and air forces, as well as other war potential, will never be maintained. The right of belligerency of the state will not be recognized.

There is an irony in the fact that the same nation that in 1945 forbade Japan from maintaining forces on land, sea, or air now clamors for Japan to support and participate in war.

By signing a peace treaty with the United States in 1951, Japan regained its independence from direct American control, but Okinawa did not. In 1960, Japan signed a Treaty of Mutual Cooperation and Security with the United States. This agreement stated that the United States would "protect" Japan from other countries in exchange for economic, political, and logistical support for the United States to maintain military bases in Japan. During the negotiations of the treaty, which continue today, I was in eastern Hokkaido chanting *"Anpo hantai!"* ("Down with the Security Treaty!") with my grade-school chums, unaware that I was protesting against the United States.

While the Jieitai (Self-Defense Forces) hold joint military exercises with U.S. forces in various parts of Japan, they also function as an emergency response team during natural disasters, such as earthquakes. On a lighter note, the Hokkaido Jieitai plays a key role in preparations for the International Snow Festival, held every February in Sapporo, the capital. They bring hundreds of truckloads of snow into Odori Park in the center of the city, where sculptors compete to carve the biggest and best sculptures and replicas of monuments around the world for millions of visitors to enjoy.

In 1964, international recognition came to Japan with the Tokyo Olympic Games, and a World Exposition followed in Osaka in 1970. In 1972, Japan normalized diplomatic relationships with China. Although the nations are diplomatically and economically connected, memories of wartime atrocities committed by the Japanese military remain in the minds of the people of China and other Asian countries. And, more than 65 years after World War II, Japan and Russia have yet to sign a formal peace treaty because of an ongoing dispute over control of four of the Kuril Islands off eastern Hokkaido. (The blue islands are so close to the shores of eastern Hokkaido that I grew up thinking Russia was located east of Japan.)

Middle Eastern oil prices rose sharply in 1973—remembered as the year of the "oil shock"—and again in 1979. Japan imports almost all its fuel, so heavy industries were greatly affected. As a result, there was a trend to develop more high-tech industries less reliant on imported oil.

THE PRESENT
Heisei Era

In 1989, the Showa emperor passed away after being the symbol of Japan for 63 years. His son Akihito became emperor and the new era, Heisei (Peaceful Rule) year 1, began. (In keeping with counting years by the emperor's reign, as well as by the Western calendar.) The early 1990s marked the end of several decades of economic growth and rapid rise in real estate and stock prices. In 1991 the stock market crashed, ending Japan's "bubble economy" (portending a similar economic crash in the United States nearly 20 years later).

On January 17, 1995, the Great Hanshin Earthquake struck the densely populated urban area of Kobe and the Inland Sea, killing 6,434 people. In the same year, the doomsday cult Aum Shinrikyo carried out a terrorist attack on the Tokyo subway system using deadly sarin gas.

A national crisis of sorts arose in Heisei 13, or 2001, when the Crown Princess gave birth to a daughter. Historically, Japanese empresses played a powerful role, but the laws were changed to allow only male succession. After public debate on changing the rule of succession to allow females, or even abolishing the emperor system itself, the "problem" was solved in 2006 when the Crown Prince's younger brother had a son— the first male child born to the royal family in 41 years.

Historically, the emperor was considered divine and the focus of Shinto worship, but religion and government were officially separated in 1945. In practice, however, many prime ministers visit Yasukuni Shrine to pray for the nation's war dead. Junichiro Koizumi, prime minister from 2001 to 2006, declared his visit to the shrine to be personal, not official. However, this did not appease neighboring Asian nations who still remember the atrocities committed against them during World War II.

Prime Minister Koizumi was the first to deploy the Japanese Self-Defense Forces overseas when he sent them to Iraq in 2004, though strictly in a noncombatant role.

This was the first foreign deployment of the Japanese military since World War II. In view of Article 9 of the constitution, which forbids maintaining armed forces or waging war, many citizens were against the prime minister's action.

Under the Security Treaty signed by Japan and the United States after World War II, 50,000 U.S. military personnel still occupy Japan—40,000 of them on the island of Okinawa. Forty percent of arable land in Okinawa consists of U.S. military bases, which has caused environmental damage and taken a physical, emotional, and financial toll on communities over the years. In particular, the U.S. Futenma Air Base, located in a dense residential area in Ginowan, poses a danger from noise, accidents, and crimes—such as the rape of a local schoolgirl in 1995 by three GIs. Successive prime ministers promised to move the Futenma base off Okinawa, only to bow to U.S. pressure. The two countries discussed plans to relocate some 9,000 U.S. troops from Okinawa to Guam, but a timetable was not set.

Japan is used to earthquakes, but the one that hit northeast Honshu on March 11, 2011, was of a different magnitude. The 9.0 earthquake triggered massive tsunami waves that wiped out more than 300 kilometers of coastline. Almost 19,000 people were killed or disappeared, and thousands of buildings and homes were destroyed in coastal farm and fishing communities. The tsunami disabled the Fukushima Dai-ichi Nuclear Power Plant operated by Tokyo Electric Power Company (TEPCO), leading to explosions of three reactors, which leaked radiation into the atmosphere. Thousands of citizens living within a 20-kilometer radius of the plant were forced to evacuate, abandoning their homes, farms, animals, businesses, and missing or dead family members.

A year after the earthquake and nuclear disaster, less than 5 percent of the rubble (including large amounts of radioactive waste) had been cleared, and the communities near the nuclear plant remained ghost towns. Despite assurances by the prime minister that the Fukushima No. 1 nuclear plant was stable, the true extent of damage inside the reactors was unknown. Before the disaster, 54 nuclear reactors had supplied one-third of Japan's energy. Within a few months, they were shut down for maintenance and stress tests. A growing anti-nuclear power movement among citizens left their future unclear, although the national government was pushing to restart some of them. With oil prices rising worldwide the gasoline prices hit ¥163 per liter (about $7.70 per gallon). Finding safe and reliable energy sources is key to the future of Japan.

A bright spot in the same year was Nadeshiko Japan's victory in the World Cup, defeating the U.S. women in soccer. The female athletes became national heroes and an inspiration to many.

GREAT EAST JAPAN EARTHQUAKE

On March 11, 2011, a magnitude 9.0 earthquake off the coast of northeast Honshu rocked Japan. Thirty minutes after the quake, massive tsunami waves as high as 133 feet inundated over 300 kilometers of coastline. In an instant, 19,000 people were killed or swept away, 270,000 buildings were destroyed, and 380,000 people lost their homes—mostly in small coastal farming and fishing communities. Japan has 3 percent of the earth's landmass, 10 percent of the active volcanoes, and 20 percent of the world's largest earthquakes. People are used to earthquakes, but a quake of this magnitude last occurred in A.D. 890—a thousand years ago.

The tsunami damaged the Fukushima Dai-ichi Nuclear Power Plant, built on the coast to supply power for Tokyo—140 miles away. It's operated by Tokyo Electric Power Company (TEPCO), and not one watt was for citizens of Fukushima prefecture. The tsunami knocked out electrical power, including emergency generators needed to cool the reactors. This led to meltdowns and explosions of three nuclear reactors, spewing radiation into the atmosphere. TEPCO and the national government were totally unprepared to handle such a nuclear accident. Hundreds of thousands of citizens within a 20-kilometer radius were forced to evacuate immediately, abandoning their homes, farms, animals, businesses, and missing or dead family members. It was unknown when, or if, they could ever return.

The vast destruction is hard to grasp from our side of the Pacific: more than 600 kilometers of coastline hit by the quake and tsunami—the distance from San Francisco to Los Angeles. Tohoku (northeast) is mostly fishing and farming villages on a narrow strip of land backed by mountains. Almost a third of residents are over age 65, because young people head to the cities for jobs and higher education.

The quake was extremely strong in Tokyo, but thanks to earthquake resistant construction, buildings were relatively unaffected. Still, it's unnerving to be on the 53rd floor and watch skyscrapers around you swaying. The quake halted public transportation—trains, buses, and subways. Millions who commute into central Tokyo had no way of getting home. So they walked. My friends walked 18 kilometers for hours to get home. Bike shops sold out of bicycles as people sought alternative transport. Convenience stores sold out of water, food, and batteries. But people remained calm. There was no looting of stores. Some restaurants handed out rice balls and water to passers-by or offered their restrooms.

During the disaster, land lines and cell phones were useless for the most part. Twitter and the Internet played a huge role in communication: Google Japan immediately set up a website where people could let family know their whereabouts, and where one could search for missing relatives. Due to radiation fears, there was an exodus of foreigners from Japan, but some stayed. There were rolling blackouts to conserve energy, and companies were ordered to cut electrical consumption 15 percent. Many embraced the "cool biz" look for the summer, letting employees show up in shirt sleeves and setting air conditioners to 28°C (82°F).

Many volunteers, Japanese and foreign, worked tirelessly in evacuation centers providing food, blankets, and medical care to refugees. TEPCO and the government were slow to provide aid and direction—a year after the disaster only 5 percent of the rubble was disposed of. Radiation levels remained high in Fukushima, and farmers and fishers were unable to sell their products due to radiation fears by consumers. One positive result after the disaster was people realizing the importance of family, consuming less, and caring more for others. The word *kizuna* (bond) was chosen by the Kanji Association as the word of the year for 2011.

Government

Japan has a British-style parliamentary form of government with an appointed prime minister. There are three branches—the legislative (National Assembly), executive (prime minister and cabinet), and judiciary (courts). The *kokkai,* or "National Diet" in English, consists of the House of Representatives *(shugiin),* with 480 members, and House of Councillors *(sangiin),* with 242 members. Every four years, Japanese citizens age 20 and older elect representatives to serve in the upper house and elect half the lower house every three years. The prime minister is not elected directly by citizens, but selected by the party or coalition of parties in power and approved by the national assembly. The prime minister appoints a cabinet whose members head various government ministries. There are two major political parties and several minor ones.

From 1955 to 1993, during the period of rapid economic growth, the Liberal Democratic Party (LDP) was the dominant political party, which, despite its name, takes a conservative stance on social and international issues. The New Komeito (NK), established by the Soka Gakkai sect of Buddhism, supports the LDP. In the 1990s several opposition parties merged to form the Democratic Party of Japan (DPJ), with more liberal and social-democratic views. The Japan Communist Party (JCP) and Social Democratic Party (SDP) generally support the DPJ. In recent years, the People's New Party (PNP) and Your Party (YP) emerged, in opposition to specific policies of the DPJ.

In order to raise finances, the government introduced the first consumption tax in 1989—a 3 percent tax on goods and services, similar to our sales tax. Not surprisingly, this was unpopular among consumers. Eight years later the tax was raised to 5

© RUTHY KANAGY

Metropolitan Tokyo is the political, economic, and educational center of Japan.

PUBLIC HOLIDAYS IN JAPAN

© RUTHY KANAGY

traditional *koto* performance at summer festival

- **January 1:** New Year's Day (Ganjitsu). People make their first visit to a shrine to pray for good fortune in the coming year.

- **January (second Monday):** Coming of Age Day (Seijin no Hi). Ceremonies are held in every town and city for 20-year-olds reaching adulthood.

- **February 11:** Foundation Day (Kenkoku Kinenbi). First emperor's reign in 660 B.C., according to ancient records.

- **March 20:** Spring Equinox (Shunbun no Hi). People visit family graves for Higan, a Buddhist holiday.

- **April 29:** Showa Day (Showa no Hi). Birthday of former Showa emperor and start of Golden Week holidays.

- **May 3:** Constitution Day (Kenpo Kinenbi). Commemorating the 1946 constitution.

- **May 4:** Greenery Day (Midori no Hi). A day to enjoy plants and nature.

- **May 5:** Children's Day (Kodomo no Hi). People fly carp streamers for each son; Golden Week ends.

- **July (third Monday):** Ocean Day (Umi no Hi). Start of school summer vacation; pools and beaches open.

- **September (third Monday):** Respect for the Aged Day (Keiro no Hi). Honors elders and longevity.

- **September 23:** Fall Equinox (Shubun no Hi). People visit family graves for Higan, a Buddhist holiday.

- **October (second Monday):** Sports Day (Taiiku no Hi). Athletic events take place nationwide.

- **November 3:** Culture Day (Bunka no Hi). Includes cultural exhibits in schools and communities and government awards for cultural achievements.

- **November 23:** Labor Thanksgiving Day (Kinro Kansha no Hi). Honoring those who work.

- **December 23:** Emperor's Birthday (Tenno Tanjobi). Birthday of the current Heisei emperor.

- **Christmas Eve** is celebrated by couples and families with KFC and Christmas cake, but Christmas Day is not a national holiday.

- Government offices and most companies are closed **December 30** to **January 3** for New Year's holidays.

- In addition, there are many traditional holidays during the year, including **Hina Matsuri** (Doll's Day) on March 3, **Tanabata** (Star Festival) on July 7, **Obon** (All Saints Day) August 12-15, **Shichi-Go-San** (festival for children ages 7, 5, and 3) on November 15.

percent. In 2001, Junichiro Koizumi was elected head of the LDP and prime minister, promising political and economic reforms. One of his proposals was to privatize the government-owned Japan Post, which functioned similarly to a bank, holding the savings accounts of millions of citizens. Shinzo Abe was elected by the LDP to be prime minister in 2006, the youngest head of Japanese government and the first born post-World War II.

The Democratic Party of Japan won a landslide victory in parliamentary elections in 2009, a year of change, ending over 50 years of rule by the LDP, with a promise to revive the economy and end corruption. Yukio Hatoyama, the first DPJ prime minister, lasted less than nine months. He was forced to resign due to a political finance scandal and over a broken campaign promise to move U.S. Futenma air base off Okinawa to another prefecture, bowing to pressure from the U.S. government. In June 2010, Naoto Kan became prime minister, but his popularity plummeted after the March 2011 earthquake. Yoshihiko Noda was appointed next, vowing to carry out social security and pension reforms and increase revenue by raising the consumption tax. In 2012, Noda and the DPJ, in conjunction with the LDP and Komeito parties, pushed through legislation raising the consumption tax (sales tax) to 8 percent in 2014 and to 10 percent in 2015.

There has long been a close alliance among politicians, business leaders, and bureaucrats who graduate from the same elite universities and do each other favors. In a practice known as *ama-kudari,* or "descent from heaven," top level bureaucrats upon retirement often join the very companies or industry they used to regulate. One of many examples in recent years occurred in the Boei-sho, or Ministry of Defense, which admitted to a long-standing pattern of corruption involving defense procurements. Another scandal was the government's admission that it had lost the pension records of 50 million citizens—almost half of the population. Japanese as well as foreign residents are required to pay into the National Pension Insurance program while employed and are eligible to receive benefits when they retire.

Due to these and many other incidents, many Japanese have little faith in elected officials and bureaucrats. There is a growing realization of the importance of *jiritsu* (self-reliance); that individuals must rely on their own judgment and make their own decisions instead of waiting for government to guide them—one of the lessons learned from the Great East Japan Earthquake when the government provided too little or inaccurate information to citizens during the nuclear crisis and its aftermath.

In the global sphere, Japan is an active member of the United Nations and participates in the Security Council, though it's not a permanent member. Japan is part of the G8 economic leaders of the world (now expanded to G20) and a member of APEC (Asia-Pacific Economic Cooperation). It provides aid to developing countries and is opening negotiations with the U.S.-led Trans-Pacific Partnership (TPP) free-trade agreement. TPP is supported by business interests seeking economic growth, but domestic agricultural and medical sectors, which have been long protected from overseas competition, oppose it.

Russia is one of Japan's closest neighbors. Due to Russia's occupation of the Kuril Islands (off eastern Hokkaido), the two governments have yet to sign a peace treaty ending World War II. Japan has demanded the return of the "northern territories" for years, to no avail. Relations with North Korea are also tense, due to the kidnapping of

Japanese citizens by North Korean agents in the 1970s and 1980s, to teach Japanese to future spies. North Korea's efforts to build nuclear weapons have not helped. Japan joined the 6-Party talks begun in 2003 in an effort to pressure North Korea to abandon its nuclear program. China's rapid military build-up in the Pacific is another worry for Japan's security.

Economy

Following the devastation of World War II, Japan enjoyed several decades of rapid economic growth. Japanese products, from automobiles and cameras to shipbuilding materials, came to be known worldwide for their high quality. Companies such as Honda, Toyota, Sony, and Mitsubishi are household words in many countries. This boom period led to the development of a consumer society in which everyone aspired to acquire the "three C's"—car, cooler (air conditioner), and color TV. Later, the three C's became camcorders, computers, and cell phones. Rapid economic growth was not without problems: air pollution from exhaust and power plants, acid rain, and the degrading water quality of lakes and reservoirs threatened aquatic life. Because Japan has few natural resources other than a few minerals, it is one of the largest consumers of fish and tropical timber, depleting Asia and other countries of these resources.

Japan's economic growth continued into the late 1980s, fueled by a rapid rise in real estate prices and speculative investment. In the early 1990s, the economic bubble burst and the economy suffered the worst recession since 1945. In the decades since 1991, slowing global trade and the strong yen affected export levels, and domestic consumption dropped, along with a shrinking and aging population.

Due to good medical care and relatively healthy lifestyles, the average Japanese life expectancy has increased to 84 years (86.4 years for women—the longest in the world). Soon one-third of the population will be over age 65, putting a strain on the rest of society to support them. In addition, the birthrate has remained low at 1.25 children per woman, though the DPJ government tried to boost births by subsidizing families with $300 per month per child. Some of the reasons for the low birth rate include higher levels of education, later age of marriage, small living space, and women pursuing their own careers. The shrinking labor pool has attracted laborers from Asia, Brazil, and the Middle East, many of whom have taken on factory positions—jobs that fewer Japanese are willing to do.

The sluggish economy in the past two decades has affected the tradition of lifetime employment and promotion based on seniority. Many workers were laid off in mid-career, too old to start fresh but too young to retire. Some turned to opening new businesses or retraining. Large companies that hired new college grads every spring cut back on or canceled recruitment altogether. This affected women graduates disproportionately. Discouraged by the lack of jobs and advancement opportunities, many women turn to foreign companies in Japan, start their own companies, or go abroad to pursue advanced degrees. Some young people opt out of the work force completely to pursue their own interests, or work very part-time, and are called "freeters."

To cut labor costs, companies are employing more and more non-contract workers, who have no job security or benefits. Currently as many as one-third of employees are *haken,* or temporary workers. A growing network of *haken* workers and local unions are campaigning for the government to change the policies of the Dispatch Work Law, which allows companies to pay them less than regular employees for the same work.

The March 2011 earthquake and tsunami, which caused unprecedented damage and loss of life, had far-reaching economic effects that will continue for some years. It crippled manufacturing in the northeast, disrupted supply chains, and halted automobile production nationwide for several months. The European debt crisis and U.S. financial crisis, along with a strong yen, put a damper on exports and resulted in record trade deficits. Japanese companies, including manufacturing, are seeking economic growth overseas, and look to expand their markets in China, Southeast Asia, and beyond. This may have an effect on foreigners who seek jobs in Japan, but there are still opportunities for those with the right skills, experience, and knowledge.

PEOPLE AND CULTURE

When you first come to Japan, you may observe things that look like cultural contradictions, a clash of East and West. For example, while waiting on a train platform, you
might see a woman in a traditional kimono using a smart phone, two businesspeople
bowing and shaking hands simultaneously, or a blonde Japanese with a mohawk.
Newcomers to Japan often perceive such phenomena as contradictions, because they've
never imagined these particular cultural elements in comfortable juxtaposition. In my
experience observing two cultures, it's no more incongruous for a woman in a kimono
to use a *keitai* (cell phone) than for a Western man in a tuxedo to do so. Though we
may regard modern accoutrements as belonging to the West, they are just as intrinsic
a part of Japanese culture and daily life.

After all, Japan has been blending foreign elements into its culture for several thousand years—Buddhist thought and arts from India, China, and Korea; Christianity
from the Middle East via Europe; literature and a writing system from China and
Europe; medicine from Germany; parliamentary government from Europe; modern
business and manufacturing practices from the United States; public school education from Europe and the United States; school uniforms from Prussia; football and
rugby from Europe; and baseball and, more recently, hamburgers, Starbucks, and
KFC from the United States.

© RUTHY KANAGY

These various components have continually merged into the Japanese way of life, resulting in the country's diverse contemporary culture. Which things are "Western," and which are "Japanese"? For children growing up among all these resources, none of this is foreign. After all, they've met Mickey Mouse at Tokyo Disneyland so he must be Japanese. Contradictions only appear when viewed from the outside. Though you may initially experience many unexpected or even curious events when you arrive in Japan, don't worry. Soon, eating curried rice with a soup spoon and ice cream with chopsticks (just kidding!), and bowing while talking on the phone will become second nature.

Ethnicity and Class

JAPANESE OR *GAIJIN*?

My Japanese acquaintances often ask, "Can you tell the difference between Koreans, Chinese, and Japanese?" Well, yes, sometimes, but I base it more on clothing, shoes, and hairstyle than facial features. I always suspect this question to be a sort of litmus test of *gaijin*-ness (outsider status), which only serves to reaffirm the gulf separating Japanese from Other. Can you tell Germans, French, and Americans apart? I wonder if the first Europeans to arrive in Japan some 450 years ago were also confronted with such questions. Every culture carries stereotypes of others based on noses, eyes, hair, and supposed national traits, but if you go back far enough, we all have a common ancestry.

Whenever I am in Japan and speak on the phone in Japanese, the person at the other end assumes I'm just your average Hanako (Jane). That is, until I tell them how to spell my name in *katakana* (script used for foreign words)—a dead giveaway. Or I meet someone at the train station, and suddenly they switch to hand gestures and talking too loudly. They're convinced a person with a face like mine can't possibly understand Japanese. Since Japanese aren't used to seeing non-Asians on a daily basis, an unexpected encounter with a sharply carved face, high-bridged nose, and sunken eyes can detract from normal communication. From the Asian viewpoint, what stands out in a European American visage is not the eyes but the high bridge of the nose. On the flip side, imagine living in Japan and being surrounded by Asian people all day, then coming home and catching a glimpse of your own face in the mirror. Does it stand out? You betcha! (Unless, of course, you are of Asian heritage and fit right in.)

Ironically, foreign models appear everywhere in advertising, and American movies and TV programs are daily fare, but to actually encounter such a face on the train or street is something else. Locals may ask for your autograph or photo, as if you were a movie star. This can feel flattering at first, but after the novelty wears off, you may wish you could blend in or be ignored. These are all normal stages while adjusting to your identity and role in a new culture.

In general, visual signals (size, appearance, clothing, hair color, piercings) seem to overwhelm the human auditory system during cross-cultural encounters. Japanese are just as startled seeing a "high-nose person" with blue eyes eating sushi with chopsticks as Americans are seeing Japanese people eat Continental-style (fork in the left hand, tines down). My happiest encounter with a stranger was when a stooped *obaachan* (granny) stopped me on the street to ask directions. I waved my hand in the general direction, and she bowed, turned, and walked away. I was so happy to be treated like an ordinary person that I wanted to run after her and give her a big hug (except then I might have scared her off by acting like a *gaijin*). For me, the ultimate insult in Japanese is being called *"gaijin-san,"* which means Ms. Outsider (or Mr. Outsider). Never mind that the *-san* title, when added to others' family or personal names, is a sign of politeness—it's never pleasant to be lumped into a category you didn't choose.

Overcoming stereotypes is a mutual process that happens as you build a relationship and get to know each other. You can't prevent anyone from having preconceptions about you, but over time, through shared activities, you can reveal who you are and invite others to do the same. In Japan, people who have had experiences in which they were the minority are most likely to understand other internationals.

If you want to get beyond the initial exchange of names and pleasantries, here are some things you can do in advance of meeting people in Japan: Keep up with the daily news online—read about what's happening in Japanese politics, economy, and society. Think about what you will say when asked about the United States and its foreign policies. When traveling around the country, learn something about the history, products, and sights of the region and inquire about them. Try to find out who's hot in Japanese music, TV, and sports, and mention them during conversations. Of course, learning to converse in Japanese will allow you to meet and interact with a much wider range of people, and most Japanese will appreciate your efforts to communicate in their language.

MULTIETHNIC SOCIETY

Despite initial appearances, Japan is neither culturally nor ethnically homogenous. The number of people in each category may be few, but nonetheless, there is much diversity in the country. Minorities living in Japan include the Ainu, Okinawans, Koreans, Chinese, descendants of the former outcast class *(burakumin),* Japanese children left behind in China after World War II, Japanese children who grew up overseas, dual citizens, naturalized citizens, non-citizens born and raised in Japan, and descendants of Japanese immigrants who have returned to Japan. Societies with relatively few visible minorities can more easily downplay or ignore diversity and promote the notion of sameness (one of the underlying themes of Japanese public education).

Foremost among these minority ethnic groups are the Ainu, the native people of Japan whose history reads like that of the Native Americans—they were pushed north into Hokkaido by the encroaching Japanese from the south in the 19th century. Many discriminatory laws were passed in the 19th and 20th centuries that destroyed the Ainu way of life and most of the language. Private salmon fishing—their main source of food and an essential part of their religion—was banned, as was use of the Ainu language in school. Today, 50,000 or more Utari (the Ainu term for "human") live in Hokkaido and on the Russian island of Sakhalin. After a century of suppression, Ainu are reviving their religion, culture, language, and music and attempting to pass it on to their children. Okinawans (called Uchinanchu in their language) to the south have a distinctive linguistic and cultural heritage that evolved from the Kingdom of Ryukyu in the 16th century. Although its people have faced discrimination from both the Japanese government and the United States, contemporary Okinawa has a rich heritage of music, dance, religion, and way of life.

More than a million Koreans moved to Japan by force or voluntarily between 1910

DOS AND DON'TS

DO . . .

- Carry a pack of tissues and a handkerchief; public bathrooms may not have paper.

- Wear slip-on shoes and clean socks with no holes—you'll be taking your shoes off a lot.

- Take a small gift when visiting someone; if you go on a trip, bring back something (sweets, rice crackers) as *omiyage* (souvenirs) for your colleagues or host family.

- Make an offer more than once, whether it's your seat, carrying something, picking up the tab, or inviting someone to your home. In Japan, it's polite to refuse once or twice, so if you offer only once, they will not have a chance to accept.

- When you see an acquaintance, always mention the previous time you were together and thank them—it builds a connection.

- Touch or put an arm around friends of the same gender only.

- Remember the people who were kind to you by sending them a Christmas or New Year's card every year after you leave Japan.

DON'T . . .

- Chew gum at work or in class.

- Stick your chopsticks in your rice bowl (looks like incense for the deceased).

- Pour *shoyu* (soy sauce) over white rice. The side dishes are well seasoned—take a bite of rice and a bite of the side dish and chew to blend.

- Sit cross-legged on the floor if you're a woman—it's just not done (although in Korea it's common).

- Hug and kiss in public unless you like being stared at—these days you do see some couples showing affection. Holding hands is fine!

and 1945 (the period of Japan's colonization of Korea). Descendants of these Koreans are now youth of the third and fourth generation, permanent residents but non-citizens, many of whom speak only Japanese and have never been to Korea. Some have taken Japanese citizenship, but others haven't, because it means adopting a Japanese name and giving up Korean citizenship. The descendants of former outcasts from the Edo era, called *burakumin* (literally, hamlet-dwellers), still suffer discrimination in education, marriage, and jobs. Ethnically, they look no different than other Japanese, but their origins can still be traced because of the Japanese *koseki* (family register system), in which each Japanese individual's family origin and permanent address are recorded in a document containing every birth, marriage, death, and other personal information (such as mental illness). A copy of this family register must be presented when entering school (from kindergarten to university), applying for a job, or evaluating marriage prospects—many people hire private detectives to check out the family background of potential suitors.

More visible minorities in Japan include naturalized citizens from other parts of the globe outside Asia: immigrant workers from Southeast Asia and South America, children of international marriages (called "half" in Japan, and considered exotic if one parent is Caucasian), and residents with European, American, or African parentage who were raised in Japan. Several more invisible minorities are descendants of Japanese immigrants to the United States and other countries—such as Japanese

HOW TO . . .

© RUTHY KANAGY

In Japan, even kids are adept with chopsticks.

USE *HASHI*

Chopsticks can be made of wood, plastic, bamboo, lacquer, or ivory. You can get elegant his-and-hers sets or high-tech *hashi* made of wood with telescoping titanium tips. Family members each have their own *hashi*. Japanese children are skilled at using chopsticks, but they started by holding them in their fist and stabbing at food. You can find "training" *hashi* for children, with loops attached to put their fingers through. To use, hold the top *hashi* like a pencil and slide the other one under your thumb, between your middle and ring finger.

Don't be surprised if someone compliments you on your skill at using *hashi* (as if it were genetic!). I've often wanted to respond, *"Fooku joozu desu ne!"* ("You handle your fork well.") As for chopsticks as a hair ornament, it's not done in Japan. How about starting a new fad–a fork in your hair! Note: Japanese hold knives and forks Continental style, with the fork in the left hand, tines down. I suppose the American way of switching the fork from the right to the left hand when cutting is considered inelegant.

EAT JAPANESE STYLE

At the table, the rice bowl is on the left and soup bowl on the right with an array of smaller dishes behind them. *Hashi* are parallel to the edge of the table. Everything is dished out so there's no need to pass food as in the United States. Hold the rice bowl in your left hand as you take bites from other dishes. Don't pour *shoyu* (soy sauce) on your white rice! Instead, take a bite of a savory dish and a bite of rice and chew to blend flavors. How do you eat soup with chopsticks? Hold the bowl in your hands and sip, then pick out the solids with your *hashi*. *Ocha* (green tea) is often served at the end of the meal. If you're drinking alcohol, keep an eye on your neighbor's glass and refill it often (and let them fill your glass). When they pour for you say, *"Ah, Domo"* ("Oh, thanks"). There may be a speech and *kanpai* (toast) before everyone takes a sip.

Americans and Japanese Brazilians who've come to Japan to seek work or education; Japanese children born in China during the colonial years, who were abandoned in 1945 during the mass exodus of Japanese but have returned to Japan as adults to look for their kin; and Japanese children of business families who lived overseas but then returned to Japan. Called "returnees," bilingual-bicultural children are often pressured by peers and teachers to give up (or at least hide) their foreign language skills and identity, as these characteristics make them different from the "average" Japanese. However, many popular singers, such as Utada Hikaru, use their bilingual background to their advantage in composing songs in English and Japanese and even holding news conferences in English.

Customs and Etiquette

When you visit another culture you inevitably run into situations where local people speak or act in ways that seem surprising or even rude, based on your internalized rules of behavior. In Japanese restaurants, you will hear people loudly slurping their bowl of ramen (picking it up with both hands) or miso soup (soybean flavored soup) or tea or coffee. If you go out to eat with a group of Japanese friends, you may be surprised that everyone orders the same thing from the menu, and that they pour drinks only for others and never refill their own glass. You may see men pick their teeth in public, spit on the street, and, if they've had one too many beers, relieve themselves in a side street.

What you don't see is adults drinking juice or coffee or eating snacks on the train, bus, or while walking down the street. This will strike Japanese as uncouth. The same goes for chewing gum in class or at work. Blowing your nose in front of others is not very polite—especially at the dinner table. It's better to excuse yourself and do it in the restroom. If you forget to remove your shoes when entering someone's house or wear the "toilet" slippers in other parts of the house, your hosts will be puzzled by your lack of manners. Special slippers are provided just for the toilet cubicle, which is often separate from the bath.

And you aren't likely to have strangers you pass on the street look you in the eye and smile or greet you, even though saying "Hi" to people you don't know is common in the United States and considered "friendly." Japanese rarely initiate conversations with strangers while waiting for a bus or train, or tell their life story to the cashier while standing in line at the supermarket. The exception is when

© RUTHY KANAGY

Don't forget to change out of the toilet slippers when you leave the restroom!

children or pets are present. Then the smiles break out and people often smile and nod "Kon-ni-chi-wa" and even offer a child a treat. I suppose foreigners could be considered a kind of "pet," too, because they bring out "Hellos" from students learning English in school, and from adults whose inhibitions are released after several rounds of sake.

Social Values

IN-GROUP/OUT-GROUP

The public behaviors described above aren't arbitrary—they represent underlying social concepts. The notions of *uchi* (inside) and *soto* (outside) are applied to physical as well as psychological space. *Uchi* (which also means house) is clean and you want to keep it that way, so you remove your shoes and change into slippers (would you wear your shoes to bed?). *Uchi* applies to family and close friends at school or work who are your in-group. Strangers are outside your sphere, so unless a friend acts as go-between and introduces them, Japanese don't normally approach or talk to strangers. It's considered an intrusion on their privacy and in-group. The exception is an emergency situation. On the other hand, *gaijin,* who are foreign "others," fall outside the norms. Brave and motivated students and adults may approach you, asking, "Excuse me, sir. May I speak English with you?" It may be their first experience speaking to a live, native speaker (as opposed to those on TV or movies or language tapes), and it's kind to indulge. In exchange, you might ask them to teach you some Japanese phrases.

AFFILIATION

In Japan you are defined by your affiliation—the group that you belong to, whether family, school, or business. Most of the time you live and operate with your in-group. In the business world, people generally identify themselves by their company affiliation, not rank. "I'm Tanaka from Mitsubishi"; "I'm Yokota and I work for Sony"—even if they're the janitor. Levels of politeness are encoded in Japanese verbs, and before you can determine what degree of politeness you should use, you need to find out the other person's relative status. Age also commands respect.

So how can you, as the ultimate outsider, or *gaijin,* break into the system? The Japanese way is to have a letter of reference or someone to introduce you personally— my friends are your friends. Or you can participate in community events and local festivals, or join a ready-made group such as a hiking or cycle club, or take classes in traditional arts or other interests. A student learning from a master is one of the most honorable and long-lasting relationships. And learning the expressions for greeting and parting is one of the best ways to establish good relationships with neighbors and workmates. There are specific phrases for when you leave home, get to work, leave work, arrive home, and invite someone in. You will hear many of these as you observe people bowing and greeting each other in different settings.

ON

On are debts that continue for a lifetime and beyond. *On* (it's a nasal "n" with tongue in midair) are owed to people who have done kindnesses and favors for you. Children owe a debt to their parents for bringing them up. *On* are owed to teachers for instructing

GLBT JAPAN

Same-sex attraction and love has long been a part of Japanese Buddhism and samurai tradition, according to historical and literary references. The Tale of Genji, written in the 11th century by court lady Murasaki Shikibu and considered by many to be the world's first novel, includes a scene in which the womanizing title character consoles himself with the younger brother of one of his objects of affection. Kabuki theater has had an all-male cast for 400 years, and male actors who play female roles (onna-gata) attract a huge fan base and are often described as being more alluring than women. Similarly, the Takarazuka musical theater in Hyogo prefecture is known for its all-female troupe and attracts a mostly female audience. Many adolescent girls express an adoration for Takarazuka actresses who play male roles.

Compared to the United States, Japanese society seems rather nonchalant toward gender, as far as dress and mannerisms go. Cross-dressing is a common feature of comedy shows and even company parties, after the men are sufficiently inebriated. There are popular male TV personalities and singers who dress as women and act "feminine." Many of these came out of the "gay boom" in the 1990s, a period of increased media exposure for gays and lesbians that paralleled somewhat GLBT attention in the West.

Sexual orientation and expression seems to be on a continuum, without strict boundaries, at least during youth. Young Japanese guys are often rather soft-spoken and gentle in dress, speech, and manner, and might be thought of as "feminine" by macho U.S. standards. But not so in Japan—girls consider them masculine. Novels and manga taking up the theme of love between the same sex are very popular, especially among teenage girls and young women. Girls having crushes on older female students in junior and senior high school is very common, and seems to be a part of adolescence. At an all-girls junior high school in Tokyo I attended, younger girls would often write "love notes" to older girls, expressing their admiration and feelings—then they'd ask another girl to deliver them, as they were too shy.

It's common to see teenagers of the same gender holding hands (girls and young women) or walking arm in arm (both genders) in public. Japan has no legal prohibitions against same-sex attraction or homosexuality. Perhaps because of this, there doesn't appear to be any movement for legalizing same-sex marriage, as there is in the United States. On the other hand, there is a lot of social pressure to marry, and being single too long is considered a handicap for men in the business world. But more and more young women are now choosing to be single and choose their own path.

Sexual orientation in Japan is not such an either/or dichotomy as in the United States, so there's less emphasis on public "outing." What you do in your private life and with your in-group is your own business. You won't see large gay pride parades, as in the United States, although they pop up occasionally on a smaller scale.

and guiding you, to a go-between for introducing a marriage prospect. As a foreigner in Japan, you owe a debt to the person who acts as your financial guarantor or who referred you to a job. Japanese are very conscientious about always remembering to return favors and kindnesses received from others, even after a long period of time. One person who visited Japan describes it as a "cataloguing of obligation," like a "favor bank" in which you deposit and withdraw favors. Gift-giving is an example of small debts being returned. Whenever you visit someone's home you bring a gift—often some fruit or cakes. When you go on a trip, whether for business or pleasure, you always bring back a souvenir, or omiyage, for your family or colleagues. The give and take is part of how Japanese society works. Other types of on can't be repaid so easily, but you always express gratitude to that person and let them know that you are aware of your indebtedness. When you go to Japan you will likely have to ask a lot of favors—going to the bank, city hall, the post office, setting up utilities, getting furniture, enrolling children in school, figuring out public transportation. Someone is giving of their time and energy to help you and it's good to be aware and think about how you can repay them—if not literally, then in a show of gratitude for their time and expertise.

GENDER ROLES

There's a general perception by many Americans that Japanese women have lower status than men, that they don't have equal rights. As evidence, we point to the majority of Japanese women who marry, quit their jobs, and stay at home to raise children (or one child, these days) while men are out in the world. If women had equal rights, our thinking goes, they would want full-time careers, no? Each of us brings our own cultural values and perceptions with us when we encounter another culture. The word "housewife" in English has a connotation of low status, as in "just a housewife." By contrast, the Japanese term *shufu* is composed of two characters that mean "master" and "woman." In other words, *shufu* is the female master of the home. Japanese wives keep track of finances, make economic decisions, and give their husbands an allowance. They budget carefully and keep meticulous records of where the money goes and make decisions about the children's education. They shop frugally and buy fresh produce daily and take pride in cooking nutritious meals. Many women take classes in flower arranging, kimono wearing, tea ceremony, and cooking in order to prepare for their career in household management. In large urban areas the husband has a long commute, gets home late, and rarely sees the children except on Sundays. Some women say it's easier when their husband's not home—he's just one more child to take care of. Husbands who retire are sometimes referred to (tongue in cheek) as *sodai gomi,* or oversized trash. After working 60 hours a week for 30 years, the husband rattles around the house and gets in the way.

Would Japanese women rather switch their job for long hours of work at a company for 30 or more years? The answer is as varied as the individual. It is true that companies often hire young women fresh out of school to be "flowers of the office," to file papers and serve tea. At least they can go home at five, while women who choose the managerial track stay overtime with the majority of male employees. On the other hand, women who work as teachers, nurses, and in other service roles often continue their careers after marriage. And it's not unknown for men who are self-employed or writers to stay home while the wife works outside the home. Women are politicians and business owners and entrepreneurs. In Japan I never met a woman who wanted to swap places with a man.

Religion

In Japan, religious freedom is guaranteed by law—each individual is free to follow a faith or not, without fear of persecution. Interestingly, if you ask the average person in Japan about religion, she will likely reply, "I have no religion." Out of 127 million people, those who espouse formal affiliation with Shinto, Buddhism, or Christianity—the three main religions—are surprisingly few. But when you move to Japan, you will notice that there are numerous religious events at temples and shrines, and even religious parades in the street, depending on the time of year. And if you visit any of the famous temples and shrines in Kyoto, Nara, Kamakura, and elsewhere, you will see busloads of Japanese tourists with cameras who are just as interested in the sites as you are. How is it possible to profess no religion, yet participate in religious events? While growing up in Japan, I observed that in this society, religious practices and social customs are woven seamlessly through the yearly calendar and each individual's life cycle. In other words, people don't worry so much about whether something is religious or traditional—you do it because you've always done it that way, and your parents and grandparents did it that way, and because it makes you Japanese.

For example, what do most people in Japan do for New Year's, the biggest holiday of the year? Each year, around 87 million Japanese visit a shrine or temple during the first three days of January. (The rest of the population is off in Europe, Hawaii, or Las Vegas.) Those who remain in Japan go to a Buddhist temple just before midnight on December 31 to hear the *joya no kane* (temple bell) ring 108 times to atone for an equal number of sins of the past year. The solemn sound is televised nationally and internationally. As soon as New Year's Day breaks, millions elbow their way to Shinto shrines to offer money and prayers, and to buy good-luck charms (promising health, wealth, exam success, marriage, pregnancy, and protection from accidents). Shrines and temples with the largest crowds January 1–3 are Meiji Shrine in Tokyo, with 3.1 million visitors in 2002; Naritasan in Chiba prefecture, with 2.8 million; and Kawasaki Taishi in Kanagawa prefecture, with 2.8 million. That's almost one million people per day going to each of these sites. On January 15, everyone again goes to the local shrine for ceremonial burning of the good-luck charms and arrows from the previous year, now rendered ineffectual.

All three religions come into play at different points in Japanese people's lives—Shinto for blessings, Christianity (increasingly) for weddings, and Buddhism for funerals. Shinto is a celebration of life and reverence for the sacred. Buddhism takes care of sins, ancestors, and the afterlife. And Christianity, though claiming as members only one-half of 1 percent of the Japanese population, still has wide influence on Japanese society, particularly in education, social welfare, weddings, and, of course, Christmas Eve. Shinto and Buddhism, as practiced in Japan, are not exclusive—members of other religions are welcome. Christianity, when strictly observed, is exclusive, but in Japan, it is not necessarily so. Almost every Japanese person makes at least one pilgrimage to Kyoto and Nara to see the famous religious and historical sites they have studied during history classes. Usually, they go as part of a three- or four-day class trip during junior high or high school, similar to U.S. students' visits to Washington, D.C., to see historical monuments and museums. How did these religions become a part of Japanese life?

SHINTO

Shinto is the native Japanese religion, rooted in the mythological past and the origins of the imperial line. Shinto focuses on reverence toward *kami* (the divine), which is everywhere in nature, and emphasizes purification. Though there is no identified leader or scripture, the Shinto priest in traditional garb performs purification rites where needed—such as blessing the construction site of a new house or skyscraper. How can you tell if you're entering a shrine? If you pass through a *torii* (gate with two vertical posts topped by two horizontal posts), it's a Shinto shrine. Usually, these buildings are made of unpainted wood or concrete, and some famous shrines are painted red.

The best-known Shinto rite is probably the wedding ceremony. The bride and groom exchange sips of sake from lacquered cups nine times, in a ritual called *san-san-kudo*. The bride wears an elaborate kimono (rented for the occasion), along with a traditional Japanese hairdo, covered with a white cloth to hide her figurative "horns of jealousy."

After a baby is born, a naming ceremony is traditionally held on the seventh day. On the 31st day, baby girls are taken to the shrine to receive the priests' blessing; boys are taken on the 30th day. If you are visiting a shrine and happen to see a young woman in a kimono with a baby, accompanied by her parents, chances are they've come to dedicate their child. Another colorful event at shrines occurs on November 15, the Shichi-Go-San (Seven-Five-Three) holiday, which honors children aged three, five, or seven. You may see youngsters dressed in kimono or fancy clothes visiting shrines with their parents and grandparents.

In addition to their New Year's trip, many people go to shrines to pray for health, good luck in exams, finding a good marriage partner, becoming pregnant, and traveling safely. At a shrine, you first ring a bell by shaking the long rope hanging in front, then clap your hands twice and hold them together briefly while you say a prayer. You can throw some coins into the offering box. There are places to buy slips of paper telling your fortune, or charms to ward off worries. You can also purchase a wooden plaque called *ema* and write your wish on it, then tie it to the rack where other *ema* are hanging.

Shinto influences can be seen as you travel around the countryside. You will often see small shrines by the side of the road or next to a field with a statue of Jizo, the guardian deity of children, sometimes wearing a red cape.

Every community in Japan has a yearly Shinto festival. Usually during the summer months, a *mikoshi* (portable shrine) is jostled on the shoulders of young men and women through the streets to bring blessings to each home. Some festivals, such as the Sanja Matsuri (Three Shrine Festival) in Tokyo in mid-May, are quite elaborate and go on for several days. Further evidence of Shinto influence in the community appears at the end of the year, when people set up *kadomatsu* (pine branches) at the gates of their homes and businesses, and car grills are decorated with charms to start the new year auspiciously.

A final manifestation of Shinto can be found in Japanese traditional wrestling, called *sumo*. The referee is dressed as a Shinto priest and stands under a suspended roof of a Shinto shrine to preside over each match. To warm up, the *rikishi* (wrestlers) first rinse their mouths ceremonially with water, then throw handfuls of salt on the earthen *sumo* ring for purification before beginning the match. In the past decade or so, many *rikishi* of foreign nationalities have joined the *sumo* world. Some, including several Americans, did quite well, rising to the highest rank of *yokozuna* (grand

© RUTHY KANAGY

Buddha at Jourenji temple in Tokyo, amidst cherry blossoms

champion)—Akebono and Musashimaru from Hawaii (now retired), and Asashoryu and Hakuho from Mongolia. So many non-Japanese wrestlers have joined that concerns have come up about the "gaijinization" (too many foreigners) of this most traditional of Japanese sports.

BUDDHISM

Bukkyo (Buddhism) came to Japan from India, via China and Korea, in the 6th century. It was adopted by the imperial court and spread by Prince Shotoku among the aristocrats. From the 13th century on, it was popularized throughout Japan and developed into numerous sects. Zen Buddhism was widely practiced by the samurai class, and other sects, such as Jodoshinshu (Pure Land), still exist today. Buddhism teaches that enlightenment is attained by encountering truths—that life is transitory, all is insubstantial, and one must attain tolerance. Buddhism has influenced Japanese art, literature, and architecture, as well as the fundamental morals of society. Whether believers or not, most people have Buddhist funerals and are given Buddhist posthumous names.

How is Buddhism practiced in daily life? Many Japanese families have Buddhist altars in their homes—usually passed down to the eldest son in each generation—where they offer food and prayers to their relatives who have passed, to speed them on their journey to paradise. When someone dies, relatives gather and a Buddhist priest is called to the home to recite the sutra after the prescribed number of days or years (49th day, one year, and so on). On Buddhist holidays, families go to their affiliated temple to clean the family gravesite and offer incense, flowers, and prayers. The family name is carved into the gravestone, and each member that passes becomes a part of the family grave. Cremation is customary, and after the urn of ashes has rested in the home for a set number of days, it is placed in the family grave with the others.

My friend, whom I'll call Masuda-san, married late in life to a widower war veteran 10 years older than herself. They purchased a comfortable condominium in Tokyo and enjoyed traveling, photography, and their pet cat; her husband died 10 years later. When I first visited her home, Masuda-san was in the kitchen whipping up a sweet red bean soup. In one corner of her dining room, I noticed a polished table holding a vertical tablet with Japanese characters. In front were a plate of individually wrapped *nashi* (Asian pears) and a box of rice crackers. On the wall was a black-and-white photo of her husband in uniform. Seeing my interest, she remarked how she still talked to her husband every day—about her newfound hobby taking flower pictures, about her volunteer work at a children's science museum, about her cat. Having an altar in the home seems to tie the living closer to their kin who have gone ahead.

CHRISTIANITY

Kirisutokyo (Christianity) originated in the Middle East, moved into Europe, and was introduced to Japan by missionary Francis Xavier in 1549. For several decades, it enjoyed the blessing of the shogun and spread rapidly; then the guillotine dropped, Japanese Christians were hunted down and killed, and the religion of the "barbarians" was banned for 250 years.

Christianity often enters daily life when parents choose what kindergarten their child will attend. Both Protestant and Catholic churches in Japan operate kindergartens for youth aged 3–5 and are regarded by parents as a good place for their children to begin their education. My parents started a church and a kindergarten in eastern Hokkaido as a way of reaching out to the community and providing a service. I started my education at Aiko Yochien (Love-Light Kindergarten), which is still going strong after 50 years. Similarly, some parents decide on Catholic school for their children— even if they are not members of the church, they still have a respect for Christian teachings. Many Japanese fondly recall their Christian kindergarten or Sunday school experience and the songs they sang. Some Japanese go to church to learn English, especially if the pastor is an English-speaking missionary.

In recent years, Christian weddings have become popular in Japan. Many couples opt for the fantasy wedding with a white gown, a tux, and a "wedding chapel" in a five-star hotel. Often, neither the foreign "minister" conducting the package wedding nor anyone involved in the planning or executing is actually Christian, but it pays well. It's customary for guests at the wedding reception to pay a specified fee, which helps out with the large expense borne by the couple's families. A Japanese reception is a veritable fashion show, with the bride disappearing and reappearing in different evening gowns, while pictures of the couple's individual childhoods are projected on a screen, along with predictions of their future together.

Officially, the number of Christians in Japan is small, about one-half of 1 percent. However, the influence of Christianity is disproportionate to that statistic—there have been numerous Christian politicians, such as the founding members of the Social Democratic Party, Nitobe Inazo, social activist Uchimura Kanzo, Kagawa Toyohiko, and Yoshino Sakuzo; the founders of the Japan Farmers' Union and the predecessor to the Japan Federation of Labor; the founders of Christian schools, including Doshisha University, Aoyama Gakuen University, Sophia University, and Obirin University; and the founder of YMCA Japan (Kozaki Hiromichi). Christian writers (Endo Shusaku, Miura Ayako, and many more) have also earned great respect in Japanese society.

The Arts

LITERATURE

The earliest Japanese written works appeared in the 8th century, one a record of *Kojiki* (ancient myths passed down orally), and the other a *Nihonshoki* (chronological history of Japan). Both were written in *kanji* (Chinese characters) and adapted to the Japanese language. *Manyoshu,* the oldest anthology of poetry, appeared in the same century, containing 4,500 poems. Many of the poems are *tanka* (short poems) consisting of 31 syllables in five-seven-five-seven-seven-syllable lines. The beauty of nature and life and, in particular, a deep sense of yearning are important elements in *tanka.* Their words evoke a wealth of associations.

Perhaps the best-known volume in the *bungaku* (literature) of the early period is *Genji Monogatari (The Tale of Genji),* written in the 11th century by court lady Murasaki Shikibu. The novel focuses on Prince Genji and the women around him.

Heike Monogatari (The Tale of the Heike), an epic tale written in the 13th century, is about the fierce battles between the Genji and Heike clans, ending in defeat for the ruling Heike in 1185. This narrative masterpiece, depicting the proud coming to ruin, was chanted to the accompaniment of a four-stringed Japanese instrument called the *biwa.* The Heike story is part of the repertoire of Noh, Bunraku, and Kabuki theaters.

In the late 17th century (the middle of the Edo period), Matsuo Basho developed an art form, taking the opening verse of a longer linked verse *(haikai renga)* and expressing nature, life, and the esthetic values of austere elegance *(sabi)* and delicate beauty *(shiori).* Later, this new form came to be known as haiku, the fixed verse form consisting of 17 syllables in a five-seven-five pattern. In the United States, students are often introduced to haiku in elementary school and encouraged to compose haiku in English. Perhaps the brevity of haiku suggests simplicity. However, in Japan, haiku are considered far too subtle and complex for children, and are often taken up as an avocation by the older generation. Winners of haiku and fixed-verse competitions often have their work published in the newspaper.

In the late 19th century, a new kind of literature influenced by the West emerged, written by authors who became well known abroad. Natsume Soseki, one of the most popular among modern writers, published the novel *Wagahai wa Neko de Aru (I Am a Cat)* in 1905. Written from the perspective of a cat belonging to an English teacher, the piece uses satirical humor to convey the author's own social views. Jun'ichiro Tanizaki wrote *Sasame Yuki (The Makioka Sisters),* about the lives of four sisters from an Osaka merchant family during the late 1930s. The novel became popular for its dreamlike depiction of a happier, more affluent life than the stark reality and militarization of prewar Japan. The Japanese title means "lightly falling snow," and the book was later adapted as a motion picture featuring lush outdoor scenes of the Arashiyama area of Kyoto in each of four seasons.

Yasunari Kawabata is a modern writer who received the Nobel Prize in Literature in 1968 in recognition of such works as *Izu no Odoriko (Izu Dancer), Yukiguni (Snow Country),* and *Koto (Ancient City).* His work carries one of the underlying themes of classical Japanese literature—the transitory nature of life. Numerous other Japanese authors, including Yukio Mishima and Haruki Murakami, have also become well known abroad.

THEATER

Japanese music, art, cinema, and *engeki* (theater) are inseparable from literary tradition and often deal with the same stories and themes through different media.

Noh

Japan's oldest theater, Noh, dates back to ancient times and developed into its present form in the 14th century. It is a very formal, stylized dance-drama accompanied by song, narration, three types of drums, and a wooden flute. ("There's no music like Noh music," as foremost Japanese musicologist William P. Malm used to say.) The masked main character performs slow dance movements enacting tales of god, man, woman, madness, and demons. The concepts are derived from Buddhist influences. Most Japanese people have never seen Noh live. For better appreciation by the uninitiated, it's helpful to do some background reading or attend a performance with a knowledgeable person. *Takigi noh* (bonfire Noh), performed outdoors in the summer at night—in a forest illuminated by fire from torches—is an unforgettable experience.

Kabuki

Kabuki originated in 1603, when Izu no Okuni, a former shrine maiden, arrived in Kyoto with a group of dancing girls and caused a stir. Their unorthodox dancing was banned, and some time later, Kabuki was limited to male actors performing male and female roles in plays and dances of the 17th and 18th centuries. During the Edo period, Kabuki became popular among the merchant class. The term Kabuki consists of three *kanji* characters meaning "song-dance-skill." Kabuki is the most popular of the traditional Japanese theater types, because of its flamboyant colors and costumes, exaggerated gestures and *kata* (form), and revolving stages, trap doors, and even flying lions. The stories center on domestic themes, such as love triangles and love suicides, or historic samurai battles.

Bunraku

Bunraku is the traditional Japanese puppet theater that developed in the Osaka area. The puppets are not suspended by string; rather, each one is manipulated by three puppeteers wearing black face covers and costumes (except the head puppeteer). The puppets are large, about two-thirds life-size, with mechanical arms and legs and moving eyes, eyebrows, and mouths, resulting in amazingly lifelike expressions. The repertoire is similar to Kabuki, covering domestic tales and historical tales, accompanied by a *shamisen* (three-stringed lute played with a large triangular plectrum) and an extremely expressive singer/narrator who is the voice for all the characters. The term Bunraku comes from the name of the man who built the Bunraku-za theater in Osaka in 1872.

© RUTHY KANAGY

The Taisho *koto* is a traditional Japanese instrument.

MUSIC
Traditional Music

The numerous *hogaku* (traditional music) genres and instruments are mostly unknown to those outside Japan, and even to many within. *Gagaku* is court music. Played on several distinctive reed instruments that produce an unforgettable sound, this musical style came from ancient China and was preserved for centuries. Performances take place mostly at the Imperial Palace on formal occasions. A four-stringed, pear-shaped lute called a *biwa* was played by itinerant Buddhist monks in the feudal age to narrate epic tales of battles (such as the *Tale of the Heike* from the 12th century) as they traveled from Kamakura, seat of the shogun, to the imperial capital of Kyoto. Another kind of lute is the three-stringed *shamisen* (one of the instruments that accompany Kabuki and Bunraku theater). It has a square body and long neck and is played by plucking the strings with a triangular plectrum. *Shamisen* accompanies numerous traditional dance types, as well as *minyo* (folk music). Each region of Japan has its own folk music, handed down through the generations. At Obon (Buddhist All Soul's Day) festivals in mid-August, local communities dance to the folk songs of their region.

Another type of music that accompanies Kabuki theater is called *nagauta* (literally, "long song"), played by an orchestra of *shamisen,* three kinds of *taiko* (drums), and flutes. The *koto* is a 13-stringed chamber instrument made of hollowed-out paulownia wood. The sound board is six feet long and a foot wide, and it has movable bridges to hold up the silk or nylon strings. The performer kneels facing the *koto* and uses three finger picks to pluck the strings. Similar instruments found in China and Korea suggest that the *koto* may have come from the Continent many years ago. The five-holed *shakuhachi* is a bamboo flute with a beautiful haunting tone. *Koto, shamisen,* and *shakuhachi* are frequently performed together as a trio. Japanese children are introduced to Japanese traditional music in middle school, but unless they take a personal interest and study an instrument, traditional music is mostly passed up in favor of more accessible contemporary sounds.

Nontraditional Music

You will hear music everywhere you go in Japan—most of it loud, and almost none of it traditional. Japanese youth listen to the same kind of *ongaku* (nontraditional music) as their contemporaries across the Pacific. Their parents or grandparents grew up listening to Bob Dylan, the Beatles, and other 1960s and 1970s rock. There are dozens of music shows on TV, with scores of live singing and dancing pop idols who participate in interview and game shows. Likewise, on the radio, J-Pop (Japanese pop music) is everywhere, with songs introduced by a hip English-speaking DJ. In addition to pop, there's also gangsta rap in Japanese and heavy metal groups such as Yellow Machine Gun (a three-woman band), Shonen Knife, and many more. Live clubs are everywhere, and often very crowded (clustered around big train stations like Shinjuku, Shibuya, or Kichijoji in Tokyo). These clubs play all genres of rock, blues, jazz, and country—yes, you can dance the two-step with Japanese cowboys. You can also be your own DJ on your MP3 player or *keitai* (cell phone).

Classical music also has a huge following in Japan. There are fine symphony orchestras in all the major cities, and educational TV broadcasts live performances. Many children start taking piano or violin lessons before kindergarten (you may hear them practicing in the adjacent apartment), then enter competitions and travel to New York or Europe for advanced study. Coffee shops catering to lovers of *kurashikku* (classical) play nothing but that. One classical music event draws a large percentage of listeners to concert halls across the countries every December. No, it's not Handel's *Messiah;* it's the well-known *Daiku,* or Beethoven's Ninth Symphony. Amateur and professional performances of the famous choral symphony continue through the month of December. Some choruses number as many as 10,000 singers, according to the *Asahi* newspaper. This all started because a German POW, confined to the island of Shikoku during the Pacific War, taught the music to his captors. The Japanese love music... and they have long memories. All of the old Stephen Foster songs are taught in school music curricula, and students still march to the tune of "Turkey in the Straw" for the annual all-school *undokai* (sports day).

ART

Many countries outside Japan have museums with fine collections of Japanese *geijutsu* (art), including paintings, calligraphy, ceramics, lacquer, cloisonné, swords, wood carvings, and Japanese gardens. These art forms are more accessible to people outside Japan than are traditional theater and music. The greatest concentration of museums in Japan are the National Museums next to Ueno station in Tokyo.

Shodo (Japanese calligraphy) is taught from elementary school to instill depth and beauty in writing *kanji* and *kana* characters. Calligraphy, created using brushes of different thickness dipped in *sumi* (ink) and applied to fine paper, expresses the artist's sense of beauty and personality. Calligraphy is traditionally displayed in the *tokonoma* (alcove) of a Japanese-style room in the home. Every year on January 2, students gather

SAKURA

Sakura (cherry blossoms) have long been part of Japanese culture, celebrated throughout history in song, verse, art, film, and on the backs of ¥100 coins. The words to a popular tune go:

> *Sakura, sakura, yayoi no sora wa . . .*
> Spring sky as far as one can see
> Is it mist or a cloud?
> Fragrance wafting in the air
> Come, oh come, let us go and see.
> (author's translation)

Why are *sakura*, with their exquisite beauty and short life, loved so much? Fragile petals emerging from hoary branches to bloom for a few days, then scatter to the earth, seem to represent the Buddhist notion of the transitory nature of life. *Sakura* were used as a nationalistic tool during World War II to rally citizens and soldiers, and also given as a sign of international friendship—3,000 *sakura* trees presented to the United States in 1912 and planted along the Tidal Basin in Washington, D.C., are still enjoyed 100 years later.

The most popular variety is the Somei Yoshino (Yoshino cherry), with five pale pink notched petals. Yaezakura, with multi-layered rich pink blossoms, Shidare-zakura (weeping cherry), and native Yama-zakura (mountain cherry) are also widespread. *Sakura* petals are used for tea and in sweets such as *sakura-mochi*, wrapped in salted cherry leaves (my favorite!). *Sakura* trees are planted around many schools and public buildings—their blooming in April marks the start of the new school year and fiscal year. *Sakura* line rivers and canals and are planted in parks. When in full bloom, there's nothing quite like strolling under a pink cloud and watching the petals fall like pink snow.'

The best way to enjoy *sakura* is, of course, to go on *hanami*, flower viewing picnics with family and coworkers. One member of the group goes early in the morning to lay a giant blue tarp to reserve a spot under the trees. *Hanami* parties can get very crowded and loud, with food, sake, and beer flowing freely, accompanied by boisterous karaoke and dancing.

Almost every town and city has a *hanami* spot. In Tokyo, popular places are Shinjuku Gyoen Park and the Chidorigafuchi Imperial Palace moat, where you can you rent a rowboat and glide under the blossoms. In Kyoto, you can walk the Philosopher's Path or stroll the Arashiyama hills. The most famous location for *hanami* is Yoshino, south of Kyoto, where 30,000 cherry trees were planted on the mountains a thousand years ago. Himeji castle is also picturesque (once restorations are completed in 2016).

The Cherry Blossom Front—predicting when *sakura* will bloom in each region of Japan—is the topic of nightly television news. Peak bloom forecasts, from late January in Okinawa to early May in Hokkaido, are watched closely by tour companies and citizens alike (see www.jnto. go.jp/sakura/eng/index.php).

---

to write auspicious sayings for the new year, a practice known as *kakizome* (first writing), and the best receive awards.

Oil and water painting are the most widespread forms among Japanese artists. Traditional Japanese painting on silk or Japanese paper using *sumi* and mineral colors is also taught. Early Japanese painting was influenced by Buddhist art from China. During the Edo period, *ukiyo-e* (wood-block prints) became the first mass-produced art. Subjects included portraits of famous Kabuki actors, beauties, and *sumo* wrestlers, as well as landscapes, historical themes, and nature.

Ceramics also play an important role in Japan. The earliest prehistoric period (called Jomon) is named for the type of pottery produced, namely earthenware with a cord design. Up to the 6th century, Japanese ceramics were influenced by Korean and Chinese craftsmen bringing in new techniques. Seto City in the Chubu region of Honshu became so famous for fine ceramics that ceramic wares are now called *setomono* (Seto objects) in Japanese. Each region of Japan has at least one or two towns famous for the type of pottery they make, and for techniques such as *rakuyaki* (Raku firing). Lacquer is a product of many countries in Asia. It uses a liquid from under the bark of a lacquer tree, which is then mixed with pigment. Applied and dried in the right kind of air, the layers of coating take on a high sheen. Lacquer was used on Buddhist images and buildings, as well as tableware and *hashi* (chopsticks).

Japanese sword-making came to Japan from China and Korea and has a long history. During the Edo period, swords were very important to the samurai class for protection (they could carry two), and they were considered the soul of a warrior. Now they are largely decorative, acquired either as heirlooms or by collectors. Traditional wood carving of various types also developed over a long period of time. For household furniture such as *tansu* (dressers to store kimonos), it was crucial that the wood be resistant to the hot and humid climate.

Japanese gardens are known the world over for their careful simplicity and asymmetry, belying close attention to detail. They require intensive manual labor to maintain. There are many famous gardens throughout the country, including Kenrokuen in Kanazawa, Suizenji in Kumamoto, and Katsura Rikyu (Katsura Imperial Garden) and Ryoanji's Zen Garden in Kyoto.

PLANNING YOUR FACT-FINDING TRIP

Many people are attracted to karate, *sumo,* Zen Buddhism, anime, or high-tech gadgetry, and imagine how great it would be to experience these things in Japan. A fact-finding trip is an important step to take before deciding on a permanent move, however. Unlike a casual tourist, you are on a mission to discover whether you can be happy living in a foreign environment for an extended period. If you've never felt what it's like to be a minority member of a society, you will experience it for the first time in Japan. Lack of fluency in Japanese will limit you until you gain more skill. Before you go, talk to people who've lived there and gather as much information as you can about jobs and housing in the regions you plan to visit. The more reading and research you do and the more contacts you make in advance, the more you will gain from the trip.

© RUTHY KANAGY

Preparing to Leave

WHAT TO TAKE
Documents
U.S. citizens who are going to Japan as a "temporary visitor" or tourist can stay up to 90 days without a visa. Make sure you have your return air ticket and that your passport is valid for at least 90 days beyond your arrival date. Foreigners entering Japan must provide fingerprint scans and have their photograph taken as part of entry procedures (with certain exceptions, including children under 16 years of age). Bring your health insurance card, emergency contact numbers, and travel insurance. There are no immunization requirements.

Books
If you speak Japanese, you're ahead of the game. Pack your guidebooks, dictionary, and clothes and you're ready to go. If you don't know Japanese but have a good ear, a sense of humor, and a skill for drawing and pantomime, take along a good phrasebook and try to absorb as much language as you can during the trip. Take along a chart of Japanese *kana* (phonetic letters). If you can memorize the 46 square-shaped *katakana* letters, you'll be able to read menus in coffee shops and Western-style restaurants, as well as foreign names and places. Invest in a good Japanese–English/English–Japanese dictionary.

Clothing
Japanese people dress up, whether shopping, riding the train, or going out to eat. Only joggers wear sweat suits, and women dress conservatively. Wearing revealing clothing, tube tops, and miniskirts may draw unwanted looks. If you're job hunting, bring a nice shirt and tie or a dress. In summer, when it's hot and muggy, light colored, moisture-wicking, quick-drying clothing is best. Bring your hat and comfortable slip-on shoes. Shorts are worn for sports, but otherwise long pants are the norm. In Hokkaido, you'll want a sweater and jacket on cool summer evenings. In fall and spring, add long-sleeve tops and, in winter, warm coat and gloves. A light rain jacket is handy. Above all, travel light! You will be lugging your suitcase up and down steps. A rolling backpack is practical.

Miscellaneous
As for toiletries, take sunblock, deodorant, skincare items, and pain medication. These are available, but somewhat more expensive. Shampoo, razors, and toothpaste are inexpensive and can be found at 100-yen shops ($1.25). You can bring up to one month's supply of prescription medications—note that U.S. prescriptions are not transferable. Reading material for wait or travel time is wise, and souvenirs or postcards from home are nice as gifts for people who help you out.

Japan has one time zone and does not change clocks for daylight savings time as in the United States. From mid-March to October, Japan is 13 hours ahead of eastern time and 16 hours ahead of Pacific time. When it's noon in Seattle, it's 4 A.M. the following morning in Tokyo. From November to mid-March (standard time), Japan is

14 hours ahead of eastern time and 17 hours ahead of Pacific time. Noon in New York is 2 A.M. the next day in Japan.

Electricity is 100 volts, while the United States is 120 volts. Most electrical appliances will work, with less power. Tokyo and eastern Japan are on 50 hertz, while Osaka in western Japan is 60 hertz. This will not make a significant difference in most electronic equipment.

MONEY
How Much to Take?

If you are frugal and stay in inexpensive hotels and eat cheaply, $200 per day is adequate for food and lodging. Bring another $75–100 per day for travel and shopping. If you're going for deluxe accommodations and food, you might budget up to $500 a day. Transportation by air or bullet train should be budgeted for separately. Travelers checks are no longer as useful because cash is available from cash machines (ATMs) that accept international bankcards. You can use a debit or credit card at 7-Eleven stores, as well as at post offices. Smaller towns may not have a 7-Eleven, and post offices are closed nights and weekends. Be prepared to have adequate cash with you each day because many smaller hotels and restaurants don't accept credit cards. Travelers checks have limited use other than in a few large department stores and shops catering to foreign tourists. Foreign exchanges at major airports have competitive rates and take less time than at banks (and not all banks have a foreign exchange service). Personal checks are not used in Japan—electronic banking is the norm. Lastly, be sure to inform your home bank about your travel plans, or they may block your ATM card when you try to use it abroad. It can take several days and numerous phone calls to straighten it out, and meanwhile, you are cashless (as I found out the hard way).

Currency and Exchange

The Japanese monetary unit is 円, *en* ("yen" in English). Common bills are *sen-en* (¥1,000), *gosen-en* (¥5,000), and *ichi-man-en* (¥10,000), distinct in color and size; *nisen-en* ¥2,000 bills are infrequently used. Coins are *ichi-en* (¥1), *go-en* (¥5), *ju-en* (¥10), *goju-en* (¥50), *hyaku-en* (¥100), and *gohyaku-en* (¥500), in different sizes and colors. Five- and 50-yen coins have a hole in the middle. Most vending machines take up to ¥10,000 bills. The foreign exchange rate for yen to U.S. dollar in 2012 fluctuated between ¥76 and ¥84. For convenience, we use the rate of ¥80 to the U.S. dollar in this book. Not all banks offer foreign exchange; those that do require your passport and may have short hours.

Taxes and Tipping

In Japan, the customer is king; shopping is a pleasure and customer service is excellent. Larger hotels, department stores, restaurants, and taxis accept major credit cards, but there are still many shops, eateries, and inns that will only take cash. A 5 percent consumption tax will be added to your bill. (In 2012 the government put forth a proposal to raise the consumption tax to 8 percent in 2014 and to 10 percent in 2015.) You don't need to leave a tip in restaurants, taxis, hotels, or elsewhere in Japan, and if you try, it will likely be refused. A smile and thanks (*"Arigatoo gozaimasu"*) will do.

HOW TO . . .

REMOVE YOUR SHOES

When you visit a Japanese school, home, inn, or traditional restaurant you remove your shoes and step into slippers. Why bring the outside dirt in? Wearing slip-on shoes makes this easier, as you'll be removing your shoes often (and make sure your socks don't have holes!). At the entry, take one foot at a time out of your shoe and deftly slide it into the slipper *without stepping on the entry floor*, which is dirty. Then turn around and straighten your shoes, toes pointing out. In college when I lived with a host family in Tokyo, I would plop my shoes down any which way in the *genkan* (entry), much to the dismay of my host mom, who thought I was rude and undisciplined. (Maybe she was right!)

BOW

When bowing, bend from the waist and don't look the other person in the eye. The depth and length of your bow signals your relationship. Students nod and say *"Ohayo"* ("Mornin'") to each other, but bow deeper and say *"Ohayo gozaimasu"* ("Good morning") to their teacher. Parents teach children to bow by gently pushing their head down when they say *"Arigatoo"* ("Thanks"). Adults use the more formal *"Arigatoo gozaimasu"* ("Thank you"). If you want to see bowing as art, visit a large *depaato* (department store) right when they open at 10 A.M. The entire staff, from clerks to managers, line up and freeze into a deep bow while saying *"Irassahimase"* ("Welcome"). They even use "bowing machines" to train employees to bend an exact number of degrees. You'll know you're Japanese when you start bowing while talking on your cell phone!

WHEN TO GO

Spring and fall are the most pleasant seasons to visit Japan. Cherry blossoms start blooming in January in Okinawa, and in late March to early April in Tokyo. Temperatures in April and May are moderate and comfortable. June to mid-July is the rainy season, after which most of Japan (except Hokkaido) turns hot and muggy. July to early October is an ideal time to visit Hokkaido, which has cool summers and no set rainy season. September can still be very warm in much of Japan. Fall colors are at their peak in late October through November, and scenic destinations, including Kyoto, are quite crowded. Winter is brisk, and as central heating is not common in homes nor in older *ryokan* inns, guest rooms may be drafty. Southern Kyushu and subtropical Okinawa are possible winter destinations. However, to gain a realistic idea of what the weather in Japan is like, you might plan a visit in summer or winter to see how it feels. If you like to ski, Hokkaido and the central mountains of Gunma and Nagano are great in winter. Sapporo holds an International Snow Festival in the first week of February, attracting millions. New Year's is the biggest holiday of the year and there are crowds everywhere. Most businesses close between December 28 and January 3, so it's not a good time to search for jobs and housing. Avoid traveling during major holidays such as New Year's, Golden Week (April 29–May 5), and Obon (August 14–17), when 127 million people are on the move or flying overseas.

JOIN A TOUR

If this is your first trip to a non-English-speaking country and you're nervous about getting around on your own, organized tours are an option. Day tours or multi-day tours of Tokyo, Kyoto, Osaka, and other regions with an English-speaking guide can provide lots of information. Japan National Tourist Organization (JNTO, www.jnto.go.jp) is a good source of information; call the U.S. office for free maps and brochures. Some cities, such as Hiroshima, Osaka, Kyoto, Nara, and Tokyo have volunteer guides—local residents who want to introduce English speakers to their city. Reserve ahead by phone or email through JNTO's website.

How about a tour on two wheels? Cycle Tokyo! will introduce you to the metropolis by bicycle on weekends, by advance reservation (http://cycle-tokyo.cycling.jp). Kyoto Cycling Project (www.kctp.net/en) offers guided tours including bike rental.

Arriving in Japan

Most international flights from North America land in Tokyo (Narita Airport or Haneda Airport) or Osaka (Kansai Airport). If your final destination is another city you will transfer to a domestic flight, or if you have a Japan Rail Pass, you can take the airport train to the nearest *shinkansen* (bullet-train) station. Information on transportation is available in English at the airport. Once you leave the airport, however, you may look around and realize with a shock that you can't read the signs! This can be very disorienting—yesterday you were a competent adult and now you're reduced to an illiterate dependent. There are some challenges in finding your way at first, but be assured that Japan is a safe place and most people are very kind if you need help.

© RUTHY KANAGY

With a Japan Rail Pass, you can ride the *shinkansen* to different areas of Japan.

CUSTOMS

During your flight to Japan, you'll receive customs and immigration forms to fill out. List any expensive items you are bringing in, such as cameras or electronic equipment, so you won't be charged duty when you leave. Bring original prescriptions along with medications. Do not even consider bringing illegal drugs or firearms into the country. Japanese laws are very strict in this regard and you may be arrested or deported. Upon arrival, you'll line up with other foreigners and show your passport and immigration and customs forms, be fingerprinted, and have your photo taken. If you are *not* entering as a temporary visitor and already have a visa as a mid- to long-term resident, you will be issued a resident card at Narita, Haneda, Chubu, or Kansai Airport (at other ports of entry, a resident card will be mailed to your place of residence after you complete residency

KO-NE (CONNECTIONS) FOR YOUR FACT-FINDING TRIP

If it's your first trip to Japan, the best entrée is to contact people and set up interviews and appointments in advance. If you don't know anyone in Japan, try these steps to establish *ko-ne* before you go (see the *Resources* section for more details).

- Does your town or state have a sister city/prefecture in Japan? Talk to your city's chamber of commerce and state office of tourism. There may be a delegation coming from Japan that you can meet. For example, Portland, Oregon, and Sapporo, Hokkaido, have annual citizen exchanges.

- Does your university have an alumni association in Japan? If so, get in touch before you go. Arrange interviews with American and Japanese alumni of your university who are living and working in Japan.

- Find out if the professional organizations you belong to have affiliates in Japan. Time your fact-finding trip with a professional conference or meeting in Japan. Some trip expenses may be tax-deductible. Japan Association of Language Teachers has chapters in many cities.

- Research language schools and universities with programs in Japan and arrange to visit students and professors.

- Search "Japan with kids" online for a list of international schools.

- Contact cycling, hiking, judo, or other interest groups in Japan and ask if they have events you can participate in during your trip. Cycling groups such as Cycle Tokyo! and the Kyoto Cycling Project will take you on a tour.

- Search www.gaijinpot.com, www.japan-guide.com, www.gojapan.about.com, and *Metropolis* (www.metropolis.co.jp) for housing, jobs, and contacts.

- Contact the American chamber of commerce in Tokyo and other cities for information on housing, jobs, and setting up your business in Japan.

- Contact the Japanese chamber of commerce, Japanese language schools, and Japanese businesses in your town or state and request information on cities you plan to visit and ask for introductions to businesses and schools in Japan.

- Read the *Nikkei Weekly* and other Japanese newspapers online (in English) to become familiar with key issues in society.

- Ask your realtor to recommend a realtor in Japan.

- A personal introduction is the best entry into Japanese society. Make sure to carry out your part and not abuse it.

procedures at your local municipal office). After completing entry procedures, pick up your bags and look for the counters selling airport-bus or train tickets. If you have more luggage than you want to carry, there are several baggage delivery service counters—called *takkyuubin*. Fill out your destination address and they will deliver your bags anywhere in Japan, including your hotel, for about $25 per piece—very convenient!

TRANSPORTATION

Airport buses and trains will take you to the center city, whether Tokyo or Osaka. Narita Airport's Limousine Bus stops at major hotels and stations in Tokyo in 1–2 hours. JR (Japan Railway) Narita Express train delivers you to Tokyo station in 60 minutes and Shinjuku station in 80 minutes. The Keisei Skyliner goes to Ueno station in Tokyo in 55 minutes.

Most areas of Japan are accessible by train, bus, or ferry. The *shinkansen* speeds along elevated rails, but not cheaply. Students and others looking for a cheaper way take overnight highway buses, between Tokyo and Kyoto or other cities. Using a 7-, 14-, or 21-day Japan Rail Pass will save you lots of yen and it's valid on all JR trains, buses, and ferries. An exception is the Nozomi *shinkansen,* which is extra. The pass is only valid for temporary visitors staying 90 days or less, and you have to purchase a voucher for it *outside* Japan (contact your local travel agent at home), which is exchanged for the actual pass in Japan. What about driving? Rental cars are available, but gasoline is around ¥160 per liter—that's $7.50 a gallon! And if you're not used to city traffic and driving on the left, it could be nerve-wracking. Many road signs are in Japanese only. If you do drive, you will need a valid international driver's license from your local automobile association.

Sample Itineraries

From Tokyo you can fly north to Hokkaido or south to Kyushu in an hour and a half. But you won't be able to see the whole country in a week or two. Since the purpose of your trip is to get a realistic picture of what it's like to live in Japan, it's a good idea to focus on one or two cities or regions if you're planning a one- or two-week visit. And unless you're set on living in an urban area, you will enjoy getting out of the cities and seeing some smaller towns and villages, where there's a different rhythm to daily life. If your vacation time is limited to one week, with good advance planning you should be able to gather information on housing and job options in one or two locations. Two weeks will allow time to visit several different regions. A one-month trip gives you many options—you can explore Japan from north to south, pick up some of the language, arrange job interviews or visits to university campuses, and look at neighborhoods you might want to live in.

THINGS TO DO

On your first visit your goal is to observe and learn as much as possible about a city or prefecture. If you arrive by train, you can start exploring the minute you step out of the station—or even before, in the underground shopping arcade. Buy an English newspaper from a kiosk. Then go outside and survey the taxi stands and buses, shops, restaurants, and hotels surrounding the station—usually the hub of the city or neighborhood. Walk into a convenience store, or *konbini,* and survey the variety of items sold. Your debit card will work at the ATMs in 7-Elevens and post offices. Department stores, or *depaato,* such as Ito Yokado, sell groceries in the basement levels and have restaurants on the top floor. Follow the narrow shopping streets, where you will find traditional noodle and sushi restaurants and maybe a 100-yen ($1.25) store.

Look for real estate offices that post rentals and housing on the windows—each posting shows a floor plan, square meters, and price, which may be in Japanese characters. English-language newspapers list realtors who specialize in Western-style houses for foreign residents. You could call and set up an appointment to see some properties, which are more expensive than Japanese-style (normal) housing, but the agent may be able to refer to you a real estate office.

If you have children, visit international schools and local Japanese schools. Japanese public schools are free and will welcome your children. If your plan is to study abroad, visit several universities and Japanese language schools. Take a look inside a hospital, pharmacy, and fast-food restaurant, and visit the city or town hall. The latter will likely have guides to life in their city for foreign residents. They may also offer Japanese language classes.

In the evenings, follow the neon lights and crowds, but be careful not to go into "hostess" type bars, which lure customers in (very persistently) and then charge exorbitant rates for drinks and conversation with a hostess or host. Many restaurants have plastic food displays in a glass case outside the door. If you don't speak Japanese, you can always point to what you'd like to eat.

Get a subway map and ride the subways to various parts of the city. Routes are color coded and easy to follow. A day pass lets you get on and off and explore different neighborhoods. To see what a daily commute is like, get on a bus or train during rush hour.

Your Japan Rail Pass allows you to ride the *shinkansen* and express trains anywhere in Japan for 1–3 weeks. The following itineraries for a one-week to one-month fact-finding tour offer sample routes and suggest how to investigate housing options, supermarkets, places where you can meet other foreign residents, and where to have fun. For help with train schedules and route planning, Hyperdia online is very useful (www.hyperdia.com). Enter your departure and destination cities and dates and a detailed schedule and fares will be displayed.

ONE WEEK

If you have only one week, choose an urban area like Tokyo as your base, with day trips to surrounding areas. During the week you could fly to another city (such as Sapporo or Fukuoka) or take a train to the next prefecture (such as Gunma or Nagano) for two days. If your interests lean toward the business culture of Osaka and traditional Kyoto, you can fly directly to Kansai International Airport and make Osaka your base, with a side trip to Kyoto or Hiroshima.

Days 1-4: Tokyo 東京

Flights from North America arrive in Tokyo the next day, as you lose a day crossing the international date line. After going through entry procedures, take the Limousine Bus or train to your hotel. You may want to sleep, but try to stay awake until evening. The front desk should have a map of the neighborhood and restaurant recommendations. Pick up a weekly English guide, such as *Metropolis,* to see what's going on. There's lots to take in—start by taking a walk around the hotel to get a feel for the neighborhood. Back in your room, spend some time looking for housing and job ads in the paper and online, and make a list of contacts for the next days.

The next morning, jet lag may wake you up, ravenous, at 4 A.M.—hopefully there's a 24-hour *konbini* nearby where you can buy a snack. Since you're up anyway, why not visit the Tsukiji fish market, which is in full swing. You can take the subway or taxi to Tsukiji. Be careful not to get in the way of the trucks and carts whizzing through the market. Step into any of the tiny restaurants for a gourmet sushi breakfast. Spend the rest of the morning walking around the Ginza shopping district and financial district near Tokyo station, taking a break at nearby Imperial Palace grounds. If your hotel is near Shinjuku, you can explore department stores and walk to Shinjuku Gyoen Park east of the station. Along the way you'll pass Kinokuniya bookstore, which has English maps; if you're near Tokyo station, there's a Maruzen bookstore. Call a realtor to set up an appointment for the next two days to view apartments. In the evening, go to a show or a movie, or check out the nightlife in Omotesando, Roppongi, or Shinjuku—but beware of hustlers and keep your hands on your belongings.

Dedicate Days 3 and 4 to visiting potential employers and surveying housing. Or if you want to study at a university, tour several campuses, visit the international student office, and, if possible, meet professors and observe several classes to get a feel for the campus. If you have children, visit international schools as well as Japanese schools and talk to teachers and parents. These types of visits should be planned in advance so they are expecting you. In the afternoon, meet your realtor to see housing in different parts of the city. Rents are lower in eastern and northern Tokyo than the central and western regions.

In each neighborhood, see what kinds of shops and restaurants there are. Go into a large supermarket and buy something tasty. Is there a launderette nearby? How many minutes does it take to walk from your potential house to the nearest subway or bus stop? What banks are in the neighborhood? Keep your eyes open for a post office and buy some stamps to mail postcards home. Can you communicate your needs with gestures and a few Japanese words? Visit city hall and ask about required procedures for foreign residents, including getting a resident card. They may have newsletters or handbooks in English for foreign residents, as well as Japanese language classes taught by volunteers.

Days 5-6: Sapporo 札幌

You can find plenty to do in Tokyo for a week, but if you want to see another part of Japan, fly north to Sapporo, Hokkaido's capital. An early morning flight from Haneda Airport gets you to Chitose Airport in an hour and a half. Transfer by train or bus to Sapporo. Sapporo (population 1.9 million) has many areas to explore. Odori Park is a wide expanse of green. In February it's the stage for the Snow Festival, with snow replicas of famous buildings and ice sculptures. The Sapporo International Communication Plaza Foundation next to Odori Park is full of information on living in Sapporo. Nearby is the Ainu Museum, also called the Utari Center, with displays on the culture of the indigenous people. If you're looking for a teaching position, visit Hokkaido University, other universities, or English conversation schools, having made appointments in advance. Arrange with a realtor to view apartments or houses. Rents are lower than in Tokyo, with more space. In the evening, head to Susukino, filled with restaurants, bars, and nightspots. Other places to visit are the Historic Pioneer Village and Makomanai—site of the 1972 Winter Olympics. If you decide to live in Sapporo, be prepared for four months of deep snow, with wonderful skiing and winter sports. Fly back to Tokyo the evening of Day 6 or the morning of Day 7 for your flight home. Note that most domestic flights connect to Haneda Airport rather than Narita Airport.

Day 7: Tokyo 東京

If you returned to Tokyo the night before, you have the morning for interviews, house-hunting, or last-minute shopping. Then head to the airport by bus or train. Most North America–bound flights from Narita Airport depart in the afternoon and early

© RUTHY KANAGY

1.9 million people – 1 out of 3 Hokkaidoites – live in Sapporo.

evening. Haneda Airport departures for North America are typically after midnight. Airport bookstores carry maps, language study books, dictionaries, and magazines about Japan. During the long flight home, summarize the information you gathered on housing, jobs, and study opportunities. List your remaining questions and people to contact. You may arrive home before you left, as you gain back the day you lost over the international dateline.

TWO WEEKS

With two weeks to explore Japan, you can visit two major cities, with side trips to several other regions. You could start by flying to Kansai International Airport near Osaka. After several days exploring Osaka, visit Kyoto, then take the *shinkansen* west to Hiroshima, and on to Fukuoka in Kyushu. Alternatively, fly to Sapporo and tour Hokkaido, then return to Tokyo and make a side trip to Gunma or Nagano by train. If you have a Japan Rail Pass, you could fly to your farthest destination (e.g., Sapporo or Fukuoka) and travel by train back to Tokyo or Osaka. Or to do the whole trip by land, purchase the 14-day Japan Rail Pass, which will allow more time to see the countryside. If you enjoy getting off the beaten path, a variation of the sample itinerary is to start in Osaka and spend four days in Shikoku, taking a ferry across the Inland Sea from Hiroshima. Either way, you're here to enjoy, discover, and learn as much as you can about Japan.

Days 1-3: Osaka 大阪

From Kansai International Airport, built on a landfill in the bay, the airport train or bus will get you to Osaka in about an hour. Osaka, with a population of 2.6 million, is a bustling port city of business and pleasure, with numerous areas to explore. Check into your hotel in late afternoon and walk around the neighborhood. Then take the subway or taxi to Namba district and Dotonbori canal, filled with shops, restaurants, street vendors, and musicians. You will see commercial neon logos of many popular foods that originated in Osaka—the Glico Man, a mechanical clown, and a giant moving crab atop a restaurant—an area where business people like to relax after hours.

The next morning, start your city tour at Osaka Castle, located in a nice park and walking distance from Morinomiya station. Then head northwest to Umeda, the major hub in northern Osaka and terminus of JR trains and Hanshin Railways. Take an elevator up futuristic Umeda Sky Building—two skyscrapers connected at the top, featuring movie theaters, auto showrooms, offices, and restaurants. Spend two days interviewing businesses, visiting campuses—such as Kansai Foreign Language University (Kansai Gaidai)—or Japanese public and international schools. Engage a realtor to show you apartments in various parts of the city and surroundings. Take a break in the underground malls and covered arcades of Kappabashi Street, with shops specializing in knives and gourmet kitchenware. Sample Osaka's famous *okonomiyaki,* a kind of Japanese pizza made with batter, chopped cabbage and onions, shrimp, beef or squid, grilled and topped with mayonnaise and brown sauce.

Days 4-6: Kyoto 京都

Kyoto is just 40 minutes north by Hankyu train. If you have a Japan Rail Pass, hop on the JR *shinkansen* gratis. Kyoto was the ancient capital of Japan for a millennium, with a thousand temples and shrines and famous festivals in spring and summer. Kyoto is easy to get around by bus, train, and subway, and worth spending two or three days in. The city streets are laid out with numbered streets going east and west, beginning with Ichi-jo (First Avenue) in the north. Shi-jo (Fourth Avenue) is the shopping district, and Kyoto station is on Hachi-jo (Eighth Avenue). The Tourist Information Office next to Kyoto station has a *Kyoto Visitor's Guide* and free Internet. Stop by Kyoto City International Foundation, near the Keage station on the Tozai subway, for housing, study abroad, and job information, and the *Easy Living in Kyoto* guide. Visit Doshisha University, businesses and language schools, and international schools, according to your interests. Evening activities include Pontocho's eateries and nightspots along the Kamo River. The best time to visit temples and gardens is early morning before the crowd of students on school trips.

Days 7-8: Nara 奈良

If you have time to visit Nara, an hour south by train, you'll see World Heritage sites such as Horyuji and Todaiji, with a massive statue of Buddha. The deer in Nara Park will also welcome you (hold on to your hat). Stay at cozy Petite Hotel Nara Club (21 Kita-Mikado-cho, Nara, tel. 0742-22-3450), whose English-speaking host can tell you about the best sights.

Days 9-10: Kobe 神戸

Kobe is an international port city of 1.5 million, between the Rokko Mountains and Osaka Bay. From Osaka, take the *shinkansen* (if you have a Japan Rail Pass) or Hanshin or Hankyu private train. The Great Hanshin-Awaji Earthquake of 1995 destroyed buildings and highways and 6,000 lives were lost. If you're looking for an international school for your children, check out Canadian Academy on Rokko Island. The business district is around Sannomiya station, where you can pick up tourist maps and information.

Days 11-12: Hiroshima 広島

Continue by train west toward Hiroshima, but make a quick stop at Himeji to see Himeji Castle, the most beautifully preserved feudal castle in Japan. It's a short walk from the station and worth a visit. Continue west by train, past Bizen, renowned for its refined pottery, then Okayama city, and Kurashiki, a well-preserved feudal town. After passing historic Onomichi on the Inland Sea you'll arrive in Hiroshima.

Hiroshima, a city of 1.1 million, was the target of the first atomic bombing by the United States on August 6, 1945, in which 140,000 people died. The Peace Memorial Park is worth a visit to learn about that day, and hear a message of peace for the world. Schoolchildren leave garlands of one thousand origami *tsuru* (cranes) as a prayer for peace. Stop at the Hiroshima City Tourist Information Center at Hiroshima station for a "Welcome to Hiroshima" brochure and map. Tour Hiroshima University and other universities, and visit Hiroshima International House, an international student residence. Visit businesses and language schools and, if you have children, Hiroshima International School and local Japanese schools. Have a realtor show you apartments and houses, and take a break at Shukkeien garden and Hiroshima Castle. Hiroshima is famous for its cuisine—*okonomiyaki* similar to Osaka's but with noodles.

Take a side trip to Miyajima Island in the Inland Sea, a short ferry ride from Hiroshima. Depending on the tides, the large *torii* gate appears to float on waves. On Day 13 it's time to head back to Osaka, taking stock of the information you gathered to help you decide where you want to live.

Days 13-14: Osaka 大阪

Take a train or bus back to Osaka for your last day, which you can use to explore neighborhoods, visit potential schools, or set up contacts for when you return. Then take a train or bus to Kansai International Airport for your flight home.

ONE MONTH

A month in Japan in spring or fall will give you time to explore rural areas as well as urban culture. With a 21-day Japan Rail Pass, leave Tokyo or Osaka by train and travel north to Hokkaido, the "last frontier," and back down through Honshu along the less touristy Sea of Japan coast to Niigata. Then turn inland over mountains to Minakami Spa and Takasaki in Gunma-ken (prefecture) and Karuizawa and Matsumoto in Nagano-ken. Continue south from Matsumoto through Nagoya, then west to Kyoto and Osaka. Follow the coast west to Hiroshima, with a side trip to Shikoku, and finally Fukuoka in northern Kyushu. Adjust your itinerary to spend more time in any of these areas.

Use the *One Week* itinerary as your guide to fact-finding in each city. Stay in a variety of accommodations, from business hotels to B&Bs and traditional inns. The more advance research you do on each city, the more productive your job, study abroad, or housing search will be. On express and local trains you will meet other travelers, students, and commuters. Sample the local boxed lunches (bento) sold by venders on

a traditional sweets shop on a Tokyo side street

express trains and on station platforms. Read Alan Booth's *Road to Sata*, about his 2,000 mile trek across Japan with insights on local culture. While you travel, try to learn as many phrases and as much Japanese writing as you can—people will be delighted to teach you and impressed that you're learning their language.

Tokyo 東京

Follow the *One Week* itinerary for Tokyo and take a side trip to Kamakura, ruled by the shogun from the 12th to 14th centuries, with many historic temples and shrines. If you have time, visit Mount Fuji by bus or train. Then head north to Hokkaido or south toward Kyushu by train.

Hokkaido 北海道

You can fly from Tokyo to Sapporo in 90 minutes, but you'll see much more by train. The Tohoku (northeast) *shinkansen* departs Tokyo station and arrives in less than four hours at Shin-Aomori in Aomori-ken, known for superb apples. Transfer to the Super Hakucho special express train, which goes through an hour-long undersea tunnel to Hakodate, in southern Hokkaido. Hakodate was the northern outpost of the Tokugawa shogunate until 1868, and fishing is the major industry. A cable car or bus takes you up Hakodate-yama for a stunning night view of city lights. Continue north by train through Onuma Quasi-National Park (with its active volcano, Komagatake) to Sapporo, the capital. After exploring the city, travel east by train to Obihiro and the eastern port city of Kushiro. Visit Akan National Park and Shiretoko Peninsula. Retrace your route through Hakodate to Aomori and down the Sea of Japan coast to Niigata, the rice basket of Japan.

Central Mountains 中部

From Niigata, take a train inland (southeast) through rugged Tanigawa Mountains to Gunma-ken and a night at Minakami hot spring resort. The pace of life is much slower along the Tone River, with traditional farmhouses and rice and mulberry fields. Continuing south to Takasaki, transfer to westbound Nagano *shinkansen,* stopping at Karuizawa highland resort and the castle city of Matsumoto, gateway to the Japan Alps. Then follow the Chuo line south to Nagoya, where you can transfer to the *shinkansen* west to Kyoto.

Kansai 関西

Soak up modern city life and traditional architecture in the imperial capitals of Kyoto and Nara. Renting a bicycle (or bringing your own folding one) makes it easy to explore the back alleys, where time seems to have stood still. Osaka and Kobe are less than an hour away by train, and you can spend several days exploring their business centers, universities, and international schools, as well as housing options. Continuing west by train you'll pass Bizen, center of Bizen pottery, and Okayama, capital of Okayama prefecture. Farther west is Kurashiki, a well-preserved feudal town with canals, willows, and old storehouses. Then you'll arrive at historic Onomichi on the Inland Sea, an area known for oyster cultivation and dotted with islands glistening in the sun. By bicycle or bus, follow the Shimanami Kaido (Island-Sea Route), with seven spectacular bridges connecting the floating islands to Shikoku. You could spend the night at a B&B on Omishima Island. Then continue south to Imabari, in northwest Shikoku.

Shikoku 四国 and Kyushu 九州

Shikoku means "four prefectures"—northeastern Kagawa-ken, Tokushima-ken in the east, Kochi-ken on the Pacific, and Ehime-ken at the northwest (*ken* means prefecture). The pace is slower here with more elbow room. Explore the mountains, gorges, rivers, and beaches, or follow the 88-temple pilgrimage path. Matsuyama, capital of Ehime-ken in northwest Shikoku, has stunning Matsuyama Castle and 400-year-old Dogo Spa. You can explore Shikoku by bus or train: south to Uwajima, with a castle and fertility shrine, or southeast to Kochi, known for sword- and papermaking. Tokushima city in the east is famous for the raucous Awa Odori (Awa Dance) in mid-August.

Return to Hiroshima and catch the *shinkansen* west through Shimonoski and cross over to Kyushu Island. The *shinkansen* terminates at Hakata station, in Fukuoka city, which is the economic and political hub of northern Kyushu. Spend several days exploring Canal City Hakata, Tenjin shopping and business area, and Fukuoka University and other schools. The subway connects Hakata station, Tenjin station, and Fukuoka Airport, where you can fly to Osaka or Tokyo, or return by train.

Practicalities

HOTEL ESSENTIALS

One of the delights of traveling in Japan is the variety of accommodations: hotels, traditional *ryokan* inns (www.japaneseguesthouses.com is a helpful resource for booking these), *minshuku* (B&Bs), youth hostels, and temples.

TOKYO 東京
Accommodations

Trains, subways, and buses take you easily around Tokyo, with map in hand. Most visitors fly into Narita Airport, east of Tokyo. If you have lots of luggage, the easiest transport is the Limousine Bus, which stops at major hotels. The Narita Express train has direct service to Tokyo, Shinjuku, and Yokohama stations.

Across from Tokyo City Air Terminal (www.tcat-hakozaki.co.jp/eng/top.html, 60 minutes from Narita) is the luxurious **Royal Park Hotel** (2-1-1 Nihonbashi-Kakigaracho, Chuo-ku, Tokyo, tel. 03/3667-1111, www.rph.co.jp/english/index.html, from $450

ENJOYING AN *ONSEN*

Being naked is a great equalizer—humans taking part in an age-old ritual, sharing abundant water. A Japanese *onsen* (natural hot springs) is a delightful experience. All you need is your comb—the inn provides the rest. Grab a towel and *yukata* (cotton kimono) from your room. Outside the baths is a *noren* curtain—red for women, blue for men. Remove your slippers and step up onto the carpeted area. There are sinks, mirrors, stools, hair dryer, and scales.

Next, remove your clothes and put them in one of the baskets in the cubbies. Take the small rectangular towel (which doubles as a washcloth), casually draping it in front of your body, and slide open the door to the bath. Take a plastic basin and stool from the pyramid in the tiled washing area and stake out your spot at one of the spigots. There are bottles of shampoo, rinse, and soap or body shampoo—good luck figuring out which is which!

Your job is to scrub every part of your body and rinse well *before* entering the tub. Sit on the stool and fill your basin with hot water (or use the flexible shower hose). Soap and rinse several times. You can wash your hair while seated. No need to skimp on water, as it's one of Japan's few natural resources. When you're squeaky clean, squeeze out your towel, fold it, and leave it on the ledge.

Now it's time to step into the bath. Depending on the temperature, you may have to enter one toe at a time. Soak as long as you like. Sometimes there's a cold bath next to the hot. Walk to the *rotenburo* outdoor spa and enjoy the view of the mountains or lake. Pull yourself out before you lose consciousness. As you leave, don't forget to put the basin and stool back on the stack.

Back in the dressing room, rub down with your wrung-out towel—your body dries in an instant. Then envelop yourself in the cool *yukata*, wrapping the right front against you first, then the left *over* the right (if you do the reverse, you could be mistaken for a corpse). To hold it together, wind the *obi* sash around your waist or, if you don't have one, wherever it fits, and tie a bow or knot. Then float down the hall to your room—but don't forget your slippers!

Note: Tattoos have an association with *yakuza*, or organized crime, and some hot springs have restrictions on bathing for people with tattoos.

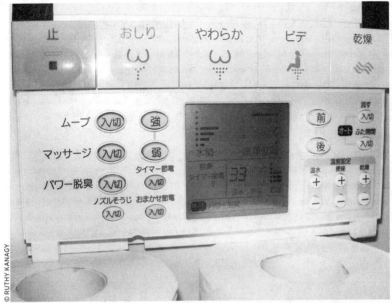

© RUTHY KANAGY

High-tech, remote-control toilets with bidets may surprise you if you don't read Japanese.

double). Wander around Ningyo-cho's traditional shops and Suitengu Shrine, a fertility shrine. From Suitengu-mae station under the hotel, take the subway to Akihabara electric city and Ginza department stores.

One subway stop east of Suitengu-mae is the moderately priced **Comfort Hotel Tokyo Kiyosumi Shirakawa** (1-6-12 Shirakawa, Koto-ku, Tokyo, tel. 03/5639-9311, fax 03/5639-9160, www.comfortinn.com/hotel-tokyo-japan-JP029, $150 twin). Walk to Kiyosumi Gardens, traditional shops, and Tokyo Museum of Modern Art. Take the Oedo or Hanzomon subway to Tsukiji fish market and the greater metropolis.

Asia Center of Japan (8-10-32 Akasaka, Minato-ku, Tokyo, tel. 03/3402-6111, www.asiacenter.or.jp/eng, $140 double) in central Akasaka is near Roppongi, known as a hangout for foreigners, with easy access to Shibuya and Shinjuku. Visit Asakusa's Senso-ji Temple and Kaminari-mon (Thunder Gate) in the heart of old Edo (pronounced "eh-doh"). To the left of the gate is **Hotel Kaminarimon** (1-18-2 Asakusa, Taito-ku, Tokyo, tel. 03/3844-0400, www.kaminarimon.co.jp/english/index.html, Japanese-style room for two from $138). Hop on a sightseeing boat down the Sumida River to popular Odaiba on Tokyo Bay, or take the train to Ueno to explore Ueno Park and National Museums.

Who says you can't sleep cheap in Tokyo? Go minimalist and spend a night in **Hotel Asakusa & Capsule** (4-14-9 Kotobuki, Taito-ku, Tokyo, tel. 03/3847-4477, http://hotelink.co.jp/english/asakusa, $28 per person). Bunk-size capsules have private TV, alarm clock, towel, and dressing gown. There's a women-only floor. In July watch the stunning Sumida River Fireworks.

Dining

Tokyo has almost an infinite variety of dining restaurants in Shinjuku, Shibuya, Ginza, Roppongi Hills, and more. You can "window shop" the plastic food displays outside restaurants clustered around train stations and subway stops as well as on the top floors of department stores and skyscrapers. See Gourmet Navigator (www.gnavi.co.jp/en) for recommendations.

In west Shinjuku on the 51st floor of Sumitomo Building is a sushi restaurant with sweeping views. **Uoichi,** pronounced "oo-oh-ee-chi" (Shinjuku Sumitomo Building 51F, 2-6-1 Nishi Shinjuku, Shinjuku, Tokyo, tel. 03/3348-0567, http://r.gnavi.co.jp/fl/en/g348505, 11 A.M.–2 P.M. and 5–10:30 P.M. daily except New Year's holidays, $45 and up) offers sushi and tempura. In Kanda, one stop north of Tokyo station on the Yamanote loop line, **Mansei** (2-21 Kanda Suda-cho Chiyoda-ku, Tokyo, tel. 03/3251-0291, www.niku-mansei.com, click on "menu," 11:30 A.M.–10:30 P.M. daily, $10–55) is a carnivore's delight—10 floors of restaurants with steak, sukiyaki, shabu-shabu, ramen, Korean *bulgogi,* and pork cutlets. Cross the Mansei Bridge from Akihabara station.

When you tire of Kanda's used bookstores and *otaku* play (referring to those obsessed with anime, games, and collectible dolls) in Akihabara, **Soba Matsuya** (1-13 Kanda Suda-Cho, Chiyoda-ku, Tokyo, tel. 03/3251-1556, http://gourmet.yahoo.co.jp/0006710892/P000887, noon–8 P.M. Mon.–Fri., until 7 P.M. Sat., closed Sun.) has refreshing noodles. It's near Awaji-cho station between Kanda and Akihabara. It serves simple and highly nutritious hot or cold buckwheat noodles ($10). Established in 1884, it survived the firebombs during World War II when most of Tokyo burned.

Tsukishima Island in southeast Tokyo is known for numerous *monja-yaki* restaurants, where you grill savory pancakes and vegetables, seafood, or meat at your table, topped with sauces and mayonnaise. At **Hiro Honten** (3-12-7 Tsukishima, Chuo-ku, Tokyo, tel. 03/5560-6732, http://r.gnavi.co.jp/b034800/lang/en, 5:30 P.M.–12:30 A.M. daily except Wed.), *monja-yaki* is $12. It's a three-minute walk from the Tsukishima or Kachidoki subway stop.

Three-star French restaurant **Quintessence** (1F Barbizon 25 Building, 5-4-7 Shirokanedai, Minato-ku, Tokyo, tel. 03/5791-3715, www.quintessence.jp/english/concept.html, noon–3 P.M. and 6:30–11 P.M. daily except Wed., closed some Sun. and on New Year's holidays) serves original cuisine by Paris-trained chef Kishida Shuzo. Reserve one day ahead for the prix fixe lunch ($98) or dinner ($210). It's a 10-minute walk from Shirokanedai station on Nanboku and Mita lines.

Feel like splurging on some of the world's best sushi? Head to Roppongi Hills' two-star **Sukiyabashi Jiro,** run by the son in the movie *Jiro Dreams of Sushi* (Keyakizaka Dori 3F, 6-12-2 Roppongi, Minato-ku, Tokyo, tel. 03/5413-6626, www.roppongihills.com/shops_restaurants/restaurants/en/japanese/201660002.html, lunch 11:30 A.M.–2 P.M., dinner 5–10 P.M., closed Wed., prix fixe lunch $223, dinner $315). When the sun goes down, enjoy the spectacular night view from **Peter: The Bar** (The Peninsula Tokyo 24F, 1-8-1 Yurakucho, Chiyoda-ku, Tokyo, tel. 03/6270-2763, www.peninsula.com/Tokyo/en/Dining/Peter_The_Bar/default.aspx, 5 P.M.–midnight daily, drinks from $14, snacks from $20). With friendly service and no cover charge, it's a short walk from JR Yurakucho station or Hibiya subway station. Find more restaurants at www.bento.com.

SAPPORO 札幌
Accommodations
Sapporo (population 1.9 million), the capital of Hokkaido, has wide streets laid out like a grid, which are numbered, so it's easy to find your way. Subway and buses link business, shopping, and entertainment districts. Budget-priced **Chisun Hotel Sapporo** (Kita 2-jo Nishi 2-9, Sapporo, tel. 011/222-6611, www.solarehotels.com/english/chisun/hotel-sapporo/guestroom/detail.html, $58 double) is a six-minute walk from Sapporo station.

Wheelchair-accessible **Art Hotel Sapporo** (2-10 Minami 9-jo Nishi 2-chome, Sapporo, tel. 011/512-3456, www.art-sapporo.com/english, from $163 double), near Nakajima Park, has luxurious hot spring baths. Nearby, **Mercure Hotel Sapporo** (2-4 Minami 4-jo, Nishi 2-chome, Sapporo, tel. 011/513-1111, www.mercure.com/gb/hotel-7023-mercure-sapporo/location.shtml, from $101 double) has a French restaurant, offers free Internet, and is walking distance from Susukino nightlife.

Dining
You haven't been to Sapporo until you've tasted Sapporo ramen and Sapporo beer. Just southeast of Sapporo station is the ESTA building, where you will find the **Ramen Republic** (10th Fl. Sapporo ESTA, North 5, West 2, Sapporo, tel. 011/209-5031, www.sapporo-esta.jp/ramen/index.html, 11 A.M.–10 P.M. daily), a collection of ramen restaurants featuring lip-smacking hot noodles with corn, crab, and more that are satisfying and easy on the wallet. Try the miso ramen ($10).

Sapporo was also the birthplace of Japanese beer in 1876. Visit the redbrick **Sapporo Beer Museum** (North 7, East 9, Higashi-ku, Sapporo, tel. 011/731-4368, www.welcome.city.sapporo.jp/english/sites/sapporobeermuseum.html, 9 A.M.–6 P.M. daily except Dec. 30 to Jan. 4) to learn the history. After going through the exhibit have dinner at **Sapporo Beer Garden** in the same building (tel. 011/742-1531, www.sapporo-bier-garten.jp/foreign/english.php, 11:30 A.M.–10 P.M. daily). Three different restaurants offer a buffet, Genghis Khan (marinated and grilled mutton and vegetables—$25–50), and king crab.

In the evening head for **Beer Inn Mugishutei** (Onda Building B1, South 9, West 5, Sapporo, tel. 011/512-4774, www.ezo-beer.com/eng/mugishutei.htm, 7 P.M.–3 A.M. daily, $8–30), serving 300 brands of beer with burgers, meat pies, fish and chips, Hokkaido cheese, and ice cream.

OSAKA 大阪
Accommodations
Dotonbori Hotel (2-3-25 Dotonbori Chuo-ku, Osaka, tel. 06/6213-9040, www.dotonbori-h.co.jp/english/index.html, $130 twin) is a three-minute walk from Namba station, centrally located for shopping, restaurants, and nightlife in the lively Dotonbori district. **Hotel Oaks Shin-Osaka** (1-11-34 Nishi-Nakashima, Yodogawa-ku, Osaka-shi, tel. 06/6302-5141, www.h-oaks.co.jp/shin-osaka/english/index.html, $130 double) is conveniently located one stop from Shin-Osaka *shinkansen* station. Nearby is **Shin-Osaka Youth Hostel** (10F KoKo Plaza Bldg., 1-13-13 Higashi-nakajima, Higashi-yodogawaku-ku, Osaka, tel. 06/6370-5427, www.osaka-yha.com/shin-osaka/shin-osaka-e/framepage1.html, $112 twin). Lights out at 11 P.M.

Near west Osaka's Kaiyukan Aquarium and Universal Studios is **New Oriental**

STAYING AT A *RYOKAN*

Have a Japanese friend show you the proper way to wear a *yukata*.

You haven't really been to Japan until you stay in a *ryokan* (two rapid syllables, "dyo" and "kan"). Rates are higher than business hotels, but include dinner and breakfast (in your room or the dining hall) and a lovely hot spring bath. When you arrive at the inn, remove your shoes in the entry and step up into hotel slippers. A staff person will guide you to your room. Take off your slippers at the entry before stepping onto the delicate *tatami* (woven rush mats).

In the center of the room will be a low table with *zabuton* cushions to kneel on. On the table is a thermos of hot water and a tea set, ready for you to make *ocha* (green tea). Put some tea leaves in the teapot and fill with hot water (push button to dispense). You won't see any beds because the futon bedding hides in a closet during the day. After dinner, a maid will lay out the futon for your bed.

There's nothing like an *onsen* (hot spring bath) after a hard day of sight-seeing or fact-finding. When you head to the public bath, take along the small towel, *yukata* (cotton kimono), and *obi* sash provided. The women's bath is often marked with a red banner and the men's with a blue banner. In the changing room, stash your clothes in a basket and enter the bath area. Take a small stool and basin and wash and rinse thoroughly before stepping into the very hot bath. Often there's a *rotenburo*, an outdoor spa among rocks and trees with screening for privacy.

Minshuku are family-run inns that usually include dinner and breakfast, and cost less than a *ryokan*. Many *ryokan* and *minshuku* accept cash only, so inquire in advance. Tipping is not practiced anywhere in Japan, but a smile and thanks—*Arigatoo gozaimasu*—are appreciated. A souvenir from your hometown for the room maid will bring delight.

Hotel (2-6-10 Nishi-honmachi, Nishi-ku, Osaka-shi, tel. 06/6538-7141, http://noh. hotwire.jp/index_e.html, $110 twin), close to Awaza and Honmachi stations.

Dining

A 21-foot-wide mechanical crab will greet you at **Kani Doraku** (1-6-18 Dotonbori, Chuo-ku, Osaka, tel. 06/6211-8975, http://douraku.co.jp.e.at.hp.transer.com/kansai/ shop/honten, 11 A.M.–11 P.M. daily, $15 and up, "Osaka Set" for two $50) in Dotonbori district, with (what else?) crab dishes for lunch and dinner. Osaka is equally famous for savory *okonomiyaki* (a vegetable and seafood "pancake" topped with bonito flakes) and *takoyaki* (octopus balls). You can enjoy them at **Takohachi** (1-8-7 Dotonbori, tel. 06/6211-7808, noon–10:30 P.M. daily except Mon., $10–65, "Osaka Set" $15), one block southeast of Kani Doraku. For a nightcap head to the **The Leach Bar** (1st F.,

FOOD IN JAPAN

In a country surrounded by bountiful oceans, food from the sea is a big part of the diet, from seaweed to fish and whales (although there is mounting international pressure to cease killing the latter). After the Great East Japan Earthquake and nuclear accident in 2011, the government set strict guidelines on the amount of radiation (cesium) allowable in seafood, vegetables, and fruit. You can be assured that restaurants and stores follow these guidelines.

Seafood seasoned with soy, along with rice and vegetables, is the main ingredient for a traditional meal. Sushi (which means "vinegared rice") is squeezed (*nigiri*), rolled (*maki*), or hand-rolled (*temaki*) and combined with strips of seafood (raw or cooked), vegetables, or eggs. Other kinds of food—Western, Korean, Indian, Nigerian, and more—are equally popular and available. You can have pizza with sun-dried tomatoes and artichoke hearts, or *ika* (squid), *nori* (dried seaweed), and corn, or have your spaghetti in a bread bowl. Order cake or *cream anmitsu* (sweet bean à la mode) for dessert or a snack.

Meat consumption has increased, as can be witnessed at any Makudo (McDonald's), MosBurger, or *yakiniku* (Korean barbecue) establishment. McDonald's offers non-American fare such as teriyaki burgers and melon shakes. MosBurger is famous for its rice burgers—two grilled rice patties with strips of meat and vegetables in between. Eating more meat has resulted in rising cholesterol levels and higher rates of heart disease.

As far as alcohol, hot or cold sake (pronounced "SA-keh," not "SA-kee") is a favorite accompaniment to traditional meals. When you arrive in Japan, you may be surprised to find vending machines supplying sake and beer. Signs warn youth under age 20 not to purchase the product, and the machines shut down after 11 P.M.

Ocha (green tea) holds an honored place in the tea ceremony and in everyday life, but coffee is extremely popular. Doutor was the first discount coffee shop chain to open in Japan. They revolutionized the market by selling coffee for ¥180 ($2.25) a cup, instead of the typical ¥400 ($5) or ¥500 ($6.25). Starbucks has expanded rapidly, and specialty gourmet coffee is becoming popular. Coffee is brewed by the cup and served in a fancy cup. While you're in Tokyo, try Cafe Bach (www.beanhunter.com/cafes/review/bach-kaffee). Where there is coffee, you will likely find smokers, although their number is decreasing. If you don't care for smoke, ask for a *ki'n-en-seki* (nonsmoking seat). Then enjoy the caffeine rush—decaffeinated coffee is unknown in Japan!

Rihga Royal Hotel, 5-3-68 Nakanoshima, tel. 06/6448-0983, 11 A.M.–midnight daily, original cocktails from $18), which has a cozy brick and bamboo decor.

KYOTO 京都
Accommodations

Kyoto was modeled after Xian, with streets laid out as a grid. Kyoto station to the south has underground shopping malls, quick access to Kansai International Airport, and hotels in every price range. **Hotel Station Kyoto** (260 Ameya-cho, Shichijo-Agaru, Higashi-Notoin, Shimogy-ku, Kyoto, tel. 075/365-9000, www.hotel-st-kyoto.com/eng/index-eng.html, $138 twin) has Japanese rooms with futons and Western-style rooms with beds, a five-minute walk north of the station.

For an authentic Japanese experience just two blocks north of Kyoto station, **Ryokan Ginkaku** (Karasuma-dori Shichi-jo Higashi-Sagaru, Shimogyo-ku, Kyoto, tel. 075/371-5252, www.ginkaku.com/english/index.html, $105 per person, includes breakfast) offers personal service, sumptuous cuisine, and huge baths. Behind it is **New Ginkaku Inn**

(Nanajo-sagaru, Higashino-Toin, Shimogyo-ku, Kyoto, tel. 075/341-2884, www.ginkaku. com/english/facilities/newginkakuinn.html, $150 twin), with clean Western-style rooms.

For the cost-conscious, consider staying at one of Kyoto's youth hostels. If you fancy an early-morning visit to Kiyomizu temple before the crush of tourists, you can't get closer than **Kiyomizu Youth Hostel** (6-539-16 Gojohashi-higashi, Higashiyama-ku, Kyoto, tel. 075/541-1651, www.key-yh.jp/fuka/index-eng.html, $50 per person, dorm). Hostels typically have lights out at 10:30 P.M., rise at 6:40 A.M. From Kyoto station bus stop D1, take bus 206, get off at Gojo-zaka bus stop, and walk up Chawan-zaka street for five minutes.

Have you ever wondered how Buddhist monks live? You can sleep like one and attend 6:30 A.M. prayers at **Ninna-ji** temple (33 Omuro Ouchi, Ukyo-ku, Kyoto, tel. 075/464-3664, fax 075/464-3665, ninnaji.wordpress.com/2011/05/21/staying-overnight-at-ninna-ji, $119–127 per person with two meals, $65 without meals), founded in 884. The rooms are spare (sleep on a futon), but the Kyoto-style cuisine is tasty. It's located in the quiet northwest, and world-famous Kinkaku-ji (Golden Pavilion) and Ryoan-ji's rock garden are a short walk; you can check out Ritsumeikan University on the way.

Dining

Long influenced by Buddhism, Kyoto developed a vegetarian tofu cuisine to serve monks. **Yudofu Okutan** was founded 370 years ago and has two locations—near Kiyomizu temple (3-340 Kiyomizu, Higashiyama-ku, Kyoto, tel. 075/525-2051, 11 A.M.–4:30 P.M. Mon.–Wed. and Fri., until 5:30 P.M. Sat., Sun., and holidays, closed Thurs., *yudofu* hot pot meal $39) and near Nanzenji Temple in Higashiyama (86-30 Fukuchi-cho, Nanzenji, Sakyo-ku, Kyoto, tel. 075/771-8709, 11 A.M.–4:30 P.M. daily except Thurs., $39). Enjoy a seven-course tofu meal in an exquisite garden.

Tofu retains its sweetness for only eight hours (there are no preservatives in Japanese tofu like there are in the United States). **Toyo-uke Chaya** (822 Kamiyagawa-machi, Imadegawa-dori Gozen-nishi-iru, Kamigyo-ku, Kyoto, tel. 075/462-3662, www.toyoukeya.co.jp/shiten.htm, 11 A.M.–3 P.M. daily except Thurs.) serves fresh tofu meals and desserts from $10. It's popular, so go early and enjoy the charming Japanese textile decor (gift shop 10 A.M.–6:30 P.M.). It's in the north, just below Kitano Tenmangu Shrine on Imadegawa street.

A few blocks east in the Nishijin silk-weaving district is **Nishijin Tori-iwa-ro** (Minami-gawa, Itsutsuji-dori Chieko-in Nishi-iru, Kamigyo-ku, Kyoto, tel. 075/441-4004, www3.ocn.ne.jp/~mao_utty/toriiwa, noon–9 P.M. daily). Delectable *oyako-don* (chicken and egg over a bowl of rice) with soup is served noon–2 P.M. ($10). A mouthwatering sukiyaki dinner is $75. Combine it with a free kimono show at Nishijin Textile Center on Imadegawa and Horikawa avenues.

Need a coffee break? You can tell your friends your coffee was brewed in a public bathhouse: **Cafe Saracca Nishijin,** pronounced "sa-ra-sa" (11-1 Fujinomori-cho, Murasakino Higashi, Kita-ku, Kyoto, tel. 075/432-5075, http://sarasan2.exblog.jp, noon–10 P.M. daily except Wed.) is inside a 1927 former *sento* (public bath) that's been transformed into a gallery, café, and boutiques. Cake and coffee sets are $10; lunch and dinner start at $8. Next door is a Japanese sweets shop, **Saraku** (11 A.M. until sold out, closed third Thurs. of every month, $9.50), famous for melt-in-your-mouth *warabi-mochi,* with cinnamon or green tea powder flavors.

After dark, head to the Gion district and you might just see a *geiko* (apprentice entertainer) in a kimono. Japanese-style pub **Kappa** (Nawate-agaru 2-suji-me, Shijo-dori, Higashi-kitakado Sueyoshi-cho, tel. 075/531-4048, 6 P.M.–4 A.M. daily) serves *robatayaki* grilled fish and other savory items to wash down with sake or beer. It's two blocks north of Shijo-dori on Nawate.

FUKUOKA 福岡
Accommodations
Fukuoka has deluxe Western-style hotels, business hotels, and traditional inns to choose from. Next to Hakata station is the **Hakata Miyako Hotel** (2-1-1, Hakataeki-higashi, Hakata-ku, Fukuoka, tel. 092/431-3025, www.miyakohotels.ne.jp/hakata/english/index.html, $125 double), with high-speed Internet connections in every room. A budget family inn, **Yamamoto Ryokan** (3-6 Reisenmachi, Hakata-ku, Fukuoka, tel. 092/291-1176, http://yamamoto-ryokan.com, $48 per person, $54 per person with breakfast, $73.50 per person with dinner and breakfast) is one subway stop from Hakata station at Gion station—or a five-minute taxi ride.

Overlooking Hakata Bay, **Hilton Fukuoka Sea Hawk Hotel** is next to the Fukuoka Yahoo! Japan Dome, home of the Hawks baseball team (2-2-3 Jigyohama, Chuo-ku, Fukuoka, tel. 092/844-8000, www1.hilton.com/en_US/hi/hotel/FUKHIHI-Hilton-Fukuoka-Sea-Hawk/index.do, doubles from $200). There's easy access by subway from Hakata station and Fukuoka Airport—get off at the Tojinmachi station. Don't miss the view of the sunset and night lights from the VJ-Bar on the 34th and 35th floors.

Dining
Fukuoka is famous for a variety of noodle dishes, including Hakata ramen. Start your gourmet tour at Hakata station. **Pikaichi** (1st floor, Chisan-mansion, 3-9-5 Hakataeki-mae, Hakata-ku, Fukuoka, tel. 092/441-3611, 11 A.M.–9 P.M. daily except Sun., $8 and up) has been in the noodle business for 33 years. Try *sara udon*—thick udon noodles with vegetables and pork on a plate—or *champon,* a rich noodle soup, for $10. For classic green tea over rice meals, **Ochazuke Dining Wan** (1-4-13 Takasago, Chuo-ku, Fukuoka, tel. 092/522-3810, 11:30 A.M.–3 P.M. and 5 P.M.–midnight daily except Sun. and holidays, until 2 A.M. Fri. and Sat., $10 and up) is a seven-minute walk from Yakuin station. *Ochazuke* is a bowl of rice topped with 27 savory toppings, such as salmon, roe, nori (dried seaweed), with green tea or broth—a quick lunch or snack, and good hangover cure.

Vegetarians and the health-conscious will enjoy **Natural Cafe Vege Garden** (1F, 1-3-29 Takamiya, Minami-ku, Fukuoka, tel. 092/524-7412, 11:30 A.M.–10 P.M. daily except Mon. and the first Sun. of the month, $10 and up) on Takamiya-dori between Hirao and Takamiya stations. Try the Healthy Plate Lunch, with three mini-veggie dishes, brown rice or bread, soup, and drink. After dark, explore the Tenjin and Nakasu district's all-night bars and *izakaya* (Japanese-style pubs). **Off Broadway** has an international clientele (Beans Building, 2nd floor, 1-8-40 Maizuru, Chuo-ku, Fukuoka, tel. 092/724-5383, 7:30 P.M.–2 A.M. daily, Fri. and Sat. to 6 A.M., drinks from $8).

DAILY LIFE

MAKING THE MOVE

After your fact-finding tour, hopefully you've narrowed down where you want to live and have chosen a university program or work you plan to do. Once you have an acceptance letter or job offer in hand, it's time to gather the necessary documents to move to Japan. You will need a valid passport and a visa specific to the activities you will be engaged in. This can take some time and requires patience. If your company is sending you, they may be covering your moving expenses. If you're going on your own, think about whether you can take everything you need in two suitcases, or whether you need to mail books and other items separately. Most things you can get in Japan, but if you are very tall or large you may not find clothing or shoes in your size. You could arrange for a family member to send your winter (or summer) clothing by post if you don't need it right away. If you're moving with children, get them involved in choosing what to take along, and introduce them to Japanese culture by reading stories and visiting a Japanese restaurant where they can practice using *hashi* (chopsticks). If you're taking your pet dog or cat, be sure their vaccinations are up to date. Moving to a new culture is hard work, and can be stressful on adults and children. Be sure to allow plenty of time to get ready, and also time to have fun.

© RUTHY KANAGY

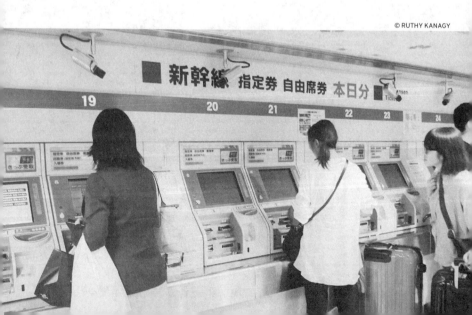

Visas and Immigration

A *sasho* (visa) is one of those necessary evils required for going international. Hopefully in the future it will be possible to simply be a world citizen and visas will be required only for interplanetary travel. In the meantime, if you are headed to Japan and want to stay longer than 90 days, you will need to obtain a visa through a Japanese consulate in the United States. Your *zairyu kikan* (period of stay) in Japan and your *zairyu shikaku* (status of residence) will be recorded in your passport by an immigration officer at the airport where you land. A landing permit will be stamped in your passport, and your date of entry and the duration of valid stay in Japan will be written in as well. Make sure not to overstay your welcome!

One more critical point: Check that your passport is valid for at least three months if you're arriving in Japan as a temporary visitor (90 days or less), and at least as long as the visa status and length of stay for which you're applying. You could be denied entry when you land if your passport expires sooner than your allowable period of stay.

TEMPORARY VISITORS

If you are an American entering Japan as a temporary visitor (tourist), you don't need a visa for a stay of up to 90 days. However, you must show a valid passport and a return ticket dated within 90 days. Authorized activities for temporary visitors to Japan include sightseeing, vacationing, playing sports, visiting family, going on site inspection tours, participating in lectures, and meeting business contacts.

What if you decide you want to stay longer? You will need to leave Japan, apply for a longer-term visa (such as a student visa, work visa, or cultural visa) at a Japanese consulate outside Japan, and then reenter the country.

VISA APPLICATIONS

If you are not a temporary visitor, but instead plan to stay for longer than 90 days and/or intend to work in Japan, you will need an appropriate visa to remain in the country. Before arriving in Japan, you must apply for a visa at a Japanese embassy or consulate in the United States. The Embassy of Japan is located in Washington, D.C., and its website (www.us.emb-japan.go.jp) gives detailed instructions on application procedures. Visit the same site for locations and contact information for all consulate-generals of Japan in the United States.

When you apply for a visa, you will need to submit the following documents in person (or possibly by mail—check with the individual consulate):

- 1. A valid passport.
- 2. A Visa Application Form to Enter Japan (Form 1-C).
- 3. One two-inch-by-two-inch photo.
- 4. *Zairyu shikaku nintei shomeisho* (certificate of eligibility) from the Immigration Bureau of Ministry of Justice in Japan (www.immi-moj.go.jp), and one photocopy. You should obtain this certificate through your sponsor in Japan.

Getting a visa will go most smoothly this way, but if you have no certificate of eligibility, you will need the first three items plus the following documents:

EXCHANGING *MEISHI* (BUSINESS CARDS)

If someone offers you their business card, receive it with both hands with a slight bow, look at it, and say their name before putting it away. When you offer someone your card, turn it so it faces the receiver. Japanese take *meishi* seriously, because it reveals information about your affiliation and rank, which are cues to the appropriate level of speech. Having someone's card is a sign that a relationship has been established. It's also used as a personal reference—showing someone's card is proof that they know you and recommend you, so you don't want to give yours out to everyone on the street.

- 5. A copy of the acceptance letter from the Japanese institution you will attend. In addition, if you are attending a vocational school, you must present evidence of your Japanese language skills (such as showing you passed Level 2 of the Japanese Language Proficiency Test—for more information, visit the Association of International Education at www.aiej.or.jp and click on English).
- 6. Documents certifying that you can defray all expenses incurred during your stay in Japan (such as a bank statement or official proof of receipt of scholarships or grants).
- 7. A photocopy of all the above documents.

The exact documents required vary depending on the particular status of residence. See the next section for more information.

TYPES OF VISAS
Student Visa

A student visa is for those entering a college or junior college in Japan for longer than 90 days. If you are going to Japan on an exchange program with your university, or have been admitted directly to a Japanese university or junior college, you need this type of visa to enter the country. Housing is often included for participants, and the host university may assist you in obtaining a student visa.

If you are already in Japan, you may be able to get a student visa if you enroll full-time in a Japanese language school or *senmon gakko* (technical school). In this case, your school may be able to act as your sponsor or guarantor. With a student visa, you are allowed to work legally up to 20 hours per week (teaching English, working in a fast-food restaurant, etc.), but first you must apply to the Immigration Bureau for permission.

Cultural Activities Visa

Cultural activities include academic or artistic activities that provide no income, or activities for the purpose of pursuing specific studies on Japanese culture or arts, or activities for the purpose of learning about Japanese culture or arts under the guidance of experts (excluding activities allowed by a student visa). The period of stay is usually six months to a year.

Work Visas

There are 14 categories of work visas. Each type has specific parameters: professor, artist, religious activity, journalist, investor/business manager, legal/accounting service,

GIVE A GIFT, SEND A CARD

When you visit someone's home, it's considered good manners to take a small gift. It can be something from your home country, or flowers, fruit, or some sweets that you bring back from a trip. In addition, there are two formal gift-giving seasons: *ochugen* in mid-July and *oseibo* in mid-December. This is a time to exchange "obligatory" gifts with business associates and people who've done you favors. Department stores display boxed gifts, ready to send. Customers can select gifts, register the names and addresses of the recipients, and have them delivered. "Regifting" gifts received from someone else is often taken up in newspaper cartoons as a humorous topic.

Along with gifts, people exchange greeting cards twice a year: *shochu mimai* ("sympathy for hot weather") cards in July, and *nengajo* (New Year's greetings) at the end of December. The post office holds all New Year's greeting cards until January 1, when they are delivered en masse to each resident. If you're in Japan during July or December, your friends and associates will be pleased to receive a card from you (you can buy them at the post office, pre-stamped). After you leave Japan, remembering to send a Christmas or New Year's card every year will be greatly appreciated by the people who have looked out for you while you were visiting or living in Japan.

medical service, researcher, instructor, engineer, humanities service/international services, intra-company transferee, entertainer, and skilled labor. You'll find detailed information on the website of the Embassy of Japan (www.us.emb-japan.go.jp).

At a minimum, you should have a college degree in any field, or prove that you have significant experience (10 years is a good length—in Japan, it takes 10 years to become a sushi chef or to master any art) in a certain field. Then you will need to seek out a school or business to give you a job and be your guarantor to obtain a work visa. Work visas are generally good for six months, one year, or three years. The longer you stay in Japan, the better your chance of obtaining a longer visa.

Instructor: This visa is for providers of language instruction and other education at elementary schools, junior high schools, senior high schools, schools for the blind, schools for disabled children, *kakushu gakko* and *senshu gakko* (miscellaneous schools), or equivalent institutions.

Artist: An artist visa is for producers of artwork that provides income, such as composers, songwriters, artists, sculptors, craftspeople, and photographers.

Humanities/International Services: This type of visa is for those who engage in service requiring knowledge pertinent to jurisprudence, economics, sociology, or other human science fields. These services must require specific ways of thought or sensitivity based on experience with foreign culture, such as interpreting, translation, copywriting, fashion design, interior design, sales, overseas business, information processing, international finance, design, or public relations and advertising based on a contract with a public or private organization in Japan.

Investor/Business Manager: An investor/business manager visa covers those involved in the operation of international trade or other businesses, investors in international trade or other businesses, and those who operate or manage international trade or other businesses on behalf of foreign nationals (including corporations) who have begun such an operation or invested in such a business. The business in question must meet certain conditions of scale. Applicants who wish to engage in business management must fulfill specific conditions concerning work status and personal history.

Professor: This visa is granted to those who perform research, research guidance, or teaching services for institutions specializing in education, such as professors and assistant professors at universities, colleges, or *koto senmon gakko* (technical colleges).

Researcher: The researcher visa is for research activities performed under contract with public or private institutes in Japan, excluding activities described under "Professor." I had this visa while I was a foreign researcher at the National Institute for Japanese Language in Tokyo. At first, my research visa was valid for one year. Then I renewed for another one-year period. The next time I went to renew my visa, they gave me a three-year research visa without my asking. Luckily, I had the proper certificate of eligibility form from my institute, and my immediate supervisor kindly agreed to act as my guarantor. (That's a big favor to ask, because if I got in trouble with the law or skipped the country with unpaid rent, my guarantor would be personally liable. Treat guarantors with care.)

NEW RESIDENCY MANAGEMENT SYSTEM FOR FOREIGN NATIONALS
Resident Card

In July 2012, the Immigration Bureau of Japan replaced the old Alien Registration system with a new Residency Management system. This applies to all foreign nationals residing legally in Japan mid- to long-term with resident status under the Immigration Control Act. This does not apply if your stay in Japan is for three months or less (i.e., a temporary visitor) or to those with diplomat or official status.

Under the new residency management system, foreign residents are entered in Japan's Basic Resident Registration System, designed to track foreign nationals who reside legally in Japan for longer than three months. The stated goal is to "improve the convenience of foreign nationals who legally reside in Japan." It will also make it easier to deport those considered "a threat to Japan's national interests or public order."

How does this new system work? During immigration procedures upon arrival, a seal of landing verification will be stamped in your passport, and if your port of entry is Narita, Haneda, Chubu, or Kansai Airport and you are a mid- to long-term resident, you will be issued a resident card. At other ports of entry, a resident card will be mailed to your place of residence after you complete residency procedures at your local municipal office. (Your passport will say "A resident card will be issued later.") You must visit the municipal office within 14 days of finding a place to live. Any time you move, you must take your resident card to the municipal office within 14 days of moving to a new residence.

The other big change is that the maximum period of stay in Japan is five years instead of the previous three years. In addition, the former requirement of applying for a reentry permit every time you leave and reenter Japan has been waived. The new system allows you to leave and reenter Japan within one year of the date of your original departure without needing a reentry permit. Be sure to present your resident card at departure. Note that you will lose your resident status if you fail to reenter Japan within one year of your departure. The maximum validity period of a reentry permit is five years.

© JPSTBCJ/FLICKR.COM

the Immigration Bureau of Japan in Tokyo

DAILY LIFE

IMMIGRATION BUREAU RESIDENCY PROCEDURES

You will need to apply at your regional immigration bureau in Japan when extending your period of stay, and for any procedure related to your status of residence (such as changing your visa category or requesting permission for any activities other than those authorized). When making such applications, you must present your passport and resident card. Foreign residents are also required to report to their local municipal office when their residence changes from one address to another in Japan.

Extending Your Period of Stay

Your *zairyu kikan no koshin* (period of stay) is determined together with your status of residence at the time you land in Japan. Foreigners are only allowed to stay in Japan within a set period of time. If you would like to remain in Japan under the same status of residence beyond your authorized period of stay, you must apply for and obtain an extension. To do so, apply at your local immigration office no later than the expiration date of your authorized period of stay (applications are usually accepted up to two months in advance). Anyone who stays in Japan beyond the authorized period of stay is subject to punishment and/or deportation by law.

Changing Your Status of Residence

Foreigners who would like to stop their present activity and concentrate on an activity that is different from what is authorized under their current status of residence must apply for—and obtain—a change of *zairyu shikaku no henko* (status of residence). The submission of such an application does not necessarily guarantee its approval. Anyone receiving income from an activity other than what is authorized under his or her status of residence, or anyone who conducts unauthorized activities with remuneration without first obtaining this permission, is subject to punishment and/or deportation by law.

Unauthorized Activities

Foreigners who would like to engage in an activity involving the management of a business or any remuneration other than what is authorized under the assigned status of residence must apply for—and obtain—permission to do so in advance. Foreigners engaging in activities other than those authorized are subject to punishment by law.

PERMANENT RESIDENCY

The main benefit of this status is not having to apply for visas every time you want to live in Japan—but keep in mind that half the "registered foreigners" in Japan are second- or third-generation permanent residents (usually Korean or Chinese). It's not impossible to obtain *eijuken* (permanent residency), but it takes connections, money, a good guarantor, and up to about 10 years. If you marry a Japanese person, the time can be as short as five years. I also know a number of internationals in Japan who got permanent residency after living in the country for five years—without being married to a Japanese. So, it's possible, albeit difficult, to move the process along more quickly.

Naturalization

What if you want to go all the way and become a citizen of Japan? Just so you know, in most cases this means giving up your present citizenship. Children born with dual citizenship don't *legally* have to give up one or the other, although the Japanese government would like them to do so. At the Immigration Bureau, there are posters of people standing on a globe, cheerfully saying, "Let's all choose just one citizenship." If I didn't have to give up my U.S. citizenship and could just add Japanese to the list, I'd do it in a heartbeat.

If you want to pursue Japanese citizenship, naturalization is the primary way for foreigners to do so. Application for naturalization must be made at the Ministry of Justice (Nationality Division, Tokyo Legal Affairs Bureau, Kudan Building No. 2, 1-1-15 Kudan Minami, Chiyoda-ku, Tokyo 102-8225, tel. 03/5213-1234).

Moving with Children

DEPENDENT VISA

If you are taking your family with you to Japan on a student or work visa, each member will need to obtain a dependent visa at a Japanese consulate office *outside* Japan in order to enter the country. A spouse or child of someone residing in Japan with the visa status of professor, researcher, or cultural activities is eligible for dependent resident status. Normally the period of stay for dependents is three months, six months, one year, or three years. If your dependent plans to stay in Japan for more than 90 days, he or she must also apply for a resident card.

MAKING THE ADJUSTMENT

Children face their own challenges when moving to a new country. Make sure to provide plenty of support—familiar books, toys, music, photographs of extended family and close friends, and some favorite foods. Allow them time to get adjusted to their new surroundings, and try not to push them to play with children they don't know. If your children are old enough, help them write a postcard or email to a friend back home. Above all, as a parent, give them your time and emotional support, even though you may be busy with the many tasks of setting up house in a new culture. When your children are ready, plan ways to learn Japanese together, go shopping, or take outings. But I recommend starting slowly—riding a subway may be a big enough activity by itself. Don't fill up the schedule too much. For helpful information on moving to Japan with children, visit this online resource: www.tokyowithkids.com.

How does a young child experience a move to a new country? I can share my personal experience of moving from Japan, where I was born, to North America for the first time at age four. My missionary parents took a one-year break from Hokkaido and moved back to Indiana. I found myself in a strange place filled with new tastes, a new language, and relatives I'd only seen in pictures. I was too young to go to school, so I stayed home and played with buttons from my grandmother's sewing basket. After a year, we went back to our home in Japan.

I don't think the transition was very difficult at that age, but when we moved again to the United States when I was in the sixth grade, it was a harder adjustment. I was used to my local Japanese elementary school and had never experienced school in English. I knew English well, but my vocabulary was somewhat limited, and I sometimes got laughed at for not knowing slang or the latest popular tune or TV show.

© RUTHY KANAGY

Your child is welcome to attend local public schools – a great way to make friends.

A preteen or adolescent needs someone who understands what they're going through (which is true when moving within the same country, as well).

Your child will face some challenges living in Japan or going to a Japanese school, but rest assured it will be an enriching experience, an opportunity of a lifetime. To ease the transition to a new school, enlist the help of the home-room teacher and find a buddy who can help your child learn the ropes and ease the transition. Keep in close touch with the school and teachers, and also try to get to know some parents.

For preschoolers, there are many good Japanese *hoikuen* (government-supported day cares) and *yochien* (kindergartens for ages 3–5).

Moving as a Single Parent

There are some challenges to being a single parent in an unfamiliar culture. Rhae Washington, a single mom who moved to Japan with her two-year-old, said:

I loved the education my son got in his *hoikuen*—they were so loving and yet taught him a lot about discipline. I loved the beach and swimming and the flowers and the temples...the aesthetic qualities of Kamakura [south of Tokyo] were extraordinary. Going to visit Daibutsu [Great Buddha] was one of our favorite things to do; we called him "our friend." I enjoyed the food very much, and learning the language, and being exposed to cultural opportunities.

On the other hand, I was also very isolated—I had only a few friends, and they weren't really friends I could count on for help or support. I made one Japanese friend by responding to an ad she'd posted seeking foreigner friends. She had a child my son's age, and she would come over for dinner and drinks a few times a month. We had a good time together, and so did the kids; we still keep in touch. She is a very nontraditional Japanese woman, though, as she's traveled extensively. Many Japanese women that I met were too shy to really engage with me, either because they were self-conscious about their English or because they found me strange—usually both, it seemed to me. I did interact socially with a couple of my students' parents, but that was not in an intimate, friendly way, but more in a very polite, business kind of way. I was very self-conscious, going to their houses, and thus didn't really enjoy myself.

In retrospect, I don't think Japan is the best place for a single parent. There just really aren't enough resources in the smaller towns. Perhaps in Tokyo one would be OK, especially with good Japanese. My advice would be to learn the language as much as possible—hiragana, katakana, and a lot of vocabulary. Try to build a support system (of foreigners, if necessary) before moving, through the websites designed for foreigners, such as www.japan-guide.com, or by contacting friends of friends—most people, Japanese and foreigners alike, will be happy to help. I would also warn anyone moving there that they will almost necessarily feel isolated, at least at the beginning. They will have to ask for help a lot—which is why it's so important to have friends to count on. But the kids will benefit! And it's one of the safest countries in the world, which is a wonderful feeling when you have kids, and also as a woman. It was the first time in my life I didn't feel the need to watch my back. My son did pick up the language easily, especially in his Japanese school, and we still use it sometimes.

Despite some challenges and the need for patience during the initial adjustment period, I strongly believe that the benefits of growing up in two cultures far outweigh the challenges. Because our brain capacity increases through mapping multiple sets of vocabularies and grammars, learning two or more languages in early childhood has been shown to stimulate and develop brain cells. In an increasingly interdependent world, knowing more than one language and culture gives children—and adults—a broader worldview and empathy for people from other places. Home is no longer limited to one country as we extend the concept of "one nation, indivisible" to "one earth, indivisible." There are practical advantages as well—being bilingual and bicultural will be an advantage when your child establishes a career. You as a parent can give your family that priceless opportunity when you move to Japan.

Moving with Pets

You may want to bring your favorite cat, dog, or other pet to Japan. It can be done, but there are many requirements involved. First of all, upon arrival (with the proper documents), your pet will be quarantined for two weeks or longer at the airport. (It is possible to arrange a home quarantine for pets who are older or require medication.) During this period, you are responsible for feeding and caring for your pet, which will be housed in a kennel. If you're landing at Narita Airport, note that Narita is located in the neighboring Chiba prefecture, not in Metropolitan Tokyo. Depending on where you are staying, it could take two or three hours to get to the airport from Tokyo. Also keep in mind that most apartments in Japan do not allow pets. A few do, but you will have to hunt for them, and an additional deposit may be required.

In my case, I decided not to bring my dog to Japan and left her with several trustworthy friends at home. I didn't want to subject her to the trauma of air travel, quarantine, and adjustment to an unfamiliar place. Moreover, there was no grass or dirt near my apartment, only concrete and asphalt—not much space to run around, and not much fun. However, if you decide to bring your pet—and you may have compelling reasons—here's how. The agency that regulates the transport of animals into Japan is the Animal Quarantine Service of the Ministry of Agriculture, Forestry, and Fisheries (www.maff.go.jp/aqs/english). Their policy is as follows:

If you bring a pet dog with you from abroad, it will be detained for a quarantine inspection for a fixed period of time after arrival in Japan in order to examine it for the presence of rabies and leptospirosis. Detention inspections are normally conducted at Animal Quarantine Stations and require that animals be isolated from people and other animals in order to check for the presence of illness or disease. Detention will continue for a period of 14 to 180 days, depending on the existence and the content of rabies vaccination and health certificates issued by the relevant authorities in the country of departure. However, if you bring a dog with you from one of the designated rabies-free areas (only Hawaii in the United States), the detention period may be as short as 12 hours.

In addition, if your dog has not had a rabies vaccination, she will be kept in detention for a period of 30 days—if you have a certificate issued by a government agency in your country of departure containing a statement to the effect that the animal was raised in isolation and that certain conditions have been satisfied. Please be aware that you will not be able to bring your dog into Japan if you do not have a health certificate

© RUTHY KANAGY

Bringing a pet to Japan involves fulfilling many requirements.

issued by a government agency. There are 17 ports and airports in Japan through which you may bring your dog (visit www.maff.go.jp/aqs/english for contact information).

There is no cost for the rabies and leptospirosis examination while your dog is held in detention. However, the dog's owner is responsible for the care of his or her dog during that time.

There is a requirement that you register a dog (91 days old or older) at the local municipal office and receive a dog license. In addition, the dog must have a rabies vaccination once a year at some point between April and June, and must receive a Completion of Rabies Vaccination Tag. The license and tag must be attached to the dog's collar at all times.

Dogs must be leashed or caged when outdoors, except in designated dog parks (see www.dog-superguide.com/dog_runs, in Japanese). Some restaurants and hotels accept pets. For further information, contact your local municipal office.

See the Ministry of Agriculture website for requirements for cats and other pets. For additional information, contact your local ward or municipal office, local public health center, or the Veterinary Sanitation Section, Living Environment Division, Bureau of Public Health, Tokyo Metropolitan Government (tel. 03/5320-4412).

What to Take

Keep in mind that your apartment or house in Japan likely will be much smaller than your present home, with limited storage and no garage. Pack as light as you can! If you're going for a short term, try to limit yourself to what you can carry on an airplane—two suitcases—plus perhaps books to ship by M-bag (contact a U.S. post office for info). Almost everything you need to set up house in Japan can be purchased after you arrive—furniture, kitchenware, linens, television, DVD players, and so on. Look for recycle shops where you can buy furniture and appliances for a reasonable price, and ¥100 stores, which have a wide selection of kitchenware, office supplies, and dried food for about $1.25 each. In a nutshell, take only what you absolutely can't live without.

MONEY

Do bring as much money as you can to cover startup costs. Cash amounts up to ¥1 million ($12,500 at the exchange rate of ¥80 to $1) in any currency are not subject to customs declaration when you enter Japan. Keep in mind that housing and apartment rents are lower in smaller cities and towns and the farther you go from urban centers. Getting the key to your apartment or house, however, can set you back $5,000 or more by the time you pay the deposit, landlord's fee, and key money. Cash is the norm for paying rent in Japan. If you plan to withdraw cash from an ATM machine in Japan using your debit or credit card, be sure to confirm with your home bank what their daily limit is on the amount of cash you can withdraw. If the limit is, say, $700 per day, calculate how many days you require to withdraw a sufficient amount of cash to pay to your landlord at the outset.

ELECTRONICS AND MEDIA

Japan runs on 100V electricity, while the United States runs on 120V. Japan operates under two frequencies—50 hertz AC (alternating current) in the east, including Tokyo, and 60 hertz AC in the west, including Osaka and Kyoto. The United States operates on 60 hertz. The slight difference should not affect your laptop computer, printer, hair dryer, or electric razor (the latter two may run a little slower), but for cycle-sensitive equipment—microwaves, stereos, and analog clocks—you should use a transformer.

Electrical outlets have two flat-blade plug-ins like in the United States—but only for equal-size blades. In other words, polarized plugs, where one blade is larger than the other, will not fit. Three-pin grounded plugs are also uncommon. The problem is easily solved if you bring a plug adaptor for polarized blades and three-pin blades to plug into a Japanese outlet.

Used electronics stores are abundant and cheap, and you can find computers, printers, fax machines, DVD players, and more. The English classifieds in the paper or online are also a good place to find them, although a Japanese keyboard has a slightly different configuration. To protect market share, DVD software and players are regulated worldwide via region-specific codes. Japanese DVDs and players are specific to region 2, while North American DVDs and players are specific to region 1 and won't work on Japanese players. DVDs from other regions sometimes can be viewed on a laptop. There are some region-free (or code-free) players available, but make sure to note whether the warranty is international or limited to the country of purchase. Standard TV frequencies and FM radio (from 76 to 90 MHz) are different than in North America, so no need to bring those. You can get English news and other bilingual broadcasts in Tokyo and other large cities.

What about a cell phone? First, check with your provider to see if your phone has international coverage, specifically for Japan. Some international phones will work in Europe but not Japan. If you plan to be in Japan long-term, it's a good idea to invest in an international 3G cell phone compatible with the Japanese system (make sure it uses the same frequency). Or, you can also rent or purchase one in Japan. To buy a cell phone and subscribe to a service, foreign residents must have a resident card or Japanese driver's license as proof that they live in Japan. If you don't want to sign a two-year contract for a cell phone, you can buy one that uses pre-paid cards of 3,000 or 5,000 yen and have a PIN to key in. When you run out of time, you can buy another card at any *konbini* (convenience store). NTT DoCoMo, KDDI (au), and SoftBank are the three main Japanese cell phone companies.

MEDICATIONS

Keeping yourself in good physical and mental health is very important when you're far from home. The last thing you want is to get sick and not be able to find the kind of pain or cold medication that you're used to. Although Japan offers a wide variety of drugs, the labeling and instructions are in Japanese, the quantity and dosage may be less, and the price high. Bringing basic, familiar brands of pain, cold, and allergy medications will be a comfort if illness strikes. You can bring up to a one-month supply of prescription medication with you. If you need to bring more, you will need to get a *yakkan shoumei* import certificate (see the *Medications for Personal Use* sidebar in the *Health* chapter for details). Take all medication in the original, labeled bottles, with the generic name, pharmacy name, and doctor's name and phone number. Take along original prescriptions to show at customs, if asked. Your prescription will not be valid in Japan, so you will need to see a Japanese doctor and get a new prescription (which may not be the same brand or dosage), or have a family member mail refills when you run out. Don't forget prescriptions for glasses or contacts, and your dental records.

CLOTHING AND SHOES

Japanese clothing and shoes are well-tailored, high quality, and expensive. Shoes may cost $200 or more, and a two-piece suit for women $300 or more. If you are a woman over 5'7" or wear shoes larger than size 7.5, it's a good idea to bring all the clothing and shoes you will need in Japan. Larger sizes are available, but only in major department stores and specialty shops, and prices are quite steep.

The same applies to men who are over 5'8" or who wear shoes larger than size 8.5. Even if the clothing fits, the sleeves may be short. You can find relatively inexpensive clothing at several chain stores, including Ito Yokado department store, UniQlo (www.uniqlo.com), and MUJI (www.muji.net/eng). If you're smaller in stature, you'll have no problem finding clothing.

WHAT TO TAKE

Some of the following items are available in Japan, but are expensive or hard to find.

TOILETRIES AND MEDICATIONS*

- Prescription medications–up to one-month supply of allowable medications in original, labeled bottles with original prescriptions

- Sunblock, deodorant, insect repellent, hair dye

- Pain medication, allergy and cold medication, hydrocortisone, multi-vitamins, contraceptives

*See the *Medications for Personal Use* sidebar in the *Health* chapter for restrictions on prescription and over-the-counter medications.

FOOD AND COOKING SUPPLIES

- Spices, seasoning mixes, popcorn

- Herbal teas, decaffeinated coffee (decaf is unknown in Japan)

- Dutch oven for stovetop (ovens are not common)

CLOTHING

- Conservative and casual clothes (if you are tall or large, bring all you will wear)

- Undergarments, shoes, boots

- A few linens and towels

CHILDREN

- Diapers and formula to get you started

- Favorite stuffed animals, books, games

TRANSPORTATION

- Bike helmet, folding bike for shopping and travel (see www.bikefriday.com)

DOCUMENTS

- Medical records, immunizations, insurance cards

- School transcripts, diplomas, birth and marriage certificates

- Bank and social security information

- Passport, U.S. and international driver's license

OTHER

- Thermometer with Fahrenheit and Centigrade

- Tape measure with inches and centimeters

- Plug adaptors, extension cords for polarized and three-pin blades (Japanese outlets are two-prong)

- Laptop computer (note that U.S. DVDs are not compatible with Japanese DVD players), international cell phone

TO SHARE

- Photographs of your town, school, family, friends

- Some treats, postcards, souvenirs from home for gifts

COMFORT FOOD

Japanese food is wonderful and varied, but sometimes you crave a taste of home. Many large department stores in urban areas have an international food section where you can find exotic items such as Skippy peanut butter, taco shells, and pretzels. If you have favorite seasoning mixes, spices, herbal teas, hot chocolate, microwave popcorn, macaroni and cheese, or tortilla chips, you may want to bring along a supply. If you love hot cereal for breakfast, for example, take it with you or request a care package from your family back home. And decaffeinated coffee doesn't exist in Japan, so bring a supply if needed. Some items, such as plants, seeds, meat, and produce, are prohibited. Check with your Japanese consulate.

I asked several friends who had moved to Japan what they recommend taking.

Most toiletries are available in Japan, but they can be expensive.

Kristy said, "There was no good coffee! I brought all my own clothing and shoes, because I knew I wouldn't find anything that fit. There were no souvenir or kimono shops in the town I lived in—I wanted to buy a *yukata*. There were no import stores or American food items or DVD stores. They did have a good selection of alcohol, including imported labels."

And Mike, who lives in Hokkaido, said, "Some foods that are not impossible to get, but sometimes a bit difficult to find, would be nice to have available. These include things such as a greater variety of cold cereals, oatmeal, and natural peanut butter, just to name a few."

DOCUMENTS

You will need copies of certain documents in order to rent a house, enroll in school, get a driver's license, and have a resident card. These include your (and your children's) medical records, including immunizations, school transcripts, diplomas, birth and marriage certificates, bank and social security information, and medical insurance cards. This is a partial list and there may be more. About Moving to Japan (http://aboutmovingtojapan.com/preparation.html) has a helpful list of things to prepare for your move to Japan.

MOVING COMPANIES

Although minimal packing is recommended, if you're moving to Japan for several years, or the move is a corporate transfer that covers your moving expenses, there are reputable moving companies that will simplify the process. They will pack and pick up your items, ship them by air or container ship, and deliver the items to your home. To get an idea of shipping costs to or from Japan, contact Nippon Express for a free estimate.

Be sure to consider the cost of shipping things home, when deciding what you will take. Often, shipping costs to Japan are much less than the cost of shipping goods home again. This is particularly true with mailing books to Japan. You can request an "M-bag"—a large canvas bag that holds up to 40 pounds of books—at U.S. post offices for a very reasonable rate. I opted for that when I moved to Japan, and then ended up paying the equivalent of $100 per 10-pound package of books (the maximum weight for book rate) to mail things home. All told, I paid about $1,000 for postage to North America. So the less you can live with, the better. Buying used or borrowing things you need after you reach your destination will help establish solidarity with your new home. Going shopping in your neighborhood stores is also an excellent way to introduce yourself to local shopkeepers and interact with your new neighborhood.

ARRIVAL PLANS

Well before you leave for Japan, make plans for how you will get from the airport to your new home (or hotel). Who will meet you? How will you transport your luggage? One of the easiest ways is to use *takkyuubin,* or home delivery service, at the airport for a very small fee. Look for ABC or Yamato counters in the arrival area of the airport. Think about where you will get food and immediate supplies for the first day or two. Keep track of all your moving expenses, as they may be tax deductible with the IRS. Check with your IRS office before you move. Lastly, don't forget to take along your sense of humor, for when unexpected things happen!

DAILY LIFE

HOUSING CONSIDERATIONS

If you've heard anything about the cost of living in Japan, you've probably been warned that housing prices in Tokyo are out of sight. A two-room rental apartment in Tokyo can cost anywhere from $800 to $18,000 per month, and the price of buying a home? Don't even ask. As in New York and San Francisco, space is at a premium in concentrated urban areas. Smaller living spaces are the result of continuous urbanization and centralization of the populace in industrial zones along the Pacific seaboard. One out of five Japanese residents reportedly lives in the greater Kanto plain, where Tokyo—the political, economic, financial, and educational center of Japan—is situated. The average Tokyo family with a salaried wage earner can never hope to own a detached house, even with a yard the size of a *tatami* mat (three by six feet), so many opt for a *manshon* (condominium) in one of the highrises sprouting like shiitake mushrooms above the traffic-choked highways. Others move to the suburbs an hour or two away from the city, or even to a neighboring prefecture, where housing is more affordable—but the family rice earner must get

© RUTHY KANAGY

used to a two- to three-hour commute on packed trains. The good news is, once you get away from the metropolis to the small towns in outlying regions, housing prices drop by 30 percent or more. It is also possible to build or buy a traditional house in the country.

Housing Options

JAPANESE- OR WESTERN-STYLE ROOMS?

In the past, Japanese houses have been described through Western eyes as "paper houses," and this stereotype contains a kernel of truth. Traditional houses were built of wood, with sliding *amado,* or rain shutters, on all sides that could be opened to air the house in hot, humid climates. Inside, rooms were partitioned off with ingenious *fusuma* (wood-framed paper doors) that, when slid back, could open up three or even four rooms into a combined great room when relatives gathered. In place of curtains, windows were fitted with pairs of sliding *shoji* (wood lattice frames covered with white Japanese paper) for privacy. The inevitable tears and rips children made poking fingers through the delicate *shoji* panes were patched with white, cherry-petal-shaped cutouts, then repapered completely at year's end. Floors were covered with *tatami* (thick, rectangular woven rush mats), and cooking areas had earthen floors. *Tatami* are still used in *washitsu* (Japanese-style) rooms, imparting a fresh scent of grasses.

If you decide to live in a small town in the rural areas of Honshu (the main island), Kyushu (southern island), or Shikoku (western island), you may be lucky enough to rent or even buy such a traditional house. It may even have a *kayabuki yane,* or

thatched roof, though very few such houses remain, other than as historical museums (such as Takayama, in central Japan). Many Japanese have abandoned traditional houses as too difficult and costly to maintain, and instead have fled to the cities. In modern Japanese housing, stucco or reinforced concrete walls have replaced sliding doors, and lace curtains flutter in place of opaque *shoji.* These days, *onsen* (traditional hot springs inns) may be one of few places you can sleep surrounded by traditional Japanese architecture.

APARTMENT OR MANSION?

In a place where land is at a premium and has been fully developed for more than 400 years, the only direction to build is up. Every day, scores of single-family homes 20 or 30 years old

13-story *manshon* constructed of reinforced concrete

are razed, then replaced with high-rise buildings known as *manshon* ("mansions"), meaning something quite different than a million-dollar estate. How do you tell a *manshon* from an apartment? A *manshon* is a newer, multi-unit, high-rise building made of reinforced concrete, with units for rent or purchase—like a condominium complex. The fancier ones come with nice landscaping, a lobby, a security guard, and an elevator. Because of its sturdy construction, a *manshon* unit keeps out noise from other units more effectively.

An *apaato* (abbreviation of "apartment"), on the other hand, is typically an older two- or three-story wood building with thin walls and lower rent. Public housing complexes subsidized by cities or local governments are often rows of rectangular five- or six-story apartment buildings, the older ones walk-up only. So many people apply for such units that they are awarded through a lottery, and the wait may be five years or more.

The Housing Search

Most apartments and houses are described in terms of the number of rooms they have in addition to the kitchen. Because most of the rooms are multi-functional—living room by day, bedroom at night—the rooms aren't designated as "bedrooms" as you might be used to in your home country. Instead of a one- or two-bedroom apartment, classifieds and postings at real estate offices will describe listings as 1K, 2K, 3DK, 1LDK. A 1K is one room plus kitchen, 2DK has two rooms plus a kitchen large enough for a small dining table, and a 3LDK has three rooms plus a living room and eat-in kitchen. A *wan ruumu* is a one-room or studio. It's rare for an apartment or house to have more than one bath and toilet, so that's usually unstated. The bathtub is normally filled to the top with cold water and heated by an auxiliary gas heater. The same hot-water bath is shared by the whole family (after washing thoroughly outside the tub, of course). The bathtub, sink, and toilet may be in separate tiny rooms, so that each can be used by different family members at the same time.

TEMPORARY LODGING

Where will you stay while searching for a place to call home? There are several alternatives less costly than paying for a hotel room.

Weekly *Manshon*

One option is a short-term "weekly mansion," which is a furnished apartment with linens, TV, and basic kitchenware for rates starting at ¥5,000 ($62) per night for a one-week stay. Unlike with long-term apartments, there is no deposit required. Weekly and monthly *manshon* are popular with Japanese business travelers and single workers who are transferred to another city short-term. Posters advertising furnished units are common on the trains and subway, as well as online. Location makes a difference in rates—in Tokyo, look in the north and east for cheaper rates than south and west. There are also cheap, dorm-style accommodations catering to foreigners. One "gaijin house" in east Tokyo charges ¥3,000 ($37.50) per night for a room shared with 2–4 people. This is also a way to meet other newbies to Japan as well as Japanese residents. (The rates quoted are based on an average exchange rate ¥80 to US$1 in 2012).

COZY QUARTERS

What might your housing be like in Japan? I asked three Americans to describe their living situations.

The apartment was similar—nice and modern, but there was no central heat. I wasn't used to waking up to the cold—you can see your breath in winter. The toilet seat was heated, which was novel. I slept on a futon. There was no dryer, so clothes were air-dried. I had to rethink how to shop because the refrigerator was so small. I didn't know how to separate the garbage and I didn't know where to get heating oil for the portable heater, but later I figured these things out.

David, who lived in Kanazawa

My space was much smaller, but more modern. We had a serious mold problem! The bathtub and heater were difficult to operate, since I couldn't read the controls.

Rhae, who lived in Kamakura

Here in Hokkaido, we first lived in an apartment complex, so space was limited, but it was adequate. Later we found a farmhouse that was empty, and were able to negotiate a rental arrangement with the elderly owners. The house is not large, but the property gives ample room for gardening and various other activities.

Mike, who lives in Hokkaido

DAILY LIFE

Japanese Host Families

Another option is to find a Japanese family to stay with for several nights—or even the duration of a school year, if you're a student. If you plan to enroll in a Japanese university, the housing office can likely match you with a host family. Be aware that living in a Japanese home may come with constraints, such as a curfew, lack of personal space due to tight living quarters, scheduled bathing order, and requests to teach English to children or neighbors. If you live with a Japanese family, you should not expect to come and go as you please, returning home only to eat and sleep. You will experience Japanese customs and cultural events as a member of the family, and you can learn a lot firsthand. For instance, observe how the family's shoes are arranged in the *genkan* (entryway)—in which direction do they point? What is the order in which family members take baths and where do you fit in? How is trash sorted and when is it taken out? Bring some small gifts from your hometown or state to present to your host family. These will be greatly appreciated as a token of thoughtfulness, as will pictures to share of your family, school, and hometown.

In most towns and cities, there are volunteer international organizations waiting to help visitors find everything from housing to jobs to Japanese language lessons. Inquire at your local city or town hall for information, or consult the *Multilingual Living Guide*, available online in 14 languages.

Renting

PRICES

How much does it cost to rent an apartment? That depends on how much space you require, as well as the location. For a luxury apartment or house in the areas of Tokyo where Western executives congregate (with American appliances too large to fit most Japanese apartments), the sky is the limit. A 1,000-square-foot one-bedroom apartment with whirlpool tub in Ebisu lists for ¥990,000 or $12,875 per month, and a 4,200-square-foot house in Shibuya rents for ¥2,150,000 or $26,875 per month—more than what some people earn in a year. You could also choose a 65-square-meter (700-square-foot) two-room apartment for ¥240,000 or $3,000 per month, or a 27.2-square-meter (300-square-foot) studio in Roppongi for ¥175,000 or $2,200 a month.

If you are willing to try Japanese-style compact living, you may be able to find a two-room apartment for ¥80,000 or $1,000 per month and up. The truly frugal could try living in a 12-square-meter (130-square-foot) room with a sink and shared toilet down the hall for ¥40,000 or $500 a month, like many Japanese university students do—if you don't mind taking your towel and basin to the public bath down the street. Again, prices depend on the size, location, type of construction, and the distance to public transportation. Housing ads usually specify, in minutes, how long the walk is to the nearest train or subway station. If you will be walking that distance twice a day or more, are you willing to walk 15 minutes each way, or is it important that you are five minutes away?

In smaller towns and rural areas of Japan, rents are much lower than in the urban areas.

In housing ads you will note that the total floor area is expressed in square meters, while each room is described by the number of *tatami,* or *jo* (one mat is roughly three by six feet). For example, a 4.5-mat room is about nine feet by nine feet, a six-mat room about nine feet by 12 feet, an eight-mat room about 12 feet by 12 feet, and so on. These descriptions apply whether the floor is wood or actual *tatami* mats. Most apartments are quite bare, with perhaps a heater/air conditioner unit on the wall and a kitchen sink. That's it. Renters must supply their own refrigerator, two-burner gas cook stove to set on the counter, microwave, washing machine, and, of course, furniture. These appliances can be found at recycle shops, which offer delivery for a fee. Clothes dryers are almost unknown, as Japanese women say they like to hang dry clothes in the sun (or if raining, indoors).

RESOURCES

Think carefully about where you want to live—how much space and how close to the train or bus station. How convenient is it to the grocery store, bank, post office, school, and restaurants? Once you have in mind a geographic area, take a look at the classified sections of *The Japan Times, Metropolis,* and www.tokyo.craigslist.jp. And let your friends and acquaintances know that you're looking for an apartment.

If you read Japanese, pick up some free real estate magazines at any bookstore or kiosk. The thick, oversized magazines are a compendium of *chintai apaato* rental apartments and *manshon* rental condos, organized by region, town, and train line. For example, if you work near the Mita subway line, look at the section of the magazine

This apartment above a rice store and dry cleaners is handy for airing futons, but not so private.

labeled "Mita Line" (in Japanese). Grouped under each train station along that line are rental listings, from cheapest to most expensive, and from one to five-plus rooms, with room sizes and a phone number to call. The same information is available online for each realtor who publishes the rental magazines: *Isize, Chintai, Able,* and *Home Adpark* are some.

If you've gotten this far and found an apartment that interests you, call the realtor listed in the magazine. If you speak Japanese, you can call directly; if not, have a Japanese friend call. Ask about availability and when you can see the unit. You may be asked to come to their office to fill out an application form. Many real estate agents in the cities have branch offices throughout Japan. Once your application is accepted, you can ask to see several listings.

RENTAL AGENTS

One of the best ways to find housing is to scout out the area you want to live in. In urban areas, realtors are clustered around train and subway stations. Look for postings on the windows with floor plans and price (in Japanese). Most neighborhood real estate offices are quite small and carry listings only for buildings in the immediate vicinity. The notices displayed outside the windows indicate whether the property is a *chintai* (rental) or *uri* (sale) and *apaato* or *manshon,* along with details such as date of construction, material, number of stories, address, number of minutes' walk to the nearest train station, perhaps a map, and features, including direction (important if you want sunshine), price (including move-in fees), floor plan, and size (counted in *tatami* mats). Even if you cannot read all the characters, you should be able to decipher

FINDING A RENTAL

In Japan you typically use a real estate agent to find rental housing. You can find realtors' offices near train stations—look for housing postings on the windows. If you tell them your budget and preferred size and location, they will help you find something suitable. If you don't speak Japanese, go with someone who does. To help narrow down your target, be prepared to give the agent the following information:

- Minimum and maximum monthly rent

- Preferred location: name of nearest train or subway station and maximum walking distance to station

- Type of housing: apartment (wood construction), *manshon* (concrete), house (*ikko-da-te*)

- Preferred floor: 1st, 2nd, etc.; do you require an elevator?

- Number of (bed) rooms

- Type of additional rooms: K (kitchen), DK (eat-in kitchen), LDK (living-dining-kitchen)

- Flooring: Japanese (*jo*, or *tatami* mat), Western (laminate or carpet), either OK

- Toilet: Western (sit), Japanese (squat), toilet with washroom

- Bath: with bath, no bath OK (go to public bath)

- Air-conditioning: required or not required

- Direction: south-facing, south or east, any direction but north, no preference

- Nearby facilities required: coin laundry, school, supermarket, park, bank, post office, hospital, public bath (*sento*), other

- Desired move-in date

QUESTIONS TO ASK THE AGENT:

- Is there parking space for a bicycle or car?

- Is there a lock on the mailbox?

- Is there high-speed cable (*hikari-faibaa*) for TV and Internet (*intaa-netto*)?

- How sound-proof is it?

- Does the front door lock automatically?

Adapted from CLAIR: www.clair.or.jp/tagengo/housing/en/h-en07.html

ROOM SIZE IS MEASURED IN:

- 1-*jo* (1 *tatami* mat) = 1.525 square meters

- 1 square meter = 10.75 square feet

- 20 square meters = 215 square feet

- 100 square meters = 1,075 square feet

the floor plan and monthly rent. For example, if you know the character for yen, then you can figure that a one-room unit listed for ¥70,000 is roughly $875 per month. Rents are often listed in ¥10,000 units (called *man* in Japanese); thus an apartment advertised for 8.85 *man-en* costs ¥88,500 or about $1,100 per month.

After perusing the housing posters from outside, you might want to go inside. You can simply point to the apartment listings that interest you—the agent may even give you a photocopy—and ask to see some of the properties. If you speak Japanese, say, *"Apaato o sagashiterun desu ga"* ("I'm looking for an apartment"); if not, ask a Japanese friend to accompany you. The neighborhood agent may make a few phone calls and take you to see the properties immediately, by foot or by bicycle.

Here I must pause to break some unhappy news. When you poke your head through the agency door, the real estate agent may take one look and shoo you away wordlessly, or cross his or her forearms in the shape of an X and say something that means, "Terribly sorry, but the landlord doesn't rent to *gaijin* (foreigners)." If this happens,

INSPECTING AN APARTMENT OR HOUSE

- Kitchen: Is there a gas stove, refrigerator, good plumbing?

- Windows and sliders: Are there screens?

- Laundry: Is there a washer and a sunny place to hang clothing to dry?

- Room size: How many jo (*tatami* mats) is each room?

- Floor plan: Do you have to walk through another room to get to the kitchen or bath?

- Construction: Wood, concrete, earthquake resistant? Year built?

- Comes with: Air-conditioning, heat, lights?

- Electrical outlets: Is there one in every room, including the bathroom?

- Switches: Check lights, plumbing, shower, and toilets to make sure they work.

- Parking: Is there off-street parking for a bicycle or car?

- Neighborhood: Is it quiet and are the neighbors trustworthy?

- Location: Is it on a busy street? How many minutes' walk to the nearest bus stop and train station?

- Rent: What is the monthly rent, maintenance fee, deposit, landlord fee, and agent's commission? How much is refundable?

- What is allowed: Pets, nailing things to the wall, subletting, ending the contract early, etc.

Note: Most apartments do not come with any appliances.

Each landlord has his/her own rules, so read the contract carefully before signing. Bring a Japanese friend or acquaintance with you to read the contract. You will need to document that you have a Japanese (financial and legal) guarantor when you sign the contract.

nothing you say or do will make any difference. You may have been born and raised in Japan, have lived there for 25 years, be fluent in Japanese, and work for the Japanese government—who promised to be your financial guarantor. I've said all of the above and more, but it didn't change a thing. When I called ahead to make an appointment, everything was fine—no one can tell my nationality on the phone, since I'm a natural bilingual. But when I stuck my "high nose" into the office, a wall came between us. If you aren't part of the majority, wishing doesn't make you so. It may not be racism so much as bad experience with a *gaijin* who didn't pay the rent on time, had raucous parties, emitted strange odors, fed the crows, put out non-burnable trash on burnables day, or eloped with the landlord's daughter. If you get the *gaijin* wave-off, turn, take a deep breath, and walk out the door. Then reflect on the difficulties that minorities and "aliens" in your home country may face on a daily basis. And even if you strike out with one realtor, most are friendly and helpful. Use your Japanese connections if you can, as well as your employer.

REVIEWING YOUR OPTIONS

You've looked at three or four apartments, following the agent to the fifth floor walk-up, wondering how you would carry your boxes of books and queen-size bed. The agent unlocks the door and takes her shoes off in the *genkan* and so do you. She pulls out slippers for herself and for you. You step up and see four bare walls. The room may be called a kitchen but all you see is a sink with a single faucet, and a round hole in the floor by the entry. This is the drain hole for the hose of your washing machine, if you decide to install one. There may not be any cupboards. You are expected to provide a one- or two-burner cookstove to set on the counter, as well as a refrigerator and heater/air conditioner. Newer *manshon* units usually have a heating/air-conditioning unit on the wall. If not, you may be able to negotiate with your landlord. When I rented an apartment in Tokyo without a heater/air conditioner, I asked my agent to persuade the landlord to provide one, and he did. I asked about high-speed Internet access and, several months later, the whole apartment building was wired (for a fee, of course).

While you're poking about the other rooms, note the number and size of closets and storage areas. Japanese-style *oshiire* (traditional closets) have a shelf where futons (cotton-filled mattresses) are stored by day, but are not so handy for hanging clothes (you can buy spring-loaded adjustable rods for that purpose). Note how the bathroom area is arranged. Are the bath, sink, and toilet all in one room or are they separated? Does each room have direct access to the kitchen and bath, or are they arranged rail-road style, where you have to walk through another room—an important consideration if you have a roommate. Note the size and direction of windows: Do they face a gray wall, or can you see a parking lot or a small patch of blue? How many hours of sunshine will you get per day?

Also note the floor covering: Is it *tatami* or *furoringu* (flooring, usually laminate wood)? Does the *tatami* look and smell new? (New *tatami* have a slightly green color and smell of rush grasses.) In better apartments, *tatami* are recovered or even replaced after a tenant moves out. Sunlight fades and dries *tatami,* so newspapers may be covering the *tatami* if the unit is unoccupied. Is the apartment unit above or below occupied? If so, you might want to visit the unit again at night or on Sunday, to check the noise level when the neighbors are home. Concrete *manshon* have thicker, more soundproof walls than wood-frame apartments. How long does it takes to walk to the bus and train station? Where is the nearest convenience store, supermarket, post office, or hospital? Proximity to public transportation is particularly important if you plan to walk to trains and buses, but less so if you have a bicycle.

CLOSING THE DEAL
Getting Your Personal Seal
Almost all legal transactions in Japan are stamped by all parties with a personal seal, or *inkan,* dipped in a red ink pad. The seal contains the family name in Japanese characters. Hand signing is not considered legally binding. It would be a good idea to purchase an *inkan* (also called *hanko* informally) with your surname in *katakana* symbols. Many larger train stations and underground shopping centers have an *inkan* shop. Some bookstores have the service. You can probably order one online. The cost depends on the material used—wood, ivory, silver, or gold. All you need is a simple wood one and a snap-open case that contains a tiny red ink pad. Japanese may have several different *inkan,* but one of them is officially registered with city hall, and is legally binding when used. An online source to order yours within Japan is www.shibuya-hanko.com/seal.htm.

Financial Guarantors and Key Money
You've now spent several days or weeks searching for your home in Japan. You found

ABOUT GUARANTORS

Non-citizens who rent property are required to have a Japanese guarantor who is legally responsible in case you fail to pay the rent or damage the property. If you have a close Japanese friend or teacher or employer, you might ask them to be your guarantor. This is a huge financial and legal responsibility that shouldn't be taken lightly. If you cannot find a guarantor, you may be able to pay a company to be your guarantor. Ask the real estate agent if they have this service or can recommend a company that does. Larger real estate offices are more likely to have a guarantor service. Or ask at your city or town hall for advice.

one you really like and have filled out an application at the real estate agent's office (again, help from a Japanese-speaking friend is valuable). Whether it's a house or an apartment, the real estate agent will not finalize the agreement without a paper signed by a financial guarantor. This is a form that has to be signed—or rather, stamped with an *inkan* (name seal)—by a Japanese citizen who trusts you enough to put her or his financial resources at risk on your behalf. If you stop paying rent or damage the apartment, your guarantor is ultimately liable. If you already have a job and an employer who will be your guarantor, you're very fortunate.

When the final papers are signed and sealed with your *inkan,* be prepared to hand over—in cash—the equivalent of six months' rent (sometimes less). That's how renting works in Japan—the costs include *shikikin* (security deposit) equivalent to one to two months' rent (refundable), as well as *reikin* (literally, "gratitude money") to the landlord, which is anywhere from one to three months' rent (nonrefundable). In addition, the real estate agent takes one month's rent as a fee for handling the contract (nonrefundable), and for a *manshon, kokyuhi* (public or common fee) is assessed from each tenant in a building.

When renting an apartment, you will typically have to sign a lease for two years, but usually there's no penalty for moving out sooner. The rent can't be raised during the lease period, but it can be raised when you renew. In addition, renewing the lease often requires another "gift" to the landlord equal to one or two months' rent.

In your apartment, you will find information on utilities—gas, electric, and water—with instructions on how to request service by telephone. Your real estate agent also has this information and may be able to help you arrange for utilities to be turned on promptly when you move in. The gas company will come after you've installed the gas kitchen ring to check for leaking tubes and to turn the gas on. There are two valves attached to the gas tubing: One is the main valve, which should be shut off in an earthquake, and the other should be turned on and off each time you use the stove. The water company will check the water flow and quality from your kitchen faucet and read the meter. The electric company will read the meter outside. In each case, you have the option of paying your monthly bill at the corner *konbini* (convenience store), or you can go to your bank to arrange automatic payment of utility bills from your bank account. In either case, you will receive bills in the mail with your meter reading and balance due. Perhaps because personal checks are not used in Japan, the automatic bank payment system is widely used, highly efficient, and reliable.

Buying

After several years in Japan, you may become attached to the culture or to someone from the culture. You might start thinking about buying a house and making it more permanent—especially when your two-year apartment lease is up and the landlord raises the rent (and you're charged one month's rent to renew). So, what are your options for buying a home? In urban areas, such as Tokyo, the price of a detached house and land is so out of reach that many Japanese families opt to buy a *manshon* instead.

To advertise high-rise condos, builders usually construct model rooms near high-traffic streets, put flags up, and hand out brochures at the station to attract buyers before the *manshon* is built. The model room is made of plywood and cheap material, then torn down after a suitable time.

The price depends on the location, size, year of construction, and amenities. For example, a four-room *manshon* with 109.5 square meters (1,179 square feet) in northern Tokyo recently listed for ¥40 million or $500,000. An search of Real Estate Tokyo (www.realestate-tokyo.com) reveals a wide range of prices for condominiums and houses. A small but centrally located 36-square-meter (390-square-feet) one-bedroom condo in Minato-ku built in 2001 lists for ¥32.4 million or $405,000. A reserved parking spot is an additional ¥50,000 or $625 per month (with no vacancies at present). A two-bedroom condo in Shibuya-ku with 61 square meters (660 square feet) of space built in 1986 is ¥44.8 million or $575,000. If you're looking to buy a house for a family, a three-bedroom house in Meguro-ku in central Tokyo with 92 square meters (985 square feet), built in 2009, costs ¥62.8 million or $807,000. In Setagaya-ku,

A single-family home in Tokyo is beyond the reach of most "salaryman" families.

© RUTHY KANAGY

a more spacious three-bedroom house with one *tatami* Japanese-style room, built in 2001 with 175 square meters (1,880 square feet), is available for ¥88 million or $1.1 million. Be sure to choose a good real estate agent and prioritize the features that are most important to you in a house or condo—location, size, age, construction, proximity to work or school, population density, and so on.

It's not unusual for Japanese families today to take out a 75-year or even 100-year mortgage to be able to afford a house in urban areas such as Tokyo—committing their grandchildren and great-grandchildren to finishing the house payments. Because of high prices, home ownership rates in urban areas like Tokyo are less than 40 percent. In outlying prefectures, home ownership is higher: 70 percent in Gunma prefecture and 60–70 percent in Hiroshima and Shikoku to the west. The national average is 60 percent, and the average amount of floor space per home is 92 square meters, or about 1,000 square feet.

While there are no legal restrictions on foreigners buying property in Japan, it's very difficult to obtain a bank loan. First of all, you must be a permanent resident, and you will need a Japanese person to sign off as financial guarantor. Banks will not loan more than three times your annual salary. However, if your spouse is Japanese, a mortgage can be taken out in his or her name.

BUILDING

Yes, it is possible to build a home in Japan. Is the process easy? No. Buying land is quite a complex process, and you're advised to engage professional assistance in the transaction to make sure it proceeds according to Japanese real estate laws. The Japanese civil code is sometimes confusing and difficult even for Japanese legal experts to interpret.

© RUTHY KANAGY

If you can't build out, build up.

Often it's wiser simply to lease a lot from the owner for a certain length of time. Many Japanese are reluctant to sell land that's been handed down for generations, but are willing to rent it out. You can build a home on a rented lot without too much difficulty. Many Japanese houses are not built to last more than 20 or 30 years, after which they are torn down and rebuilt, or sold to the highest bidder, who constructs a 12-story *manshon* on the lot.

Outside urban areas, land prices are of course much lower and it's possible to consider building a house there. A former classmate, Phil Bennett, and his wife, Akiko, built their home in the mountains of Gunma-ken, north of Tokyo. The building, which is their house as well as a restaurant, Café Manna, is on the banks of the Tone River. Kamimoku village is three hours north, and many lifestyles removed, from Tokyo. Phil elaborates:

A friend of Akiko's found the spot on the riverbank where we are and introduced us to the landowner, who agreed to lease 100 *tsubo* (330 square meters/3,550 square feet) for ¥10,000 ($125) a month. Since most of the land sloped down to the river, in order for us to have some flat land to build on, our contractor had to haul in huge preformed L-shaped concrete slabs as retaining walls for the filled-in land. Building the base for the house cost ¥6 million ($75,000), and our contractor spent a lot of time at the Numata Civil Engineering Bureau trying to persuade the inspectors that the project was safe. Given that we were building on a riverbank, the bureau was very skeptical and delayed construction for several months until they finally gave the OK. The next year, we learned that the civil engineers had good reason to be cautious, when the river flooded and washed away two-thirds of the riverbank below our house.

The building cost ¥11 million ($137,500), and the interior and restaurant fittings cost about ¥2.5 million ($31,250). There are no restrictions that I know of on foreigners buying land or building per se, but it is hard to get a bank loan if you don't have permanent resident status. In our area, many landowners are reluctant to sell land that has belonged to their families for many generations and would rather rent it instead. Akiko got a ¥10 million ($125,000) loan from her bank, payable in 10 years at an interest rate of about 1.5 percent, with a monthly payment of about ¥60,000 ($750).

Many Americans and other internationals from Tokyo escape to a cottage in the mountains during the summer. Many have Japanese spouses, who serve as the registered heads of the household, and they were able to build second homes and get a mortgage in their spouse's name. The resulting village near Phil and Akiko's home in Gunma is referred to by the townsfolk as the *gaijin-mura,* or "outsiders' village."

Moving In

UTILITIES

Most Japanese homes use natural gas for cooking and for heating water. There are usually two gas outlets in the kitchen next to the sink, each with two on-off valves. When you move into an apartment or house, there is usually a tag attached to the valve with a telephone number to call to begin your gas service. In urban areas, gas lines are city operated. In smaller towns, you may have a stand-alone natural gas tank, called *gas-u bom-be,* outside the kitchen window that you can refill when empty. There should also be a tag with a phone number for the water and electric company. If you used a realtor to find your place, they can help make the calls. How much do utilities run for a typical apartment in the city? I asked one Tokyo resident, who lives in a 2K (two rooms plus kitchen), 33-square-meter (355-square-foot) apartment in Tokyo, what his utilities cost. Electricity is ¥5,000 or $62.50 for 205 kilowatt hours, natural gas is ¥7,800 or $98 for 47 cubic meters, and water is ¥3,500 or $43.75 per month. The total comes to about ¥16,300 or $204 per month, on average. For high-speed Internet, he pays ¥5,800 or about $72.50 a month for a fiber-optic connection and ¥2,800 or $35 to the Internet service provider. Cable television costs vary, of course, according to the number of channels you subscribe to. In urban areas you can get satellite broadcasts of news and shows in English. In rural parts of Japan, there may be only two channels and no cable service.

When my translator brother moved into his Tokyo apartment, the only kitchen equipment supplied was a sink and a wall-mounted gas water heater above the spigot. Most Japanese homes have an instant water heater that fires up automatically when you turn on the hot water spigot, heating the cold water on demand. A large American-style tank of hot water with temperature maintained at a certain setting is not common in Japan. His kitchen came without a refrigerator or cook stove, nor was there a washing machine or air conditioner. These had to be purchased. Many Japanese, when they move, don't bother taking appliances with them because of the difficulty and cost of transport. Instead, people prefer to buy new appliances for their new residence. This is why, once a month on large trash collection day, you can find mountains of perfectly good used appliances, televisions, stereos, and furniture out on the curb. If you know what day of the month *sodai gomi* collection day is in a particular neighborhood, you can outfit your apartment for free (ask at city hall).

HOW TO PAY RENT AND UTILITIES

Rent is commonly paid in cash, either to the landlord or at the real estate office that helped you find your place. They may give you a booklet and mark each month with a stamp when you pay your rent. Personal checks are not used in Japan, and many transactions are done in cash. For utilities, you can set up an automatic payment system from your Japanese bank account. If not, you can take all your utility bills and cell phone bill, etc., that come in the mail to the nearest *konbini* and pay in cash. If you can't read Japanese, just show them the card and they will tell you how much.

FURNISHINGS

To outfit your apartment or house, you will need to purchase shower and window curtains, and often curtain rods, light bulbs, and ceiling lights. These items do not always come with a rental. Furniture can be bought relatively inexpensively at any number of *risaikuru shoppu* (recycle shops, or secondhand stores). *Risaikuru shoppu* have become quite popular and well stocked in recent years. Some are very large and will deliver for a fee. You will find the best selection of used furniture in March, national moving month, before the new school year and fiscal year begins in April. Many cities have a *shohisha sentaa* (consumer center) to handle complaints and give advice regarding shopping for commercial goods, door-to-door sales, etc. They may have a *risaikuru sentaa* (swap shop) of used clothing and furniture.

NEIGHBORHOOD PROTOCOL

Once you've moved in, there are several things you can do to break the ice with your new neighbors. Tradition dictates that you present a small gift, such as a hand towel, to your neighbors living on either side and in the three houses across the street. However, in a 20-story *manshon,* only the sky or a view of distant mountains (if you're lucky) will be across from you; more likely, you'll see a solid wall. The taller the building, the more anonymous: You may rarely see your neighbors, and thus gift-giving is not so common these days. In these close quarters, it goes without saying that you should avoid making excessive noise (e.g., talking in a loud voice or playing loud music) in your apartment, especially at night.

But even if you never see your neighbors, be sure to follow the system for putting out trash on designated days or you'll risk annoying your neighbors as well as the trash collectors. Divide trash into burnable items (wood, clothing, kitchen garbage, and non-recyclable paper), nonburnable items (some plastic containers, metal, glass, rubber and anything that would be toxic to burn), and recyclables (glass bottles, tin, aluminum, paper, magazines, cardboard, some plastic containers and PET bottles or plastic drink bottles). The local supermarket usually has bins to recycle plastic drink bottles, white Styrofoam food trays (from the grocery store), and washed and flattened milk and juice cartons. For detailed instructions on how to classify trash and to receive color-coded trash bags, contact your local municipal office. As far as collection schedules, in Chofu city, for example, nonburnables and PET bottles are collected on alternate Mondays, burnables and cans on Tuesday, paper and clothing on Wednesday, designated plastic on Thursday, and burnables and glass bottles on Fridays at a designated spot on the street (you may have to walk a block or two to get to your nearest collection site). At many collection sites, trash bags are covered with blue netting to dissuade pesky crows, which is why your neighbors will not look at you kindly for putting the trash out the night before pickup day.

Doing your wash at the local coin laundry, which may double as the neighborhood public bath, is a creative way to meet the neighbors, if you are adventurous. Most of your neighbors will do the wash at home on days that it's not raining, then hang the laundry out to dry on poles strung horizontally across the balcony. On sunny days, you see a colorful array of thick futon mattress covers, sheets, and blankets hanging out of windows and balconies, and even draped over bicycles to catch some rays. Due to the humid climate, bedding gets damp and musty unless aired out. Giant spring-loaded clothespins prevent the family bedding from leaping off 13th-floor balconies.

One reason people may not initiate conversations with you is that they may feel embarrassed that they cannot speak English well, even though everyone in Japan studies English starting in grade seven. On occasion, take the initiative and strike up a conversation with someone. You can ask your neighbors for help finding a supermarket, post office, bank, or drugstore. Hopefully you will develop some friends over time, but don't be surprised if they don't invite you to their home. Most homes are simply too small to entertain. Instead, people go out to eat or drink together and enjoy kara-oke. If you do get invited to a Japanese home, don't expect to get a tour of each room like we do in North America. The bedrooms and kitchen are private; they feel most comfortable entertaining you as a guest.

A *Daily Living Guide,* published by Itabashi City in Tokyo, offers tips for settling into your new neighborhood: "Japanese are traditionally community-oriented, and it is important to have good relationships with your neighbors. Even though you may not be able to speak Japanese fluently, you will find that you can get a lot of support from your neighborhood. By exchanging information and helping each other, your life will become more fulfilled and enjoyable, so try to initiate contacts with your neighbors."

Every neighborhood has a residents' association, or *chonaikai/jichikai.* They circulate information from the city or town office to residents in a kind of folder called *kairan-ban.* They also take part in crime prevention and neighborhood watch, disaster drills, and often hold neighborhood events and festivals. They collect subscriptions from residents to finance their activities. Anyone can join the local neighborhood association. You can find out more when a representative calls in your area.

Moving is hard enough in your home country, and doubly so in a new culture. It requires a lot of time and patience and can be very stressful, mentally and physically. Be sure to take time to exercise, go on walks, and eat balanced meals. Give yourself time—at least three to six months—to feel acclimated to your new home and neighborhood.

LANGUAGE AND EDUCATION

Nihongo 日本語 (Japanese language) is spoken throughout Japan, taught in schools, and used in public and private life. Though the writing system is complex—it combines 2,000 characters borrowed from Chinese, along with two sets of phonetic letters— Japanese people are highly literate. Nine years of schooling are devoted to learning to read and write all the *kanji* characters.

Spoken Japanese is not as difficult as you might imagine. If you learn how to pronounce foreign words with a good Japanese accent, you'll have an instant vocabulary of hundreds of words. This is because over the past 500 years of contact with the West, the Japanese language has absorbed thousands of words from English, German, French, Portuguese, and other languages. These words accompanied new information about government, economy, medicine, education, sports, cuisine, and clothing. Many new terms continue to arrive (or are created) with new forms of technology. Does that mean you can get by in English if you decide to live in Japan for an extended period? Perhaps, but it will probably limit you to being an outsider.

Most people in Japan will appreciate your attempts to speak Japanese. Being able to greet your Japanese neighbors and shopkeepers with *Ohayoo gozaimasu* (Good

© RUTHY KANAGY

morning) in the morning, along with being able to ask prices and answer questions about your home country, opens doors. With effort and discipline, you can learn to carry on basic conversations in a matter of months, especially if you surround yourself with Japanese speakers and good resources. You can set a goal for yourself to recognize a certain number of Japanese signs per day on your daily route.

REGIONAL DIALECTS

Japanese dialects can be broadly divided into east and west from Nagoya, in the middle of Honshu, halfway between Tokyo and Osaka. There is still a rich variety of *hogen,* or dialects, due to extremely mountainous terrain that separates one community from the next, but in recent years the use of dialects has begun to diminish. The Tokyo dialect has come to be regarded as the standard since 1868 and has spread, due to television and a common school curriculum. Depending on where you live, there may be more or less of a local dialect, as in Tohoku or northeast Honshu, central and western Honshu, and in the cities of Osaka, Kobe, and Kyoto. Shikoku and Kyushu have regional dialects, and Okinawa has its own language. But no matter where you are in the country, most people can speak "standard" Japanese.

Learning the Language

WRITTEN JAPANESE

Most Japanese words are written in Japanese script, but the Latin alphabet is also used for special effects in advertisements and music, and as an aid for foreign visitors. Signs in train stations are generally transcribed alphabetically underneath the Japanese script for the benefit of those who cannot read the characters.

The writing system combines *kana* letters and *kanji* characters. *Kana* are 46 phonetic syllables. *Kanji* are 2,000 characters borrowed from China in the 6th century, when the Japanese had no written form. Japanese characters took the shape and meaning of *kanji,* but incorporated Japanese pronunciations, in addition to retaining some Chinese pronunciations. *Kana* come in two versions, both with the same pronunciation (think of cursive versus printed writing). *Hiragana* are smooth and rounded in shape, while *katakana* are square and angular. Unlike the American alphabet, where a letter is either a single consonant or a vowel, each *kana* is a whole syllable, such as *ka* or *shi.*

Hiragana are used to show verb endings (past, present, polite, and so on) and appear in many native Japanese words. In contrast, *katakana* are used to write words borrowed from Western languages, as well as sound effects (for example, in anime action). They are also used for emphasis, similarly to our use of italics. If you go to any coffee shop or fast food restaurant, the menu will be written almost entirely in *katakana,* because most items originated in the West. Thus, "ko-o-hi-i" (coffee) contains four *katakana* letters, and "ha-n-ba-a-ga-a" (hamburger) has six *katakana.* Spelling is not a problem for Japanese children, because the name of each *kana* and its sound are one and the same. Once they learn the 46 *kana,* first graders can write long compositions.

Kanji are another story. The Ministry of Education, Culture, Sports, Science, and Technology (hereafter called the Ministry of Education) has designated approximately 2,000 *kanji* as official characters for use in written Japanese. Learning this many

WRITING JAPANESE

Four kinds of script are used to write Japanese—*hiragana, katakana, kanji,* and the Roman alphabet. *Hiragana* (rounded letters) is for verb inflections (past, present, polite, etc.), grammatical markers (subject, object, topic, etc.), and many native words (as opposed to loan words from Chinese or English). *Katakana* (square letters) is for Western words and for sound effects (important in anime), as well as for emphasis, like our use of italics.

The rest is written with *kanji* characters

borrowed from China around the 6th century, when there was no written form of Japanese. The shape and meaning of *kanji* came from China, but their pronunciation is Japanese. Note that Chinese and Japanese are completely unrelated languages—Chinese is tonal, while Japanese is not. Chinese is written using thousands of characters, but Japanese uses "only" 2,000 *kanji*. It takes Japanese students nine years to learn 2,000 *kanji,* so don't be discouraged if you can't learn them in a few months.

characters takes time. In school, students learn 100 to 200 *kanji* a year and have weekly *kanji* quizzes. Since it takes nine years for Japanese children to learn all the *kanji* characters, anyone new to Japan should not expect to master them in a year or two.

Take your time learning *kanji,* a few every day. When you are surrounded by them, you will soon recognize the names of cities, your local train station, and the characters for your favorite department store. There are many good books on learning *kanji.* It may take a while before you can read a newspaper (you have to know most of the *kanji* to be able to read a newspaper and feel comfortably literate), but if you become familiar with the most frequently used *kanji,* you'll learn how to guess the rest. *Kanji* are your friends, once you get acquainted with their shapes, strokes, characteristics, and common traits.

SPOKEN JAPANESE

Basic Japanese conversation is not as difficult as you may think. A lot can be said in a few words. Unlike with many European languages, you don't have to worry about gender markers, plurals, the future tense (it's the same as present tense), or conjugating verbs for the first person, second person, and so on. The subjects of sentences are generally understood from context and omitted when understood, just as in Spanish. The pronouns I, you, she, they, etc., are used infrequently; instead, names or titles are used when referring to or talking with other people.

Desu is the Japanese "be" verb and is very handy, because it doesn't change form when you talk about "I" or "she" or "they" as it does in English (am, is, are, etc.). Unlike in English, the verbs come at the end of the sentence. So if someone says to you, *"Yamada desu,"* it means "I'm Yamada." If you want to say "I'm Tom," you say *"Tomu desu."* If you want to refer to your wife and say, "She's Jasmine," all you need to say is *"Jasmine desu."* Referring to a group of friends, you say, *"Tomodachi desu,"* which means, "These are my friends." Context plays a big part in Japanese communication, so things that are obvious or understood by everyone don't have to be repeated.

Japanese language is very sensitive to social status, and there are several levels of politeness expressed in your choice of verbs and other words. If you are speaking in a formal situation, you might use the polite form of "be" and say, *"Tomu de gozaimasu,"*

© RUTHY KANAGY

Written Japanese is complex, but 99% of Japan's citizens are literate.

a very polite way of saying, "I'm Tom." That's why many Japanese greetings have more than one form: *Arigatoo* is a casual "Thanks." The more polite way is *Arigatoo gozaimasu*. It works the same way with "Good morning": *Ohayoo* is "Mornin'" and *Ohayoo gozaimasu* is a polite version. Age, social status, and in-group/out-group relationships all enter into deciding what level of speech to use. That's why exchanging business cards is considered so important (for career-track business people). A glance at the card tells you the counterpart's rank and position in the company so you can adjust your level of politeness.

STUDYING JAPANESE

If you don't know Japanese, you will have a difficult time getting around Japan. You may be able to get by with English and gestures in urban areas, but you will miss out on the pleasure of Japanese daily life and culture. If you know the appropriate greetings for various times of day, when leaving and coming back, before and after eating, and when offering and receiving something, your interactions in Japanese society will become much smoother.

David, who taught English in Kanazawa for two years, talks about his Japanese ability when he first moved to Japan:

> I knew next to none—it was very basic. I could introduce myself. You must learn Japanese, as it was almost a sink-or-swim feeling. I also feel it's insulting not to learn the local language. You have to linguistically bend toward them, not the other way around. Also, Japanese often communicate through feeling and atmosphere, whereas spoken words may not carry as much weight. Spoken words don't necessarily have the same face value.

DIALECTS

Everyone knows standard Japanese from school and television, but when they want to be warm and intimate with their family, friends, and neighbors, it's natural to speak *hogen*, the local dialect. My friend Yoshida-san speaks Hiroshima-*ben* (Hiroshima dialect). She says it's partly a matter of using different vocabulary, like saying *"dekin"* instead of the standard Japanese *"dekinai"* ("can't do"). Accent and intonation also vary by region. Take the words "thank you": Tokyoites say, *"a-RI-ga-to"*; people from Kobe say, *"a-ri-ga-TO"*; and Hiroshimans say, *"a-ri-GA-to,"* with the capitalized syllable spoken at a higher pitch. I wish I could rattle off in a dialect like my friend Yoshida-san, but Hokkaido is so new, it doesn't have a dialect.

Rhae, who lived in Kamakura, says:

> I had some vocabulary through the Pimsleur tapes and learned *hiragana* from a friend, who made me flash cards—but not enough to become literate. I took a language class in Japan and learned more vocabulary.

Kristy, who lived in rural Iwate, recalls:

> I learned all the *hiragana* and *katakana* letters, but no *kanji*, which was a handicap. I knew random vocabulary from anime, which was in informal style, and no grammar. Not being able to read was tougher than not being able to speak. There were very few English speakers in the town I lived in.

At least one year, but preferably two or three years of intensive study of Japanese is one of the best preparations for living in Japan. It typically takes twice as long for English speakers to learn a completely unrelated language such as Japanese, compared to an Indo-European language. Many colleges and universities in the States offer Japanese, and many have intensive summer programs where you can learn a year's worth of Japanese in nine weeks. If you aren't near a university, check for online Japanese learning sites (such as www.japanese.about.com). Another option is to find a private tutor—a Japanese student or visitor living in your town—although being a native speaker does not guarantee that one knows how to teach effectively. As for the writing system, memorize at least the 46 *katakana* syllables and learn how to write your name.

STUDY ABROAD

Many universities in the United States have study abroad and exchange programs with universities in Japan that include housing, language studies, and cultural activities for three months to a year. Once you arrive in Japan, you can find a language school in any sizable city, and perhaps volunteer citizens who offer Japanese classes for local residents. Check with the *shiyakusho* (city hall)—or *kuyakusho* (ward), if you're in Tokyo—for details.

If you are a student at a college or university that has a direct exchange program with a Japanese university, you will be able to apply through your international programs office. For example, the University of Oregon has exchange programs with seven universities in Japan, including Waseda University, Keio University, and Senshu

DAILY LIFE

ENGLISH WITH A JAPANESE TOUCH

If you know how to pronounce English words with a Japanese accent, you'll have an instant vocabulary of a thousand words! And it will be easier for people to understand your English.

Japanese has five vowels sounds and each has only one pronunciation. Here's how they are pronounced, transcribed into our alphabet:

- **a** like p*a*pa
- **i** like p*i*zza
- **u** like p*u*t
- **e** like p*e*t
- **o** like p*o*rt

In contrast, "a," "e," "i," "o," and "u" in English are unpredictable because they can be pronounced many different ways depending on the word. How does "a" sound in these words: *apple, ate, father, Paul, beautiful?* Five different ways to pronounce "a"! No wonder English is hard for Japanese speakers.

Japanese words consist mostly of consonant-vowel syllables, just like Spanish. Most words end with a vowel sound, except for "n." Note that the Japanese consonant transcribed as "r" by English speakers sounds nothing like the American "r"! Instead, it's a flap, similar to the Spanish "r," almost a soft "d". We produce the identical sound when we say *karate, party,* *photo,* and *butter* (tongue flap on the roof of the mouth), except that we spell it with "t". If you see "r" in a transcribed Japanese word, think "t" as in "par*t*y."

Practice saying these English words with Japanese pronunciation:

- bed – be-d-do
- pet – pe-t-to
- cheese – chi-i-zu
- McDonald's – Ma-ku-do-na-ru-do (Ma-ku-do for short)
- orange juice – o-re-n-ji ju-u-su
- pineapple – pa-i-na-p-pu-ru
- steak – su-te-e-ki
- skirt – su-ka-a-to
- computer – ko-n-pyu-u-ta-a
- girlfriend – ga-a-ru fu-re-n-do
- smart phone – su-ma-ho (for short)

"Nativizing" foreign words is nothing new. How do Americans say *sake, karaoke, karate, Paris,* and *Renault?* Not even close to how native speakers say them! We naturally Americanize foreign words, and Japanese automatically say English words with a Japanese accent. If you pronounce English words the Japanese way, communication will be easier.

University. These programs offer Japanese language classes and a range of courses taught in English. If your school doesn't have a direct exchange program in Japan, your study-abroad office should be able to tell you about consortium programs, i.e., groups of U.S. universities that offer programs in Japan. The Associated Kyoto Program at Doshisha University in Kyoto is a two-semester study-abroad program sponsored by a consortium. Some American universities have set up a branch campus in Japan. For example, Temple University in Philadelphia has a branch campus in Tokyo (see www. temple.edu/studyabroad). CIEE (Council on International Educational Exchange) offers a program at Sophia University in Tokyo (see www.ciee.org). You can also apply directly to Japanese universities that have international programs, such as Hiroshima University, Hokkaido University, Kansai Gaidai University, and Kyushu University. For a detailed description of study-abroad programs in Japan, check the website of the American Association of Teachers of Japanese (www.aatj.org/studyabroad/scholarships.

DOS AND DON'TS

DO . . .

- Call others by their family name plus -*san*. Don't use -*san* for yourself; say "Erin *desu*" or "Johnson *desu*" instead.

- Dress conservatively when you go out—people dress up even if they're just shopping.

- Use both hands when receiving a *meishi* (business card) or gift.

- Refuse once or twice before accepting something—it's considered polite.

- Be on time—Japanese are very punctual and so are the trains. Early is even better!

DON'T . . .

- Put your hands in your pockets in formal situations like job interviews or during introductions.

- Cross your legs in formal situations; take your cue from others.

- Talk loudly on the street, elevator, bus, or subway—people are trying to sleep!

- Blow your nose in front of others—excuse yourself and do it privately.

- Don't yell, swear, gesticulate in public—it's considered immature, unless everyone is drunk—then anything goes!

NONVERBAL LANGUAGE

- Pointing to your nose means "me."

- Forearms crossed in front mean "no."

- Palm down, fingers bending toward you means "come here."

- Honking a horn means "Excuse me, I'm coming up behind you" rather than "Get out of my way."

- A raised middle finger has no impact, although some people know what it means from American movies.

html). Study-abroad programs are too numerous for a complete list, but here are descriptions of several programs.

Waseda University

Earlham College in Indiana and several other Midwest colleges operate a study-abroad program in Tokyo. Participants live with a host family and study at Waseda University. Students can join extracurricular activities with Japanese students at Waseda. The program lasts 10 months, long enough for students to improve their Japanese language skills. A minimum GPA of 3.0 is required. Prerequisites include at least one semester of Japanese language. Scholarships are available under the Japanese government's program for overseas students. The program costs $34,500 for a full academic year for students from consortium colleges. Airfare, National Health Insurance, books, and personal expenses are extra (see www.earlham.edu/~jpns).

The University of Oregon also offers a one-year Japanese language and liberal studies program at Waseda University. Students must have a GPA of 3.0 or higher. Students are registered at the University of Oregon. The cost is around $22,750 for tuition, housing, and meals, plus $1,050 study abroad fee. Airfare, National Health Insurance, books, and personal expenses are not included (see http://oregonabroad.ous.edu/documents/costsheets/Waseda_year.pdf).

Kyoto Consortium for Japanese Studies

This one-year program for advanced Japanese language and Japanese studies is sponsored by 14 American universities, including Columbia, Harvard, and Stanford Universities. It requires two years of prior Japanese language study. Students outside the consortium universities are charged $16,000 tuition plus $5,000 program fee for housing and some meals. Airfare, health insurance, books, and personal expenses are extra (see http://ogp. columbia.edu/pages/noncolumbia_students/fall-spring-ay/kyoto/index.html).

If the cost of these programs seems prohibitive, there are scholarships available from the Japanese government to encourage more international students to study in Japan. The Japanese Ministry of Education, Culture, Sports, Science, and Technology (www. studyjapan.go.jp/en/index.html) has scholarships for foreign students who wish to enroll in a Japanese university for a year or more. These programs offer the advantages of a sponsor and a student visa; one drawback is that there are restrictions on working while enrolled as a full-time student.

DAILY LIFE

Education

Public school education in Japan began in the early Meiji period (1868) and was modeled on European and American systems. Until that time, education was limited to males of the upper class. Today, all Japanese children must complete ninth grade, the final year of junior high school. After age 15, school is no longer compulsory—yet more than 95 percent of the students complete high school, because without a diploma, job options are severely limited. Boys and girls take all their classes together, from science and language to home economics and shop, and starting in the first grade, they learn to clean their classrooms and their school every day in teams. The school year begins in April and ends the following March, with 220 school days divided into three terms. Summer vacation is the longest, lasting from July 20 (Ocean Day) to the end of August, with some variations. The national government has always been a strong presence in Japanese education, as indicated by the Ministry of Education, Sports, and Culture, which screens school textbooks and establishes a uniform curriculum. When students move to another part of Japan, they may very well continue using the same textbook on the same page where they left off.

Every culture teaches certain values to its youth at home and in school. Japanese schoolchildren learn the social rules considered essential for their educational years and for life as an adult member of society. One key notion is *minna issho* (everyone together/the same). Rather than praising a child's innate ability or IQ, teachers repeatedly reinforce the idea of *ganbaru* (trying hard). Before high school, students are not tracked by ability level into different reading or math levels; instead, each class represents a heterogeneous mix of talent and interests. All students are expected to put great effort in their studies, as well as in the mandatory after-school clubs that commence in junior high. Students who move on to high school must call forth strenuous effort—most are coached on passing the stiff subject-based entrance exams at an after-school *juku* ("cram school") that they attend on a daily basis. Almost half of Japanese young people seek a university degree, many with the goal of interviewing for jobs with

© RUTHY KANAGY

an urban elementary school

prestigious firms. Some students may choose to take a break by traveling or studying overseas before starting a career.

CURRICULUM

School organization is fairly uniform throughout Japan, under the direction of the Ministry of Education. The Ministry issues elementary and junior high school curriculum guidelines and screens textbooks. There is much less autonomy at the level of the school district compared to the more decentralized U.S. model. On the other hand, scholastic achievement is higher in Japan, according to the results of comparative studies. Also compared to the United States, classroom size is large, with up to 40 students. Another difference is that the same group of classmates studies all their subjects together in the same classroom in elementary and junior high school. In junior high, teachers of different subjects rotate through the classrooms while the students stay put. Students are not tracked according to reading level, math skills, or other abilities during the first nine years of their education. Instead, they learn to study in heterogeneous groups (a wide range of abilities) and work cooperatively in *han* (teams).

Every Japanese student studies English in grades 7–12 and in university. However, the primary goal of English class is to pass the entrance exams to get into high school and university. Because the students are so busy with homework and after-school cram school, they don't have much opportunity to use English for communication. In addition, most Japanese teachers of English rarely have the chance to speak the language. Teaching methods still involve translation and memorization of vocabulary, again in preparation for exams.

CHOOSING A SCHOOL FOR YOUR CHILDREN
Japanese Schools

Boys and girls receive equal education from preschool to high school. Advancement from junior high forward is based on passing difficult entrance examinations—both have an equal chance to get into high school and university. Both are active in sports and in after-school clubs.

Although children of foreign residents are not obligated to attend Japanese educational institutions, they will be welcomed and it will be an enriching experience for the parents, as well. Children of the appropriate age can enter or transfer to the local elementary and junior high schools. If you would like your child to attend a public Japanese school, you can obtain information from your local city hall. In some cities, foreign parents whose children go to private kindergarten (ages 3–5) may be eligible for a subsidy from the city. Municipal elementary and junior high schools provide school lunches. Some financial support is also available for elementary and junior high school students.

International Schools

International schools may be a good choice if you live within reasonable commuting distance and are prepared to pay the fees. Tuition and fees can run $10,000–20,000 per year. International schools in Tokyo with instruction in English include Nishimachi International School (in Minato-ku), American School in Japan (in Chofu), and Christian Academy in Japan (west of Ikebukuro).

With all these options, how do you choose between Japanese and international schools? Consider the following factors: Is the school within walking distance, or does it require a bus or train ride? (There are no public school buses.) Where do the children in your neighborhood go to school? Who will your child play with after school? If your children don't know Japanese, is there a teacher at the school who can communicate in English and coach them in Japanese? How much will it cost? Choosing a school also relates to your worldview as a parent—namely, whether you prefer that your children associate primarily with Americans and other internationals in Japan, or if you want to immerse them in Japanese language and culture during your stay in Japan.

One more point to consider—do you want to give your child the opportunity to become bilingual and bicultural? My experience of attending Japanese kindergarten, elementary, and junior high schools laid the foundation for my career and contributed to my multicultural perspective. Childhood is the best time to become a natural bilingual and to understand another culture through its language. Whether your stay in Japan is more or less than a year, it's a once-in-a-lifetime chance for your child to learn Japanese and make Japanese friends. English-speakers can travel the world and insist that everyone speak *our* language, but understanding the values and culture of another country comes only through learning the local language.

HEALTH

People in Japan enjoy one of the longest life expectancies in the world. The average life expectancy of Japanese women is 86.4 years—the longest in the world—while men have an average life span of 79.6 years (2011 data). The lifespan has grown considerably since World War II and suggests that Japanese society must be doing something right, health-wise. Could it be related to the fact that basic health care is guaranteed to everyone in Japan—young, old, urban, rural, rich, poor—through a system of public medical insurance? The practice of immunizing babies at public health clinics and school-age children at school may also contribute. Foreign residents living in Japan for longer than a year can join in the National Health Insurance and public health care systems.

Types of Insurance

For those moving to Japan, there are a several options for medical insurance: private health insurance, traveler's insurance from U.S. providers, and Japanese public health insurance. Public medical insurance in Japan comes in two varieties, Employee Health Insurance and National Health Insurance.

PRIVATE INSURANCE

If you're visiting Japan for a short time and need to see a doctor, you can go to any hospital, wait with others in the waiting room, be seen, pay, and get a receipt—which you can then submit to your own insurance company back home. They will decide how much to reimburse, and hopefully your bill will be at least partially covered. Costs for medical treatment and hospitalization, though significant, are generally lower in Japan than in the United States. If you're only in the country for the short term, this plan may be manageable. But for those who plan to stay in Japan longer, the following options may make more sense.

TRAVELER'S INSURANCE

Before going to Japan, it's a good idea to obtain traveler's insurance to cover examinations, treatment for an accident, or a medical emergency. Read the terms of your traveler's insurance carefully, as some illnesses with preexisting or chronic conditions, as well as dental care, may not be covered. It's a good idea to get treatment for any medical conditions before going overseas.

PUBLIC MEDICAL INSURANCE

As a resident of Japan, you will be required to enroll in a public medical insurance plan to ensure that you are covered at all times. The following several sections are based on an official description of the plan from the Tokyo Metropolitan Government website.

The aim of the Japanese insurance system is mutual assistance in case of illness or injury. Subscribers pay regular insurance premiums according to level of income, and medical expenses are paid from the general fund. There are two types of public medical insurance: Kokumin Kenkohoken (National Health Insurance) and Shakaihoken (Employee Health Insurance), both described in more detail below; the latter is organized within the workplace, and subcategories include Kyosai Kumiai Hoken (Mutual Aid Association Insurance) and Sen'in Hoken (Seaman's Insurance).

National Health Insurance

Those not covered by Employee Health Insurance at their workplace must join Kokumin Kenkohoken (National Health Insurance). For eligibility information, inquire at the National Health Insurance counter of your municipal office about application procedures. Foreigners who have completed foreign resident registration and have a status of residence of one year or longer must join.

Insurance premiums are calculated depending on municipality, and everyone aged 40–64 must pay a Long-Term Care Insurance premium as well. Premiums may be paid in installments at your local municipal office, bank, or post office, or by automatic debit

THE FAMILY REGISTER SYSTEM

Japan has a family register system, which records each person's personal details, such as birth and marriage, and is notarized in a joint document for the whole family. Every time you want to do something official, such as register for school, get a job, or get married, you have to submit an official copy of your *koseki* (family register) to the appropriate office. The register contains births, deaths, marriages, divorces, mental illnesses, crimes, adoptions, and other events in your clan, going several generations back. When reaching adulthood (age 20), citizens can opt to establish an individual register, naming themselves as head.

Although foreigners living in Japan are not subject to the family register system, they are required to notify the government of any birth, death, marriage, or divorce that occurs in Japan, in accordance with the Family Register Law. To make a report, go to the family register section of your local municipal office. The information you submit will be kept and used as evidence of your family status in Japan; you should also notify the government of your home country.

from a designated bank account. For foreign residents who earned no income in Japan the previous year, the premiums for the first year (April to the following March) may run as low as ¥2,000 ($25) per month. However, if you do earn money in Japan, your premium will rise accordingly. For a family, it can be as high as ¥50,000 ($625) per month.

Each insured household is provided with one copy of an insurance card. If you present this card at the medical facility where you receive treatment, you need only pay 30 percent of the charged medical expenses. However, part of the cost of outpatient medications and meals during hospitalization must be paid separately. You will receive the benefits when you submit your insurance card at the reception desk of the hospital or other medical institution and receive medical treatment. If you receive emergency medical treatment and do not have your National Health Insurance card on hand at the time, you may initially be required to pay the full medical bill. Take the hospital bill receipt to the National Health Insurance section of your local municipal office, which will refund 70 percent of the cost of any treatment covered by the insurance.

Some types of expenses are covered as special categories. When a child is born, a lump sum benefit of ¥300,000–350,000 ($3,750–4,375) is paid per child. If an individual pays more than a designated amount of medical expenses at one medical institution during one month, he or she can obtain a refund of the amount in excess by applying to the local ward or municipal office. When a member of the household dies, ¥30,000–70,000 ($375–875) is provided.

Promptly notify the National Health Insurance section of your municipal office of any of the following changes: You move out of (or into) your municipality; you leave or enter Japan; a child is born in your household; a household member dies; there is a change in your address, your name, or the head of your household; you reach the age of 70 and/or become eligible for Retirees' Medical Treatment; you lose your insurance card; or you join or withdraw from another public insurance plan.

Medical Fee Subsidy System for Foreign Students

Foreign students in Japan are also obliged to join the National Health Insurance plan.

MEDICAL CULTURE

Every culture has different notions of how to stay healthy and what to do when you get sick. In Japan, the stomach is the center of wellness, so it should always be covered. At night, kicking your futon covers off and exposing your stomach to the air is a sure way to catch a cold. Parents sometimes tease younger children by saying, "If you don't cover your stomach, the Thunder God will come and snatch your *oheso* (belly button)."

Also according to local belief, gargling with plain water as soon as you come home is a good way to prevent sickness, especially in crowded urban areas. If you do catch a cold, wear a white mask over your nose and mouth, so you don't pass it on to someone on the busy trains and streets. If your cold doesn't get better in a couple of days, go to the hospital to get checked out. Meanwhile, eat a bowl of steaming *okayu* (rice porridge) and *umeboshi* (pickled plum). It will surely make you feel better.

In conjunction with the plan, the Association of International Education, Japan, operates a subsidy system in which it pays 80 percent (of the 30 percent of medical fees) of individually borne expenses.

Employee Health Insurance

The plan for Kenkohoken (Employee Health Insurance) is designed for full-time employees, such as salaried workers in companies, factories, stores, or offices. All employees are obliged to enroll in this plan regardless of nationality, sex, or personal preference.

The Employee Health Insurance premium is calculated by multiplying the subscriber's standard monthly income, determined on the basis of his or her salary, by the insurance premium rate. A portion of the premium is paid by the subscriber and the remainder by the employer.

This insurance covers illness, injury, childbirth, and death for the insured person, as well as for his or her dependents. By presenting the insurance card when receiving treatment for illness or injury, the insured pays 30 percent of charged medical expenses. Dependents pay 30 percent of medical expenses for outpatient care and 20 percent for inpatient care. Part of the cost of medications for outpatients, in addition to meals during hospitalization, must be paid separately.

TAKING YOUR CHANCES

What if you have no insurance and don't or can't enroll in National Health Insurance? If I were uninsured, I'd feel safer taking my chances in Japan than in the United States. However, it's much wiser to be safe than sorry. While riding my bicycle in Tokyo, I was hit by a motorcycle that went through a red light. I was taken to the emergency room by ambulance and received good care. Since I was covered by National Health Insurance, my out-of-pocket cost for the ambulance, X-rays, and tests came to ¥55,000 ($688)—much less than what I would have paid in the United States.

If you need to find a hospital with an English-speaking doctor, call the Tokyo Metropolitan Health and Medical Information Center (tel. 03/5285-8181) or see the *Resources* section.

Medical Services

PHARMACIES AND PRESCRIPTIONS

Previously, *yakkyoku* (pharmacies) were located inside hospitals. You picked up your prescriptions (different-colored powders) in little white unlabeled bags to take home. Today, hospitals and pharmacies operate separately, but doctors will usually direct you to the pharmacy right next door, and most patients follow the recommendation because it's convenient.

Not all drugstores dispense prescriptions—some handle only over-the-counter drugs and cosmetics. You can find out which type of drugstore you've entered by asking, *"Shohosen?"* ("Prescriptions?"). A prescription from your doctor in the U.S cannot be filled in Japan, but a Japanese doctor may be able to prescribe similar medication following a consultation. Sometimes the same medication will be un-available, or it may come in a slightly different format—for example, the time-release capsule you took back home may only come as a fixed-dosage tablet in Japan. If you are concerned about staying on the same medication while overseas, ask your doctor at home to prescribe the maximum allowable supply (usually 1–2 months, by Japanese regulations).

If you receive a prescription from a doctor in Japan and are enrolled in National Health Insurance, up to 70 percent of the cost is covered (the remainder is your copayment). Don't be surprised when medications come in blister packs in a small white paper bag, instead of a sealed plastic bottle. Each medication is described in Japanese on a sheet of paper enclosed in the bag; ask the pharmacist for help if you can't tell which medication is which. It seems that patients are more trusting of doctors in Japan, and don't ask many questions—but that doesn't mean you shouldn't. Doctors often have some training in English and German, and they may be able to understand your questions.

HOSPITALS

About a third of the hospitals in Japan are privately owned. Many are named something like Yamada Internal Medicine Clinic or Suzuki Pediatric Hospital, from which you may assume that Yamada or Suzuki is the name of the doctor. In other words, most doctors not only have an examining office, but an entire hospital with anywhere from a few to many beds. Individual ownership seems to result in a high ratio of hospitals in every community; in general, the larger the hospital, the better its reputation. This is especially true for university research hospitals—consequently, they are always crowded, and wait time can be long.

Typically, you don't need to make an appointment to see a doctor. You just show up and sit in the waiting room, and you'll be seen in order of arrival. At the Itabashi Chuo Byoin (Itabashi Central Hospital) in my neighborhood, the doors to the waiting room open at 6:30 A.M. Each person who arrives sits in order on benches. At 7 A.M., the line shuffles toward the row of appointment machines, into which patients insert their hospital ID card, select the appropriate department for examination, and receive an appointment number (starting with the person who arrived first that morning). Since examining hours begin at 9 A.M., you can go home or run errands until your turn. If you don't arrive early you may have to wait an hour or more to be seen.

MEDICATIONS FOR PERSONAL USE

There are specific and strict regulations regarding medications that are allowed or prohibited from being brought into Japan for personal use.

OVER-THE-COUNTER MEDICINES

You may bring up to two months' supply of allowable over-the-counter medication into Japan duty-free. Note that some over-the-counter medicines common in the United States, including inhalers and some allergy and sinus medications, are illegal. Products containing more than 10 percent pseudoephedrine (such as Actifed, Sudafed, and Vicks inhalers) and products containing more than 1 percent codeine are prohibited.

PRESCRIPTION MEDICATIONS

You may bring up to one month's supply of allowable prescription medicine for personal use. Bring a copy of your doctor's prescription and a letter stating the purpose of the drug. If you need more than one month's supply (except prohibited drugs and controlled drugs) or are carrying syringes (pumps), you are required to obtain a *yakkan shoumei*, or import certificate, in advance and show the certificate with your prescription medicines, if requested, upon arrival at customs.

Once you arrive in Japan, a doctor may be able to prescribe a similar medication to what you are taking. (See the *Resources* section for a list of English-speaking medical facilities in Japan.) You could consult a Japanese doctor by phone before your arrival to get information on medications that are available and/or permitted in Japan.

FURTHER INFORMATION

If you have questions about prescription and nonprescription medication that you want to bring to Japan for personal use, contact the Japanese Embassy or a consulate in your home country before you leave. You may also contact a Pharmaceutical Inspector at the Ministry of Health, Labour, and Welfare in Japan (fax +81-48/601-1336, yakkan-shomei@mhlw.go.jp).

For details on how to obtain a *yakkan shoumei* certificate, see www.mhlw.go.jp/english/policy/health-medical/pharmaceuticals/dl/qa1.pdf.

- If you are arriving in Tokyo, contact: Kanto-Shin'etsu Regional Bureau of Health and Welfare, tel. 048/740-0800

- In Osaka, contact: Kansai Regional Bureau of Health and Welfare, tel. 06/6942-4096

- In Okinawa, contact: Okinawa Narcotics Control Office, Kyushu Regional Bureau of Health and Welfare, tel. 098/853-7100

Sources:
"Importing or Bringing Medication into Japan for Personal Use," Embassy of the United States, Tokyo (http://japan.usembassy.gov/e/acs/tacs-medimport.html)
"Information for Those Bringing Medicines for Personal Use into Japan," Ministry of Health, Labour, and Welfare (www.mhlw.go.jp/english/policy/health-medical/pharmaceuticals/01.html)

Examining rooms are organized differently as well. When you go to see a doctor in the United States, a nurse guides you to a private room with a door that locks, and you wait, perhaps flipping through magazines, until the doctor comes in, shuts the door, and sits down. In Japan, the doctors all line up behind a curtain to see patients. Sometimes there's also a curtain partition between doctors. Patients sit on a bench in the hallway outside the main curtain. You can't see anything, but you can hear everything that's going on. When it's your turn, the nurse calls your number and you draw the curtain aside, go in, and sit down. The doctor will have just finished seeing another patient and will stay put while new patients file through. I observed few doctors wearing latex gloves or washing their hands between patients, but everyone got examined eventually.

a Japanese hospital

PUBLIC HEALTH CENTERS

There are public health centers in every town and city throughout Japan, offering a wide range of services, including health consultations, mental health and welfare counseling (including alcohol abuse and promotion of appropriate treatment), and guidance on specific diseases. They are staffed by physicians, public health nurses, nutritionists, and various kinds of inspectors. Different public health centers have different procedures and provide different types of services. If you can't speak Japanese, it's a good idea to have a Japanese speaker accompany you when you visit your public health center for the first time. Many centers have evening hours, and some are open on Saturdays.

In addition, local health centers provide consultations and education to encourage citizens to take care of themselves throughout their life cycle. Such services are directed at pregnant women and infants, adults, and the elderly.

Public health care covers non-citizens. If you have applied for a resident card at the municipal office, they will have your name and address on file and will contact you when it's time for a specific type of check-up for your age bracket. I received letters from the public health department of Itabashi city telling me which tests were due for women my age. Over several years, the tests included a vision check, a chest X-ray (called *rentogen,* from the German), a mammogram, a Pap smear, urinalysis, and a fecal exam. All you need to do is call, make an appointment, and show up on the assigned day. Everything is free!

STD Testing

Public health centers offer free anonymous consultations for AIDS. Some public health and local health centers also have checkups for other sexually transmitted diseases.

Nishi-Shinjuku Public Health Center in Tokyo also conducts AIDS tests and consultation services, and there is an AIDS Telephone Service by the Japan Foundation for AIDS Prevention.

IMMUNIZATIONS

In Japan, the government takes care of immunizations for designated diseases to prevent epidemics among children. Babies are immunized at hospitals at no or minimal cost, and each school sets aside days for the whole student body to be immunized against such diseases as polio, diphtheria, whooping cough, measles, rubella, Japanese encephalitis, and tuberculosis.

Throughout the year, specific days are also set aside for annual physicals for all students, including a heart exam, urinalysis, a fecal exam, and a dental exam (with certificates for students with no cavities). Doctors, nurses, dentists, and X-ray trucks go to each school. Students also take fitness tests, in which they perform such tasks as running, pull-ups, push-ups, and grip tests (much like presidential fitness tests in the United States, before they were eliminated due to budget shortages in some states). Public health is carried out with little privacy—as students get older, it can be rather embarrassing for them to line up in the gym, boys in one line and girls in another, waiting to see a male doctor behind a curtain—but everyone is treated equally, and no one falls through the cracks.

PREGNANCY AND CHILDBIRTH

In Japan, when you get pregnant you go to the municipal office to file a pregnancy notification. In exchange, you receive a Mother and Child Health Handbook. This handbook is used to keep a written record of your physical and dental health, as well as that of your child (from birth to age six). Take the handbook along when receiving various types of prenatal checkups and services. Maternity classes on health management during pregnancy, preparation for childbirth, and care for newborn babies are also offered. After the baby is born, local health centers provide health checkups for infants aged 3–4 months, 18 months, and 3 years. The mother's checkups after giving birth are given at the same time as the health checkups for infants 3–4 months old. Local health centers also offer BCG (Bacille Calmette-Guerin) vaccinations against tuberculosis.

However, please note that delivery costs are not covered by National Health Insurance, and must be paid personally. The average cost is about ¥300,000 ($3,750), including seven days of hospitalization. However, if you are enrolled in National Health Insurance, you will receive a one-time childbirth benefit of ¥300,000. For detailed information, contact your nearest local health center or other health facility.

DAILY LIFE

Environmental Factors

POLLUTION

Air and water pollution certainly exist in Japan. Power plant emissions result in air pollution, acid rain, and acidification of lakes and reservoirs, degrading water quality and threatening aquatic life. Air pollution from vehicle exhaust is concentrated in urban areas. In recent years, the government has passed increasingly stringent exhaust emissions regulations, and these have improved the air quality noticeably. Still, if you suffer from asthma or allergies, you might think twice about living in Tokyo or other large urban concentrations.

Another urban disease is caused by cedar pollen, which triggers widespread allergies from January to April each year. During this period, you will see thousands of commuters wearing surgical masks to work or school. The cause, ironically, is due to the reforestation of denuded mountains surrounding the cities. In the Kanto plain, cedar seedlings were planted everywhere, creating a monoculture forest; decades later, the pollen from the flowering trees blows into the metropolis. I've been told that even if you have no allergic reactions for five or six years, you can suddenly develop a sensitivity to cedar pollen. Be sure to take precautions.

The extremely high humidity throughout most of Japan means that mold, fungus, and dust mites flourish in bedding and in woven *tatami* mat floors. To combat mildew, homemakers hang futons and bedding over balcony railings to dry in the sun as often as possible. You can also purchase portable futon dryers, so you're not limited to cleanliness on sunny days.

It is safe to drink tap water everywhere in Japan. Many people prefer bottled water, but unless marked otherwise, tap water is fine to drink. As for swimming in rivers and

Smoking on sidewalks is banned in many of Tokyo's financial and business districts, but a few provide a smokers' car, such as this one in Chiyoda-ku.

© RUTHY KANAGY

the ocean, it makes sense to stay within designated areas. Many previously polluted rivers have been cleaned up by citizen environmental groups and local governments, and as a result, fish now swim in areas where there were none for many years.

RADIATION

After the Great East Japan Earthquake and Fukushima Dai-ichi Nuclear Power Plant explosions in March 2011, the national government set strict guidelines on the amount of radiation (cesium) allowable in foods. You can be assured that restaurants and stores follow these guidelines. Due to fears among consumers, many food producers and those in the fishing industry in the Tohoku region are unable to sell their products even if they meet the safety standards.

This Japan radiation map shows 2,000 up-to-date radiation measurements from around Japan: http://jciv.iidj.net/map.

PRESERVING RESOURCES

Japan consumes a large amount of scarce resources, such as imported fish and tropical timber. On the other hand, the country has been active in joining with other nations to sign international agreements on environmental issues, such as banning nuclear tests; protecting the Antarctic, endangered species, the ozone layer, and wetlands; and controlling whaling (which remains controversial). Japan also hosted the United Nations Framework Convention on Climate Change–Kyoto Protocol.

Recycling has become more widespread in Japan. Glass, cans, paper, magazines, and drink cartons are picked up and recycled. Many communities also have ecology centers, with classes for children and adults on how to conserve, reuse, and enjoy the earth's resources.

Safety

ACCIDENTS

Traffic accidents do happen, but there is a difference in the way the law assigns liability. In an accident between an automotive vehicle and a pedestrian, the driver is always held responsible. Similarly, if a bicycle hits a pedestrian, the cyclist is held liable. Traffic fatalities in Japan numbered about 6,350 in 2006, a 30 percent decline in 10 years. If you don't come from a country where cars drive on the left, be extra cautious when crossing roads in Japan. Look to the right for on-coming traffic, then to the left, then right again. Children are trained to raise their hand high when crossing the road, the better to be seen by drivers. At crossings near schools, there is a container filled with yellow flags at each side, which schoolchildren hold as they cross. Even so, narrow streets with no sidewalks, and only a painted white line to divide pedestrians from cars and bikes, can be very dangerous. There are many illegally parked cars, and to go around them means stepping into oncoming traffic.

Another problem is the issue of where bicycles belong. According to traffic laws, bicycles are considered to be vehicles and should be ridden in the street. However, in practice, the streets are too dangerous for bicyclists and so they ride on the sidewalk, where they pose a danger to pedestrians. Helmets are rarely worn, and although lights are required after dark, they are also rare. Here's a tip for walking on a sidewalk: Be cautious about making sudden turns or stops. Always be aware that there are bicycles approaching from behind.

House fires are also a danger, particularly because most houses are constructed of wood and are close together. Gas cookstoves and gas water heaters need proper ventilation when in use. After cooking and before leaving the house, check all gas valves to be sure they are turned off. Although severe earthquakes are not frequent, they can damage gas lines and cause fires. It's a good idea to bring several fire alarms and install them in your new home. Each community has a designated place for emergencies. Find out from your local city hall where this is. Create fire- and earthquake-escape plans and practice them regularly with your family.

The emergency number for police is 110 throughout Japan and 119 for fire and ambulance.

CRIME

Japan has a relatively low crime rate compared to many countries, resulting in part from social values that emphasize getting along with others, despite crowded conditions. The low rate also stems from strict laws against drugs and weapons. In Japan, handguns are illegal, and crimes committed with guns—usually carried out by the *yakuza* (similar to the Mafia)—attract national attention. Crimes such as bank robberies and hold-ups are most often committed using a knife—with a knife, there's a chance to run away. Illegal drugs are less readily available and the consequences of carrying even a small amount of a drug, such as marijuana, are severe. For example, there was a case of two university students who grew marijuana from seed and gave some to their friends—they were sentenced to one and a half years in prison.

Sadly, as in any country, there is violence within families, in schools, and on the street. But on the whole, Japan feels safe, and riding trains and subways is fine even at midnight (although a drunk businessman may try to practice his English on you).

Police officers patrol neighborhoods on bicycles, enforcing public safety.

If you are female—and especially if you're young—it makes sense to stay in groups and know your surroundings. There have been cases of young Western women being abducted by Japanese men from bars frequented by foreigners. Don't go with strangers—the same advice as back home. Tell a friend where you are going and when you expect to be home. Women commuting on rush hour trains are sometimes groped by men, who take advantage of the crush of bodies. If this happens, yell *chikan,* which means molester or pervert. Some people recommend grabbing the offender's hand, if you see it, and raising it up so others can see. To safeguard women, some train lines have designated women-only cars during peak times—usually at the front of the train. Nowadays you can even find tutorials on dealing with *chikan* on YouTube.

Whatever your age or gender, use common sense in regards to your safety. Find out where all the *koban* (police boxes) are located in your neighborhood, and introduce yourself to the police officers patrolling your street on bicycles. If you ever get lost, or lose something, the *koban* is the best place to go, and the police officers on duty will do their best to help.

Travelers with Disabilities

There was a time in Japan when being disabled meant being forgotten and invisible. But there are now laws protecting the basic rights of persons with disabilities and promoting their participation in society. There are more ramps and elevators in public buildings and train stations, though not all. Building codes require accommodation for those with disabilities, but this does not apply to older buildings. Many train stations and sidewalks have raised Braille paths to follow and crosswalks that play a tune, indicating when it is safe to cross. Each *shinkansen* (bullet train) has a car with one or two spaces for a wheelchair and an accessible toilet. These can be reserved in advance. This is true of the Narita Express and other express trains. Buses with ramps and low floors have been introduced in larger cities. Many of the better hotels have accessible accommodations.

The best advice when traveling to Japan is to plan ahead and research the accessibility of transportation, lodging, and restaurants. There are several online resources: Japan Accessible Tourism Center (www.japan-accessible.com) has accessibility information for various cities. Another group, Accessible Tokyo (http://accessible.jp.org/tokyo/en), provides information and offers tips on arrival and departure from airports and a guide to hotels, shopping, museums, and parks with inclusive accommodations.

Many Japanese go out of their way to help foreign visitors. Don't hesitate to let people know what your needs are so they can help to make your visit enjoyable. Sometimes it helps to write down words in English to aid communication, if you don't speak Japanese.

EMPLOYMENT

The employment situation in Japan has changed markedly in the past decade. Although the economy has shown a slow recovery, hallmarks of Japanese business health, such as guaranteed lifetime employment and advancement by seniority, have virtually disappeared. The number of employees working under "temporary" status, or *haken,* has tripled in recent years. Graduates from top universities have difficulty landing jobs with prestigious firms, many of which have reduced campus recruiting. Female graduates have difficulty accessing corporate jobs, based on the assumption that they would get married within a couple of years and "retire." But many graduates don't necessarily want to work for a big *kaisha* (company).

A growing number of Japanese youths choose to become *freeters* (part-time workers), working part-time and pursuing their own interests over a career—a life far removed from overworked *salary men* (white-collar workers) in neckties and suits on crowded commuter trains. Compared to their peers of the past, who went straight from university to a company job, the earning power of young people has diminished considerably. On the other hand, many still live at home, which frees up more yen. A number of youth also choose to pursue nontraditional paths, such as going overseas to work, travel, or earn an advanced degree.

© RUTHY KANAGY

Where do foreign residents fit into the employment picture? Thousands of immigrants from Brazil, the Middle East, and other parts of Asia have flooded into Japan to take factory employment and other jobs that most Japanese don't want. In contrast, English-speaking foreigners have earned a living in Japan for many years by teaching their native language. If anything, interest in learning English at increasingly younger ages has intensified, so teaching is still an option—provided you come with solid training, the appropriate degree, and, preferably, an introduction. In Japan, connections *(kone)* are important. Getting an introduction from someone in a position of authority carries weight.

The Job Hunt

Before you go to Japan, it's worthwhile to research the job market by reading online newspapers, magazines from Japan, and job-related websites. You could also search trade magazines or journals in your field. Through professional associations and on-line discussion groups, you may be able to find contacts in Japan who are working in fields that interest you. Search the websites of Japanese companies—many have overseas branches you might contact. The same technique may help if you're looking for teaching jobs at academic or commercial schools. When you take your fact-finding trip to Japan, write or call ahead and arrange to visit businesses and universities (if you want to teach) for an informational interview. Keep in touch regularly to let them know of your interest.

JOB LISTINGS

As you might expect, Tokyo has the most jobs, but also the greatest concentration of people competing for them. This reason may compel you to widen your search to cities in other regions of Japan, such as the Kansai area (Osaka, Kobe, and Kyoto), Shikoku, Kyushu, or Hokkaido. English-language newspapers, such as *The Japan Times* and the free weekly magazine *Metropolis* (www. metropolis.co.jp) have help-wanted ads in numerous fields. It's not uncommon for job ads to specify age limits, gender, Japanese language ability, and other restrictions. If you don't meet all the criteria, it isn't worth your time to apply, unfortunately. If you're looking for a teaching job, remember that the Japanese school year begins in April. That means most schools recruit new staff between December and February.

© RUTHY KANAGY

Many urbanites endure long commutes.

INTERVIEWS

When interviewing for jobs in Japan, remember that attitude and personality count just as much as your background. At the entry level, companies often prefer to hire a "blank sheet," then train the employee to fit into their corporate culture. A few simple dos and don'ts can make or break your interview:

- Be on time. If you're unsure of the location, go the day before to scope out the area.

- Dress appropriately. The key word is conservative—look conservative, act conservative, be conservative. The Japanese prefer no facial hair on men, trim haircuts, no visible tattoos, no facial piercings, and no earrings on men. Suits in dark colors are the standard uniform, with polished shoes. If you're interviewing at a public school, slip-on shoes are best for removing and changing into slippers.

- Maintain a respectful demeanor. Wait to sit until your interviewer indicates where. Be attentive, and don't talk too much. Wait to be asked questions, and don't chatter on or boast about your background and experiences. Your interviewer may want to know why you came to Japan, how tall you are (in centimeters), if you're married, if you have kids, and how you like sushi. English-speakers tend to talk with their hands, but in Japanese settings, it's more polite to keep your hands down. You may also notice less eye contact—it's considered more respectful not to stare, so try not to gaze directly for too long.

- Bring your credentials. It's a good idea to carry your résumé and credentials in a folder or binder. Japanese companies typically ask for a photograph (passport-size) affixed to the résumé, as well as date of birth. Education and job experience are listed from your first (oldest) position up to your most recent. Be sure to list any certificates you have earned (such as for the Japanese Language Proficiency Test), licenses (include the date you acquired your driver's license), computer skills, and personal interests. Japanese university seniors practice mock interviews and read numerous interviewing advice books. Students who usually wear jeans and T-shirts suddenly show up during campus recruiting season in dark suits—their overnight initiation into the uniform of the working world.

Questions to Ask a Potential Employer or University Program

If you're moving to an urban area, some answers are obvious. But if you're going to a small town or rural area, the answers may surprise you. It pays to ask in advance so you know what to expect.

CITY LIFE

- What is the terrain—mountains, hilly, plains, seacoast?
- How many people live in the immediate town or city? What are the primary age groups?
- If it's a small town or village, how far is it to the nearest major city?
- What part of town will I be living in?
- Are there any special features of the town?
- Are there any universities or high schools?

TRANSPORTATION

- How do I get around—by car, bike, train, or bus?

- How far is the nearest train station and nearest airport? How do I get there?
- How long will it take to get to school or work?

LANGUAGE
- Are there many fluent English speakers in town? Any English-speaking foreigners?
- Are there Japanese language classes?

SOCIAL
- What kinds of entertainment, outdoor activities, and sports are available?
- Are there places to hang out with English speakers?
- Are there any classes in traditional arts?

COMMUNICATION
- Is high-speed Internet available? Is a computer provided? Are there any Internet cafés?
- How many TV channels are there? Are there any bilingual programs?
- Are English radio programs, newspapers, and magazines available?

SHOPPING
- Are there coffee shops and Western-style restaurants?
- What kinds of grocery stores are there? Are there any American food items?
- Are there large department stores? Are English-language books available?

WORK
- What are my duties? Is there any training or orientation?
- Who is my supervisor? How many employees are there?
- How many hours do I work? What about benefits and paid vacation?
- If teaching English, are a curriculum and teaching materials provided? What do I need to bring? Will I be team teaching? How many classes and what ages?
- Will someone help with discipline?
- Is socializing with students allowed?
- What is the contract period and pay? Are any deductions taken from pay? When do I get my first paycheck?

HOUSING
- Will I be living alone or with a roommate?
- How old is the house/apartment?
- What kind of heat and air-conditioning does it have? How do I get fuel?
- Is there a washing machine, dryer, cookstove, refrigerator?
- What kinds of furniture and bedding are included?

DAILY LIFE

HEALTH

- Where do I go if I get sick? Are there any doctors or dentists who speak English?
- Where can I get medications—cold or allergy, etc.?
- Is health insurance provided?

LEISURE

- How many paid vacation days and holidays do I get?
- How easy is it to travel to other areas of Japan or overseas?
- Who can I spend holidays with?

Employers

A wide range of jobs may be found in Japan in such fields as information technology, research and development, administration, finance, sales, consulting, Web design, marketing, teaching, translating, and many others. If you have the relevant degree and sufficient experience, don't hesitate to apply for a position that interests you. At the same time, keep your competition in mind—young Japanese men and women who have returned to Japan from overseas with MAs and MBAs. They're bilingual and prepared to work hard, and they don't just apply to Japanese companies; they apply to *gaishikei* (foreign affiliate companies). Recently, many highly skilled Japanese women have begun flocking to foreign companies, where there is a greater chance of promotion based on merit.

LANGUAGE SKILLS

Without Japanese language skills, you will have a tough time competing with bilingual applicants. If you have studied the language, one way to demonstrate your ability is to show that you have a certificate at a certain level. Japan has standardized tests and certificates for skills in every possible field, from abacus and calligraphy to IT and foreign languages. Many people take extracurricular classes in certain skills to prepare for these tests so that they can list them on their résumés.

You can get a certificate to prove your ability in Japanese by taking the Japanese Language Proficiency Test (JLPT), which is administered every December in locations within Japan and around the globe. Level 4 is the beginning level, and Level 1 the highest. Outside Japan, contact the Japan Foundation Los Angeles Language Center (tel. 213/621-2267, fax 213/621-2590, www.jflalc.org/jlpt.html) for information. In Japan, contact the Association of International Education Japan (AIEJ), JLPT Section, Testing Division (tel. 03/5454-5577, www.aiej.or.jp). If you study Japanese before arriving in the country, you won't regret investing your time and effort.

It's true that some help-wanted ads specify "no Japanese language required." However, you will get much more out of your experience if you understand what's going on around you.

TEACHING ENGLISH

If you're interested in teaching English in Japan, bring along your diploma, ESL certificate, transcripts, awards, birth certificate, letters of recommendation, résumé, and passport photos—you will need all these materials to apply for teaching and other jobs. You might also pick up a good book on how to teach English, along with a grammar reference book.

English teaching jobs in Japan have become more competitive, with longer hours, more duties, and less pay. At a minimum, you should have a college degree, and preferably a license in teaching English as a second language. Private English conversation schools are everywhere in Japan, or you can teach English privately, but in that case you'll need a working visa and a guarantor. It's best to avoid the large chain English-language schools, as they often overwork and underpay teachers. NOVA, one of the largest chain schools, went bankrupt in 2007, leaving many American and British teachers with unpaid wages. The Japanese government has a program to place assistant English teachers in junior and senior high schools in Japan (www.mofa.go.jp/j_info/visit/jet), but you're not allowed to pick your own placement location. Many elementary schools have also begun offering English as part of global studies for kids; if you're interested, bring picture books and teaching materials for children.

Government-sponsored and commercial organizations recruit thousands of native English speakers from around the world annually, bring them to Japan, and assign them to elementary, junior, and senior high schools to serve as assistants to Japanese teachers of English. In this type of position, you will be expected to keep school hours (8:30 A.M.–4 P.M. or later) Monday through Friday, and to attend some school events on weekends. The average pay is ¥250,000 ($2,270) per month (less 7 percent in income taxes). These organizations hold interviews overseas in late fall or winter; teaching begins in April. Housing may or may not be subsidized. One of the best known is the Japan Exchange and Teaching Program (JET, www.jetprogramme.org), begun 20 years ago. The Ministry of Foreign Affairs notes in its official materials that "it is desirable that applicants are adaptable and develop a positive interest in Japan and its culture."

WORKING ON A FARM

A more casual employment option is to work on organic farms and other small businesses in different parts of Japan in exchange for room and board. An international organization known as WWOOF (www.wwoofjapan.com) has a membership program under which people can experience Japan at little or no cost, in return for helping business proprietors with their work. Hosts include organic farms, family inns, healing centers, ski resorts, and more. A one-year membership costs around $55.

TEACHING IN RURAL JAPAN

© RUTHY KANAGY

Kristy Lawton moved to a small town in northern Honshu and taught English for six months before returning to the United States for graduate school in biology.

What influenced you to move to Japan?
My interest in Japan developed over many years. I knew people from Japan and had Japanese friends since high school. I like to travel and wanted to learn more about Japanese culture. I wanted a break before grad school and liked the idea of living somewhere different.

How did you find a job and get a visa?
I searched online for ESL jobs. I graduated in the summer, which was out of season for job hunting. The Japanese school year starts in April, so there were fewer jobs. The English school where I ended up teaching got me a one-year work visa, renewable up to three years. The visa process takes several months, so you have to apply well in advance.

How did your work in Japan differ from working in the United States?
I found a big cultural difference in the relationship between employers and employees. The level of formality was different. The teachers worked very hard for little pay and were expected to sacrifice for the employer's business, a private language school.

Were there any frustrations?
Not being able to read, especially in grocery stores and restaurants. Small-town restaurants have no plastic food displays, and there were no McDonald's or Starbucks. The TV had only two channels—the cooking channel was interesting, but I couldn't understand much. I had no Internet for the first three months, so I couldn't communicate with friends back home.

What were the biggest rewards?
Ten days in Tokyo with two different friends' families were wonderful. I experienced growing pains and learned about the adult working world. I got to see such a different culture—it expanded my mind. I did pick up a little Japanese in six months. Now I miss the food!

Was it easy to make friends?
I was teaching small children and adults (whom I wasn't supposed to see outside class), so it wasn't easy. I made a few good Japanese friends—a coworker, and someone who'd visited my hometown in the United States years before.

Any advice for people from the United States who are moving to Japan?
Know what questions to ask before you go! What exactly will I be doing, what ages, and how many in a class? Will I be teaching with someone? If you're going to Japan for the first time and don't know Japanese, do not go to a small town. It's much easier if you know Japanese before you go. Be aware when looking online for English teaching jobs—some are almost scams. Don't teach for huge chains—they are teaching mills.

© RUTHY KANAGY

Working on a farm is one employment option for visitors to Japan.

Employment Laws

Japanese labor laws generally apply to all workers in Japan regardless of nationality. The Japanese Labor Standards Law, the Industrial Safety and Health Law, the Minimum Wages Law, and other labor-related laws apply to foreign workers. The Labor Standards Law states that employers shall not discriminate with regard to wages, working hours, and other working conditions by reason of nationality, creed, or social status of the worker. Foreign workers are also entitled to basic labor rights, such as the right to organize a labor union and act collectively to maintain and improve their working conditions. When a foreign worker is employed, the employer must draw up a labor contract specifying the conditions under which he or she will work. The following materials must be given to the employee in writing: the period of labor contract, place of work and job duties, existence of overtime work, start and finish times of work, breaks, holidays, and annual vacation. In addition, the wages and their methods of calculation, paydays, and procedures for pay increases must be written, as well as retirement policies. If working conditions differ from the actual conditions stated, an employee has a right to cancel the labor contract immediately.

Employment agreements may be for a fixed term (up to three years) or unlimited term. Fixed-term employment is the norm for foreign workers. Japan has minimum-wage laws, which vary by region since they are based on actual cost of living. Tokyo has the highest minimum wage, at ¥791 per hour, but it would be difficult to live on that wage. Pay is generally provided in cash, directly to the employee. The maximum full-time work period is eight hours per day, 40 hours per week, with a one-hour break each day. Overtime pay of 25 percent for additional work over 40 hours per week must be provided. Ten days of leave per year must be granted after six months of work. The law provides unpaid leave, such as maternity, child care, family care, and sick leave. If an employee is fired, 30 days advance notice or 30 days of pay must be provided. By law, women must be afforded the same hiring, job training, promotion opportunities, and retirement plans as men, but many companies get around this by separating "office track" and "management track" positions. Translations of Japanese laws are available online (www.japaneselawtranslation.go.jp).

There are government benefits and support that are extended to all residents, whether citizens or foreigners. Rhae Washington, an American single mom, reports:

> I received very generous single-mom benefits when I lived in Japan. Americans are always amazed—as I was myself—when I tell them about the monthly stipend I received (roughly $400); free medical insurance for myself and my son; and free tuition for my son that the Japanese government awarded me, a foreigner. Of course, it wasn't just offered to me—it required a lot of help from my sponsor to go through the application process.

Knowing about these extra benefits may make a move to Japan more financially feasible than you think. Offering and even requiring foreign residents to join National Health Insurance and the national pension, if you're employed in Japan, is certainly a contrast to the way the United States treats its citizens and immigrants.

Self-Employment

Some people come to Japan knowing that they want to start their own business. Others work for an employer for a few years, perhaps teaching English, then decide to branch out on their own. Whatever the path, many Americans and other internationals have found a niche doing what they like and calling all the shots. Among the self-employed people I know in Japan are Web designers, video producers, photographers, restaurant owners, translators, English-school operators, agribusiness owners, and more.

Benefits of self-employment include being your own boss, having control over the product or service you sell, setting your own hours, choosing who to hire, and possibly hand-picking your clients. On the other hand, it takes capital to start a business, and if you are not a Japanese citizen or a permanent resident, it is difficult to obtain a bank loan. You will need a Japanese sponsor in order to get a proper working visa and help secure funds. Language skills also play a pivotal role—if your business targets only English-speakers, you may be able to get by without knowing much Japanese. However, if you hope to work with Japanese customers, advanced language skills are a must. One solution may be to have a Japanese partner (or spouse) to help with the business. Finally, keep in mind that your customers will demand very high standards of quality and customer service.

OPENING A BUSINESS

You don't need to be a citizen or even a permanent resident to start your own company in Japan. Under a Japanese law passed in 2003, you can incorporate for just one

MAKING A LIVING AS A TRANSLATOR

Dan Kanagy started his own translation business, WordWise, and has lived in Tokyo for the past 20 years.

What was the impetus for moving back to Japan (after living there as a child)?
I wanted to improve my Japanese.

How did you go about finding a job? How did you get a visa?
I was in Japan on vacation and interviewed for a translator position. The company hired me and sponsored my work visa, although I first had to return to the United States until the visa was issued.

How does your work in Japan differ from your work in the United States?
I'm not sure how to answer that. It differs like computer programming differs from translation. Or like working for a company differs from working for your own company.

How is your living situation similar to or different from in the United States?
I live in an urban environment with public transportation like I did in the United States. There are more similarities than differences in how I live my life day to day.

Are there any frustrations about living in Japan (as a foreigner)?
No.

What are the biggest rewards of living in Tokyo? Is it easy to make friends with Japanese?
Language is what drew me here and continues to hold my interest. Being bilingual and being in an environment where I can exercise that provides great satisfaction. Making friends has been difficult for me in the United States and in Japan. Even so, I've made a handful of great friends in Japan.

Is there anything you can't buy in Japan that you wish you could?
I've not felt that, but then my needs are modest.

Any advice for people considering a move to Japan, including what they should take?
The more Japanese you know, the better.

yen. If you have a proper working visa, all you need is a website or another means of publicizing your existence.

Small Businesses

Support for small businesses comes from many sources. In Tokyo, the Metropolitan Government works with the Tokyo Metropolitan Small Business Promotion Agency to offer training, financial assistance, equipment loans, facilities, and facility management services to help small businesses get started. Under the Small and Medium Enterprises Support Law, the Small Business Promotion Agency (www.tokyo-kosha.or.jp) has been designated a support center to provide comprehensive advice services throughout Tokyo.

If you incorporate, your company can write off many types of business expenses—check with your local municipal tax office for specifics. Another agency called JETRO (Japan External Trade Organization) helps foreign companies invest in Japan. They provide Japanese market reports with information about specific segments of the market designed to help business owners look at opportunities for investing and for exporting manufactured products to Japan.

Invest Japan! (www.jetro.go.jp) is an online journal put out by JETRO that provides comprehensive information on the investment environment in Japan, including macroeconomic data, laws and regulations, and examples of foreign companies operating

The Japanese government encourages small businesses like this neighborhood flower shop.

in the country. JETRO also publishes books, such as *Setting Up Enterprises in Japan,* that summarize national investment laws and procedures. Visit the organization's website for a complete list of titles.

TYPES OF BUSINESSES

With a proper work visa you could open a restaurant, online retail business, Web design business, translation company, English school, bagel bakery, or another business in Japan. Bed-and-breakfasts, known as *penshon* (as in a European-style pension), are quite popular in resort destinations, and may be a viable option as well. When deciding on the type of business you'd like to run, consider the cost of property in your area, your customer base, and your Japanese language ability (there are likely to be more English-speakers in urban than rural areas). Conduct thorough market research and become familiar with consumer trends and preferences in Japan—the *Nihon Keizai Shinbun (Japan Economic Newspaper)* and *Invest Japan!* may prove helpful, as well as the Small Business Promotion Agency and Japan External Trade Organization. Observe successful American businesses in Japan and consider how they adapted to Japanese consumer preferences. For example, what changes in operation did 7-Eleven, Kentucky Fried Chicken, McDonald's, Kinko's, and Starbucks make when they came to Japan? How did they adapt their business models to fit their new customer base? What are their most popular products? If you don't have a business background, you might consider taking business or marketing classes at Temple University in Tokyo.

Once you decide on your product or service, talk to as many people as you can in that business. A good real estate agent will not only help you find a suitable property to rent or buy, but can also introduce you to local business owners. Consult your local municipal office for advice, and make certain that you have the right type of working visa to operate a business legally in Japan (see the *Making the Move* chapter for details on visa requirements). Nonpermanent residents may incorporate in Japan, but they must produce the proper paperwork and register with the Justice Department. If you have nonpermanent status and wish to take this route, you must register a *teikan* (notarized article of incorporation) and provide a copy of your company seal registration and evidence that you have deposited the required amount of capital (¥3 million/$27,272) in the bank.

Philip Bennett and his wife Akiko own and operate Café Manna, far from the neon city lights, in the mountains of northern Gunma prefecture. They serve homemade pizza and pasta alongside the rushing Tone River. According to Phil, the requirements for a foreigner operating a restaurant are no different than for Japanese citizens. One must obtain a certificate from the Hokenjo (Public Health Department), which visits the restaurant twice a year.

Dan Kanagy of Tokyo owns WordWise translation company. After working for a Japanese translation agency for several years, he decided to go freelance and incorporated as a *yugen gaisha* (Limited Liability Company). He comments:

> I incorporated more for positioning myself in the market. Some companies will only order translations from companies and not individuals. Being incorporated indicates a level of commitment to working in Japan. You may also be perceived as being more reliable and trustworthy than an individual. There is a tax advantage, but that wasn't the main reason.

Tax benefits vary by your level of income. Forming your own *yugen gaisha* also depends, in part, on your visa status. His visa status, Jinbun Chishiki Kokusai Gyomu (Humanities Specialist/International Services), requires an employment contract. As far as the Immigration Bureau is concerned, he is an employee of a Japanese translation agency.

English Schools

A number of people have started their own English schools after teaching for a Japanese agency or school for several years. Considerations for this type of venture include real estate costs for renting a building. Another significant factor is competition from large commercial English chains, such as Aeon, which have huge advertising budgets. In smaller towns, you might be able to spread the word about your school by word of mouth without spending a lot on advertising. Once you find a suitable building, the most difficult step is to secure a bank loan. A Japanese bank will not extend a loan any longer than the validity of your visa (maximum three years, unless you have permanent residency). You will need a guarantor who is willing to carry the financial risk. Having a Japanese spouse who can act as the guarantor can speed things up. Once you start your school, if you decide to hire a foreign teacher, you will need to incorporate as a *yugen gaisha* (Limited Liability Corporation) in order to sponsor your employee's visa.

Volunteering

Whether you're in Japan to study or work, why not spend some time volunteering to give back to your host society? There are many organizations that would welcome an extra hand, where you can contribute your talents and energy. This includes, but is not limited to, organizations working to rebuild the Tohoku northeast region of Japan affected by the 2011 Great East Japan Earthquake.

Second Harvest (www.2hj.org/index.php) is Japan's largest food bank, and they need donations as well as volunteers. The bilingual organization distributes food to soup kitchens, orphanages, the elderly, emergency shelters, single mothers, the homeless, migrant workers, and many others.

It's Not Just Mud (http://itsnotjustmud.com) is a nonprofit volunteer organization specializing in disaster relief and grass-roots support and rehabilitation of disaster-affected individuals and small businesses. They are based in Ishinomaki, Miyagi prefecture, in the Tohoku region.

Peace Boat (http://peaceboat.jp/relief/volunteer) is a Japan-based international non-governmental and nonprofit organization that works to promote peace, human rights, equal and sustainable development, and respect for the environment. They provide opportunities to volunteer in Tokyo and also in the Tohoku region.

YMCA Volunteer Center in Sendai https://sites.google.com/a/sendai-ymca.org/volunteer_support/home) was set up in March 2011 to support and coordinate YMCA volunteers from all over Japan. They work with people in the coastal areas who were evacuated from the disaster.

FINANCE

If you've decided to live in Japan, you are probably concerned about how to make your dollars stretch. You've kept an eye on the dollar–yen exchange rate and watched the dollar drop to a low of ¥76 in 2011 then fluctuate around ¥81–82 to the dollar—not a whole lot compared to five years earlier when a dollar was worth ¥120 yen. You might be asking yourself: How much will it cost to live? How much money do I need to bring with me? Can I open a savings account in a Japanese bank? How will I transfer funds to and from my U.S. bank? How will I get paid? You may have heard that personal checks are uncommon in Japan, and wonder how to pay your utilities and other bills. All of these concerns and more are addressed in this chapter.

The cost of living in urban centers of Tokyo and Osaka is high, although rents fluctuate depending on the area of the city you choose to live in. Outside larger cities the cost of living is lower. Keep in mind that if you try to maintain the same lifestyle you had in your home country, it will be expensive. However, if you adopt a more Japanese lifestyle—living in smaller spaces and eating Japanese food—it will be easier to keep a balanced budget. When you shop, you will pay a 5 percent consumption tax (sales tax) on purchases, which will rise to 8 percent in 2014 and 10 percent in 2015. On the other hand, there is no custom of tipping for service in Japan and no bargaining on the price of new items.

© RUTHY KANAGY

various denominations of Japanese currency, the yen (international symbol: ¥; Japanese character: 円)

Balancing Your Budget

Housing costs vary by size, age, and location of the apartment or house. The average Tokyo family can't hope to own a house, so many settle for a flat in a *manshon* (condominium). Other families choose to live in another prefecture where housing is more affordable, leaving the "rice-winner" with a two-hour commute each way to work. A tiny studio in Tokyo may be ¥70,000 ($875) a month, and rents go up as you get closer to city center. Moving in may require a damage deposit, landlord's fee, realtor's fee, plus two months rent. That can be the equivalent of six months rent—in cash—just to get a two-year apartment lease and a foot in the door! As you move away from the metropolis to outlying regions, you can expect to pay up to 30 percent less for housing; it may also be possible to buy a traditional house. If possible, try to allot no more than a third of your monthly income for housing.

How much do utilities run for a small traditional apartment in the city? When I lived in a 2K (two rooms plus kitchen), 33-square-meter (355-square-foot) apartment in Tokyo, electricity averaged ¥4,585 ($57), natural gas ¥6,800 ($85), and water ¥3,000 ($37.50) a month. High-speed Internet was about ¥5,460 ($68) for fiber-optic connection and ¥2,625 ($33) for the Internet provider. Cable television subscription

SMART CARDS

© RUTHY KANAGY

You may already have a smart phone, but do you know about smart cards? They're

a convenient alternative to cash or credit cards: a prepaid smart card that you can use for shopping, subways, and trains. In Tokyo, JR East issues a Suica rechargeable smart card that can be used as electronic money in participating electronics stores, *konbini* (convenience stores), and drink vending machines. It is also valid on JR trains nationwide and subways and buses in Tokyo. (Suica stands for "super urban intelligent card"–and it is!) Prepaid cards can be purchased at Narita airport or JR train stations for ¥2,000 plus a ¥500 deposit and can be reloaded at recharging stations. Tokyo has another smart card called PASMO. If you're traveling or living in the Osaka and Kyoto areas, you can get an Icoca smart card from JR West stations (Icoca also means "Let's go" in Japanese). Use it as e-money and for the Osaka subway and JR and private railways in Osaka, Kobe, and Kyoto.

Many Japanese prefer using a prepaid card over credit cards so they don't overspend.

costs vary by provider and the package. J:COM, the largest provider, offers a digital TV package for ¥5,200 or $65 per month.

Your food budget will stretch farther if you develop a taste for Japanese cuisine. If you shop like the locals do and eat vegetables, fish, tofu, and rice instead of steak, you can maintain a healthy diet without breaking your budget. You may even discover the secret to Japanese slimness.

Once you start your new job, you typically won't see a paycheck until you have worked for six weeks if wages are paid once a month, which is the norm. At a research institute in Tokyo where I was employed, I began working on October 1, but did not get my first paycheck until November 20. I ended up having to borrow cash from a friend. So it's critical that you bring sufficient funds to live for the first two months. At first you will need to pay cash for everything, from rent to utilities to insurance, until you set up a bank account. Once you've established a bank account you can arrange automatic payment of your bills from your Japanese bank account. If not, you can pay bills at your local convenience store.

When choosing the time of year to arrive in Japan, keep in mind that the Japanese fiscal, educational, and employment year cycle begins April 1 and ends the following March 31. Therefore, the latter half of March is not a good time to be traveling, as everyone is changing schools, transferring from one job location to another, or traveling on spring break.

Banking

© RUTHY KANAGY

Many shops don't accept credit cards.

BANK ACCOUNTS

Having a Japanese *ginko koza* (bank account) is a convenient means of receiving your salary and paying bills. Automatic bank transfers and cash-based transactions are widespread and efficient, eliminating the need for personal checks, which aren't used in Japan.

Major Japanese banks include the Bank of Tokyo-Mitsubishi UFJ, Mizuho Bank, and Sumitomo Mitsui Banking Corporation. In addition, each prefecture and city has regional banks. Tourists with temporary visitor status (staying in the country for 90 days or less) generally cannot open bank accounts; at least a six-month visa is necessary. Some banks, such as Citibank Japan, require ¥300,000 ($3,750) cash and a visa valid for at least one year to open an account.

To open an account, you must show your foreign resident card, passport or driver's license, and *inkan* (a name stamp or seal; also called *hanko*). In Japan, the *inkan* is the legal equivalent of a signature in the United States. Have one carved to your specifications (with the characters of your family name) in plastic, wood, or ivory. The stamp is kept in a small oblong case, and some have a round built-in container of red ink called *shuniku*. When you open an account, the bank will take an imprint of your name stamp, and you will need your stamp for future transactions. Your official stamp is registered at city hall, which issues certificates of authenticity needed for many types of transactions.

If you don't have an *inkan,* you may be able to use your signature, but some banks hesitate to allow your signature in place of a name stamp. From the Japanese perspective, signatures are considered too easy to forge, as compared to a registered *inkan.* You will use your registered stamp (or signature) when making withdrawals from your account at the teller window, and when closing your account—but only your debit card is needed for using a cash machine.

When you go to a bank to open an account, first take a number from the machine on the counter that indicates your place in line. Then complete an application form for new accounts, also available at the counter. If you're unsure which form to complete, say, *"futsu yo-kin koza,"* which means "regular savings account," and someone will help you. In Japanese banks, someone in uniform (often an older man) usually works in the waiting area to help customers. You won't see lines of people waiting for an open teller window. Everyone takes a number, sits down, and waits until their number is displayed and called.

After you fill out the forms and present some cash to open an account, you will receive a bank account booklet and a small gift. Once you have an account, you can apply to have all your utility bills paid by automatic transfer. You will need one statement from each of the utilities addressed to you to prove your residence. You may also apply for a *kyasshu kādo* (debit card), which will be mailed to you along with your *ansho bango* (PIN) to use at the ATM.

At the ATM, you can make withdrawals and deposits, check your balance, and print entries in your bank book (by opening and placing the book in the slot face-up). You can also transfer money from your account to other banks to make payments. Cash machines are usually located inside the bank and are not accessible 24 hours (generally 9 A.M.–7 P.M. weekdays and 9 A.M.–5 P.M. Sat.–Sun., but be sure to confirm ahead of time). The interest rates in Japan on savings accounts are extremely low—as low as 0.5 percent. So, you won't get rich on your savings. On the other hand, interest rates for borrowing money, such as educational loans or house loans, are also low.

JAPAN POST BANK

The government-controlled Japan Post was privatized in 2007 and separated into four businesses: Japan Post Service, which handles mail; a post office management company; Japan Post Insurance, which offers life insurance; and Japan Post Bank, the world's largest savings bank, with assets of $3.2 trillion. Having an account at Yucho Ginko or Japan Post Bank is convenient because there are many more branches than regular banks. Debit machines are open 9 A.M.–5 P.M. Monday–Friday, and some are available on weekends and holidays.

To open a post office account, fill in the savings deposit application form available at the counter. Show some form of identification, such as a Japanese driver's license, a foreign resident card, or a passport. You will also need your *inkan,* or you may be able to use your signature. Even if you don't have an account at the bank, their ATMs recognize most debit cards from major American banks. This is a great convenience, as there are many more post offices throughout Japan than branch banks. In this case, a small fee is charged for each transaction—around ¥200 ($2.50).

TRANSFERRING MONEY
Sending Money

You can transfer money overseas from both banks and post offices. To do so, you must present some form of personal identification, such as a foreign resident card, passport, or driver's license. To send money from a bank, you have three choices. Telegraphic transfer is the fastest method; notification of the transfer is sent electronically by telegraph. You will normally pay the cost of the transfer plus handling charges.

With an ordinary transfer, notification of the transfer is by airmail (5–7 days to the United States). The third way is a demand draft, which operates like a money order. It is purchased at a bank for a specific amount, then mailed directly to the recipient, who can cash it at a bank. Many banks also offer online financial services, enabling you to transfer money between accounts or to an overseas account—for a fee.

Within Japan, cash can be mailed easily from any post office. Ask for a *genkin kaki-tome* (registered cash envelope), and they will give you a special envelope for sending cash (bills only, no coins). The envelope is sealed with a special stamp on which you affix your *inkan.* It's also possible to send money internationally through any post office that handles savings accounts. Again, there are three methods: sending money directly to the person's address, postal book savings, or bank account.

Automatic Payments

Thanks to a highly developed system of *jido shiharai* (automatic payments) in Japan, the easiest way to pay utilities and other bills is to have the money deducted from your bank or postal account each month. Several weeks before payment is due, you will receive monthly electric, gas, and telephone (domestic) statements through the mail (water/sewerage statements come every two months). Once your payment system is set up, the correct amount will be deducted from your account. Utility and other bills, such as National Health Insurance, can also be paid at a bank, credit association, post office, or convenience store.

CONSUMER RIGHTS

If you purchase something with a credit card or cash and later decide you don't want it, you're in luck—consumers in Japan are, by law, allowed a cooling-off period. In its *Guide to Living in Japan,* the Tokyo Metropolitan Government explains that the cooling-off period allows consumers to cancel a contract, such as one with a door-to-door salesman, even after the contract has been finalized. The consumer must write to the retailer in Japanese within eight days from the time the proper written contract was received from the retailer. Notify the retailer of your desire to cancel the contract by postcard. Keep a photocopy of the postcard and send it by registered mail or another certified delivery service. The government provides a sample written notice to send via postcard, as follows:

> On [date], I contracted to purchase [item] for [amount] yen with a salesperson of your company named Mr./Ms. [Name]. However, I now wish to cancel this contract. Accordingly, please send me a refund of [amount] yen (equal to the sum I paid) as soon as possible. In addition, please arrange to pick this product up promptly.

There is a spot to write in the date, your name and address, and the name and address of the retailer. If a credit contract has been finalized, the consumer must also write to the credit company. The cooling-off period applies only to unused merchandise. For more information, contact your local consumer center in Japan.

At the Tokyo Metropolitan Comprehensive Consumer Center (tel. 03/3235-1155), books and videos related to consumer life may be viewed on-site or borrowed. Consultations concerning problems with merchandise, services, and contracts are also conducted.

Taxes

JAPANESE TAXES

Everyone living in Japan, regardless of nationality, is obliged to pay *zeikin* (taxes). The 5 percent consumption (sales) tax is the most obvious tax in daily life. Two additional types include national taxes, which are levied by the national government; and local taxes, which are levied by prefecture and municipal governments. Each person in the country must pay an income tax (national tax) and a resident's tax (local tax).

Income Tax

For foreign residents in Japan, whether or not you will be taxed—and, if so, the income on which your taxes will be levied—depends on your resident status. There are three types of resident status, defined as follows:

A "resident" is someone who has lived in Japan continuously for more than one year. The two subcategories of resident include: 1) a nonpermanent resident who has lived in Japan for five years or less and does not intend to become a permanent resident; and 2) anyone who does not fit that first qualification, in which case he or she is regarded as a permanent resident. A "nonresident" is someone who has lived in Japan for less than one year.

Both types of residents are taxed on income generated in Japan, whether paid in Japan or outside Japan, as well as on income generated outside Japan and paid in Japan. Of the income earned outside Japan by nonpermanent residents, only the amount sent to Japan is subject to taxation. For income earned outside Japan, the amount kept outside Japan is not subject to taxation.

As a rule, nonresidents are taxed on income generated in Japan, whether paid in Japan or outside Japan. Nonresidents are not subject to taxation on income generated outside Japan.

Personal *shotokuzei* (income tax) is a national tax collected by district tax offices and levied on personal income earned between January 1 and December 31. It is assessed on the total income for the year, so you must file a tax return if you have earned any income. Personal income is calculated as total income minus "necessary expenses" (defined as expenses involved in gaining the income). Tax returns must be filed at the local municipal office between February 16 and March 15.

If your total income for the year is less than ¥380,000 ($4,750), an income tax report is not required. When a foreigner leaves Japan permanently and his or her income for the year exceeds ¥380,000, he or she must designate a proxy to file an income tax report during tax season, or file a return in person and pay any taxes before departure.

There are two methods of income tax payment, one for nonsalaried workers and the other for salaried workers:

Nonsalaried taxpayers must calculate their own income and tax for the year, submit an income tax report, and pay the necessary taxes. Income tax reports must be filed at the tax office administering to the area of residence during the period between February 16 and March 15 for the previous year.

Salaried employees must deduct their personal income tax from their salary (under a tax withholding system). Since the employer carries out a year-end adjustment every December to calculate excesses or shortfalls in taxes paid for the year, salaried taxpayers do not need to file an income tax report. However, the following persons must file a personal income tax report: 1) salaried employees with an annual income of more than ¥20 million ($250,000); 2) salaried employees with additional income amounting to more than ¥200,000 ($2,500) in the year; and 3) salaried employees earning separate incomes from two or more employers.

When filing income tax reports, taxpayers can claim deductions for the following items: 1) *(not applicable to nonresidents)* if medical expenses for the previous year, excluding the portion covered by health insurance, totaled more than 5 percent of the individual's annual income or more than ¥100,000 ($125); 2) if the taxpayer suffered losses from disaster or theft; and 3) *(not applicable to nonresidents)* if the taxpayer took out a loan to purchase a home. In addition, taxpayers can claim a spouse deduction and spouse's special deduction if the spouse's income for the year did not exceed a certain amount. To claim these deductions, the taxpayer must submit documented evidence, such as receipts for medical expenses, to the tax office.

Residential Tax

Juminzei (residential tax) is paid to the municipality in which you resided on January 1. You must pay the tax if you were living in that municipality on January 1, lived in Japan for the previous 12 months, and earned income during that period. Taxes are based on the previous year's annual income and consist of two amounts—one proportionate to the level of income, and the other uniformly applied to all (on a per capita ratio) regardless of income level.

Nonsalaried workers usually pay the residential tax computed on the basis of the income tax report in four separate installments in June, August, October, and January. Notification is sent by the ward or municipal office, and payment can be made through banks, credit associations, credit unions, agricultural cooperatives, and post offices. The salaried employee's residential tax is computed by the ward or municipal office on the basis of the employer's report. The residential tax is deducted from the individual's salary in 12 installments from June through May of the following year.

For Tokyo residents, a *Guide to Metropolitan Taxes* (in English, Chinese, and Korean) is available from the Consultation Section of the Metropolitan Taxation Office, or from the Tokyo Metropolitan Citizens Information Room (3F, Main Bldg. No. 1, Tokyo Metropolitan Government, 2-8-1 Nishi-Shinjuku, Shinjuku-ku, Tokyo, tel. 03/5321-1111).

Asset-Based Tax

The *koteishisan-zei* (municipal property tax) and *keijidosha-zei* (light motor vehicle tax) are based on assets. The former is paid by persons who own land, a house, or a depreciable asset, and is collected by the Tokyo Metropolitan Government Tax Office (for Tokyo residents). The amount of tax payable is based on the value of the asset. The light motor vehicle tax is paid by owners of motorcycles and light cars. Contact your local municipal taxation office in Japan for requirements.

U.S. TAXES

How about income taxes to the U.S. government for American citizens residing in Japan short- or long-term? The answer is yes, you must file an income tax return each year by June 15—a two-month automatic extension is granted to citizens living abroad. You may also be required to file a state income tax return with your home state.

The Bona Fide Residence Test requires that you have spent at least 330 days outside the United States in the previous year. The maximum foreign earned income exclusion is adjusted annually for inflation. For 2011, the maximum exclusion was $92,900. Detailed instructions and forms are available online. A good starting point is IRS Publication 54, Tax Guide for U.S. Citizens and Resident Aliens Abroad (www.irs.gov/publications/p54/index.html). The U.S. Embassy in Tokyo and U.S. Consulates throughout Japan can also answer your tax questions.

Investing

The Japanese government is eager to promote more investments in their country. Under the government's plan to revitalize the economy and promote new growth, three targets were laid out to achieve by 2020: to promote Japan as an ideal location for Asia regional headquarters and research-and-development facilities, to double the number of employees of foreign enterprises, and to double the volume of direct investment into Japan.

A resource for foreign investors is the Japan External Trade Organization (JETRO), which organizes seminars and individual consultations in Japan and abroad to provide information about investment opportunities. They can provide information on trends in the Japanese market, the regional investment climate, laws, and procedures. JETRO's online journal, *Invest Japan!* (www.jetro.go.jp/en/invest), offers detailed information on the investment environment, including macroeconomic data, laws and regulations, and foreign companies operating in Japan.

A LOOK AT THE MARKETS

Japan has five equities exchanges, located in Tokyo, Osaka, Nagoya, Sapporo, and Fukuoka. The Tokyo Stock Exchange (TSE) offers market information in real time. The Nikkei All Stock Index is a market value–weighted index that serves as a benchmark against which investment results can be measured. Stocks in the Nikkei 225 Stock Average can be found at www.nni.nikkei.co.jp. The Nikkei Stock Index 300

© RUTHY KANAGY

the Tokyo Stock Exchange

(also known as Nikkei 300), a representative gauge of the overall market, is a market value–weighted index of 300 major selected issues on the Tokyo Stock Exchange. The Nikkei JASDAQ covers most over-the-counter issues.

STOCKS

Nikkei Interactive provides business news, market data, and current information on *kabu* (stocks), backed by Nikkei, Inc. Nikkei publishes the Japanese daily newspapers *Nikkei (Nihon Keizai Shimbun)* and *Nikkei Business Daily (Nihon Sangyo Shimbun),* covering economic news, investment, and management strategies. English readers can access this information through the *Nikkei Weekly* newspaper and online at eNikkei.com. Nikkei Indexes provide real-time stock data and analysis.

SECURITIES

These are some of the *shoken* (securities) companies in Japan.

Japan Securities Agents, Ltd. (JSA), a subsidiary of JBIS Holdings, Inc., is engaged in services related to securities transfer, custody, close inspection, clearing, and financing. The company is affiliated with Japan Securities Finance Co., Ltd., which holds 36.61 percent of issued stock. Securities transfer, transit, and other related services accounted for 99 percent of the company's fiscal revenues in 2000; calculation and data processing services accounted for the remaining 1 percent. Japan Securities Agents has one consolidated subsidiary based in Tokyo. The group's operations are entirely domestic.

Established in 1973, Jafco Co., Ltd. invests in unlisted medium- and small-sized companies with high potential, and offers related services, such as leasing, installment, and commercial loans. The company provides information, consulting, and other support services to investor companies to enhance their performance and provide assistance in their initial listing on the stock markets, as well as help them form investment enterprise partnerships and manage the collected funds.

DIRECT INVESTMENT

Foreign direct investment in Japan has grown steadily in recent years. The Japanese government is aiming to double foreign direct investment (FDI) under the Program for Acceleration of Foreign Direct Investment. Key market sectors include automotive parts, retail, ICT, biotechnology, medical care, and the environment. In the aftermath of the Great East Japan Earthquake of 2011, the government established a new Reconstruction Agency to coordinate rebuilding and assisting companies in the affected areas. Five prefectures of the Tohoku (northeast) region were designated as a Special Zone for Reconstruction, and efforts were made to attract foreign companies and FDI into the region.

The Japan External Trade Organization provides analytical reports on key industries, covering their products, services, business and industrial environments, regional enterprises, and current market trends. Among the advantages of investing in Japan are consumer sophistication and purchasing power, unique and innovative products and services, commitment to long-term partnership, and a rapidly growing broadband society. For more information on investment opportunities and how to set up your business in Japan, contact one of JETRO's overseas or Japan offices (www.jetro.go.jp/en/jetro/network).

DAILY LIFE

COMMUNICATIONS

Communication has been an art form in Japan for thousands of years, from ancient times when wandering monks narrated tales of samurai battles accompanied by the *biwa* (stringed lute), and myths about Japan's origin were being recorded in elegant calligraphy. One of your first impressions upon arriving in Japan may be the manner in which people communicate. You may see people bowing to each other on the street, tracing *kanji* characters on their palms (to show how a character in their name is written, for example). And everywhere people are tapping on their cell phone keys and smart phone and tablet screens. Watching Japanese rapidly typing messages on their phones is amazing when you consider the complexities of their script, with 2,000 *kanji* characters and two syllabaries. With so many electronic forms of communication, traditional land-line use has diminished and newspaper circulation has dwindled. However, mobile phones and tablets have not fully displaced other forms of communication. Old-fashioned telephone, fax, postal service, print, and visual media are still in use. Read on for details on how to obtain Internet service and access news and information while you are in Japan.

Internet Access

Although a majority of Japanese access the Internet through their mobile phones, there are numerous Internet cafés clustered around train stations and in high-rise buildings. Manga cafés, supplying magazines, manga, drinks, food, and private space are popular as all-night hangouts. Each cubicle has a computer that you can use for around ¥400 ($5) an hour. There may be an initial membership fee of ¥500 ($6.25), valid for a year. Some JR train stations have Internet cafés, such as at Ueno station in Tokyo—the coffee isn't the best, but you get 30 minutes free access on one of a dozen laptops. Most hotels have LAN and/or WiFi access, but free WiFi outside is very limited, unless you sign up with a WiFi provider in Japanese. A good option is to rent a pocket WiFi hotspot (WiMax) from a mobile phone rental company.

Want to buy an iPad for your stay in Japan? With the proper ID and a 25-month contract, you can get an iPad WiFi + 4G model with no down payment from SoftBank for a basic flat-rate data plan of ¥4,410 ($55) per month and basic Internet service fee of ¥315 ($4) per month (http://mb.softbank.jp/en). If your stay in Japan is shorter than two years, you can subscribe to SoftBank's prepaid plan for the iPad and get Internet access through their 3G coverage areas for 30 days (or when the data usage limit is reached). The 1 GB plan costs ¥4,410 for 30 days or when 1GB of data has been used; the 100MB plan is ¥1,510 for 30 days or when 100MB of data has been used. Both plans have an auto-recharge option.

FTTH (fiber-optic) and ADSL broadband connections are available for your home

DAILY LIFE

Japan is on the cutting edge of technology.

and workplace through Internet providers such as ASAHI Net, J:COM, KDDI, Nifty, and SpinNet. You can choose to subscribe to Internet service alone (typically about ¥5,500/$68.75 and up a month) or package plans including cable TV, telephone, and mobile phone services. KDDI "au" offers FTTH from ¥5,460/$68 a month for a single family home and ADSL for ¥4,284/$54 for Internet only and ¥315/$4 additional per month for phone service. Rates vary, so check their websites and choose the service that best meets your needs.

Telephone Service

MOBILE PHONES

Japan has more *keitai* (literally, "portable") users than landlines, and far more people connect to the Internet via their mobile phone and smart phones than from computers. Japan was first to introduce 3G technology and i-mode service in the early 2000s, connecting mobile phones to text-only and mobile-specific websites.

Today, mobile phones are used not only as voice and message tools, but as an electronic wallet, train pass, GPS navigator, video on-demand, camera, TV-viewer, music player, dictionary, library, trip planner, and game device with a multitude of other functions. With the advent of smart phones (called *sumaho*), such as iPhones and Androids, the landscape has expanded, enabling users to access all of the Internet.

Buying a Mobile Phone

The big three telecommunications companies are NTT DoCoMo, KDDI "au", and SoftBank, and the competition is fierce to continually introduce new features and technology for the *keitai*. NTT DoCoMo released the first 4G LTE smart phone, the Samsung Galaxy S II LTE in 2011, with a 1.5GHz dual core processor and speeds up to 10 times faster than the previous 3G. Basic use plan is ¥780 ($9.75) per month with a two-year contract plus ¥42 (53 cents) per minute for calls and ¥63 (79 cents) per KB for data. KDDI and SoftBank offer a wide variety of mobile phones and smart phones (called *sumaho*), including the iPhone and iPad as well as Android. SoftBank's standard price plan for an iPhone 4S is as low as ¥2,900 ($36.25) per month with a two-year contract. This includes the basic White Plan (i) for ¥980 ($12.25) per month, S! Basic Pack (MMS) for ¥315 ($4) per month, and Standard Price Plan Unlimited Packet Discount for Smartphone.

How do you sign up to buy a cell phone? There are strict requirements for foreigners to purchase a mobile phone and subscribe to a service in Japan. You must be a resident with the proper form of ID, such as a resident card that is valid for at least 90 more days plus a passport, or a student ID plus National Health Insurance Card, or a Japanese driver's license.

If you are not staying long enough to sign a two-year contract, another option is to buy a prepaid phone. You must prove that you are eligible to stay in Japan for at least 90 days or more after the service application has been accepted, and show a form of ID such as a Japanese driver's license, passport, or resident card, and proof of current address. A basic prepaid phone costs around ¥5,000 and you can buy prepaid cards worth ¥3,000 ($37.50) or ¥5,000 ($62.50) at mobile phone stores and *konbini* convenience

USEFUL TELEPHONE NUMBERS

- Police: 110
- Fire/ambulance, medical emergency: 119
- Directory inquiries: 104
- Other inquiries: 116
- Time: 117
- Weather forecast: 177
- Telephone repairs: 113

- Collect call (reverse charges): 106
- International phone call inquiries: 0057
- AIDS information: 0120/461-995
- Japan Helpline (24-hour English-language hotline with free advice and practical aid from anywhere in Japan): 0120/46-1997

Source: www.jhelp.com/en/jhlp.html

DAILY LIFE

stores. See http://mb.softbank.jp/en/prepaid_service. If you're not sure whether you want to buy a cell phone, renting is another option.

Renting a Mobile Phone

Can you use your cell phone from home in Japan? Only if your phone is a 3G international mobile phone that is WCDMA/UMTS/HSDPA 2100MHz compatible. The widespread U.S. GSM phone will *not* work in Japan. Contact your service provider to verify. You have several options if you decide to rent. One is to sign up for an international roaming plan and international data plan with your home service provider and take your own SIM card along to use in a rented Japanese 3G phone (for about ¥945/$11.80 a day). You keep your own phone number in Japan but pay international roaming rates for calls and data usage, which are quite costly. Another option is to obtain a 3G SIM card in Japan—either buy (about ¥3,150/$40) or rent (about ¥105/$1.32 a day) one to use in your own 3G phone (after verifying that it is unlocked and compatible). In this case you will have a local Japanese phone number. If you rent an iPhone SIM Card or 3G SIM Card from SoftBank, local calls are ¥105/$1.32 per minute with free incoming calls; sending SMS is ¥15 per message, and receiving messages is free.

A third option is to rent a Japanese mobile phone with SIM card. You can rent one at the airport when you arrive or reserve one online in advance. One rental plan gives you a 3G handset and local phone number with free incoming calls for ¥250 ($3.13) per day for the handset. Local calls are ¥105 ($1.32) per minute and calls to North America are ¥200 ($2.50) per minute. If you make a lot of international calls, it may be cost effective to rent a phone by the week for ¥3,900 ($48.75), with free incoming calls. If you use a special discount number, your local calls are ¥35 (44 cents) per minute and international calls to the United States are ¥45 (56 cents) per minute. Companies that rent cell phones for use in Japan include JAL ABC, PuPuRu (iPhone and Android rentals), Rentafone Japan, and SoftBank Rental.

LANDLINES

If you need standard telephone service you can apply at the nearest Nippon Telegraph and Telephone (NTT) office. Obtaining a conventional phone line used to require purchasing a "telephone line" (subscription) from NTT for ¥75,600 ($945) plus a contract and labor fee, for a grand total of $1,000 or more! (and that does not include telephone service). Fortunately, this requirement was dropped when NTT started offering a "Lite Plan" where you can pay a monthly surcharge to "rent" subscription rights instead of buying the subscription. For Japanese residents, phone subscription happens only once in a lifetime, because it follows you when you move to other parts of Japan. If you're staying in Japan more than three years, it may be worth buying a subscription—the street price these days is as low as ¥10,000 ($125). Check the classifieds online (www.metropolis.co.jp). Once you find a seller, set up a time to meet at a NTT office to sign over the subscription rights. Then schedule a date to have your landline installed in your apartment or house.

You can find a variety of new or used telephones and fax phones. There are many choices of long-distance companies, and it pays to shop around for the best rates. Prices are listed in three-minute units, such as ¥9 (12 cents) for local calls, ¥20 (25 cents) for a wider area. Every area code in Japan begins with zero, and you must omit the zero when calling Japan from another country. Japan's country code is 81 and the country code for the United States is 1.

INTERNET-BASED LANDLINES
Use of Internet-based services, such as Skype and Hikari Denwa digital phone service by NTT, is the least expensive way to make international phone calls. NTT Hikari Denwa's basic IP phone service is around ¥525 ($6.57) per month, with domestic calls for ¥8.4 (11 cents) per three minutes and international calls to the United States for ¥9 (11 cents) per minute. Packaged with Internet service, the monthly rate is around ¥5,500 ($69).

PAY PHONES
With the spread of mobile phones, it is increasingly hard to find pay phones (koshu-denwa). They are usually located in train stations, outside convenience stores, and near kiosks. Pay phones are green or gray and take coins (¥10 coins or ¥100 coins—but if you use the latter, no change is given at the end). When your money is about to run out, you'll hear a beep reminding you to add more coins. Prepaid phone cards, for ¥3,000 ($37.50) and ¥5,000 ($62.50), with scenic pictures, are available from station kiosks and convenience stores for use with the green phones. When you insert the card into the phone, it displays how many units remain on the card (100 units per ¥1,000). The gray pay phones take a different sort of card—ICC phone cards—and have analog outlets to connect laptops. Only telephones displaying an international telephone call sign can be used to make calls internationally.

HOTLINES
Hotlines connect you to emergency service, directory assistance, and other service from landlines and mobile phones. The number for police is 110; for fire and ambulance, dial 119. Directory assistance is 104, and the fee is ¥63 per inquiry by day, ¥158 late night, and ¥100 from pay phones.

© RUTHY KANAGY

All gray phones and some green phones can be used for international calls.

Postal Service

You can recognize a post office anywhere in Japan by a 〒 symbol in red. This symbol is also used on maps. Postage stamps are also sold at convenience stores, train station kiosks, tobacco shops (look for a red sign saying *tabako* in *hiragana*), and stores displaying the postal mark. The domestic rate for a postcard is ¥50 (63 cents), and letters up to 25 grams (0.88 ounces) are ¥80 ($1). International airmail postcards are ¥70 (88 cents), and letters up to 25 grams (0.88 ounces) are ¥110 ($1.38) to North and Central America, Europe, and the Middle East. Envelope size is strictly regulated and must be 14–23.5 centimeters (5.5–9.3 inches) long, 9–12 centimeters (3.5–4.7 inches) wide, and less than one centimeter (0.4 inch) thick. You can drop stamped mail into any square red postbox marked with the English word "Post" and the postal sign. Pickup times for weekdays and weekends are noted on the box. There are usually two slots—one for domestic and the other for international and special delivery mail. A chart with detailed postal rates is available at the post office, or check online. Small parcels can be mailed from the post office or a *konbini* displaying the sign Yu Pakku (sounds like "You Pack").

To send parcels overseas, there are several rates: *kokubin* (airmail), *funabin* (surface mail, which takes 4–6 weeks to the United States), and *sarubin* (SAL). SAL is on a "space available basis" and takes longer than airmail, but is faster than surface mail. There is a small green form to fill out, declaring the contents and value. When sending books, refer to the rate chart carefully, as there are restrictions on maximum weight for books and printed matter. International mail can be sent from your local post office,

HOW TO READ A JAPANESE ADDRESS

Japanese addresses are organized spatially rather than lineally as in the United States. While houses in the United States are numbered consecutively along named streets, in Japan imagine having a pie that you cut into six pieces, then each slice into smaller pieces, then each of those pieces into tiny morsels, where each morsel represents a house. It's a bit like Paris, which is organized spatially into 20 *arrondissements* (districts) and then smaller *quartiers* (neighborhoods). And New York is organized by boroughs (the Bronx, Queens, Brooklyn) and neighborhoods (Williamsburg, Bushwick, and so on).

Another difference is that Japanese addresses list the largest unit first (the country), on down to the smallest unit: your name. U.S. addresses begin with smallest unit (the name), then street, city, state, zip code, and finally, the country. Here's an example:

> Nihon, 174-0051 Tokyo-to,
> Itabashi-ku, Azusawa 2-23-
> 10-101. Kanagy, Ruthy, Dr.

Nihon is the country, followed by the postal code, prefecture (state), Itabashi city, Azusawa district, area 2, neighborhood 23, building 10, apartment 101. And your family name comes before your given name. Perfectly logical, once you know the system.

Since houses aren't numbered along named streets, how in the world do you find a building based on the address? Take a look at telephone poles—they have a plaque showing the address of that particular location. A GPS is handy, too.

Tokyo Central Post Office, or Tokyo International Post Office. Note that post offices also provide packaging services.

If there is a package that's too large to be delivered to your mailbox (mail slot) or requires your signature, the mail carrier will leave a delivery notice at your door. Take the notice, along with identification (resident card or other verification of name and address) and your *inkan* (name stamp) to the designated post office. It's usually the largest one in your area and some are open 24 hours a day. If you move house in Japan, fill out a change of address postcard at the post office. Mail will be forwarded for one year within Japan, but not overseas. If you expect to receive important mail after you leave Japan, it's a good idea to make arrangements with a friend to receive it for you.

DELIVERY SERVICE

For transporting packages and suitcases in Japan, *takkyuubin,* or delivery service, is widespread, inexpensive, and easy to use. Many Japanese travelers use it to ship their luggage to the airport to pick up before their flight, and have their luggage delivered to their house after their return flight. You can ship bags to or from hotels and travel light. You can call and have items picked up at your home, or go to a local shop that handles delivery service. Well-known companies are Yamato (with a black cat logo), Sagawa Express, and Nittsu (with a pelican logo). Most items are delivered the next day and cost from ¥1,200 ($15) to ¥2,000 ($25) per piece, depending on the size and weight. Look for the delivery service counters when you arrive at the airport.

DAILY LIFE

JAPAN POSTAL RATES

© RUTHY KANAGY

You'll know it's a post office by the red post symbol.

DOMESTIC MAIL

- Post cards: ¥50/$0.63
- Letters up to 25 grams: ¥80/$1
- Letters up to 50 grams: ¥90/$1.13 (regular-sized letters)

INTERNATIONAL AIR MAIL

- Postcards: ¥70/$0.88
- Aerogramme: ¥90/$1.13
- Letters up to 25 grams: ¥110/$1.38 (North and Central America, Europe, Middle East)
- Letters up to 50 grams: ¥190/$2.38

PACKAGE UP TO 2,500 GRAMS (5.5 POUNDS) TO THE UNITED STATES

- Express Mail Service (EMS): ¥4,700/$59 (3 days)
- Airmail: ¥5,900/$54 (7 days)
- Economy Airmail (SAL): ¥5,000/$63 (2 weeks)
- Surface Mail: ¥2,900/$37 (2 months)

Based on exchange rate of ¥80 = $1.

Source: *Japan Post* (www.post.japanpost.jp/english/index.html)

Media

NEWSPAPERS AND MAGAZINES

English-language newspapers include the *Japan Times, Daily Yomiuri, Asia Wall Street Journal,* and *Nikkei Weekly.* These are sold in train stations and newsstands in larger cities. You can also subscribe and arrange delivery through a branch office in your neighborhood or read them online. There are numerous national and local newspapers in Japanese. Weekly and monthly periodicals in Japanese are plentiful, ranging from tabloids to literary and news analysis, spilling out over the racks at bookstores and newsstands. *Time, Newsweek,* and other popular English-language magazines are available in bookstores such as Kinokuniya, Maruzen, and Junkudo in larger cities.

TELEVISION

Television channels abound, if you subscribe to cable, with many popular song shows, game and quiz shows featuring "talent" starlets, Japanese traditional comedy, drama, film, news, and outstanding documentaries about Japan and the world. Some shows are bilingual in English and Japanese and are marked as such in program guides. Analog broadcasting ended in 2011 as all six nationwide channels switched to digital broadcasting. The public television channels are NHK (Nihon Hoso Kyokai or Japan Broadcasting Corporation), NHK Education, and BS1 and BS2 satellite stations, available to subscribers. The latter often carry NFL and NBA games from the

English-language newspapers are sold in train stations and newsstands in larger cities.

United States. NHK collects a subscription fee from viewers, which ranges from ¥15,000 ($188) to ¥28,000 ($350) per year. There is no penalty for nonpayment, but the solicitors will keep coming back. If you buy a television in Japan, get one with bilingual broadcast reception via cable or satellite if you want to watch movies, NHK news, and other programs in English. In outlying areas only one or two channels may be available, so many people subscribe to satellite or cable. Watch news from Japan online at NHK World.

RADIO

FM radio in Japan is broadcast at 76 to 90 MHz, which is a lower frequency than in the United States. You will need a radio purchased locally to hear these stations. Wide-band radios, which cover both Japanese and U.S. frequencies, can be purchased at some electronics stores. If you're in Tokyo, Akihabara Electric City or any large electronics store, such as Yodobashi Camera, will have a wide selection of radios, televisions, and all manner of the latest electronics. There are a number of J-pop (Japanese pop) stations, such as J-WAVE (81.3 MHz in Tokyo), that have bilingual DJs who chat in a mixture of Japanese and English. InterFM (JODW-FM 76.1 MHz Tokyo) is an English-format station with international pop music and information for the foreign community of Tokyo and Yokohama. The other English station is the U.S. Armed Forces Network (AFN), at 810 kHz in Tokyo and 648 kHz in Okinawa.

SOCIAL MEDIA

Social media has taken off in a big way in Japan. Mixi is the Japanese social network with 15 million active users. Facebook and Twitter were slower to catch on until 2011, when they played a critical role in communication during and after the Great East Japan Earthquake, when other means of communication, including mobile phones, went down. During the immediate aftermath of the 9.0 magnitude quake, tsunami, and nuclear explosions, emergency numbers and information were communicated in real time via Twitter. People around the world used it to try to locate evacuation shelters and verify the safety of relatives. Skype Internet phone service and Google also played a big role. Facebook users in Japan grew to 5 million by the end of the year.

DAILY LIFE

TRAVEL AND TRANSPORTATION

Most people land in Japan at an airport near one of the major cities—Narita (NRT) or Haneda International Airport in Tokyo; Kansai International Airport (KIX) in Osaka; or Nagoya International Airport in Nagoya. If you're continuing on, you can transfer to a domestic flight to your final destination. How long will your flight be to Japan? From New York or Washington, D.C., it's about 14 hours nonstop, and from Chicago, 13 hours. From the West Coast it's about 10 hours from Seattle, 11 hours from San Francisco, and 12 hours from Los Angeles. From Hawaii, it's just 6 hours. Depending on the strength of the jet stream, the return flight can be up to an hour less. Japan is all in one time zone, which is nine hours ahead of GMT.

Japan has an extensive and efficient transportation network covering almost 1,800 miles from north to south—airplanes, trains, buses, ferries, subways, taxis, cars, motorbikes, and bicycles traverse the country. The train system, including the high-speed *shinkansen,* fans out like a web, centered in Tokyo. In most of the country you can get around quite easily using public transportation—train, subway, taxi, or bus. In Tokyo or Osaka, a car is not really necessary, and if you do own a car you can pay up to $800 a month for a parking place. A car is convenient, though, in rural and mountainous

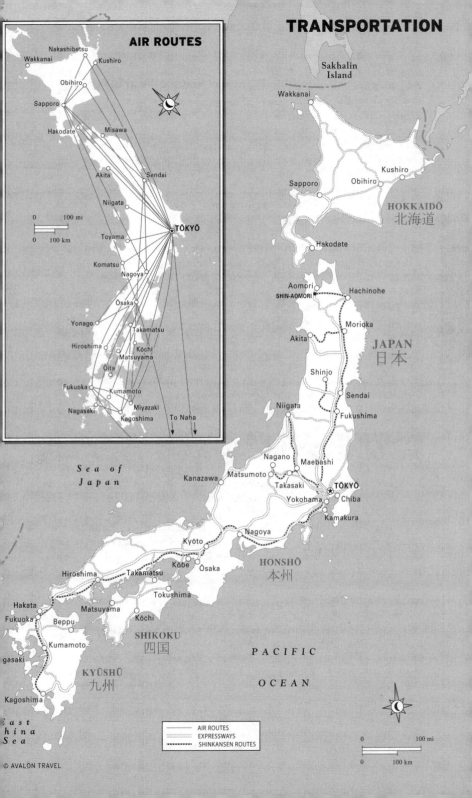

TRANSPORTATION

AIR ROUTES

Nakashibetsu
Wakkanai
Kushiro
Obihiro
Sapporo
Hakodate
Misawa
Akita
Sendai
Niigata
Toyama
Komatsu
Nagoya
Ōsaka
Yonago
Takamatsu
Hiroshima
Kōchi
Matsuyama
Ōita
Fukuoka
Kumamoto
Nagasaki
Miyazaki
Kagoshima
TŌKYŌ
To Naha

0   100 mi
0   100 km

Sakhalin
Island

Wakkanai

Sapporo
Obihiro
Kushiro

HOKKAIDŌ
北海道

Hakodate

JAPAN
日本

Aomori
SHIN-AOMORI
Hachinohe
Morioka
Akita
Shinjo
Sendai
Fukushima
Niigata
Nagano
Maebashi
Kanazawa
Matsumoto
Takasaki
TŌKYŌ
Yokohama
Chiba
Kamakura
Nagoya
Kyōto
Kōbe
Ōsaka
Takamatsu
Hiroshima
Tokushima
Hakata
Matsuyama
Fukuoka
Kōchi
Beppu
Kumamoto
gasaki
Kagoshima

HONSHŌ
本州

SHIKOKU
四国

KYŪSHŪ
九州

Sea of
Japan

PACIFIC

OCEAN

East
hina
Sea

AIR ROUTES
EXPRESSWAYS
SHINKANSEN ROUTES

0   100 mi
0   100 km

© AVALON TRAVEL

areas, including Hokkaido and Shikoku, and smaller towns no longer served by trains. Train service used to cover almost every town and village in the nation, but in the past 30 years many of the lines lost ridership and were abolished. The few train lines that remain in rural areas have just one train car—called "One-Man Car," taking students to junior and senior high schools in larger towns.

To help you plan your travels within Japan, you can find detailed schedules and prices at the websites of each airline, train, or ferry operator. Some of this information is also available in English. To find train schedules and routes, Jorudan Route Finder (www.jorudan.co.jp/english) and Hyperdia Timetable are handy (www.hyperdia.com). Enter the name of your departure and destination cities and it displays detailed schedules and fares.

And no matter how you travel, you don't have to drag your suitcases with you on trains, buses, or subways. If you've been to Japan, you may have noticed how everyone seems to travel light. The secret lies in door-to-door delivery services, such as Yamato, Nittsu, and Sagawa. When you arrive at the airport, take your suitcases to one of the delivery counters, fill out a form, pay the fee ($18–25 per suitcase), and the next day your bags will arrive at your hotel or your home.

If you're taking a trip within Japan, you can arrange to have your luggage shipped from your home to the airport, or better yet, to your final destination. Weight limits on domestic airlines are quite restrictive—usually 15 kilograms (33 pounds) for combined luggage. So it is often cheaper to use a *takkyuubin*. Give the delivery service a call a couple days ahead and schedule a pickup. Or you can take it to the nearest convenience store. It's well worth the cost, since many local train stations have stairs and no elevators, although more are becoming accessible.

By Air

The two largest Japanese airlines serving both domestic and global cities are Japan Airlines (JAL) and All Nippon Airways (ANA). Major airports include Tokyo's Narita International and Haneda International Airports, Kansai International and Itami Airport (in Osaka), Nagoya's Komaki International Airport, Sapporo's Chitose Airport, and Fukuoka Airport in northern Kyushu. Skymark Airlines operates between Tokyo and Sapporo, Kobe, Fukuoka, and Naha. Air Do flies between Tokyo and Sapporo and other Hokkaido destinations. Peach Aviation is the newest low-cost carrier with domestic and international flights. You can reserve flights online or at travel agencies such as JTB. Standard fares are expensive, but look for discounts for early morning and late evening flights, booking early, and specials for New Year's and your birthday.

If you're headed north, there are dozens of flights daily from Tokyo and other cities to Hokkaido. ANA takes you from Tokyo to Sapporo (New Chitose Airport) in 90 minutes for ¥30,000 ($375) one-way. Air Do's fare for the same route is as low as ¥20,000 ($250). You can fly from Tokyo to Hakodate in 75 minutes and to Obihiro or Kushiro in 90 minutes.

From Osaka's Itami Airport domestic flights link to all of Japan. Flying Osaka to Fukuoka (Hakata) in Kyushu takes about 80 minutes with fares as low as ¥13,000 ($163) round-trip on Peach Aviation. This is less than the bullet train, which takes 2 hours and 40 minutes and costs ¥29,000 ($365) round-trip. Nagano and Gunma in the central mountains are easily accessed by *shinkansen,* and flights from Osaka's Itami Airport to Matsumoto City in Nagano take just one hour. For southern destinations such as Naha and Ishigaki in Okinawa, flying is the quickest and most convenient way to get there. This is true also for traveling from Kyushu to Hokkaido (unless you have sufficient time and a Japan Rail Pass). Otherwise, trains are often just as fast, if you take into account the time it takes to travel to an airport, check in, fly, retrieve your baggage, and transfer to your destination.

TO ASIA AND EUROPE

While you're in Japan, why not explore the rest of Asia? By air, it's just two hours to Seoul, 2.5 hours to Beijing and Shanghai, and three hours to Hong Kong. Manila is four hours, Bangkok is five, and Singapore is just over six hours away. If you're in Hiroshima you can fly to Seoul, Hong Kong, Singapore, Shanghai, Beijing, or Honolulu. Fukuoka and other cities in Kyushu—Kagoshima, Nagasaki, and Kumamoto—have handy connections to China and Korea. If you want to explore down under, you can fly to Sydney in 10 hours and Auckland in 11. Moscow is 9.5 hours away and Paris is 11.5 hours.

By Train

Japan has a very efficient public transportation network, which is usually the quickest way to get around metropolitan areas and between major cities. Trains and subways interconnect cities such as Sapporo, Tokyo, Nagoya, Osaka, Kobe, and Fukuoka like a web. They are used by millions of riders daily and are punctual and convenient, but not necessarily cheap.

Japan Railway (JR) operates about 70 percent of the 23,670 kilometers (14,709 miles) of railways in Japan; private railway companies operate the remaining 30 percent. Tokyo is at the hub, and by convention, trains headed in the direction of Tokyo are considered to be *nobori* (ascending or inbound) trains, even if they are local lines within Hokkaido or Kyushu, far from Tokyo. Similarly, trains headed away from Tokyo are known as *kudari* (descending or outbound) trains. Train arrival and departure schedules posted electronically inside train stations are grouped by the *kanji* characters *nobori* or *kudari* to indicate the direction of the train. For example, if you're in Osaka headed to Tokyo, you will look at the *nobori* train schedule, and if you're going to from Osaka to Hiroshima, you should check the *kudari* schedule.

SUBWAYS

Subways are often the fastest way to get around major cities such as Sapporo, Sendai, Tokyo, Yokohama, Nagoya, Kyoto, Osaka, Kobe, and Fukuoka. You don't have to worry about weather or traffic conditions, and can usually get across town faster than by bus or car. Much of daily life in urban areas is organized around subway and train stations. Most large department stores, bookstores, Internet cafés, and restaurants fan out in a radius from each station. When searching for housing and when giving directions, people generally state how many minutes' walk it is from such and such station, e.g., "The hospital is a 15-minute walk from Takashima-daira station." Rental and housing costs are usually higher closer to the subway or train stations ("One-room apartment, only three minutes' walk from Azabu station") and less costly farther away. Taking the train is such an intrinsic part of urban life that just five minutes' difference in walking time, when multiplied by 365 days per year, makes a huge difference in terms of convenience. Tokyo has 12 subway lines, color-coded and operated by Tokyo Metro and Toei lines. Both offer one- or two-day passes for tourists, which will save you a considerable amount if you're riding all day. There are many types of prepaid cards, which you can buy from vending machines; some are now valid for subways and buses. *Teiki-ken,* or commuter passes, are available for students and workers who commute between two stations everyday.

TYPES OF TRAINS

When you want to cover more ground (and enjoy the view) there are local trains, express trains, and super-fast *shinkansen* to choose from. Almost everyone has heard of Japan's "bullet trains." The amazing thing is that they are almost 50 years old. The first *shinkansen* (literally, "new trunk line") was completed just in time for the Tokyo Olympics in the summer of 1964. Traveling by *shinkansen* is fast and convenient (and expensive). But *shinkansen* have an excellent safety record; because they travel on elevated lines, there are no railroad crossings. They operate from early morning to late night, departing major cities at 10- to 15-minute intervals. The three types of *shinkansen* on the Tokaido line are *nozomi, hikari,* and *kodama. Nozomi* is the fastest and makes fewest stops, traveling 550 kilometers (340 miles) from Tokyo to Osaka in just 2.5 hours. The fare is about ¥14,000 ($175) one-way. Note that the Japan Rail Pass

The Japan Rail Pass is good on *shinkansen* high-speed trains.

is not valid for fastest *nozomi* and *mizuho* trains on the Tokaido, Sanyo, and Kyushu *shinkansen* lines.

The high-speed *shinkansen* connects most of Honshu and Kyushu: JR West operates the Tokaido *shinkansen* line west from Tokyo to Nagoya, Kyoto, and Osaka. Sanyo *shinkansen* continues from Hiroshima to Shimonoseki at the western end of Honshu, and through an undersea tunnel to Hakata (Fukuoka) in northern Kyushu. The JR Kyushu *shinkansen,* completed in 2011, speeds you from Fukuoka to Kagoshima in the south in 80 minutes. JR East operates the Tohoku *shinkansen,* taking you northeast from Tokyo to Shin-Aomori at the northern tip of Honshu in 3 hours and 10 minutes. You can also take the branch Akita *shinkansen* from Morioka west to Akita on the Sea of Japan coast and the Yamagata *shinkansen* northwest from Fukushima to Shinjo in Yamagata prefecture. Joetsu *shinkansen* crosses Honshu from Tokyo on the Pacific side to Niigata on the Sea of Japan. Nagano *shinkansen* links Tokyo to Nagano city in the central mountains. There is no *shinkansen* in Hokkaido, but *tokkyu* express trains cover this region. The *shinkansen* is fast, but also quite expensive if you're on a budget. Because Japan is so mountainous, the *shinkansen* often spend more time inside tunnels than out in the open and you don't get much of a view.

If you have the time and want to save money, you can see more of Japan by taking one of the many *tokkyu,* or express trains. For example, if your destination is Sapporo, capital of Hokkaido, you can take the Tohoku *shinkansen* from Tokyo to Shin-Aomori, transfer to the Hachiko limited express through a 54-kilometer-long (33-mile-long) undersea tunnel to Hakodate, in southern Hokkaido, and then take the Super Hachiko to Sapporo. Travel time is about 9 hours and 30 minutes and you can see lots scenic views, buy boxed rice *bento* and tea, and see how many Japanese families and students travel.

Another option for long-distance travel is by "Blue Train," or sleeper train *(shin-dai-sha).* These include the Akebono from Tokyo to Aomori, and the Hokutosei and the deluxe Cassiopeia (private suites) operating between Ueno (Tokyo) and Sapporo. Sleeper trains bring back memories of the years when I attended high school in Tokyo and would travel 26 hours by train to my home in Hokkaido during school vacations. That was before the undersea tunnel linking Honshu and Hokkaido, and involved a four-hour ferry ride sandwiched by two long train rides. If you like falling asleep to the clickety-clack of the rails, I highly recommend it. If you use the Japan Rail Pass, there will be a separate extra charge for the sleeping berth.

There are numerous privately operated trains in Japan, such as the Hanshin and Hankyu lines in the Osaka and Kobe area.

BUYING TICKETS

If you're traveling on a local train, you need just one ticket covering the basic fare. You can buy tickets from vending machines located the station or at the ticket counter. Most tickets have a black magnetic strip on the back, and you slide the ticket into a slot at the gate and pick it up when it pops up again. Even more convenient are prepaid passes that can be used for subways and trains and even shopping. JR East has a Suica rechargeable smart card valid on JR trains nationwide and subways and buses in Tokyo, and as electronic money in participating stores and some vending machines. The PASMO is a similar rechargeable card for Tokyo subways and buses. JR West has its own smart card, Icoca, valid on the Osaka subway and JR and private railways in

DAILY LIFE

TYPES OF TRAINS AND TICKETS

TRAINS

- *shinkansen:* super high-speed train, "bullet train" (means "new trunk line")
- *tokkyu:* limited express or special express, the fastest train on regular rails
- *kyuko:* express, makes more stops than the *tokkyu*
- *tokubetsu kaisoku:* special express commuter train
- *kaisoku:* express commuter train, makes more stops than *tokubetsu kaisoku*
- *futsu:* slow train, stops at every station
- *chikatetsu:* subway

TICKETS

- *kippu:* ticket
- *josha-ken:* basic fare ticket
- *tokkyuken:* special express ticket— you need this in addition to the basic fare ticket if you're riding anything faster than a commuter or slow train
- *ichi-nichi josha-ken:* one-day ticket
- *teiki-ken:* monthly commuter pass
- *kaisu-ken:* multiple trip tickets

Osaka, Kobe, and Kyoto areas. It is interchangeable with the Suica card for JR East lines. Prepaid cards can be purchased at train stations for around ¥2,000 plus a ¥500 deposit and reloaded at recharging stations. To use, just hold the card in your wallet next to the reader as you pass through the gate—super-convenient! Foreign passport holders arriving at Narita airport can purchase a Narita Express ticket plus Suica card for a discount (see www.jreast.co.jp/e/suica-nex).

You can also buy JR train tickets up to 30 days in advance at a *midori-no-madoguchi* ("green window") ticket office at major stations. You can reserve a seat or *shitei-seki* on any express train or *shinkansen.* You will need two kinds of tickets for these trains: a basic ticket, or *josha-ken,* and a *tokkyu-ken* (special express ticket). If you're splurging and getting a seat in the *guriin-sha,* or "green car" (first class), you will need a special ticket for that. This is true as well for a *shindai-sha,* or sleeper train. When you make your reservation you can ask for the nonsmoking car. If you buy your ticket at the *midori-no-madoguchi* office you can pay by credit card, unlike the vending machines, which take cash only (albeit up to ¥10,000 bills).

There are many types of discounted train tickets and passes for students, young people, or for a set number of days at a particular destination that can save you yen. The Seishun 18 ticket is the cheapest way to travel by "slow train" (JR local and rapid trains) anywhere in Japan for five days for ¥11,500 ($144). It goes on sale three times a year (see www.jreast.co.jp/e/pass/seishun18.html). Unlike the Japan Rail Pass, these discounted rail and bus passes have no visa restrictions.

JAPAN RAIL PASS

If you come to Japan as a tourist, a one- to three-week Japan Rail Pass (www.japan-railpass.net) will save you a lot over buying individual tickets, if you're planning long-distance train travel. The pass is valid on any JR-operated train, bus, or ferry (excluding the fastest *shinkansen, nozomi* and *mizuho*). Only temporary visitors to Japan staying

90 days or less can use the pass. Use it for your fact-finding trip, because you won't be able to once you get a work or student visa. You must buy a voucher for the pass in your home country before entering Japan. A one-week pass costing ¥28,300 ($353) is about the price of a round-trip ticket from Tokyo to Osaka by *shinkansen*. You can purchase an Exchange Order at your local travel agency to take to Japan, where you exchange it for the actual dated Japan Rail Pass. You can exchange it at any major JR ticket office (Sapporo, Tokyo, Yokohama, Kyoto, Osaka, Hiroshima, or Hakata) or JR Travel Service Center. You will need to show your passport with a valid, temporary visitor stamp in it. If you arrive at Narita Airport in Tokyo, you can exchange the order for the Japan Rail Pass there and use it immediately for JR transportation. The pass can be used for the Narita Express train to Tokyo, which costs ¥3,500 ($344) purchased separately. The period of validity begins the first day you use the pass.

By Bus

CITY BUSES

Municipal and private buses operate in most cities and towns in Japan. Some inter-city buses replaced JR train lines that were abolished over the years. In smaller towns and rural areas, buses are often the only means of transportation for the elderly and students. Bus schedules are usually posted at each bus stop—but you have to be able to read the characters for your destination. The charts show the schedules for *heijitsu* (weekdays), as well as *doyobi* (Saturday) and *nichiyobi/shukujitsu* (Sunday/holidays). On some buses, you board from the front and exit from the rear; on others, it's the other way around. Just follow the person in front of you. When you want to get off, push one of the buttons near the window or on the ceiling and it will beep and light up, indicating that the bus will stop at the next location.

Bus Tickets

Some city buses have a fixed fare. When you board from the front, you will see a fare box next to the driver where you should insert the correct change. If you don't have the exact amount, you can slide a larger bill or coin into a change machine attached to the fare box. If you have a prepaid card or *teiki-ken* (commuter pass), all you have to do is show it to the driver. If the bus doesn't have a single fare, you take a slip of paper with a number on it from a machine as you board. Watch the electronic chart at the front of the bus and check your fare by matching the number on your boarding ticket to that number on the chart. Children under age six ride free, and those under age 12 pay half price on both buses and trains. On city buses, you can also use a prepaid card. This is handy because you don't need correct change each time you ride, and you also receive a discount with a card. You can buy these cards, along with *ichi-nichi josha-ken* (one-day pass) or *futsuka josha-ken* (two-day pass), from bus drivers or at the bus terminal. *Teiki-ken* (one- to three-month commuter passes) are also available at a discount.

LONG DISTANCE BUSES

Long-distance highway buses offer an cheaper alternative to *shinkansen*. The cheapest long-distance travel is by intercity highway bus. Some are operated by JR, and others

© RUTHY KANAGY

a typical bus stop

by private regional companies. Many travel overnight. For example, one bus leaves Tokyo at 9:30 P.M. and arrives at Osaka at 6:30 A.M. the next morning, with tickets as little as ¥4,300 ($54). You can save the cost of a hotel and get to your destination by morning (see www.jrbuskanto.co.jp/bus_route_e).

By Boat

If you have enough time and want to save money, consider taking a ferry from Tokyo or Osaka to another part of Japan. On many of them you can take your bicycle, motorcycle, or car on board. Many university students choose this popular option in the summer and head to cooler Hokkaido for a motorcycle or cycling tour. A ferry from Oarai near Tokyo takes you to Tomakomai in Hokkaido (south of Sapporo) in 20 hours. Some cities with seaports are Chiba, Himeji, Hiroshima, Kawasaki, Yokohama, Tokyo, Muroran, Tomakomai, Osaka, and Kitakyushu. You can take a ferry from Osaka through the Seto Inland Sea to Shikoku or Kyushu.

If you're feeling adventurous, why not take a ferry to explore other parts of Asia? There's an overnight ferry as well as a high-speed boat from Fukuoka to Busan, Korea (also from Hiroshima and Osaka). You can also book a ferry from Niigata on the Sea of Japan coast to Vladivostok on the east coast of Russia. Vladivostok is the gateway to the Trans-Siberian Railway all the way to Moscow.

By Car

Japanese cars are highly regarded for their quality and innovation and are popular around the world. Japanese cars are expensive, and their owners take good care of them. One thing you will not see on the streets in Japan are beat-up, rusted out cars with missing headlamps and doors held together with duct tape—as is common in my home state of Oregon (where we don't have mandatory car inspection). Where I live, if it runs, it's good to go. The other reason you don't see old cars is because car registration and inspection fees increase every year; the older the car, the higher the fees. There is a network of expressways connecting northern Hokkaido to the southern end of Kyushu. There is a toll for using them. During holidays the highways near urban areas are extremely congested, with vehicles backed up for many kilometers. The main roads in Hokkaido are newer, with wide shoulders and less traffic, but in other parts of Japan, roads may be quite narrow with no shoulder and ditches on each side. Away from urban areas, road signage may be in Japanese characters only, posing another challenge. On the other hand, GPS (in Japanese) may help you find your way.

Another challenge with car ownership is that houses with garages are almost non-existent and parking the car is a huge problem. Walking down residential streets, you will see family cars parked one centimeter from the wall, partially protruding onto the street. Be prepared to pay a lot for gas since Japan relies 100 percent on imported oil. In 2012 a liter of gas cost about ¥160 per liter or $7.50 a gallon. Renting a car is one option for trips to the countryside.

Compact cars are perfect for compact spaces like this vertical parking lot.

TAXIS

During your first few days in Japan, you will probably have an occasion to use a taxi. Taxis in Japan are clean, even sparkling. The drivers are uniformed and usually wear a hat and white gloves. In the cities, plenty of *takushii* cruise the streets, so all you have to do is raise your hand at the left side of the road. You can get a taxi at the stands in front of train and bus stations, or call ahead for a ride. The "flag-drop" fare for the first two kilometers is around ¥710 ($8.80), with a surcharge after 10 P.M. All taxis are equipped with meters that display the correct charge. Since there is no tipping in Japan, you pay the displayed amount only. Some drivers are reluctant to get out of the driver's seat to open the trunk, so you may have to put your bags in yourself. And don't touch that passenger door handle—it opens automatically.

Japanese businesspeople often use taxis after a night on the town, since the trains stop running around midnight.

DRIVER'S LICENSES

The minimum age for driving in Japan is 18 years. If you do plan to drive in Japan, you should obtain an international driver's license in advance from a national automobile association in your home country. An international license is valid for one year from the date of issue, and no more than a year from the day you enter Japan. If you are a resident of Japan (i.e., have a resident card), you should apply for a Japanese license even if it has been less than a year. Otherwise, you may face a stiff fine. The Driver's License Testing and Issuing Center of the police department lists the procedures for changing from an international license to a Japanese license. The required items include a foreign driver's license, a copy of a resident register listing your permanent address, a photograph, certified translation into Japanese of your driver's license, your passport, fee for ordinary vehicles, and a written and driving skill tests.

TRAFFIC LAWS

One of the first things to get used to, if you're used to driving on the right, is to start thinking and driving on the left. The Japan Automobile Federation (JAF) issues a *Rules of the Road* manual in five languages for foreign motorists to help prevent traffic accidents involving foreign residents and promote their safety on the road. They suggest that foreign drivers should pay special attention to the following traffic rules:

- Drive on the left side.
- Drivers and passengers are required to fasten seat belts.
- Children under age six are required to use child seats.
- You must not drive while using a mobile phone.
- Driving under the influence of alcohol is prohibited.
- Park only in proper parking spaces. Cars parked on the street may be towed away if they violate parking laws.

Drivers who violate traffic regulations imposed under road traffic laws must pay a fine or face criminal punishment. In addition, they receive penalty points according to the seriousness of the violation. When penalty points accumulate to a certain level, offenders will have their licenses suspended or cancelled, and will be banned from driving (or riding) on the roads.

RENTING A CAR

If you're planning a trip to the mountains or a tour of national parks in Hokkaido or Shikoku, it's handy to have a car—especially if you're going with a group. Mazda, Nissan, and Toyota all have car rental programs, but their information is usually only in Japanese. Avis and Hertz also offer rentals, but they tend to have higher rates. A company that acts as a go-between between foreign customers and rental agencies is ToCoo Car Rental. The staff is bilingual and their website is in English (www2.tocoo. jp/?file=rentcar_inbound/main). Rates depend on the location, size of car, season of the year, and number of days. For example, renting a compact car in Sapporo for four days costs around ¥22,000 ($275) including insurance. Drop-off charges, GPS navigators, and child seats are extra. After reserving the car online or by email, you need to bring your original driver's license, international driver's license, passport, credit card, and copy of your reservation confirmation.

BUYING OR LEASING A CAR

Buying a car in Japan is a complex process requiring trips to the car dealer, District Land Transport Bureau, city hall (to register your *inkan,* or name stamp), the police, and a translation agency, to list a few. The cost of buying a new car includes the car itself, acquisition tax, tonnage tax, automobile tax, compulsory insurance, plus additional insurance for personal protection in case of an accident. When purchasing a car, you sign a contract with the car sales company. Then the car has to be registered with the District Land Transport Bureau or an automobile inspection and registration office before you can drive it. Where you go to register your car depends on the type of vehicle: Ordinary cars and motorcycles go to the District Land Transportation Office or automobile inspection and registration office in your area. Items required for car registration are a certificate of signature issued by your embassy (or a *inkan* registration certificate for Japanese citizens), a parking space certificate issued by a police superintendent providing evidence that a parking space has been secured, and a resident card.

When you purchase or scrap a car, change your address, or transfer ownership, you must notify the District Land Transport Bureau or an automobile inspection and registration office, as well as the municipal office. If you are planning to leave Japan, you must complete ownership transfer and other necessary paperwork before leaving the country. New cars are expensive, but since registration and inspection fees go up with the age of the car, many people trade in their cars in less than 10 years. If you don't mind an older car, you can find some good deals on a used car from a car dealer.

If your stay is Japan is short-term and you don't want the hassles of buying a car, leasing is another option. Monthly lease fees typically include maintenance and insurance policies. At least one leasing company offers services and contracts in English and their staff is bilingual (www.leasejapan.com). Under a lease plan, you basically pay for the portion of the car's value that you use during the lease term. Added to that are insurance, registration fees, and options (such as GPS navigation). Monthly payments are typically 30–60 percent lower than payments on a car loan.

When your lease ends, you return the car to the leasing company. Documents needed to lease a car include a resident card, *inkan* (name stamp) registration certificate, and a car park certificate showing that you have a legal place to park the car.

BY BICYCLE

Bicycles are officially categorized as vehicles in Japan and are supposed to follow the same road use laws. However, in reality bicycles are not taken seriously—they are seen as a utilitarian extension of your legs, one that gets you places more quickly. That is why many riders are so casual about operating their bikes and don't pay attention to pedestrians and other vehicles. Likewise, pedestrians and cars tend to ignore bicycles. As a result, accidents involving pedestrians, bicycles,

DAILY LIFE

BICYCLE SAFETY IN JAPAN

The following bicycle regulations are distributed to residents of Itabashi city in Metropolitan Tokyo, and are typical of many cities.

- Be sure to observe traffic rules and ride a bicycle that is properly inspected and maintained.

- Keep to the left side of the street when you ride your bicycle.

- Bicycles can be ridden on sidewalks if there is a sign that reads Bicycles and Pedestrians, or the like. Generally, however, pedestrians have priority on sidewalks. When trying to move along a crowded sidewalk, it is best to get off your bicycle and push it.

- It is usually illegal to park your bicycle in front of a station with a lot of foot traffic. Illegally parked bicycles may be removed, and will be disposed of after two months if not reclaimed. There are usually free or inexpensive bicycle parking lots available near the station, so make good use of them.

- Bicycle Crime-Prevention Registration: All new bicycles must undergo crime-prevention registration after being purchased. Even if you receive a used bicycle from a friend or acquaintance, you should re-register the bicycle. If you leave a bicycle registered under the name of the previous owner, you may face problems. The fee is ¥525 ($6.60), and most bicycle shops handle crime-prevention registration.

and automobiles are fairly common, and sometimes fatal. Cyclists often ride on the wrong side of the street and are preoccupied with their cell phone, cigarette, or umbrella, and almost no one wears a helmet. At night, few people use lights on their bikes, and many riders wear dark clothing. Technically, bicycles are supposed to ride in the street. But in reality they often ride on the sidewalks. If there are no sidewalks, that means the shoulder of the street is shared by bicycles, pedestrians, concrete telephone poles, and illegally parked cars—a challenging obstacle course. If you're riding a bike, be constantly aware of pedestrians, other bikes, and obstacles in your path.

If you can bring a high-performance folding bike with you to Japan it will pay for the cost in convenience and freedom. Most of the bikes you see in Japan for running errands are the heavy, steel *mama-chari* (Mom's shopper) variety. Too big and heavy to bring inside, they are left at train stations and on side streets with thousands of other bikes to rust in the rain. By contrast, a folding bike can be stored in the smallest Tokyo apartment and gives you a two-wheeled advantage anywhere in Japan. Of course, you can use it for grocery shopping, trips to the convenience store, river-path riding, and more. I took a custom, foldable, packable bicycle from Bike Friday (www.bikefriday.com), and it was a handy thing to have. I could quickly fold my bike and bag it to take on the bus or train, then unfold it at my destination to ride again. Smaller wheels mean that these bikes pack in a suitcase for air travel, so unlike with traditional bikes, there's no surcharge.

Traditional (heavy steel) bikes can be purchased at department stores and corner bike shops for a couple hundred dollars. If you're looking for a road bike, mountain bike, or high-quality folding bike, you can find them in specialty bike shops in larger cities. There are also bike clubs and races and excursions by bicycle. Joining a bike club is a great way to make connections. To buy a high-quality folding bike in Tokyo, visit Ehicle in Shinjuku or Cycletech-IKD in Takasaki. Ito Cycles in Osaka also sells custom folding bikes. For information on cycling in Tokyo and free guided tours, contact Cycle Tokyo! The Kyoto Cycling Project near the station offers two-wheeled tours and has rental bikes and maps.

PRIME LIVING LOCATIONS

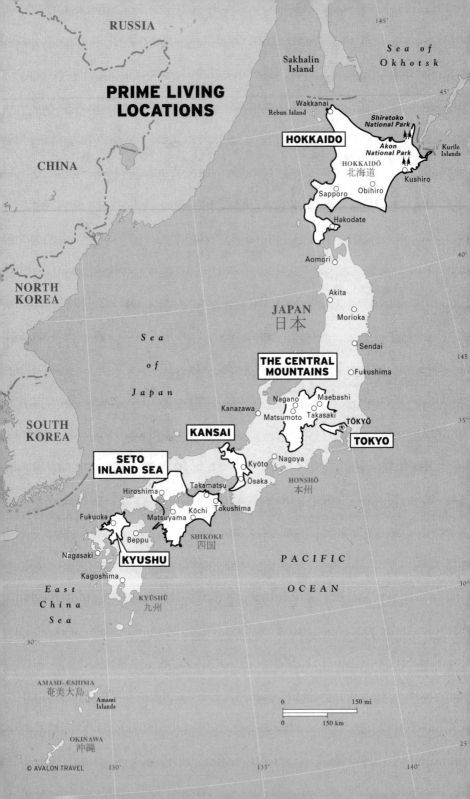

OVERVIEW

The prime living areas selected in this book represent contrasts in climate, environment, industry, population density, history, cultural traditions, and dialects. If you're lucky enough to be able to choose where to live in Japan, the information provided in each chapter will help you narrow down your choices, according to your interests. If your study plans or employment are already determined and are in one of the prime living locations covered here, the information can supplement what you already know about the location and help stimulate you to plan trips to different parts of Japan for your vacations.

We consider Tokyo, the nation's capital, as a potential living site; the northern island of Hokkaido; Gunma and Nagano prefectures in the central mountains of Honshu; the Kansai region, including ancient Kyoto and Osaka, center of commerce; farther west to Hiroshima and Shikoku Island, facing each other on the Seto Inland Sea; and finally, Fukuoka, a major city in the southern island of Kyushu.

TOKYO 東京

When we think of Japan, most of us visualize Tokyo—a megalopolis where crowds of dark-haired people in suits are jammed onto trains by hired pushers; a city of skyscrapers where everything is digital and high-tech, and sushi and anime abound. With a population of 12.8 million, Tokyo has the highest population density in the country

© RUTHY KANAGY

WHERE TO LIVE . . .

. . . if you want to learn Japanese.
Choose: a smaller city or town where you will have to speak Japanese, such as rural Hokkaido or Shikoku, Gunma, Nagano, or Hiroshima prefecture.

. . . if you want to get by in English.
Choose: an urban area with lots of English speakers, such as Tokyo.

. . . if you want to make a career move.
Choose: a city of commerce, such as Osaka, Kobe, Tokyo, or Fukuoka.

. . . if you want to live in a city of more than 1 million.
Choose: Tokyo, Osaka, Sapporo, Kyoto, Fukuoka, or Hiroshima.

. . . if you want to live in a city of 300,000.
Choose: Matsuyama, Nagano, Takasaki, Takamatsu, Kochi, or Hakodate.

. . . if you want to live in a small city.
Choose: Tokushima, Matsumoto, or Kushiro.

. . . if you want to live in a small town.
Choose: Minakami or Karuizawa.

. . . if you want to save money and live frugally.
Choose: a smaller city or rural prefecture, such as Shikoku, Gunma, or Nagano.

. . . if you want to party all night.
Choose: Tokyo, Osaka, or Fukuoka.

. . . if you want to be near temples, shrines, and gardens.
Choose: Kyoto, Nara, or Shikoku.

. . . if you want to travel cheaply and see Japan.
Choose: outside of an urban area, or any location if you use long-distance bus, slow train, ferry, and bicycle.

. . . if you want to visit other Asian countries.
Choose: Fukuoka (overnight ferries to Korea); Niigata (ferry service to Vladivostok); Tokyo, Osaka, or Hiroshima (flights to Australia and Southeast Asian destinations).

. . . if you want to interact with minority cultures.
Choose: Hokkaido, for indigenous Ainu culture; Okinawa, for Ryukyuan culture; Osaka, Tokyo, or Fukuoka for Korean culture.

. . . if you dislike hot, muggy summers.
Choose: Hokkaido and mountainous regions of Gunma and Nagano; avoid Tokyo and anywhere south or west.

. . . if you dislike long, cold winters.
Choose: Hiroshima, Seto Inland Sea, Fukuoka, or Okinawa; avoid Hokkaido and the mountains and Kyoto.

. . . if you need top-quality Western medical care.
Choose: Tokyo and Osaka, Sapporo, Fukuoka.

. . . if you have asthma or environmental allergies.
Choose: Hokkaido (best); avoid areas with a rainy season, mold, and fungus; avoid Tokyo's cedar pollen season (Jan.-Apr.); and avoid industrial cities.

. . . if you are vegan.
Choose: Kyoto, which is known for tofu dishes; soy drinks are available, soy cheese is not. Rice, vegetables, seaweed, and soy products, such as *miso*, are everywhere; eat *shojin-ryori*, the traditional Buddhist diet.

© RUTHY KANAGY

In Hokkaido, houses are more spacious and well insulated.

(Osaka is second). Tokyo is the seat of the national government and the best universities and companies. Summers are hot and sultry, and winters, though not long, are cold, with one or two snowfalls. It's not all urban, however—within the metropolitan boundaries there are also mountains, gorges, hot springs, and eight semitropical volcanic islands. There's still a lot of old Tokyo, if you look for it, in the neighborhood festivals at shrines and temples and traditional shops.

The advantages of living in Tokyo include excellent public transportation, availability of nearly every type of food, clothing, electronics, and printed material you may need, and a wealth of museums, international schools, universities, and businesses with job opportunities. If you're seeking lots of English-language resources, a large English-speaking community, and a job that requires minimal Japanese, you may find it in Tokyo. On the other hand, it's crowded, expensive, hot and muggy, and can aggravate the health of asthma and allergy sufferers. If you decide to live in the eastern capital, be sure to explore the six other prefectures that make up the Kanto region—Chiba-ken (location of Narita Airport), Kanagawa-ken, Saitama-ken, Tochigi-ken, Ibaragi-ken, and Gunma-ken (*ken* means prefecture or state).

HOKKAIDO 北海道

Hokkaido, the frontier island to the north, is strikingly similar in geography and climate to the Pacific Northwest in the United States, with cool summers, snowy winters, open spaces, and largely unspoiled nature. Hokkaido is the largest prefecture in Japan in land area (about the size of the state of Indiana). Less than 5 percent of the population of Japan (5.7 million people) lives near mountain ranges, lakes, wetlands, and plains. The land is 70 percent forested, with 16 percent used for agriculture and only 1.8 percent used for residences.

People in Hokkaido often say that the island's wide-open space contributes to communities that are less bound to tradition, with more open attitudes. Based on my experience growing up in eastern Hokkaido, I would say this is true. You're allowed to be an individual and move off the beaten track. If you want to work for, or start, a business related to food, agriculture, nature, or outdoor sports, Hokkaido has room for you. If you enjoy cosmopolitan city life, Sapporo (the capital) has 1.8 million people and scores of foreign entrepreneurs, teachers, and house builders, as well as an excellent subway system.

The western half of Hokkaido, including Sapporo, is buried in snow from December to March. Skiing and winter sports are fabulous and the annual Snow Festival draws millions of visitors. The eastern side has less snow but is frigid, with temperatures as low as -27° C (-16.6° F), but is often sunny. Summers are relatively cool and ripe for hiking, cycling, camping, and hot air balloon riding. The roads are excellent and less crowded than in the rest of Japan. If you want to, you can fly to a meeting in Tokyo in 90 minutes, or take a 10- or 12-hour scenic journey to the capital by train—that is, if you need to go south at all once you've made your home in Hokkaido.

THE CENTRAL MOUNTAINS 中部: GUNMA 群馬 AND NAGANO 長野

What if you want it all—to live close to Tokyo, but be able to go rafting on rushing rivers, snow shoeing in the mountains, and gather *sansai* (wild vegetables) in the spring? What if you want to rent or own a traditional farmhouse with room to raise organic food? All of these activities are possible in the mountains of Gunma-ken and Nagano-ken, just two hours north of Tokyo by special express train (or one hour by *shinkansen*). Many Tokyoites head for the mountains during the sweltering summer months. One enterprising village rents out rice paddies to Tokyo families who want the experience of planting seedlings by hand in the mud and harvesting their own rice in the fall. Less urbanization and more traditions are what you'll find here, although most of the local young people head for the city lights as soon as they're old enough.

Nagano prefecture, gateway to the Japan Alps and host of the 1998 Winter Olympics, is west of Gunma. If you'd like to live surrounded by snowcapped mountains, you can find a place here. Some areas of Nagano are filled with summer homes for city folk, the most well known being Karuizawa. You can experience a rural lifestyle, connected to the earth and strikingly scenic, yet only two hours from urban Tokyo by *shinkansen* (high-speed train) tracks laid down in time for the Nagano Winter Olympics. If you're looking for peace and quiet, fewer Westerners, historic towns and villages, proximity to Tokyo, and opportunities to climb and ski, head for the central mountains.

KANSAI 関西: KYOTO 京都 AND OSAKA 大阪

The Kansai area west of Tokyo includes the urban areas of Osaka, Kobe, and Kyoto. Kansai is the western end of the Pacific industrial zone stretching from Tokyo, where almost 70 percent of the Japanese population lives. Economically, Kansai plays a vital role second only to Tokyo. The three Kansai cities have distinct characteristics, yet are only an hour or less apart. Kyoto has a 1,200-year-old historic and cultural heritage,

LIFE IN RURAL JAPAN

I asked my friend Kristy about her experience living on the rugged coast of Iwate in northeast Honshu, where she taught English.

What was it like to live in rural Japan?
The official population was 50,000, but that included a bunch of tiny fishing and farming villages that were strung out over a wide area. My town seemed more like 800 people. The coastline was very rugged and the roads to the next town were steep and winding. Major cities were three hours away. The town was very isolated. It seemed like 80 percent of the townspeople were over the age of 70. There were lots of small grannies pushing carts down the street. The population was decreasing because there were no jobs and young people left for the cities for school and work. The English school where I taught was struggling financially because there were fewer and fewer children and rising costs.

How was your living situation similar to or different from in the United States?
I lived in an upstairs room in the school. It was a large room with a kitchenette consisting of a single burner camp stove! I had to buy gas cartridges from the ¥100 store. It had a dorm-size refrigerator, microwave, and rice cooker. The bed was a metal cot with futon that wasn't too comfortable—I bought an extra foam mattress for it. The only heat was a kerosene heater that wasn't very efficient because of the high ceiling. It used up a tank of fuel if I left it on overnight—not to mention the fumes—so I turned it off at night. I slept in lots of sweaters and blankets. The washer was cold water only and there was no dryer, so I hung-dry all my clothes on a rack. Sweaters took four days to dry, so I had to plan what I was going to wear. My diet was different—I ate Cup Noodles a lot because I couldn't read the labels at the grocery store. The school where I taught was in an industrial part of town, not residential, and there were no *konbini* (convenience stores) nearby. I had an old car to drive, but the nearest city was a three-hour drive through mountains, so I took a lot of long walks along the coast.

Osaka is the commercial center, and Kobe has a multinational feel. In this region, you'll find historic spots, many designated as World Heritage Sites, as well as skyscrapers, business districts, restaurants, shopping malls, and Universal Studios Japan. There are many universities, language schools, and job opportunities, and several international schools.

In Osaka, the legend goes, people greet each other by asking, *"Mokari makka?"* ("Making any dough?"). This supports the common notion that Osakans are more direct, pragmatic, practical-minded, and impatient. These qualities have nurtured many innovative products and ideas. Osakans speak Osaka-ben (*ben* means dialect), and are the only dialect-speakers in Japan who don't switch to standard Japanese when they're around Tokyoites—or so I've heard. In other words, they're proud of their dialect and don't try to hide it, as do speakers from other regions.

Kyoto is a good area for those interested in Buddhism, traditional architecture, or ancient arts, and also offers thousand-year-old festivals, an international community, and many good universities for teaching or studying. The Kyoto dialect is considered refined—or a soft touch. In Kyoto, people welcome you saying *"Oideyasu"* (instead of *"Irasshai"*), and thank you with *"Okini"* (rather than *"Arigatoo"*). Kansai food is flavored differently than Kanto food; the latter is saltier, with a soy flavor, while Kansai cuisine tastes sweeter. Kansai is only three hours away from Tokyo, thanks to the *shinkansen.* If you're attracted to urban convenience but are looking for a place with

Seto Inland Sea is dotted with islands.

distinct culture and history (as opposed to Tokyo's blandness), you might fall in love with the Kansai area.

SETO INLAND SEA 瀬戸内海:
HIROSHIMA 広島 AND SHIKOKU 四国

Hiroshima-ken (prefecture) is about two hours west of Kansai by *shinkansen* in western Honshu. The culture of western Honshu is influenced by the Setonaikai (Seto Inland Sea), which was the scene of numerous fierce battles between clans during the feudal period. Hiroshima has mountains, the sea, small towns, and superb oysters in winter, cooked a dozen ways. The climate is mild, with less wind and rain because of the protection of the Seto Inland Sea. The Hiroshima dialect is used in daily life, as is "standard" Japanese. Hiroshima-shi (city) is a regional city and very international, with a message of peace for the world. I strongly believe that every head of state ought to visit the Peace Memorial Park and listen.

Across Setonaikai (Seto Inland Sea) is Shikoku, the smallest of Japan's four main islands. Meaning "four countries" or prefectures, Shikoku comprises Kagawa-ken, Tokushima-ken, Kochi-ken, and Ehime-ken. Outside the capital cities, the lifestyle is rural and agricultural, with a slower pace, which gives you time to enjoy the mountains, gorges, rivers, and beaches. Resident Americans and other English-speakers are active in their communities, producing English newsletters, radio programs, and websites. Many universities hire native English speakers for their teaching staff. You can get to Shikoku by highways that bridge the islands between Honshu and Shikoku, and by train, bus, ferry, and bicycle.

KYUSHU 九州: FUKUOKA 福岡

Return to Hiroshima and catch the *shinkansen* west through Shimonoski and cross over to Kyushu Island. The *shinkansen* terminates at Hakata station, the name of the port area of Fukuoka city. Fukuoka (population 1.4 million) is the economic hub of Kyushu and is known for its IT-related industries and concentration of universities in a comfortable urban environment. Spend several days exploring Canal City Hakata, Tenjin shopping and business area, and Fukuoka University and other schools. The subway system connects Hakata station, Tenjin station, and Fukuoka Airport, which has flights to every part of Japan as well as overseas.

TOKYO 東京

Tokyo, situated on the broad Kanto plain in the middle of Honshu, is the geographic center of Japan and home to 12.8 million people. If you include the citizens of the neighboring Saitama, Kanagawa, and Chiba prefectures, one out of every five Japanese resides in the Kanto region.

Although Tokyo is commonly referred to as a "city" in English, Tokyo-to is actually a prefecture (state) known as Metropolitan Tokyo, with a governor, containing 23 core *ku* (city wards) and 26 other cities, five towns, eight villages, and Izu and Ogasawara Islands, dotting the Pacific like skipping stones. The narrow piece of land on which Tokyo proper is situated is 25 kilometers (15.5 miles) north to south and 90 kilometers (56 miles) east to west.

Tokyo (pronounced "to-o-kyo-o," in four syllables) is not only the political seat of the government, but also the economic, commercial, transportation, educational, cultural, and psychological center of Japan. Almost all major corporations have their headquarters in Tokyo. All the prestigious universities are here, including renowned Tokyo University. The emperor and his family reside in the Imperial Palace grounds—a green oasis in the middle of the capital city. And although the idea of moving the capital elsewhere has been debated in recent years, the national government and ministries are firmly planted in the Kasumigaseki district.

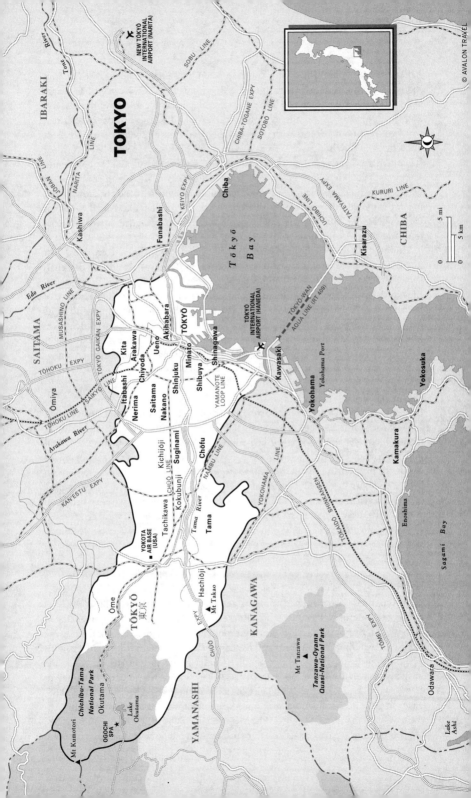

Loud, exciting, and filled with concrete, neon, museums, concerts, theater, and sports, Tokyo is a consumer's paradise. It's as if Washington, D.C., New York, Chicago, and Los Angeles were combined into a giant megalopolis in the middle of Kansas, and 26 percent of the U.S. population moved there. Sound a little crowded? Certainly, when you're rubbing elbows with eight million people in the core *ku*. Even so, most Tokyoites—or New Yorkers or Parisians—would very likely say, "So what if it's crowded? It's convenient," and disparage the countryside as too "backward" and inconvenient.

How will you know if Tokyo is right for you? If you love 24-hour amenities, enjoy being carefree and car-free, and adore art museums, theater, live concerts, crowds, and noise, you should thrive in Tokyo—or Osaka or Sapporo or Fukuoka. And if you're not keen on learning Japanese, you will be closer to English-language resources in Tokyo than anywhere else in Japan.

However, if you have health issues, such as allergies or asthma, Tokyo's exhaust (though much reduced of late) and cedar pollen season (January–March) will be a challenge. Mold and dust mites are another problem. Tokyo has few trees and green spaces, though the rows of potted trees and planter gardens lining the streets are evidence of residents' love of nature (there's nothing like a potted plum tree, blooming with all its might). If you have children, there are few safe places for them to play or ride bikes unsupervised (or even supervised) unless you live next to a large park. If your goal is to immerse yourself in traditional Japanese arts, Kyoto may be more to your liking, although there are some artisans and craftspeople in Tokyo.

HISTORY

If you know where to look, evidence of Tokyo's long history is abundant. In 1603, the spotlight fell on the village of Edo, when Tokugawa Ieyasu ascended to the shogunate (military general) and established political rule over Japan. Tokugawa set about building a castle city, and the population grew rapidly to more than one million by the 1800s. To maintain a grip on the *daimyo* (regional lords) who might have designs on him, the shogun instituted a system of *sankin kotai* (alternate attendance). All *daimyo* were commanded to pay a visit to Edo every other year, leaving their wives and children behind, effectively as hostages. Long processions of *daimyo,* samurai retainers, and servants carrying household goods from outlying regions to the capital became a common sight. The routes leading east from Kyoto to Edo included the Tokaido (east sea way) and the Nakasendo (middle mountain way). The journey took three months on foot.

Four hundred years later, one of these ancient routes is called the Tokaido train line, which Japan Railway (JR) began operating in 1914 with service to Kobe, west of Kyoto. Now, the trip to Kyoto is just two hours and 40 minutes by the Tokaido *shinkansen* (high-speed train). Nakasendo is now Route 17, a major truck route commencing at Nihonbashi, east of the present Yamanote loop. Just as mile markers stand along the old highway linking Philadelphia and Lancaster, Pennsylvania, a stone marker stands where the ancient highway began; another marker stands in Itabashi-ku, beside the busy highway. During the 250 years of the Tokugawa era, the emperor remained in Kyoto, which had been the capital city for a thousand years. This changed in 1868, when the rule of the shogun ended, and the emperor was "restored" and brought to the new "eastern capital"—Tokyo. The Meiji period (1868–1912) saw the introduction of brick buildings, paved roads, telecommunications, public education (first for boys, later for girls), and steam locomotives. In 1885, the first prime minister was selected and a cabinet form of government (with a constitution) established. Former samurai cut off their topknots and replaced their swords and kimonos with Victorian-style bowler hats, suits, and walking sticks; women donned high collars and full skirts. The nation's first zoo opened in Ueno in 1882—you can still visit it today.

In the early 1900s, more people moved into the city for work, and the consumer lifestyle was born. In 1923, the earth shook, and the Kanto region experienced its worst natural disaster. More than 140,000 people died or disappeared, and 300,000 houses were destroyed in fires. Following the Great Kanto Earthquake, the city formulated an urban reconstruction plan, but did not have the budget to implement it. This may account for the mixture of residences, factories, schools, and commercial establishments that make up Tokyo neighborhoods. In 1926, at the beginning of the Showa era, the first subway line opened between Asakusa and Ueno. In 1931, the airport at Haneda (now mostly used for domestic flights) was built, and in 1941, the Port of Tokyo opened. By this time, Tokyo was a city of 6.3 million, on the scale of New York and London.

In 1943, Tokyo-to was formed, and the first governor appointed. During the last two years of World War II, Tokyo was bombed 102 times by U.S. forces. (March 10, 1945, was the worst day; more than 100,000 people perished.) Five months later, Japan surrendered and the war ended. During the war period, schoolchildren were evacuated to the countryside with their teachers. Tokyo's population dropped to 3.4 million. Today, you can see documentary accounts of the firebombing, along with pictures drawn by children about their experience of *sokai* (evacuation), at resource centers maintained by many of the *ku* (city wards).

The 23-*ku* system of Tokyo was organized in 1949. The next three decades saw economic growth and mass production. By 1962, Tokyo's population reached 10 million. Japan hosted the Olympics in 1964, and in preparation built the first *shinkansen* line (Tokyo to Kobe, paralleling the Tokaido route) and the Metro Expressway. As a result of rapid industrial expansion, Tokyo suffered the effects of congestion and air, water, and noise pollution. During the late 1980s, land prices and stocks shot up in a bubble economy, then crashed in the early 1990s. This was followed by economic recession and financial crises for banks and government. Tokyo is looking to attract more tourists and residents as a partial solution.

The Lay of the Land

The saying "All roads lead to Edo" rings as true today as it did 200 years ago, when Edo (now Tokyo) was just an overgrown castle town of one million inhabitants. Every day, hundreds of *shinkansen* depart and return to Tokyo station, scores of planes depart and land at Haneda and Narita airports, and close to 100 ships dock at Tokyo Port. Unlike car travel in the United States, where interstate highways are designed to bypass cities, Tokyo's highly developed transit system takes you through multiple layers of densely populated metropolis. If you're not used to urban areas, it can be a bit overwhelming. However, once you understand how the metropolis is organized and linked to the transportation systems, it won't seem so confusing.

© RUTHY KANAGY

Tokyo embraces both modern and traditional Japan, as seen in its contrasting architecture.

If you look at a transportation map of Tokyo, you will see a green loop line called Yamanote-sen (*sen* means line). Along the Yamanote loop, Ueno is in the northeast section, Tokyo station is east, Shinagawa is southeast, Shibuya is southwest, Shinjuku is on the west, and Ikebukuro is in the northwest. The green Yamanote loop contains the four busiest cities, or *ku*, in Tokyo—Bunkyo-ku, Chiyoda-ku, Minato-ku, and Shinjuku-ku. Chiyoda-ku contains the Imperial Palace grounds, government buildings, and Marunouchi business district. Only 40,000 people actually live (and sleep) in Chiyoda-ku, but almost one million people work and spend their days there. Minato-ku's resident population of 160,000 swells to 850,000 by day with the influx of commuters. Outside the metropolitan core, dozens of train lines radiate in all directions. Every point where a train line intersects the Yamanote loop is a major transportation, shopping, and entertainment hub, and a transfer point to other trains carrying you to suburban Tokyo and neighboring prefectures. Underground there are 12 color-coded subway lines crisscrossing 23 *ku* in every direction.

Imagine that your train has arrived in Shinjuku—the busiest train station in the world, for the record—at the west side of the Yamanote loop. No matter what direction you exit from the station, you will see large department stores, high-rise office buildings, theaters, and restaurants, some of them built into the train station itself. Shinjuku station is always crowded with commuters and shoppers. Walking west from the station, you will pass shops, restaurants, hotels, and a cluster of skyscrapers. Giant gray towers 202 meters (663 feet) tall rise from the Tokyo Metropolitan Government Building, designed by architect Kenzo Tange and open to the public. The courtyard of the Metro building is also the starting point for the Tokyo City Cycling event in September, with more than 2,000 participants. Go east from Shinjuku station, and you will arrive at Shinjuku Gyoen (the Shinjuku Gardens), covering 58 hectares and incorporating Japanese, French, and English styles. People come to view pink *sakura* (cherry blossoms) in the spring, purple iris in June, and red and yellow leaves in autumn. The wide expanse makes this a favorite spot for walkers, couples, families, and photographers.

The farther west you travel away from the Yamanote loop, the more greenery you see. The westbound Chuo (central) line traverses the broad Tama region above Tamagawa (Tama River), with stops at major stations, such as Ogikubo, Mitaka, Kichijoji, and Kunitachi. After an hour or more, you will notice fewer high-rise buildings and a bit more space between houses, maybe a vegetable garden or two; then the houses yield to green trees entirely, and you reach your destination deep in the mountains of Oku-Tama. Hiking trails, hot-springs inns, and rushing streams abound, and it's hard to believe that you are still in Tokyo. If you pick a weekday to visit, you may have a quiet outing. But if it's the weekend or a national holiday, don't turn around, because half of Tokyo will be gaining on you!

Back in Tokyo's east and northern sectors you will find less expensive cities to live in, including Arakawa-, Koto-, Kita-, Itabashi-, and Nerima-ku. When you exit the subway or train station, you will find yourself in a neighborhood that fans out from the station. Buses and taxis are lined up to take you where the trains don't go. Covered arcades and narrow shopping streets are filled with small shops—the greengrocer, bakery, butcher, seafood, tea, rice, sake, and tofu shops. There are also multiple *konbini* (convenience stores), fast food, beauty salons, Pachinko (pinball) parlors, restaurants, schools, realtors, police box, and post offices. The streets are unnamed and impossibly narrow, with concrete telephone poles jutting into the lanes—in short, a jumble of pedestrians, bicycles, motorcycles, cars, buses, taxis, and trucks. Compact neighborhoods like these, by the thousands, are what make up sprawling Tokyo. They are home to millions of Tokyoites, one of whom could be you.

CLIMATE

Tokyo is cold in winter, and generally hot and muggy from July to September. The average temperature in February, the coldest month, is 6°C (43°F), and in August, it's 28°C (83°F). Also in February, dark pink plum trees bloom. In late March, *sakura* (cherry trees) unfurl. The rainy season begins about the same time as iris season in June, while typhoons in late summer and fall bring rain and strong winds. In November, when the air turns chilly, rows of gingko trees lining the Tokyo University campus and many city streets turn golden, and December is so busy with "forget-the-old-year" parties and gifts that even teachers have to run. (*Shiwasu* is the traditional name for December, literally meaning "even teachers run.") Oshogatsu (New Year's) is the biggest holiday of the year. Millions desert the metropolis for their annual visit to the homestead or a junket overseas, and for three short days, you can hear the *hashi* (chopsticks) drop in Tokyo.

CULTURE

Tokyo offers many places to explore, including parks, historic neighborhoods, museums, antiques shops, live shows, and at least 13 amusement and theme parks (including Tokyo Disneyland and Disney Sea). Ueno, on the northeast side of the Yamanote train line, is the place to go if you're a museum buff. The National Science Museum, National Museum of Western Art, Tokyo National Museum, Tokyo Metropolitan Festival Hall, and the Shitamachi Museum are in front of the train station. Next to the museum complex are Ueno Zoo and Shinobazu Lake, a lovely oasis where *sakura* bloom in the spring, and water lilies and rowboats decorate the summer. It is also home to residents who live under blue tarps.

East of Ueno in Asakusa is Sensoji Temple, with the great Kaminarimon (Thunder Gate). A souvenir arcade with throngs of people leads to the temple and a shrine. The streets behind the temple continue the traditions of old Tokyo. Asakusa is along

SUNDAY SOUNDS IN A JAPANESE NEIGHBORHOOD

Yakii-imooo, yakii-imoooo,
Yams, yaaams, yaaams,
Roasted yaamsss,
Stone-roasted yaaaams,
rooooasted yaaams.

Plodding down side streets, calling out the familiar three-tone tune from my childhood, an old man clad in a tattered blue jacket and faded black pants pushes a rickety *riya-kaa* (cart) laden with stone-roasted yams sizzling over charcoal. Smoke fills the air with a robust burnt scent. The old man pauses, then stoops to greet a tiny tan dog in a bright orange sweater. Intimate scene on a sharp winter afternoon.

A small white pickup truck crawls along the back streets of the neighborhood and a loud monotone voice on tape loops endlessly:

Broken black-and-white
TVs, color TVs,
Video decks, CD-radio-
cassette players,
Mini-components, stereo
amps and more,
We'll take them off your
hands for free,

Old or broken, no matter, we
dispose of them for free.

The round headlamps of the truck are a dim yellow.

Then from a distance comes the tinkling of an *orgel* (music box) playing a melancholy tune, "Far away in a moonlit desert," off-key. As it comes closer, a voice blasts from speakers:

Put your poly-containers outside your door as a signal,
we offer fast, safe service.

A silver tank truck carrying fuel oil rumbles by, offering to fill family homes with warmth.

At 5 P.M., a different melody rings out the close of day throughout the city:

Sunset, sunset, day is dying,
Mountain temple bell rings,
Holding hands, all go home,
Go home with the crows.

A few seconds later, another loudspeaker chimes in, creating a cacophony in dual keys, and reminding another generation of children that it's time to go home for dinner.

the banks of Sumidagawa (Sumida River), a favorite spot since the Edo era for viewing 1,200 *sakura* blooming in spring. In midsummer, millions stand on the shores of the river to see the Sumidagawa Fireworks. You can take a riverboat ride down to the Odaiba waterfront on Tokyo Bay. The Edo-Tokyo Museum and Kokugikan Hall, where *sumo* wrestling takes place in January, May, and September, is two stops on the yellow Sobu line going east from Akihabara. Towering over the landscape in Sumida-ku is Tokyo's newest landmark, which opened in 2012—Tokyo Sky Tree. At 634 meters (2,080 feet), it's the tallest structure in Japan and second tallest in the world and was built for TV and radio broadcasting, dining, and shopping and as an observation tower.

Two stops south of Akihabara on the Yamanote line is Tokyo station. (Yes, there is a Tokyo station in Tokyo.) The Renaissance-style, redbrick station was built in 1914; there's also an elegant restaurant upstairs. Walking west from Tokyo station, you soon come to the moats and gates of the Imperial Palace, attesting to the former Edo Castle. The Gaien Gardens are open to the public, and the wide boulevards make it

© RUTHY KANAGY

Vestiges of old Tokyo remain.

an ideal place for cycling on Sundays when the streets are blocked off. South of the Imperial Palace is the Diet (National Assembly) building, erected in 1936 in a blend of European and Japanese styles. Note the bronze statues of famous Meiji politician Ito Hirobumi and others. The closest subway stop is Kokkai-Gijido Mae.

Curious about Kabuki? Take the Hibiya subway east to Higashi Ginza station. The Kabuki-za (Kabuki Theater) was built in 1951 in the style of the Momoyama period. The cheapest tickets are for the fourth balcony, where you can rent a radio and earphones to listen to an English explanation of the drama.

Seeking an escape from urban life? If you take the Chuo line train traveling west from Tokyo and change to the JR Ome line, it will take you to a green oasis, a mountain hideaway that is still within Metropolitan Tokyo boundaries. Oku-Tama is popular with hikers on weekends and holidays. Takao-san (Mount Takao) is another cool, forested mountain that you can reach on the Chuo line or Keio line from Tokyo. On weekends you may be jostling with others, like Shinjuku station at rush hour, but on weekdays the two nature spots are a pleasant getaway.

Where to Live

If you've already firmed up a job or study program in Tokyo, it will simplify your housing search. Ask yourself the following key questions: How far am I willing to commute? (The average Tokyoite commutes an hour each way to work or school, and two hours is not unusual.) What's my budget? What kind of neighborhood do I want to live in? How close do I need to be to the train station, parks, rivers, airport, and schools? Housing decisions often come down to a question of convenience versus affordability. Japanese listings always specify how many minutes it takes to walk to the nearest train station and how many minutes it takes by train to central Tokyo. When calculating your commute, note how many times you will need to transfer to another line. A 90-minute commute on a single train is less tiring than three 25-minute rides with three transfers, especially if one involves a 15-minute hike underground—and you must repeat it all on the way home. Note if there are elevators, escalators, or only stairs in the closest station. Unfortunately, Tokyo transit has many barriers for people in wheelchairs and those who can't walk the many steps. If you have the luxury of flextime and can avoid rush hour, that makes a longer commute much more tolerable.

Rental housing is listed in the classifieds section of the weekly *Metropolis* (http://metropolis.japantoday.com/classifieds). H&R Consultants (www.japanhomesearch.com) also lists properties in Tokyo.

CHIYODA-KU AND MINATO-KU 千代田区、港区

Of the four wards, or cities, located within the JR Yamanote loop, Chiyoda- and Minato-ku are considered prime real estate because of their proximity to the political, economic, and financial districts. Minato city has the fourth largest registered foreign population in Tokyo, with about 16,000. Roppongi, Azabu, and Hiro are areas popular with Westerners. If your company is transferring you to Tokyo with all expenses paid, or if cost is not an issue, there is an attractive and convenient array of housing close to American-style supermarkets, private international schools, and fancy nightclubs where you can meet many other expatriates. However, the downside of living among concentrations of foreigners is the lack of urgency to learn Japanese, as well as fewer opportunities to interact with Japanese neighbors.

Roppongi Residences in Minato-ku has 1LDK and 2LDK units starting at ¥172,000/$2,150 a month with a ¥10,000/$125 monthly maintenance fee. Moving into a 43-square-meter (433-square-foot) unit requires a ¥344,000/$4,300 deposit, ¥172,000/$2,150 agent fee, and ¥52,500/$650 per month for parking. Shiba Heights in Hamamatsu-cho near Tokyo bay has two-bedroom apartments for ¥245,000/$3,062 with a two-month equivalent deposit and ¥245,000/$3,062 agent fee. This 30-year-old *manshon* is an eight-minute walk from JR and Toei subway lines. Upscale Western-style apartments and houses in this area can cost as much as ¥3 million/$37,500 per month for 2,000 to 3,000 square feet of living space (parking included). When you pay that kind of rent, you're paying for a fashionable address in central Tokyo where you can walk to an international school or a job in the financial district and shop for American food at the supermarket. The U.S. Embassy, Tokyo American Club, Nishimachi International School, Sacred Heart International School, the British School, and Meidiya (American-style) Supermarket are all located in this district.

SHIBUYA-KU AND SOUTHWEST SUBURBS 渋谷区

Shibuya station is a major hub on the southwest side of the Yamanote loop and is a transfer point to subways and private train lines heading toward suburban districts to the west. Shibuya station is a mad scramble of people with boutiques, cinemas, cafés, and hundreds of people crowded around looking for their friends by the statue of a dog

On Sundays, suburban Harajuku is where people-watchers go.

named *Hachiko,* a popular meeting spot. The sidewalks are so crowded that sometimes you can't walk in the direction you want to go.

Harajuku is one stop north of Shibuya on the Yamanote line, and another great place for people watching. On Sundays, you can mingle with the crowds of young Japanese girls (and boys) dressed in Gothic or Little Bo Peep costumes, and watch impromptu band performances. Right across the bridge are Yoyogi Park and the Meiji Shrine grounds.

Heading southwest from Shibuya, the Toyoko line takes you to suburban and western Meguro, which was built with lots of space and greenery. This area is popular with well-to-do Japanese and Westerners who can afford it. You could live in a studio with 33 square meters (355 square feet) for ¥152,000/$1,900 plus ¥10,00/$125 maintenance fee, along with two months' equivalent deposit and ¥152,000/$1,900 agent fee, or in a spacious 230-square meter (2,500-square foot) penthouse with stunning view of the metropolis for ¥1,750,000 /$21,875 per month (the deposit is ¥7 million/$87,500). Century 21 offers three-bedroom houses from ¥450,000/$5,625 and up per month with parking space for one car. Aoba International School, Daiei Supermarket, and Tokyo Kyosai Hospital are located in this district.

SHINJUKU-, NAKANO-, AND SUGINAMI-KU 新宿区、中野区、杉並区

Nakano-ku and Suginami-ku, located west of Shinjuku on the Chuo line, are convenient areas to live in if you work or go to school in Shinjuku or anywhere in central Tokyo. JR lines, private train lines, and the Shinjuku, Oedo, Marunouichi subway lines cover the area. Shinjuku city has the largest population of foreign residents in the metropolis. Thirty-thousand Korean and other nationalities live here. Excellent Korean restaurants and shops are clustered around Shin-Okubo station on the Yamanote line. Waseda University on the east side of Yamanote attracts many foreign students. The Metropolitan Tokyo government buildings, hotels, and high-rise office buildings dominate the west Shinjuku skyline. Shinjuku Gyoen Gardens in east Shinjuku provide a quiet retreat from the crowds and noise.

Shinjuku-ku offers attractive *manshon* (condominiums) for sale. For example, you could purchase a 1LDK condo in west Shinjuku with 50 square meters (538 square feet) of floor space for ¥26.5 million/$315,000 plus ¥12,800/$160 monthly maintenance fee. As for rentals, if you don't mind a one-room or very small two-room apartment some distance from the train station, you may find one for ¥100,000/$1,250 and up. Proximity to the popular Chuo line and Yamanote loop requires a larger housing budget, but cheaper rentals can be found in older buildings. My brother lives in Suginami-ku on the Chuo line with quick access to Shinjuku. His tiny apartment in a 30-year-old three-story wood and stucco building is ¥90,000 ($1,125) per month for 355 square feet. The Aoba Japanese International School and Tokyo Korean School are located in Shinjuku, with numerous large department stores and two Kinokuniya bookstores carrying English and other foreign language books and magazines.

ARAKAWA-, KITA-, ITABASHI-, AND NERIMA-KU 荒川区、北区、板橋区、練馬区

If you're looking for more affordable housing, check out the eastern, northern, and northwestern areas of Tokyo. Cheap apartments are usually older and smaller, but if you're close to a river with jogging and cycling paths, or neighborhood parks with cherry trees, you might not mind the limited space. In exchange, you have the convenience of walking to all the essential shops, and with no skyscrapers, you get a better view of the sky.

I lived in Itabashi city in northern Tokyo for three years and I was puzzled when people said, "Itabashi-ku is rural Tokyo." The 13-story *manshon* and truck-choked Route 17 didn't strike me as country living. But after looking at apartments with an agent I found a two-room unit on a quiet side street just a five minute walk from the subway. Central Tokyo was less than 30 minutes away on the Mita line. Two six-mat (9-by-12-foot) rooms with a small kitchen, and bath and storage, were ¥83,000/$1,038 a month. There were also move-in fees. You can rent a 2LDK from ¥115,000/$1,438 and up, including a compact three-story house with space for one car for ¥200,000/$2,500 a month. After paying a deposit equivalent to one month and a ¥400,000/$5,000 landlord's fee you can enjoy 75 square meters (807 square feet) of living space.

If you want to buy a property, Itabashi *manshon* condos start at around ¥21 million/$262,500 for a 1LDK with 35 square meters (377 square feet) in Shimura 3-chome. Fifteen minutes on foot from Ikebukuro, a 51-square-meter (550-square-foot) 3LDK lists for ¥46.6 million/$582,500. It's close to the Yamanote loop line with a 24-hour supermarket nearby. Single-family homes are increasingly scarce, as most of them have been torn down and replaced with up to *four* "houses" on a postage-stamp-size plot. The houses are three stories tall, with one room on each floor, and

ARAKAWA RIVER

Tokyoites, like urbanites everywhere, spend much of their days confined to vertical slots. Narrow streets, commuter trains, high-rise office buildings, and compact apartments allow no room to stretch. For relief from the constraints of daily life, thousands escape to the mountains or sea. They endure hours of packed trains or traffic jams to reach their destination. Others head for the green spaces along Tokyo's rivers.

Arakawa River springs from the mountains in northern Saitama and flows through three cities before emptying into Tokyo Bay. "Rough River" was tamed long ago and hemmed in by massive concrete dikes and wide bands of grass and willows. Itabashi city maintains baseball practice diamonds, a golf course, and biking paths in Arakawa Green Space. Every weekend, scores of uniformed kids and adults bat, kick, swing, run, and ride the grassy expanse. There's room to relax, play catch, train for a marathon, or ride a bike without fearing for your life.

Old men in white undershirts under beach umbrellas perch on the embankment, waiting for fish to bite. A passing speedboat tows a water skier, though the water isn't recommended for drinking. Park workers haul heavy mowers up giant, grassy steps. Every July, the banks are crowded with citizens watching the spectacular Itabashi fireworks on the south bank.

One Saturday I ride my "Sat-RDay" recumbent bike along the path. Leaning back into the seat, I rest my hands on the underseat handlebars. Around me children clutching nets chase *akatombo* (red dragonflies), grasshoppers, and praying mantis. A horizontal *gaijin* on a bike attracts stares, waves, and comments: *"Nan da korya"* ("What the heck is that?"). Other cyclists nod as they speed by on their road bikes.

Gliding along, I watch nature shifting into fall mode. Silky *susuki* pampas fronds wave above yellow blooms. Showy cosmos with filigreed leaves sway in pink. Birds hop on one foot, pecking at the ground.

I take a deep breath. The air, though not pristine, is better than city exhaust. It's Saturday, and there's room to run, stretch, meditate, and claim a piece of horizontal space on the Arakawa.

barely wider than the minivan parked on the ground floor. If you stretch, you can reach your neighbor's wall.

STUDENT HOUSING NEAR UNIVERSITIES

If you're planning to study at one of Tokyo's many universities, you may be interested to know how Japanese university students can afford to rent a place. There are still a number of older, very small apartments and boarding houses near universities with one room, a toilet, and no bath, for around ¥50,000 ($625) a month. The shared kitchen is down the hall. How do you take a bath, you ask? At the *sento,* or public bath, down the street. To find it, look for someone carrying a basin and towel in the evening, and follow him or her (men and women bathe separately). You can bathe for ¥400 ($5) or so, and even do your laundry at the same time at the coin laundry in the same building. You can find such minimalist rooms in rental magazines such as *Chintai* or *Isize* (published in Japanese) at bookstores and train station kiosks. Another option is walking around different neighborhoods looking at vacancies posted on realtors' office windows.

SAITAMA-KEN AND CHIBA-KEN 埼玉県、千葉県

Another option for cheaper housing is to do what so many Tokyo commuters do—live in Saitama-ken (Saitama prefecture) north of Tokyo, Chiba-ken to the east, or

Kanagawa-ken (near Yokohama) in the south. You will have to endure a longer commute to work or school in Tokyo. Or get a local job. In Funabashi city, just 40 minutes from Tokyo station on the Tozai subway line, a 2DK unit in a 20-year-old reinforced concrete *manshon* is available for ¥82,000/$1,025 a month. The security deposit (equal to two months' rent) is refundable with no landlord's fee. A benefit of living outside Tokyo is that you are closer to the sea and mountains, or at least you can get there faster than the 12 million people living in the metropolis.

If you want to buy a single-family home with room for a vegetable garden, you may want to choose one in Saitama-ken (north) or Chiba-ken to the east. If your work or school is in central Tokyo, you'll have to resign yourself to a one- to two-hour commute each way. This is a choice that many Japanese families have made. My friends, the Inoues, built a house near Chiba city, not too far from Narita airport. Mr. Inoue rises at 4:30 A.M., eats breakfast and leaves the house at 5:15 A.M. After a brisk walk to the train station, he takes the 5:35 to Tokyo. An hour and 15 minutes later, he transfers to another train and then walks to his office, arriving at 7 A.M. The process is repeated in the evening. It's no wonder that many children with "salary-man" (white-collar) dads hardly see them except on Sundays.

Daily Life

FOREIGNERS IN TOKYO

Almost 371,000 people, or three out of ten Tokyoites, are "registered foreigners"—i.e., they've lived in Japan for more than six months and are registered at city hall. Of these, about 33 percent are Chinese and 30 percent Korean. Many Chinese and Koreans living in Japan are third- or fourth-generation residents, but are not granted citizenship. Of the other nationalities, around 9 percent are Filipino, 5.5 percent American, plus British, Thai, Brazilian, and others. Shinjuku-ku, where Korea town is located, is home to 30,000 foreign residents. Adachi-ku has 21,000, and Edogawa-ku—where many Indian families live in Nishikasai—has 21,000 foreigners. Minato-ku, where many Westerners congregate, has 16,000. Tokyo has not only temples and shrines, but also synagogues, mosques, and churches (Tokyo Union Church in Shibuya-ku has English services).

Shopping

Ginza is a shopping paradise, with many department stores and name-brand shops selling everything from pearls to handbags to haute couture. Other large department stores, bookstores, and do-it-yourself shops (Tokyu Hands) are located in Shibuya, Shinjuku, and Ikebukuro on the Yamanote line. From Ginza, you can walk southwest to the Shinbashi station and board the Yurikamome transit line. The train goes over the Rainbow Bridge and makes a stop at Odaiba Seaside Park on Tokyo Bay. The shops, boutiques, and a waterfront atmosphere make Odaiba popular with young people. There is a Statue of Liberty replica from France, and the night view of Rainbow Bridge, Tokyo Bay, and the giant Ferris wheel at Palette Town is memorable.

Popular with bargain hunters, Ameya Yokocho (American Corner; Ame-Yoko for short) is a shopping street extending from Ueno station at the northeast side of

© RUTHY KANAGY

Ginza offers shopping, dining, and proximity to central Tokyo.

Yamanote, south to Okachimachi station. With dried fruit and fish, cheap (imitation) luggage, and clothing, it's always lively with shoppers. Akihabara Electric Town, with a concentration of electronics stores and "otaku" goods, is two stations south of Ueno.

Getting Around

RAILS AND HIGHWAYS

Tokyo's extensive web of public and private trains, subways, and buses makes it easy to get around without a car. Every day at least 2.7 million workers commute from surrounding prefectures (Saitama-ken, Kanagawa-ken, and Chiba-ken) into Tokyo. Along with that number, around 400,000 students commute to schools in the metropolis. At the same moment, almost 500,000 Tokyoites do a reverse commute to work or school in surrounding prefectures. Commuters like these add up to 8.3 billion train passengers a year. Shinjuku station alone is a transit point for one million people *daily*. It's easy to get lost in the maze, but look for signs with colored circles that match your train or subway line.

Due to the lack of street signs, illegally parked vehicles, and plentiful pedestrians and bicycles, driving in Tokyo is downright difficult—even hazardous. Even if you manage to reach your destination, parking spaces are as rare as cherry blossoms in August. The subway is much faster. Owning a car is also expensive—up to $600 a month for a parking space near your apartment. Gasoline has shot up to ¥167 per liter ($7.50 a gallon). The older your car, the higher the inspection and registration costs. Despite these obstacles, many Tokyo families do own a car to use for outings. Intercity expressways radiate from Tokyo to north, central, and western Honshu, but on holidays they can be virtual parking lots.

When I moved to Tokyo I took two folding bikes with me—a heavy-duty one for shopping, and the other, a Bike Friday, for cycle touring. I highly recommend pedal power for convenience and health. Plus, almost everyone in Japan rides one for daily transportation. Riding your bicycle to school or work gets you in a lot better shape than driving or standing on a rush-hour train. On a bike, you can choose less crowded back streets and get to your destination quickly. Just be sure to watch for unexpected moves by pedestrians and other cyclists. Make eye contact with drivers when you signal to turn, to be sure that they see you. If your bike folds, you can ride to the station, fold and bag it, and hop on the bus or train to your destination. The Arakawa and Tamagawa river paths are wonderful for cycling—the former down to Tokyo Bay and the latter as far as Oku-Tama in the mountains. For valuable information on cycling safety and free, personalized tours of the metropolis, check out Cycle Tokyo's English site (http://cycle-tokyo.cycling.jp). To buy a high-performance folding bike, visit Ehicle in Shinjuku or Cycletech-IKD in Takasaki.

HOKKAIDO 北海道

Life in Hokkaido feels different from the rest of Japan. Maybe it's the wide-open spaces and houses without fences. Maybe it's the sense of opportunity, of being empowered to do something wild and creative. Hokkaido is considered to be Japan's "last frontier," and even today, homesteaders from *"naichi,"* or the south, migrate north to take up dairy farming or start a business. Until the mid-1800s this land was called Ezo, just a northern outpost of the Tokugawa shogun (military general). But it was not empty. Indigenous Ainu, who were pushed north from Honshu into Hokkaido, had occupied this lush and fertile land for millennia. After a long period of oppression Ainu today are reviving their language and rituals and beliefs and teaching them to the next generation.

Proximity to Russia is another unique feature of Hokkaido. Sakhalin Island to the north and the four Russian-held (and contested) islands to the east are clearly visible and have a stronger presence in Hokkaido's consciousness than do Tokyo and the rest of Japan. There are still areas of wild, untamed nature: brown bears, *tancho-tsuru* (red-crested cranes), seals, northern foxes, Ezo deer, many birds, and salmon are all at home here. The short summers are marked by a wild profusion of native wildflowers.

The primary industries in Hokkaido are agriculture, forestry, fishing, manufacturing, construction, and distribution. Housing costs are 30–50 percent lower than in

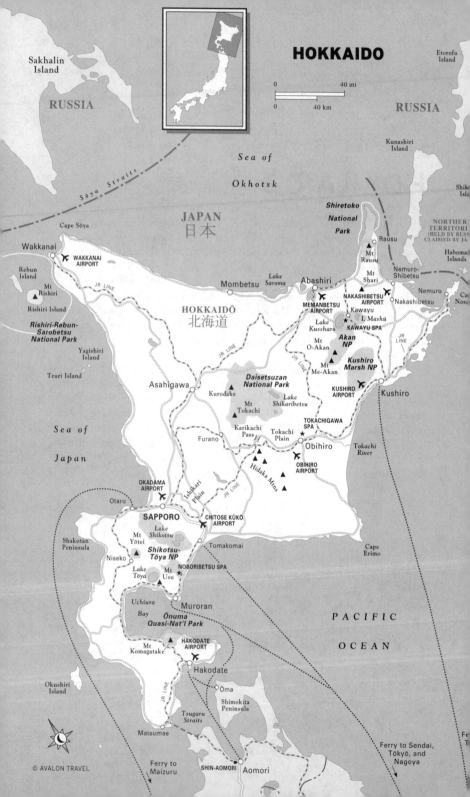

Tokyo, and the language is standard Japanese. Foreigners don't create much of a stir, in part due to more than a century of interacting with native Ainu, Americans, and Russians. Some of the stated goals of the Hokkaido government are "to create a society where everyone can live safely, where men and women participate equally, and where Ainu pride is respected, their language and culture promoted, and their social and economic status improved." The government encourages tourism, creative technology, and the information industry, and offers support to "small- and medium-sized enterprises with a global vision."

What about jobs? Commerce and industry abound in Sapporo and Hakodate. Foreign entrepreneurs have small businesses in these cities and also in Obihiro. Teaching and research opportunities are widely available in Sapporo's eleven universities, Kushiro's four universities, and Obihiro's agricultural university. Teaching English is also possible in all of these cities, and all are good candidates for self-employed translators, writers, editors, and naturalists. A great resource to Sapporo and Hokkaido life for English speakers is the *Hokkaido Insider News,* an email newsletter produced by 20-year resident Ken Hartmann (www.ne.jp/asahi/hokkaido/kenhartmann/index.html). Besides job notices, subscribers frequently post housing for rent, furniture for sale, and events of interest to the English-speaking community.

THE LAY OF THE LAND

Hokkaido is shaped roughly like a diamond, with a "boot" like Italy dangling from the southwest. It's Japan's largest prefecture, the size of Indiana, with a population of 5.7 million. Almost a third of Hokkaidoites live in Sapporo, the capital (population 1.9 million), on the Ishikari plain. Hokkaido's coastline faces the Pacific Ocean, Sea of Japan (or East Sea), and Okhotsk Sea to the north. The Daisetsuzan and Hidaka mountain ranges divide the island into east and west. As in the rest of Japan, there are active volcanoes, clear caldera lakes, and springs. Summers are relatively cool with low humidity, and winters are cold and snowy, but invigorating. If you're drawn to the wild seacoast and fresh seafood, Hakodate, at the southern tip of the "boot," or Kushiro on the eastern coast may fit the bill. If pastoral vistas, cows, sheep, and digging potatoes with your hands are your style, Obihiro, in the fertile Tokachi plain, might be just the place. The distances are easily traversed by car, train, or bicycle. From Sapporo, Hakodate (population 279,000) is four hours south by train; Obihiro (population 167,000) is three hours east, tunneling through the mountains. Two hours farther east is the seaport of Kushiro (population 181,000), near the Kushiro Wetlands and Akan National Park.

Climate

Hokkaido is an outstanding summer destination for hiking, camping, and cycling, but the ocean is rather cold for swimming (which is why I never learned to swim). There is no rainy season like in the rest of Japan, and some summers are cool and rainy while others may have a hot and dry spell. The roads are straight and smooth, with less traffic than the congested south, but speeding is a problem, sometimes resulting in major accidents. Roads are icy in January and February, requiring caution when walking. Deep snow in the central and western regions requires chains, and the heavily salted roads are hard on cars.

© RUTHY KANAGY

Some Hokkaido homes have their own snow plows, which come in handy in winter.

Sapporo's average annual temperature is 9°C/48°F, with summer temperatures around 20°C/60°F. The first snowfall begins in late October, and up to 1 meter (3.3 feet) of snow covers the ground from December to April. In January and February, temperatures drop as low as -15°C/5°F—ideal for the Snow Festival. Ice and snow begin to melt in April and green vegetation flourishes in May and June. July and August are summer, September to October fall. Annual total snowfall is around 5 meters (16.4 feet). Obihiro winters are rather cold, with lows of -27°C/-17°F and snow, but less than Sapporo. Summers are comfortably warm, but without the humidity of southern Japan. Obihiro is the number-one sunshine city in Hokkaido, making it a great location for solar power.

Kushiro is situated at 43°N latitude between the Pacific Ocean and the Kushiro Wetlands (home to the red-crested cranes) and the mountains. The average annual temperature is a cool 5°C/41°F, compared to 6°C/43°F in Obihiro and 17°C/63°F in Tokyo. Spring and summer are cool, with highs up to 20°C/68°F, and are when damp fog rolls in from the sea. Fall and winter are crisp and sunny, with lows of -15°C/5°F; average snowfall is only 90 centimeters (3 feet), far less than Obihiro and Sapporo. Hakodate's average temperature in August is 22°C/77°F, and in January, -3°C/27°F. Hakodate winters sparkle and you can admire the snow from an outdoor hot spring. The air is clear in winter and fish and other seafood are abundant and fresh.

Sapporo 札幌

Just 90 minutes by air from Tokyo, cosmopolitan Sapporo is a near twin to Seattle—with snow instead of rain. More than one in three Dosanko, or Hokkaidoites, lives in the capital city. Sapporo is Japan's fifth-largest city, with a growing population of 1.9 million.

THE LAY OF THE LAND

The city was founded as an agricultural outpost in the mid-19th century and has become the pivotal urban area of northern Japan. The main industries are wholesale and retail, construction, transportation and communication, manufacturing, finance, and insurance. Sapporo has 11 universities with 48,000 students and 11 junior colleges with 7,400 students. The most prestigious is Hokkaido University, a national college with agricultural roots. In 1877, educator William Smith Clark came from Massachusetts to establish the Agricultural College of Sapporo (now Hokkaido University). After a one-year stint, Clark returned to the United States with the parting words, "Boys! Be ambitious!"—a phrase that has inspired many Japanese and is taught in school textbooks.

In Sapporo, the outdoors is always in fashion, whether summer or winter. Sapporo hosts the annual Snow Festival in February, drawing millions of visitors from around the world. You can explore the Winter Sports Museum and take a chairlift to the top of Okurayama Ski Jump, and cross-country ski for free at Nakajima Sports Center in Nakajima Park (near Horohira-bashi subway station). In the summer, you can go hiking, mountain climbing, cycling, or spa-hopping, and swim at the Yoichi beach. Sapporo is close to numerous national parks, mountains, and spas, all within an hour

PRIME LIVING LOCATIONS

© STEPHEN GIBSON/123RF.COM

Sapporo

PRIME LIVING LOCATIONS

BOYS, BE AMBITIOUS!

In 1876, William Smith Clark, president of the Agricultural College of Massachusetts (now the University of Massachusetts), was invited by the Japanese government to come to Hokkaido and establish an American-style university. Clark accepted the offer and became vice president of the new college, which had only 50 students. Clark had a positive impression of Japan and the climate of Hokkaido, and he wrote to his family that it was pleasant to teach hard-working, polite, and grateful Japanese students.

When Clark departed Sapporo in 1877, he left these farewell words with his students: "Boys, be ambitious! Be ambitious not for money or for selfish aggrandizement, not for that evanescent thing which men call fame. Be ambitious for the attainment of all that a man ought to be." You can see these famous words next to the statue of William Clark at Hokkaido University today. Students throughout Japan read about this 19th-century American, one of the many foreigners who contributed to modern Japan, in their textbooks.

Among Clark's students were Paul Nitobe Inazo, author of the book *Bushido (The Code of Samurai)*; Christian activist Uchimura Kanzo; and other prominent Meiji-era figures.

or two. Lake Shikotsu and Lake Toya are both caldera lakes formed by volcanoes; Mount Usu, which last blew its top in 2000, is still steaming; and Niseko ski area, with its Olympic ski courses, is just an hour away from Sapporo.

WHERE TO LIVE

Sapporo stretches 42 kilometers (26 miles) east to west from the Ishikari River and Nopporo forest to the Teine mountain range (pronounced "teh-ee-ne"). Wide city streets are numbered and laid out like a grid, north (Kita)–south (Minami) and east (Higashi)–west (Nishi), so it's easy to find your destination. There are many Japanese language schools. Sapporo has a wealth of shopping and entertainment choices, available and accessible. Kinokuniya bookstore has an extensive collection of English books, magazines, and newspapers. Enterprising foreign residents have opened a bagel bakery, several restaurants, the Gaijin Bar, and private English schools. There are many attractive areas in which to live.

In the south, Fukuzumi residential area is a bus and subway hub that provides easy access to downtown and to New Chitose Airport. It's also the home of the new, climate-controlled Sapporo Dome, where the Consadole Sapporo soccer and Nippon-Ham Fighters baseball teams play to loud fans. Southwest Sapporo is situated around the Toyohira River, which flows through the city; farther south the foothills turn into mountains. Hokkaido International School, which follows an American curriculum, is located in the Hiragishi area of Toyohira-ku (district). North of Sapporo railway station is the spacious campus of Hokkaido University, a convenient location to live if you want to teach or study there.

For example, a 3LDK duplex (three rooms plus living-dining-kitchen area) with 80 square meters (860 square feet) of space, built in 2008, is available for ¥83,000/$1,040 per month—far less than in Tokyo. Similarly, 2LDK units in a *manshon* rent for ¥50,000/$625 and up, with one month's equivalent deposit and no landlord's fee.

© RUTHY KANAGY

Hokkaido prefecture building in Sapporo

Rentals are listed online and in real estate magazines—pick one up at the train station or purchase one at a bookstore.

Public housing units managed by the city or prefecture are available at reasonable rates. Because of high demand, occupants are selected by lottery. If you work or live in Sapporo and have a resident card, you can apply at the Sapporo Housing Management Corporation. Information on prefecture-managed apartment houses is available from the Hokkaido Housing Management Corporation, and there are also public apartment houses operated by the Hokkaido Housing Supply Corporation. If you would like to build or renovate a house, an application must be submitted in advance for approval. Keep in mind when purchasing land that housing construction is prohibited in urbanization control areas. For details, contact the Building Permit and Inspection Section (tel. 011/211-2846, in Japanese); for land purchase, contact the Housing Land Section (tel. 011/211-2512, in Japanese).

GETTING AROUND

Sapporo has a superb transportation system, with three subway lines, JR lines, a streetcar, a network of buses, and two airports—New Chitose Airport and Okadama (flights within Hokkaido). The subway links the main business, commercial, and entertainment areas, along with Sapporo station and residential areas. Shuttle buses operate between shopping areas and event venues, as well as between the two airports. Discount one-day passes are available.

Sapporo is easy to reach by plane from Tokyo and other cities down south. Flights from Tokyo (Haneda) to New Chitose Airport outside Sapporo take just over one hour. Or you can catch a *shinkansen* from Tokyo to Shin-Aomori, where you transfer to a *tokkyu* special express that passes through an undersea tunnel to Hakodate and then on to Sapporo. If you have plenty of time but not a great deal of money, consider taking a ferry from Tokyo to Hokkaido. The trip from Oarai (near Tokyo) to Tomakomai, south of Sapporo, takes 20 hours.

Obihiro 帯広

Three hours east from Sapporo through the Hidaka Mountains is Obihiro (population 167,000), in the center of Tokachi plain, filled with patchwork fields and a snowy backdrop of Daisetsuzan Mountains. The city's website describes Obihiro as a "pastoral city building the new century." Major businesses are agriculture, food processing, construction, and transportation.

THE LAY OF THE LAND
The first Japanese settlement of Tokachi formed 120 years ago, although the Ainu knew these lands intimately for millennia. In recent years Hokkaido has experienced a U-turn phenomenon, in which Hokkaido-born young people who left the island to go south (read: Tokyo) for university and work decide to go home to where the air is crisp and clear. One such young man I knew worked for a big-name car manufacturer down south, then returned to Obihiro to start a language school, which he calls Joy English Academy. That was 25 years ago. Today he offers classes for children through adults and has a translation service. He hires several native speakers each year.

Obihiro University of Agriculture and Veterinary Medicine is a national university with about 1,000 students. Foreign students, many of whom are Asian, live in the International House. There may be openings for a foreign teacher. For more information on living in Obihiro, contact the International Relations Section of Obihiro City Hall. They handle phone calls in English and Chinese. The city built an International Center to enable people from around the world to study agricultural technology and other fields.

WHERE TO LIVE
Obihiro's wide streets are laid out like a grid, so it's easy to find your way around. Addresses consist of the east–west block first, followed by the north–south block. Go to Nishi 5 (west five blocks), Minami 7 (south seven blocks), and you will find city hall—blocks are counted from Oodori (Main Street). In Obihiro, you can rent a small 1DK (one room plus dining room/kitchen) apartment for as little as ¥35,000/$440 per month with a deposit equal to one month's rent. You can find a 3DK in the center of the city for ¥70,000–80,000 ($875–1,000) per month with one month's deposit and equivalent realtor's fee. The city owns about 3,000 public housing units, varying in size, location, age, price, and requirements. Foreigners are allowed to rent public housing under the same conditions as Japanese, if they meet the following three conditions: they are in need of housing, they have a family (single elderly or handicapped persons allowed), and they meet certain income requirements. Contact the Public Housing Section to apply.

A HOME IN HOKKAIDO

Mike Buckwalter, a builder, lives with his wife, Yoko, and two daughters in rural Hokkaido.

What was the impetus for moving to Hokkaido?

My wife is a native of Hokkaido and I, too, was born and raised here. Though I am not a citizen, in a variety of ways, this has always felt like home.

How did you find a job and get a visa?

Before I married my Japanese wife, Yoko, visas were a problem. Now I am a permanent resident. We found work when we returned from living in Ohio for eight years. It is a great feeling to have permanent residence, because I am not limited to certain kinds of work, such as English teaching.

How does your work in Hokkaido differ from your work in the United States?

No difference currently. I do construction-related work, which I did in the United States. I currently work at Kyodo-gakusha, an intentional community, helping to build a residence there. Yoko is a visiting home health nurse for a nonprofit organization, serving primarily elderly patients who need care. In her case, her Japanese registered nurse's license was not valid in the United States, so she could not practice there. In the United States I worked full time, and my wife part time. Now our roles are reversed, which is still fairly uncommon here.

Are there any struggles living in Japan?

As I said before, I am technically a foreigner, but I have lived here many years, and therefore am quite comfortable in this culture. Written Japanese is still a challenge. I attended Japanese elementary school for several years, then switched to English schools. My speaking skills developed over time, but my reading and writing lagged behind. But now I have help—I can ask my wife to read for me, or get help from the Internet and word-processing tools. I keep absorbing more with years of use. Am I gaining or losing ground with age and forgetfulness? I don't know.

What are the biggest rewards of living in Hokkaido?

One big reward is that I have the benefit of an international experience and perspective. Being an outsider allows me to have a slightly different world view. When I live in America, I am an insider there, but always a bit of an outsider, too. Here, I am by appearance an outsider, but able to be an insider, too. Aside from that, there are specific qualities of Hokkaido that are rewarding—the beautiful landscapes, the change of seasons, and the cultural "melting pot"—originally occupied by the Ainu, and then people from all over Japan. It's less traditional than the rest of Japan.

DAILY LIFE

The many recycle shops in Obihiro are a cheap source for household items. Every October, the Obihiro Autumn Recycle Festival takes place at the Public Sanitation Section. Reusable goods collected during the year are for sale.

Chonaikai (neighborhood committees) are groups of residents that provide information on festivals and other events, trash pickup days, and other daily needs. When you move into a new house or apartment, don't be surprised by a visit from your local *chonaikai* representative; or ask a neighbor how to join. Obihiro has six TV channels, including two NHK (National Broadcasting Corporation) bilingual channels. If you own a television, you must pay an NHK reception fee. English-language papers, such as *Japan Times,* are available by subscription through a local newspaper agent for around ¥5,000 ($45) per month. You can exchange money at the main post office and several local banks, wherever you see the sign Authorized Foreign Exchange Bank. When changing from yen to foreign currencies, only U.S. dollars are available on demand. The maximum daily exchange limit is $1,000 or equivalent.

The Tokachi area is ideal for cycling, hot-air ballooning, kite flying, and other recreation. All winter, you can cross-country ski everywhere and ski downhill at Memuro or on the advanced slopes at Karikachi Pass to the west. Ice hockey, skating, and curling are also popular winter sports. Obihiro has an Ice Festival in January and a homemade river-rafting race in the summer. In the fall, you can watch salmon swim up the Tokachi River to their spawning grounds. Tokachigawa Onsen (Tokachi River Hot Springs) is a spa resort with many traditional inns, popular for New Year's parties. Daisetsuzan National Park is only an hour or two away. Dominated by Kurodake (Black Peak), the highest peak, the whole area is an outstanding hiking and wildflower-viewing destination. Pristine Lake Shikaribetsu is hidden among the mountains, with two quiet hot springs inns. In the winter, when the lake freezes over, an igloo and snow and ice sculptures are built on the lake.

GETTING AROUND

Bus routes traverse the city and the Tokachi area from the central bus terminal, adjacent to Obihiro station. The cheapest long-distance travel is also by bus. The trip from Obihiro to Sapporo is about four hours, and to Kushiro, 2.5 hours. Taxis are readily available downtown or just a phone call away. Train travel is extremely convenient, as Obihiro is located on the main JR line between Sapporo and Kushiro. Each day, a dozen super-express trains take passengers west toward Sapporo and east toward Kushiro and Nemuro (the end of the line). Obihiro Airport is just 30 minutes south of city center, accessible by airport bus from Obihiro bus center next to the train station. Parking is available. You can fly directly from Obihiro to Sapporo and other cities in Hokkaido, as well as to Tokyo (Haneda Airport), Osaka (Kansai), and Nagoya.

Kushiro 釧路

Kushiro (population 181,000) is situated on the eastern Pacific seaboard of Hokkaido. In the 17th century, the Matsumae clan of Hakodate established posts to trade with the Ainu who were living where the city now stands. The first Japanese settlers came in 1870 from northern Honshu and Hakodate. The Port of Kushiro opened in 1899. One of the preeminent fishing grounds is just off the coast and feeds the city's marine food-processing industry. The West Port has an international terminal. Kushiro's paper industry began in the Meiji period and produces newsprint, corrugated paper, and other paper products.

THE LAY OF THE LAND

The sound of foghorns and the smell of fisheries and pulp/paper factories are part of daily life in Kushiro. In the center of the city is a prominent hill—Tsurugadai—with a view of the port, Pacific Ocean, and mountains of Akan National Park. Hokkaido University of Education's Kushiro Campus is located on this hill. The Kushiro Public University of Economics may have possibilities for teaching positions.

Kushiro is the gateway to Kushiro Wetlands National Park, which you can reach

© RUTHY KANAGY

Kushiro is near Akan National Park – a sacred place for native Ainu.

by bus, car, or bicycle via a cycling path. Kushiro Marsh Observatory overlooks the wetlands, which are inhabited by many species, including the once almost extinct *tancho-tsuru* (red-crested crane), found only in eastern Hokkaido and Siberia. Akan National Park is located about 1.5 hours by bus or car north of Kushiro. The park encompasses three volcanoes and three caldera lakes surrounded by relatively untouched wilderness. The inhabitants of an Ainu village called Kotan, on the shore of Akanko (Lake Akan), perform authentic dances and music for visitors and offer many shops with wood carvings and other handcrafts. In January, when Lake Akan freezes over, people set up tents on the ice and bore holes to fish for smelt, which they grill on the spot to enjoy. In the summer, the whole Akan area is a hiker and cyclist paradise. You can join a cycle tour and explore Akan and Shiretoko National Parks in eastern Hokkaido (http://livingabroadinjapan.com/cycling.htm).

Today Kushiro faces the dual challenges of an aging society and a declining birth rate, as does the rest of Japan. Young people continue to leave rural areas for the big-city lights of Sapporo and Tokyo. At the same time, Kushiro citizens are internationally minded and promote exchanges with their sister cities of Burnaby, Canada, and Kholmsk, Russia. The Port of Kushiro has economic links with the ports of Seward, Alaska, and New Orleans, Louisiana. Kushiro Public University is affiliated with Simon Fraser University in Canada, and the city has an official relationship with Kooragang Nature Reserve in Australia (see http://international.city.kushiro.hokkaido.jp).

WHERE TO LIVE

Downtown Kushiro is bordered by the Kushiro River to the west, the Old Kushiro River to the east, and Kushiro Harbor, Fisherman's Wharf, and the Pacific Ocean to the south. Southeast of Kushiro station, across the Nusamai Bridge and the Old Kushiro River, is a bluff called Tsurugadai (Crane Hill) that overlooks the city. Hokkaido Educational University, Kushiro City Hospital, and Tsurugadai Park are in this area. Farther east are the Kushiro City Museum and Lake Harutori, a popular spot for relaxing and strolling. The city expands west to the Tottori district, with shops, residences, and factories—the largest is a paper mill. Farther west are the airport and zoo, and to the north are the Kushiro wetlands and roads leading to Akan National Park. Choosing where to live depends on whether you like to live in the hills, near the sea, near a university, or out in the countryside north and east of the city. City bus service covers all parts of the city. There are 17 hospitals and clinics, nine high schools, and one library.

Compact 1DK rentals range from ¥50,000/$625 to ¥63,000/$788 a month, depending on the age of the building. A 2LDK unit with 58 square meters (625 square feet) in a brand-new building costs ¥70,000/$875 a month with one month's deposit and no landlord fee.

DAILY LIFE

Downtown Kushiro has department stores, bookstores, shops, and restaurants. Supermarkets and convenience stores are distributed throughout the city. On the downtown waterfront is Fisherman's Wharf, with events to attract visitors from Japan and overseas. The morning fish market, called Wasyo, offers just-caught seafood in the form of sushi, sashimi, and other delectable dishes.

GETTING AROUND

The city is served by taxis and local and long-distance buses. JR trains link Kushiro to Obihiro in two hours, and to Sapporo in four hours. Kushiro Airport has flights to Sapporo and Hakodate, which take about an hour. You can be in Tokyo or Osaka in 90 minutes.

Hakodate 函館

Hakodate is the southernmost city in Hokkaido, at the bottom of the "boot." If you're coming by train from Honshu through the undersea tunnel, Hakodate is the gateway to Hokkaido. In the 18th and 19th centuries Hakodate was the northernmost outpost of the shogun's military government. When feudalism ended in 1859, Hakodate was opened as an international trade port, along with Yokohama and Nagasaki.

THE LAY OF THE LAND

As a result of a long tradition of international exchange and cultural contact with many countries, Hakodate (population 279,000) has an "exotic" atmosphere (read: non-Japanese), with buildings in foreign architectural styles and many historic areas. The city has many foreign residents and tourists, who are drawn to Hakodate for its historic Western architecture and for the stunning night view from Mount Hakodate. In recent years, the city of Hakodate has promoted exchanges with its sister cities (Halifax, Canada; Vladivostok, Russia; Lake Macquarie, Australia) and other foreign cities.

Hakodate has three universities—Hakodate University, Hokkaido Education

© RUTHY KANAGY

Onuma Quasi-National Park, north of Hakodate

University Hakodate Campus, and Future University—Hakodate. Future University—Hakodate (FUN) is the youngest, founded in 2000 with a focus on information and communication technologies and the concept of complex systems. A graduate school was added in 2003. Excellent teaching opportunities are available. There is also a private Catholic school, Hakodate LaSalle Junior and Senior High School.

North of Hakodate is the beautiful Onuma Quasi-National Park, with large and small lakes great for cycling and hiking around. The park is dominated by Mount Komagatake (1,131 meters/3,710 feet), which erupts occasionally (as volcanoes tend to do). Fall colors are spectacular. The park is a 50-minute drive from Hakodate and three hours by train from Sapporo.

WHERE TO LIVE

The Hakodate train station is the geographical center of Hakodate city (this is true of most cities in Japan); within walking distance are the bus terminal, city hall, fish market, and numerous department stores and hotels. West Hakodate spreads out on a peninsula jutting into the sea, with Hakodate Port, the waterfront, and a ropeway taking you up Mount Hakodate. There are many historic buildings clustered in the area, including Catholic churches, a Harrist Church, former Russian and British consulates, historical museums, and the foreigners' cemetery. The eastern part of the city features Gorykaku Park and Tower as a backdrop, with the Northern Regions Museum, the Prefectural Art Museum, and *Hokkaido Newspaper* offices in the area. In southeastern Hakodate, you'll find the Yunokawa Hot Springs, the City Cultural and Sports Center, a tropical arboretum, a beach, racetracks, and a nearby Trappist monastery. The choice of where to live is wide open, perhaps influenced by your work location.

Hakodate station

During the stock and real estate bubble economy of the late 1980s and early 1990s, many older buildings were demolished and replaced with condominiums funded by investment capital from Honshu, which has, unfortunately, "uglified" parts of the city.

While you're looking for a place to rent, you can stay at a hotel, *ryokan* (Japanese-style inn), or youth hostel. Hakodate has many facilities, such as a municipal spa, library, city museum, fort museum, historical museum, community center, women's center, northern sea fishery museum, literature museum, art museum, gym, swimming pool, baseball stadium, and track.

Rent for a 2DK (two rooms plus eat-in kitchen) ranges from ¥45,000/$563 per month in older apartment buildings to ¥63,000/$788 in newer buildings. A 2LDK rents for ¥67,000/$840 and up, and a family-size 3LDK (three rooms, living room, and eat-in kitchen) can be rented for around ¥80,000/$1,000. Most locations are served by buses or streetcars. If you're interested in building a house, you can purchase a lot for ¥10 million ($125,000) and up.

DAILY LIFE

Most of your shopping needs can be met in neighborhood supermarkets, convenience stores, and larger department stores in downtown Hakodate. Be sure to check out the Hakodate morning fish market—you can't get any fresher than that. Mount Hakodate is known for its outstanding night view, and historic Gorykaku Park is a popular tourist destination. Special events held by Hakodate citizens include a Winter Festival in February, the Goryokaku Festival in May when *sakura* (cherry trees) are in bloom (one to two months later than Tokyo), and the Port Festival and Yunokawa Spa Fire Festival in August. There is open-air theater from July through August, and a half-marathon in September. Hakodate's symbols are yew trees, azalea flowers, the varied tit bird, and the squid.

GETTING AROUND

Hakodate is easy to get around by bus, streetcar, taxi, or train. Timetables are posted at each bus or streetcar stop. You enter from the rear on most buses and streetcars, and exit from the front. When boarding, take a boarding ticket from the machine and signal your stop by pushing a button. The fare chart at the front of the bus displays the fare. Prepaid cards, one- or two-day passes, and *teiki-ken* (commuter passes) are available for city buses and streetcars. *Takushii* (taxis) can be reserved by phone or flagged down on the street or at taxi stands.

You can buy Japan Railways (JR) tickets at the ticket window, or from the ticket vending machine at the station. JR Hakodate station has a Midori-no-Madoguchi (Green Window) office where you can make reservations a month in advance for train travel. Sapporo is four hours north via special express, and Tokyo is about six hours by special express train and *shinkansen*. Hakodate Airport is a 20-minute bus ride from the city and serves airports in Hokkaido and points south. You can fly from Hakodate to Sapporo's New Chitose Airport in 35 minutes, and to Tokyo (Haneda) in an hour and a quarter, with seven flights daily.

THE CENTRAL MOUNTAINS 中部

If you like clean air, mountains, rushing rivers, and hot springs, the Chubu, or central region of Honshu, could become your *kokoro no furusato* (home of your heart). Gunma- and Nagano-ken (prefecture) are only 100–150 kilometers (62–93 miles) northwest of Tokyo, but a world away in lifestyle. Gunma-ken begins at the northern edge of the broad Kanto plain and continues north to where it hits the Tanigawa Mountains. On the other side are Niigata-ken and the Sea of Japan (or East Sea). Gunma is known as the primary vegetable basket for the Kanto region because of its proximity to the consumer market of Metropolitan Tokyo. As vegetables, arrowroot, and rice flowed south, industry and urbanization have crept north.

Nagano-ken is west of Gunma and often called the "roof of Japan," for good reason—16 of its mountains tower over 3,000 meters (9,842 feet). Nagano's castle towns and temple towns were an important part of the transportation system in the feudal period, when samurai and itinerant priests walked these mountain routes from Kyoto to Edo (now Tokyo). The mountains, which used to be a barrier, have been cut open and overlaid with highways and rails. Today *shinkansen* high-speed trains bore through tunnels, emerging in brief, silver flashes. Tourism and outdoor sports

© HIROTAKA IHARA/123RF.COM

are major industries in the central mountains. Residents and visitors in Gunma and Nagano enjoy superb Alpine and Nordic skiing in the winter and mountain climbing and river rafting in the summer.

Gunma-ken 群馬県

Gunma prefecture is home to two million people living in 11 cities, 33 towns, and 25 villages. The four largest cities—Maebashi, Takasaki, Isesaki, and Ota—all have populations over 200,000. Maebashi, the capital (population 280,000), is situated in the southern plain in a direct line to Metropolitan Tokyo. In the mountainous north, tourism is the main industry, with numerous *onsen* (hot spring) resorts and ski areas. Agriculture is an important part of Gunma's economy. In the past, the primary products were silk, wheat, and rice. Today the region is known for producing the most *konnyaku* (arrow root), cucumbers, and shiitake (mushrooms) in Japan. The cooler climate produces high-quality vegetables, such as cabbage, leeks, and spinach, which are shipped to Tokyo.

Sericulture, or silk production, was Gunma's major industry during the latter half of the 19th century and early 20th century, as was true in neighboring Nagano-ken. As Japan's economy took off in the 1950s, Gunma experienced rapid economic growth based on industry and commerce—so much so that by the mid-1960s revenue from manufacturing surpassed agriculture. Old farmhouses that raised mulberry bushes and silk worms sit empty, and the old way of life is disappearing as young people go south to the cities.

Isesaki and Kiryu cities are the center of traditional textile and clothing-related industries. The manufacture of transport machinery and electronic goods is a major part of Gunma's industry, concentrated in the southeast cities of Oizumi and Ota. A large number of foreign workers, especially Brazilian, have moved to this area to work in factories, due to the shrinking Japanese labor pool. Today 16 percent of Oizumi's population of 41,000 is Brazilian, many of whom are descendants of Japanese immigrants who settled in Brazil a century ago.

THE LAY OF THE LAND

The upper two-thirds of Gunma-ken is mountains. On the western border between Gunma and Nagano-ken is Asamayama (Mount Asama), an active volcano that is 2,500 meters (8,200 feet) high. When Asama erupted in 1783, it spewed forth lava and formed a hardened lava field known as Onioshidashi (Goblin Rocks). The most recent eruption was in 2004.

Directly north of Asamayama is Kusatsu *onsen* hot spring resort, with many traditional *ryokan* (Japanese-style inns). The area is filled with skiers in the winter and hikers in the summer. East of Kusatsu at the northern border of Gunma is Minakami *onsen* hot spring along the Tone River (pronounced "toh-neh"), backed by the majestic Tanigawa Mountains. You can take the easy way up the mountain by ropeway, or join other hardy mountaineers in the summer. In November, the Suwa Gorge is ablaze with red and yellow, and with weekend traffic jams. Tonegawa (Tone River) is one of Japan's three longest rivers at 322 kilometers (200 miles) long. It springs from Mount

rice harvest in Gunma

Ominakami in northeast Gunma and forms the Tonegawa River Basin, which, along with other rivers, forms a huge river basin of 16,840 square kilometers (6,502 square miles), the largest in Japan.

On the northern border of Gunma is a fragile, high elevation marshland called Oze. At 2,000 meters (6,561 feet) above sea level, Oze is filled with rare flora and fauna. In the spring, urbanites crowd the wood-plank paths in Oze to see the vast colony of white and green *mizubasho* (which, oddly enough, are called "skunk cabbage" in English and are unappreciated). Japanese children sing about Oze's blue sky and *mizubasho* flowers in elementary school—*Natsu ga kureba omoidasu, haruka na Oze, tooi sora* . . . (or at least they did when I was in elementary school).

CLIMATE

Southern Gunma's plains have a Pacific climate, with a great deal of rain in summer and less in winter. The average annual temperature is 14°C/57°F. The mountainous north has more precipitation and lots of snow. Frequent thunderstorms in the summer and strong winds in winter are characteristic of the area.

WHERE TO LIVE
Minakami 水上

Minakami, in the northern mountains of Gunma, is a hot springs resort and out-door mecca: rafting and kayaking on Tonegawa (Tone River), climbing or skiing the Tanigawa Mountains. The official population of 22,000 is spread out over a wide area. With a low population density of 29 persons per square kilometer (compared to Tokyo's 13,500 per square kilometer), there's still room for enterprising people who'd

© RUTHY KANAGY

The Tanigawa Mountains in northern Gunma attract hikers, cyclists, and skiers.

like to live in a natural setting. The pace of life is much slower along the Tone River, which rushes by traditional farmhouses and rice and mulberry fields. A *gaijin mura* (foreigners' village) of sorts has sprung up over the years in Tsukiyono area. A few permanent exiles from the urban scene live here year-round, while others come in summer to escape Tokyo's sweltering heat. One enterprising American and his Japanese wife operate a homemade pizza and pasta restaurant in Tsukiyono called Café Manna. If you'd rather be outdoors, there are plenty of places to explore. Minakami has one high school and four junior high schools.

Apartments in this rural area are modest and inexpensive, ranging from ¥39,000/$487 for a 2K to ¥55,000/$687 for a 2LDK with one month's rent as security deposit. As a hot-spring and skiing destination for urban dwellers, high-rise condominiums (many built during the bubble economy of the late 1980s) have one- and two-bedroom units available from ¥500,000/$62,000 and up—handy for your weekend getaway.

Local buses and JR trains serve Minakami and northern Gunma. The Joetsu line of the *shinkansen* goes direct to Tokyo in about two hours, and also takes you north to Niigata on the Sea of Japan coast. To catch the train, take a 20-minute bus ride from Minakami to the Jomokogen station. A less expensive way to travel is to take the *tok-kyu* (limited express) or local train from Minakami to Tokyo, which takes up to three hours. A bicycle is convenient to get around the area, and a mountain bike is great for exploring the mountains.

Takasaki 高崎

Takasaki city (population 371,000) is west of Maebashi, Gunma's capital, and has

© RUTHY KANAGY

Minakami offers an escape for city dwellers.

fine views of Mount Akagi and Mount Haruna to the north and Mount Myogi to the west. Takasaki was a castle town in the Edo period (1603–1868) and is now a center of transportation and commerce. The local Daruma-ji temple is famous as the origin of Daruma dolls, supposedly representing the Buddhist monk Bodhidharma, who sat in meditation for nine years. The round, red dolls with white circles for eyes are bought for good luck: Make a wish and paint in one eye black. When your wish comes true, fill in the other eye. Huge Daruma dolls are used during election campaigns by politicians, who make a big show of filling in the eye if they win the election. Takasaki has a number of universities with teaching possibilities, including Takasaki University of Commerce, Takasaki University of Health and Welfare, and Takasaki City University of Economics. Takasaki is a sister city to Battle Creek, Michigan.

Housing prices are quite reasonable. A 1DK (one room plus eat-in kitchen) apartment in Takasaki city starts at ¥30,000/$375 per month (if you can live in 300 square feet), and a 2DK rents from ¥40,000/$500 and up. They typically require two months' equivalent deposit to move in. A spacious 3LDK (83 square meters/895 square feet) in a four-year-old *manshon* rents for ¥87,000/$1,088 a month. One month's equivalent deposit along with the landlord's fee gets you in. Stop by any of the realtors near Takasaki station to see properties, or search online.

Takasaki station is at the junction of several railways, including the Joetsu *shinkansen,* which takes you south to Tokyo in just one hour. The west-bound *shinkansen* passes through Karuizawa highland resort and turns north to the capital city of Nagano. An airport limousine bus from Takasaki and Maebashi will take you to Narita or Haneda Airport in about 3.5 hours.

For complete cycling information for this region, visit Cycletech-IKD (tel. 027/324-2360, www.ikd21.co.jp/ikd/about/access.html), where you can test-ride bikes and talk to bike shop manager Mr. Yoshida "man." He has cycled all over Japan (as well as Nepal and Ireland). He can tell you how to travel with your bike on local trains and where the best sake breweries are located.

Ota 太田

Would you like to teach at a total immersion English school? Ota (population 213,000) is an industrial city in eastern Gunma where the enterprising mayor established a new type of school in 2005. At Gunma Kokusai Academy, native speakers teach most subjects in English. The mayor was convinced that not being able to communicate

MOZAEMON, PEASANT OF TSUKIYONO

Probably the most famous person to come out of Tsukiyono in northern Gunma prefecture was Mozaemon. He was a wealthy 19th-century peasant and village leader who went to Edo (now Tokyo) to protest to the shogun about excessive taxes in his area. Despite crop failures and near-famine conditions, Sanada, the lord of Numata Castle, insisted on taxing the rice crop as if it were a bumper year. Mozaemon knew it meant death to be insubordinate and to break the law forbidding peasants from leaving their home district, and he ended up being crucified. However, the shogun heard his complaint, deposed the Sanada clan, and tore down Numata Castle. Mozaemon's spirit is revered at a large shrine near Gokan station.

in English (i.e., learning English grammar and translation skills just to pass entrance exams) is a handicap. The school receives many applications from Japanese parents, eager for their children to get ahead by acquiring a black belt in English. Northern Ota city is mostly agricultural, with rice as the main crop. Subaru has a large manufacturing plant here. The Aeon Ota Shopping Center in the northwestern part of the city is the largest shopping center in the region. One of the famous local sites is Kanayama Castle, which was built in the Kamakura era (1185–1333) on top of Mount Kanayama, north of the downtown.

Brand-new 1K apartments five minutes from the train station are available for ¥45,000/$563 a month (with an equivalent amount as security deposit and as landlord's fee). Farther out from the station, a 3DK in an older apartment building rents for ¥41,000/$513 a month (with a security deposit equal to two months' rent), while a roomy 2LDK in a 30-year-old *manshon* rents for ¥47,000/$587 a month with a small pet allowed.

Ota station is a major hub of the private Tobu Railway, and also a stop on the JR Ryomo line. Ota is an hour southeast of Takasaki and an hour and 20 minutes north of Tokyo by express train on the Ryomo line. The Kita-Kanto expressway interchange is also nearby.

Nagano-ken 長野県

Nagano is the name of the prefecture, or *ken,* and also the name of the capital, Nagano-shi (city). The prefecture is the fourth largest in area in Japan, and has a population of 2.2 million. Of this number, some 43,000 are foreign residents. The largest groups come from Brazil, China, Korea, Philippines, and Thailand. Many Westerners call this region home, drawn by the fabulous scenery and outdoor sports.

Tourism is actively promoted, and close to one million tourists visit Nagano each year. Three of their favorite destinations are Karuizawa, a highland resort in the east; the capital of Nagano in the north; and the castle town of Matsumoto in the center. Nagano welcomes tourists, offering old-fashioned hospitality at thousands of Japanese-style inns.

Nagano's history is closely tied to the rise and fall of the silk industry. Before World War II, most farmers were engaged in raising silkworms and the mulberry plants they ate. Both silkworms and mulberry leaves were prone to disease and damage by the weather, thus affecting the fortunes of silkworm farmers from year to year. The silk-reeling industry peaked in the 1920s, but due to the depression that began in 1929, the silk industry collapsed and farmers were hard hit. The silk industry also floundered because of poor working conditions, wages, and living conditions for factory girls, who were little more than indentured slaves. Today the main industry besides agriculture is the manufacture of computer-related electric machinery.

THE LAY OF THE LAND

Nagano-ken (prefecture) is in the Chubu (central) region of Honshu, the main island, surrounded by eight other prefectures—Gunma, Saitama, Yamanashi, Shizuoka, Aichi, Gifu, Toyama, and Niigata. A whopping 78 percent of Nagano's land area is forested, and 21 percent is designated as natural parkland. The mountains here are majestic. The four tallest peaks—Okuhodaka, Yarigatake, Akaishi, and Kitahodaka—are all higher than 3,100 meters (10,000 feet). Nagano boasts that its primary resource is snow. The deepest snow recorded at a municipal office in Nagano was almost 4.5 meters (14.5 feet). Nagano built the first ski lift in Japan in 1946 and manufactured the first snowplow in 1896. The city was also the first to build a *kemonomichi* (underpass) in 1923 to allow wild animals to pass under the road safely. The prefectural bird is the ptarmigan, its flower the gentian, its animal the Japanese serow (slightly smaller than a goat), and its tree, white birch. The longest river is Shinano (or Chikuma) River, which is 367 kilometers (228 miles long).

CLIMATE

Nagano-ken is situated in the center of Honshu and is one of only eight prefectures in Japan that do not border the sea. The interior location and high elevation result in summers that are exceedingly refreshing (like Hokkaido), and cold winters with lots of sunshine. Nagano city, the capital, has an average annual temperature of 12°C/54°F, with the hottest days up to 36°C/97°F and coldest winter days around -12°C/10°F. Karuizawa to the east is a bit cooler, with an average yearly temperature of 8°C/46°F. Summer highs are up to 32°C/90°F, and the winter lows are -18°C/0°F.

Nagano and Matsumoto have an annual precipitation of 93 centimeters (37 inches), while Karuizawa gets nearly 160 centimeters (63 inches) of rain. Matsumoto is the third sunniest city in Japan, with an average annual temperature of 12°C/54°F. Summers can get up to 36°C/97°F. Winter temperatures can reach down to -12°C/10°F. The rainy season lasts mid-June–mid-July, with the highest rainfall in July.

WHERE TO LIVE
Nagano City 長野市

The Nagano-shi, capital of Nagano-ken, has a population of 381,000. It is surrounded by the mountains of Joshinetsu National Park and Zenkoji Plain, at the confluence of the Chikuma and Sai Rivers. The city grew up around Zenkoji Temple and is rich in historical and cultural assets. In the same region are numerous castle towns from the feudal period, such as Suzaka, filled with old storehouses; Koshoku, known as Apricot Country; Obuse, known for Japanese chestnuts; and Hokusai, birthplace of the famous *ukiyo-e* (wood-block print) artist by the same name. The main industries include electrical and general machinery, food, and printing, along with agriculture and forestry. The 1998 Olympic Winter Games were held here, triggering international

LEARNING TO LIVE WITH CULTURAL AMBIGUITIES

David Gracon taught English in Kanazawa for two years. He had previously taught English in Poland and traveled to Russia and England.

What was the impetus for moving to Japan?

I wanted to immerse myself in another culture and gain international experience, and you can't get that kind of experience merely from traveling. I was interested in Japanese cinema (Ozu and Kurosawa), literature (Kawabata, Murakami), and Eastern philosophical thought. My friend recommended the Japan Exchange and Teaching Program (JET), sponsored by the Japanese government. I thought this would be an enriching experience to have before doing my doctoral studies.

How did you find a job and get a visa?

I filled out an online application for the JET program. The application was lengthy, and I was interviewed by three people at the same time—so it's an in-depth process. Once accepted, I filled out some paperwork, and JET took care of the rest, in terms of the visa.

How did your work in Japan differ from working in the United States?

There was much emphasis on group dynamics. People work hard, are dedicated, and take their job very seriously. I felt the need to conform to Japanese standards; i.e., wear nice clothes, be punctual, work with a team. I "team taught" English with 18 different teachers at two junior high schools and various elementary schools. It took me a full year to understand the system, know how to teach to the students' level, and get used to each teacher's style and personality. It was a lot more challenging than I expected and at times isolating, because you're the only native English speaker at the school.

I didn't eat school lunches because I'm vegetarian. I brought my own lunches but felt I should eat the same thing as others. If you're vegetarian, come up with some explanation other than a moral one, like you have an allergy—that is accepted. The pluses were that I experienced a wildly different culture, gained confidence as a teacher, impacted students, met friends from around the world, was paid well, and got to travel around Asia and Australia.

Was it easy to make friends?

I would say it's more difficult to make friends in Japan, at least on a deep and emotional level. I think Japanese people take more time to let others into their personal world. The meaning of friendship is different. Once friends, they really go out of their way for you. Their selflessness was at times unbelievable. Friendships take a long time to nurture and don't just happen.

What was it like coming back to the United States?

I went through reverse culture shock, definitely. My English had become much slower and I had developed some Japanese mannerisms (I still say "un, un" during conversations). My whole conception and appreciation of food had radically changed, which has become much healthier. Your friends and family will be excited to hear about Japan for about a week, and then it gets old for them, which can be isolating. I actively sought out people who had experienced Japan, or were Japanese. I had developed more organizational skills, and felt the need to be more productive, as the Japanese were such movers and shakers. I also thought more about maintaining harmony, especially at work, which gave me much respect, as opposed to being confrontational. I understood race relations in the United States more because I had been a minority for two years—thus, I have more empathy for minorities and social inequalities. It took me about a year until I felt "Americanized" again. I no longer was a novelty, and I missed people being really polite, selfless, and going above and beyond for me in very kind ways.

cultural and sports exchanges with cities around the world. The International Exchange Corner (IEC) of Nagano city provides support for foreign residents and offers Internet, a library, and Japanese-language classes.

You can rent a studio or one room plus kitchen for ¥42,000/$525 to ¥57,000/$713 a month, depending on the age of the building, or a new 2LDK apartment for ¥54,000/$675 (one month's deposit required). A new 3LDK house is available for ¥96,000/$1,200 with a roomy 93 square meters/1,000 square feet. Be prepared to hand over two months' rent equivalent as a deposit and another two months' rent to thank the landlord. Public housing is also available for residents who qualify. Contact the Nagano Prefecture Housing Management Public Corporation or Residential Housing Section, City Hall.

There is good bus service, and taxis are available. From Nagano to Tokyo takes just one hour and 40 minutes by *shinkansen* Asama. The Hokuriku *shinkansen* line and Hokuriku Expressway were completed just before the Nagano Winter Olympics in 1998.

Karuizawa 軽井沢

Karuizawa is the eastern gateway to Nagano-ken. It is located between Mount Asama, an active volcano that erupts frequently (most recently in 2004) and Mount Yatsugatake in the south. The town was originally a summer retreat for foreign missionaries. An English missionary, A. C. Shaw, helped develop Karuizawa as a summer resort beginning in 1886. Today it has grown into an international health and tourist resort with a lush green environment. Resort owners and town residents share a desire to preserve the culture in a setting where low buildings blend into the landscape. The imperial family summered in Karuizawa for many years, and the present Heisei emperor and empress met here in the 1950s, playing tennis. The town is surrounded by farms raising highland cabbage, lettuce, and other crops. Karuizawa holds a "Young Leaves" festival in the spring, with horseback riding, as well as an international women's tennis tournament. There are grand fireworks in the summer, a festival of fall colors, and ice sculpting and international curling in the winter. Karuizawa is the nearest mountain getaway for millions of city-dwellers who come to enjoy golf, tennis, hiking, camping, skiing, and hot springs.

Karuizawa's highland resort environment is an important asset. There is always a high demand for condominiums and other types of housing. To keep the skyline unblemished, the government of Nagano decreed that new condominiums cannot be higher than two stories, and a single complex can't have more than 20 units. Studios with 260 square feet of space cost about ¥55,000/$687 a month, and a 2DK (two rooms plus eat-in kitchen) goes for ¥62,000/$775 and up, with a one-month equivalent deposit to move in. Need more space? You can rent a 4LDK house for ¥120,000/$1,500 a month plus two months' equivalent deposit and two months' rent as landlord's fee. If you're interested in owning a property, a newer 3LDK log house can be yours for ¥33 million/$412,000 on a 3,000-square-foot lot.

Most residents and visitors to Karuizawa get around by car. But the traffic can be horrendous on weekends, when Tokyoites invade the peaceful town. A bicycle is a faster and better way to get around because the town is small enough to navigate easily. Bus service is available. The Kanetsu Expressway links Karuizawa to Tokyo, a distance of 142 kilometers (88 miles); how long it takes depends on traffic conditions. The only train service is the *shinkansen,* which speeds you to Tokyo in 70 minutes for a $50 one-way ticket (on weekends you might have to stand up the whole way). The *shinkansen* replaced the old Shinano Railway, which used to run to Karuizawa. The only cheaper travel option is an infrequent bus.

Matsumoto 松本

The city of Matsumoto, situated at the center of Honshu, is a picturesque castle town with a striking backdrop of snowcapped mountains. The Northern Japan Alps, Utsukushigahara Highlands, Kamikochi, and Norikura Highlands offer year-round outdoor recreation. The Kamikochi resort is a pristine wilderness that is open only mid-April–mid-November, with no cars allowed to enter. In the late 1800s, an English missionary named Walter Weston introduced Western-style mountain climbing in the Kamikochi Highlands and named the mountains the "Japanese Alps."

Matsumoto city maintains a balance between modern life and preserving historical traditions. Matsumoto has flourished as a castle town since the 16th century and was the capital of the region known as Shinano, or Shinshu. The striking, five-story Matsumotojo castle tower was built in 1592. In those days, samurai warriors traveled the Nakasendo Highway, a winding, interior route through the mountains from Kyoto to Edo (Tokyo).

The city is home to 243,000 residents, who enjoy galleries, museums, hot springs, historical sites, and clean air. About 4,500 registered foreign residents from 51 countries live in Matsumoto. They include an owner of an English school, teachers, and translators. A group of foreigners and Japanese launched the Matsumoto Welcome Project, an English website and blog about life in Matsumoto (http://welcome.city.matsumoto.nagano.jp). Major industries include precision and agricultural machinery, furniture,

With the Japanese Alps as a backdrop, Matsumoto is an attractive city for living.

food, medical supplies, and tourism. A wide variety of fruits and vegetables is produced, including apples, grapes, watermelons, tomatoes, rice, and Japanese horseradish. The region's soba (buckwheat) noodles and apples are famous throughout Japan. Matsumoto is the home of Shinshu University and the Talent Education Research Institute, better known for the Suzuki music method. Matsumoto has sister-city relationships with Salt Lake City and Katmandu.

Housing in the city and surrounding towns is available at low cost compared to urban areas. You can rent a studio with a loft in a newer *manshon* (reinforced concrete condo) for as little as ¥25,000/$313 per month, with one month's equivalent deposit and landlord's fee. A 2LDK (two rooms plus living/dining/kitchen) in an older, wood-frame building runs ¥50,000/$635 and up with about 55 square meters (590 square feet) of space. A three-bedroom house rents for as low as ¥68,000/$850 a month with a two-month security deposit. Public housing is available for residents of Nagano-ken, including foreign residents. Foreign residents must have resided in Japan for one year or longer, or have a status of residence of one year or longer, or have permanent resident status. In addition, they must live or work in Nagano-ken, earn a low income, and need housing. There is also public housing managed by cities and towns—apply at the local municipal office.

To get around Matsumoto you can ride the local bus, catch a taxi, or hop on one of the free bicycles scattered about town. Velocycles and rickshaws are available during tourist season. For help with bus routes and schedules, stop by the tourist office inside the train station. From Matsumoto, the JR Chuo line express trains (Azuza or Super-Azusa) speed you southwest to Nagoya and east to Tokyo in about 2.5 hours. The Shinonoi line trains take you to Nagano city. To get to Kamikochi resort, you can take the Matsumoto Electric Railway to Shin-shimashima and then transfer to a bus (cars are banned from the pristine highlands). If you're in a hurry, head to Matsumoto airport. You can fly to Osaka (Itami Airport) in an hour or catch a flight to Sapporo or Fukuoka. Matsumoto Airport, at 660 meters (2,165 feet) above sea level, is the highest airport in Japan. Three expressways—the Chuo, Nagano, and Joshinetsu—provide easy access to Nagano prefecture by car, provided there's no one else on the road.

KANSAI 関西

Kyoto, Osaka, and Kobe are three major cities in the Kansai area of west-central Honshu. The Kansai region includes six *ken,* or prefectures: Osaka, Hyogo, Kyoto, Nara, Wakayama, and Shiga. People in Kansai are pegged as having several distinct characteristics, such as a love of new things and being practical-minded and impulsive. Osakans don't beat around the bush; they say what they think. Osaka is a bustling port city of commerce and pleasure, while Kyoto has a gentler pace with a coexistence of modern and traditional architecture. The local dialect, called Kansai-ben, has a distinct flow and intonation, but is not so different from "standard" Japanese that you can't understand it.

Kyoto was the imperial capital for 1,000 years and is a living museum of ancient culture, religion, arts, literature, and architecture (as well as modern, not-so-beautiful concrete buildings). On broad and narrow streets between timeless temples, shrines, imposing palaces, and gardens, modern Kyoto goes about daily life. A mix of office workers, tourists, and uniformed students thread their way between banks, department stores, teahouses, and construction zones, while consumers fill the boutiques, restaurants, and coffee shops.

A point worth noting, if you're choosing a place to live, is that Kansai has a high population of foreign residents. About 460,000 foreign residents in Japan live here,

© RUTHY KANAGY

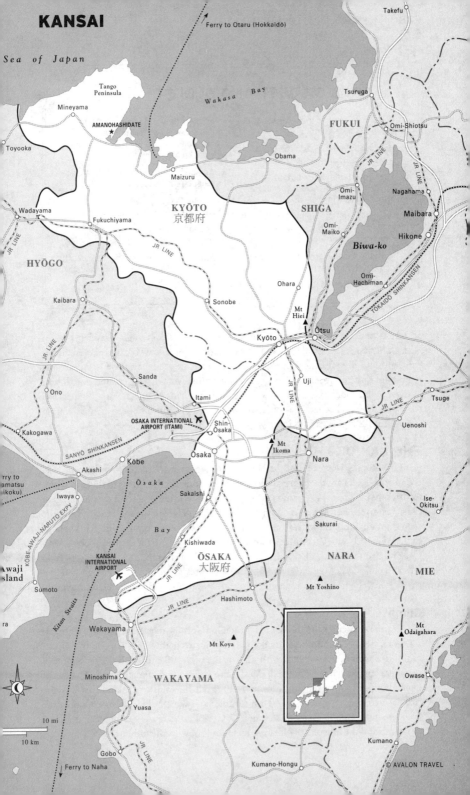

KANSAI'S BIGGEST AND OLDEST

- Daisenryo Kofun is the largest burial mound in the world.
- Horyu-ji's Golden Hall is the oldest wooden structure in the world.
- The Great Buddha (Daibutsu) at Todai-ji temple in Nara is the largest bronze statue in the world.
- The Main Hall of Todai-ji temple in Nara is the largest wooden structure in the world.
- Lake Biwa is the largest lake in Japan and the third oldest lake in the world.
- Izumo no Okuni founded Kabuki in Kyoto.
- Kongo Gumi is the world's oldest continuously operating business and constructed several of Japan's cultural assets.
- Amanohashidate is one of the three most beautiful views in Japan.
- Sen no Rikyu, a merchant from Osaka, perfected the tea ceremony.
- Japan's tallest pagoda is at To-ji temple in Kyoto.
- Nintendo became the most successful company in the video game industry.

or almost one out of four. As much as 93 percent of Osaka's foreign residents are of Korean heritage; i.e., third- and fourth-generation Koreans who came or were forcefully brought over during Japan's occupation of Korea. The city of Osaka and the region are quite active in promoting human rights, women's rights, and equality in housing, education, and jobs. This consciousness seems to operate at a higher level than in Tokyo and other areas of Japan, which is a plus for foreigners contemplating a move to this region of the country.

THE LAY OF THE LAND

Kansai occupies 11 percent of the land area of Japan, with about 24 million people. Kyoto and Osaka are the names of the two cities, and also the names of the urban prefectures. Kyoto-fu (the prefecture) is long and narrow, extending from the Sea of Japan (East Sea) to the north, over mountains to Osaka and Nara in the south. Kyoto-shi (the city) is in the Kyoto Basin, surrounded on three sides by mountains with Kinki plains to the south. Osaka-fu (the prefecture) is southwest of Kyoto on the Kinki plain, with Osaka Bay on the west. Osaka-shi (city) is centered on the mouth of Yodogawa (Yodo River) facing Osaka Bay. Mie and Shiga prefectures are to the east, Hyogo-ken and the city of Kobe lie to the west, and Nara and Wakayama prefectures are to the south.

Climate

The bay makes winters in Osaka milder than in Kyoto, with average January temperatures of 5.8°C/42°F. Summers are hot and humid, averaging 28.4°C/83°F in August. Humidity is high year-round, with an average of 1,300 millimeters (51 inches) of precipitation. The Tamba range divides Kyoto-fu into two climate zones: The Sea of Japan dumps moisture onto the northern half, while the southern, inland area of Kyoto city has extreme temperatures in both summer and winter. The average temperature in Kyoto-fu is 4°C/39°F in January and 27°C/81°F in August. Yearly precipitation is around 1,660 millimeters (65 inches), including snow in the mountains.

© RUTHY KANAGY

the Yodo River in Osaka

Osaka 大阪

The city of Osaka has 2.6 million residents and a population density of 11,800 people per square kilometer (second to Tokyo). The daytime population swells by an additional one million commuters who come to work.

THE LAY OF THE LAND

Osaka is known as a city of commerce, culture, international sports, and history—an environmentally advanced economic and industrial center. Osaka is home to a World Trade Center, Osaka Business and Investment Center, and Osaka Business Partner City. Science industries are concentrated in northern Osaka. More than 123 foreign firms have headquarters in Osaka. The city offers a number of investment incentives to foreign-affiliated firms, such as a business establishment promotion subsidy, office rent subsidy, and tax incentives that reduce Osaka's prefectural corporate business tax.

Osaka's comprehensive plan for the 21st century includes becoming a "City of International Cultural Exchange." To this end, the city aims to create an environment where Japanese and non-Japanese residents can live together in harmony. Osaka has many minorities, the largest group being resident Koreans. There are 121,000 registered foreign residents, or almost 5 percent of the city's total population. Many universities, with potential teaching positions, are located in the Osaka area—Osaka University, Kansai University, Osaka University of Economics, Osaka University of Arts, and Osaka University of Education, to name a few. Osaka International School is an English-language-based, pre-K–12, coeducational college-prep school, and

MADE IN OSAKA

Osaka has been a center of commerce for 1,400 years. It's said that a typical greeting is *"Mokari makka?"* or *"Making any dough?"* Osakans are known for their love of new things, their practical minds, and impulsive nature—all qualities that have shaped their enterprising spirit. These innovative products all came from Osaka:

- Chicken Ramen—the world's first instant noodles, by Nissin Foods
- Prefabricated housing
- Moving walkway—at Hankyu Umeda station

- Automatic ticket machines—at Hankyu line stations
- Automatic teller machines
- Automated ticket gate machines at railway stations
- Cup Noodles—the world's first ramen in a cup, by Nissin Foods
- Karaoke
- Home video game console—by Family Computer (Fami-Con)
- Breadmaker

Tezukayama Montessori International School offers instruction in English for children from age 18 months through age six.

WHERE TO LIVE

To begin your housing search, you can go through a real estate agent, look through housing information magazines or online (in Japanese), check postings outside realtors' offices, and search the classifieds of *Kansai Scene* online. The Osaka Municipal Housing Information Center provides information in English, Chinese, and Korean. Rental costs depend on the distance from train or subway, age of the building (anything over 10 years is considered old), and whether it's a wood frame or reinforced concrete structure.

In older buildings, a 1DK (one room plus eat-in kitchen) can be as low as ¥55,000/$688 plus a maintenance fee of ¥10,000/$125 per month for 35 square meters (375 square feet) of space. A ¥150,000/$1,875 landlord's fee is required to move in. Older 2DK units are typically ¥75,000/$938 and up for 45 square meters (484 square feet). A 2LDK (two rooms plus living room and eat-in kitchen) near Osaka harbor is available for ¥80,000/$1,000, while a similar size apartment in a newer building downtown is ¥160,000/$2,000—both require a landlord's fee equivalent to one to three months' rent.

A centrally located 2LDK unit in Shinsaibashi rents for ¥150,000/$1,875 per month. With 60 square meters (about 645 square feet), it is suitable for a family or shared with roommates. It's offered by a company that works directly with owners, so there's no agency fee, no landlord's fee, and a guarantor is not needed. A short-term lease is available (see AB Housing Osaka).

DAILY LIFE

Osaka Castle, the premier symbol of the city's heritage, is located inside a large park popular for sports, walking, and learning about history. The main tower of the castle contains a historical museum. Near the castle are the Osaka City Museum,

Nishinomaru Garden, and Osaka Business Park. There are many shopping areas and department stores around the JR Osaka, Hankyu, and Hanshin Umeda stations, including underground shopping. The neighborhood surrounding Tennoji Temple in the northeast contains both old and new Osaka, with lots of greenery. Shitennoji temple was built in the 6th century. At the end of January, the Osaka International Women's Marathon is held at Nagai Park.

Osaka is also known as the gourmet capital of Japan, and Dotonbori is the place to find it. Osakans have an expression, *kuidaore,* which means "eat till you drop." You'll find *okonomiyaki* (a sort of Japanese-style pizza), *takoyaki* (grilled round octopus balls), *kushiage* (skewered portions of meat, seafood, and vegetables to dip in batter and deep-fry at the table), and much more.

Osaka is the home of Bunraku, traditional puppet theater developed in the 17th century. The puppets are very expressive, two-thirds life-size, each manipulated by three puppeteers dressed in black. Historical tales and domestic dramas are narrated by a singer and accompanied by *shamisen* (three-stringed lute). Many Japanese have never seen a Bunraku performance, but you can. Osaka has many museums, including the Municipal Museum of Art; Museums of Oriental Ceramics, History, Natural History, and Liberty; a Science Museum; and Osaka International Peace Center.

GETTING AROUND

Osaka has city-operated subways and buses. The subway connects the city center and many outlying cities. Seven subway lines and one new tramline provide a fast, easy way to get around. Each line is color-coded and operates 5 A.M.–midnight. For details, visit the Osaka Municipal Transportation Bureau's website.

In addition, there are private and public JR trains, airport transportation, and taxis. A JR loop line goes around the city, with access to major terminals. JR trains for Kyoto and Kobe depart from Osaka station, while *shinkansen* depart from Shin-Osaka (New Osaka) station. If you're headed to KIX (Kansai International Airport) on JR, depart from Namba station.

Private railways offer service to some of the same places as JR. Hankyu Railways has service to Kyoto and Kobe, and Hanshin Railways goes to Kobe and Himeji further west. You can also ride the Keihan line to Kyoto and the Nankai line to Kansai International Airport. Kintetsu goes to Nara and destinations farther east. In short, public transportation is intense and thorough. Get a good transportation book or map.

Kyoto 京都

About 2.6 million people live in Kyoto prefecture, many concentrated in the city of Kyoto, which borders Osaka. Kyoto city (population 1.47 million) was the capital of Japan for 1,000 years, from the start of the Heian court in A.D. 794 until the end of the Tokugawa era in 1868, when the emperor and the capital moved east to Tokyo. Kyoto-fu (the prefecture) produces computer and electronic equipment, transportation, beverages, food, tobacco, and general machinery. Brand names originating in Kyoto include Kyocera (short for Kyoto Ceramics), Omron, and Wacoal. Traditional industries that are still going strong are *nishijin-ori,* a 1,200-year-old technique for

© RUTHY KANAGY

Many commuters in Osaka and Kyoto take the subway to work or university.

weaving kimono cloth; *yuzen* silk dying; *tango chirimen* (silk crêpe); and *kiyomizu-yaki,* or Kiyomizu pottery.

Kyoto has long fostered international gatherings, from the 7th and 8th centuries, when they actively welcomed Chinese and Korean people and cultures, to hosting important conventions critical to the world today. In 1997, the Third Session of the Conference of the Parties to the United Nations Framework Convention on Climate Change, better known as the Kyoto Global Warming Conference, took place in the city. Kansai Science City and its world-class research institutions have a strong international focus.

THE LAY OF THE LAND

Kyoto's streets were modeled after the T'ang dynasty capital of Chang-An (Xian) in China, with wide main boulevards laid out in a grid. East to west avenues are numbered, starting with Ichi-jo (1st) in the north, then Ni-jo (2nd), San-jo (3rd), and so on. Kyoto station and the *shinkansen* trains are located on Hachi-jo (8th Avenue). Three of the main north–south streets are Kawaramachi-dori, Karasuma-dori, and Horikawa-dori.

The city is further divided into 11 *ku* (city wards): Kita-ku (north), Ukyo-ku (west), Sakyo-ku (northeast), Kamigyo-ku (north-central), Nakagyo-ku (central), Shimogyo-ku (south-central), Higashiyama-ku (eastern hills), Yamashina-ku (southeast), Nishigyo-ku (west), Minami-ku (south), and Fushimi-ku (Fushimi district). Kyoto's ancient temples, gardens, and shrines were spared from the firebombs of World War II (by the United States) because of its ancient world heritage.

With six national and public universities and 19 private universities, Kyoto-fu (prefecture) has many teaching opportunities. There are more universities here per person than in any other prefecture. A total of 140,000 Japanese and foreign students study at Kyoto University, Kyoto Institute of Technology, Doshisha University, Ritsumeikan University, and many other universities. Kyoto University has a strong engineering program, and the Faculty of Sciences produced a Nobel Prize winner. There are also several research-oriented technical and polytechnic colleges.

WHERE TO LIVE

In Kyoto, as in other cities, housing prices rise as you move from the outskirts to the center. For example, a 1SK unit (studio plus loft and tiny kitchen) in Kita-ku (northern Kyoto) rents for ¥50,000/$625 per month plus security deposit of ¥50,000/$625 and landlord fee or *reikin* of ¥50,000/$625 with a two-year lease. Floor space is a compact 20 square meters/215 square feet. A brand-new central Kyoto 1LDK *manshon* six minutes' walk from Shijo station rents for ¥160,000/$2,000 per month. Add ¥150,000/$1,875 security deposit and another ¥200,000/$2,500 for the landlord and your total move-in cost is ¥510,000/$6,375 for 65 square meters (700 square feet) of living space. If you're looking for something more affordable, an older 2DK apartment in Fushimi in southern Kyoto lists for ¥64,000/$800 per month, with ¥88,000/$1,100 security deposit and ¥63,000/$788 landlord fee, plus ¥6,000/$75 maintenance fee per month.

Need space for a family? An older two-story townhouse (3LDK) in northeast Kita-Oji is ¥140,000/$1,759 per month with 78 square meters (840 square feet). The deposit and landlord's fee are ¥200,000/$2,500 each with a two-year lease. Free parking space is available. As in other cities, most rentals require a two-year rental lease, but there is usually no penalty for moving out early, as long as you give 30 days' notice. When the two years are up, you pay a month's rent to renew for another two years, and it's likely that the landlord will raise the monthly rent.

© RUTHY KANAGY

Buddhist deity in repose

PRIME LIVING LOCATIONS

Public housing is another option, if you meet the conditions. For information, contact the Housing Division of the Department of Public Works and Construction. One final tip: Sometimes you can rent old, traditional-style houses that the owners no longer live in but don't want to sell. They may cost as little as $650 per month to rent, but may require an equal amount to heat in winter. If you've always wanted to live in an authentic house, it's worth asking a real estate agent about such properties.

DAILY LIFE

Kyoto has thousand-year-old festivals, an international community, and many good universities for teaching or studying. Ni-jo (2nd Avenue) is the location of the former shogun's castle and also Kyoto International School. Shi-jo (4th Avenue) is the business and shopping hub, with numerous department stores and restaurants. Karasuma-dori (*dori* means "street") extends north from Kyoto station to the Imperial Palace. The Kamo River, which flows through the city from north to south, has walking and cycling paths. Nearby is Pontocho's eateries and nightspots.

Kyoto station is on Hachi-jo (8th Avenue). On the 3rd floor of the station in the Kyoto Tower Book Center you can pick up the latest issues of *Kansai Time Out* and *Kyoto Journal,* both excellent resources for foreign residents. The Tourist Information Office on the east side of the Kyoto Tower building, opposite the Karasuma exit, has maps, visitor guides, and free Internet. Another resource is the Kyoto City International Foundation, with extensive housing, study abroad, and job information. It's near the Keage station of the Tozai subway line and across from Nanzenji temple (closed Mondays). Ask for their *Easy Living in Kyoto* guide. Medical services include Japan Baptist Hospital in Sakyo-ku, Kyoto City Clinic for Emergency Illness, and East-West Psychotherapy Service, sensitive to the needs of foreign residents.

GETTING AROUND

The best way to shop in Kyoto is via bicycle or public transportation. There is abundant information in English on how to get around, both on the Internet and in print. There is an extensive network of buses and two subway lines. The Karasuma subway line goes from Takeda, south of Kyoto station, north to Kokusaikaikan (Kyoto International Conference Hall) in the northeastern part of the city. The Tozai (east–west) line runs from Ni-jo (2nd Avenue) in the west to Daigo in the east.

Many local trains and streetcars crisscross the city and prefecture. Kintetsu Railway serves Kyoto and Nara, while the Keihan Railway starts from northeast Kyoto and goes to Osaka and other areas. Hankyu Railway goes from central Kyoto southwest to Umeda in Osaka, with a branch line to Katsura and Arashiyama areas in northwest Kyoto. Another way to go to the northwest hills is by *keifuku dentesu* (electric streetcar) from Shi-jo Omiya (at the intersection of 4th and Omiya Streets). Confusing? Perhaps at the beginning, but take your time and have an adventure. You can pick up English maps at the station, or check out the Kyoto Municipal Transportation Bureau's Kyoto City Bus and Subway Guide online. A Kansai Thru Pass is valid on subways, private railways, and buses in Kyoto, Nara, Osaka, Kobe, and Wakayama for two or three days. Passes may be purchased at train stations in any of the cities.

The most efficient (albeit expensive) way to arrive in Kyoto is by *shinkansen. Nozomi,* the fastest type, whisks you from Tokyo to Kyoto in 2.5 hours. The *hikari* takes slightly longer, and *kodama* takes about four hours from Tokyo. The latter two trains travel almost as fast but make more stops. Long-distance buses cost about half as much as *shinkansen* and often involve an overnight journey. To get from Osaka to Kyoto, the Hankyu or Keihan Railway is your best bet; trains operate every 15 minutes, take 40 minutes, and cost less than the *shinkansen*.

Two airports serve the Kansai area. Kansai International Airport (KIX) is on an island in Osaka Bay, an hour from Osaka. Itami (Osaka International Airport) is farther north and a bit closer to Kyoto. The JR Haruka train has direct service from Kyoto station to KIX in just under 1.5 hours. Two expressways cross Kyoto-fu: The Meishin runs east–west through Kyoto city and southern Kyoto-fu; the Kyoto expressway runs north–south through the prefecture. Maizuru Port is a major port on the Sea of Japan, which handles domestic shipping and foreign trade. You can take a ferry from Maizuru to Otaru in Hokkaido—an inexpensive and adventurous way to travel (and your bicycle can travel with you).

PRIME LIVING LOCATIONS

SETO INLAND SEA
瀬戸内海

Imagine that you've boarded the *shinkansen* ("bullet train") in Osaka. As you travel west through Kobe, skyscrapers are gradually replaced by traditional architecture and more open space. Houses with blue-tiled roofs are interspersed with fields. As the train pauses in Himeji, you can see Himeji Castle—the most beautifully preserved feudal castle in Japan and well worth a stop. You'll pass the town of Bizen, center of Bizen pottery, and Okayama, capital of Okayama prefecture. Farther west is Kurashiki, a well-preserved example of a feudal town, with canals, willow trees, and old storehouses. Then you'll cross into Hiroshima prefecture and arrive at historic Onomichi on Setonaikai—the Seto Inland Sea.

The Seto Inland Sea, known for oyster cultivation, is dotted with islands glistening in the sun. Here, you can continue west to Hiroshima city, or make a left turn (south) and cross the sea (by bus or bicycle) via the Shimanami Kaido (Island Wave Route), a series of spectacular bridges hopping across tiny islands to Shikoku. On the way, you might want to pause at Shiraishi Island, population 800. American humor columnist Amy Chavez lives on the island and writes about life in Japan—you can read her columns in the *Japan Times* and online.

POPULATION OF PRIME LIVING CITIES

- Tokyo: 12.8 million
- Osaka: 2.6 million
- Sapporo: 1.9 million
- Kobe: 1.5 million
- Kyoto: 1.4 million
- Fukuoka: 1.4 million
- Hiroshima: 1.1 million
- Matsuyama: 517,000
- Takamatsu: 419,000
- Nagano: 381,000

- Takasaki: 371,000
- Kochi: 343,000
- Hakodate: 279,000
- Tokushima: 264,000
- Matsumoto: 243,000
- Kushiro: 181,000
- Obihiro: 167,000
- Minakami: 22,000
- Karuizawa: 19,000

Shikoku, which means four districts, is divided into Kagawa-ken and Tokushima-ken in the east, Kochi-ken in the south, and Ehime-ken in the northwest. You can get away from it all in Shikoku. If you're observant, you may sense a difference in the culture and mannerisms of people here, compared to wound-up urbanites. Perhaps it's the influence of the mild climate or the bond among people who've been intimately connected to the sea for generations. At any rate, people in this region have a reputation for being frank and unpretentious. They take an interest in others (sometimes to the point of nosiness) and, in general, form friendships more readily. If you love the sea and the slow life, you may feel at home in Hiroshima or Shikoku. It's worth a visit anyway, to get off the beaten tourist path.

Hiroshima 広島

Hiroshima-ken, one of the four prefectures in the Chugoku region of western Honshu, is sandwiched between mountains to the north and the sea to the south. About 2.9 million people live in this area of 8,477 square kilometers (3,273 square miles). The capital, Hiroshima-shi (city), is set along Setonaikai (Seto Inland Sea), which is dotted with myriad islands. With a population of 1.1 million, Hiroshima city is the economic, cultural, and administrative hub of the Chugoku region. The city is divided into seven *ku* (wards). Today, the city promotes itself as an International City of Peace and Culture, with sister-city relationships with Honolulu and Montréal, among others.

On August 6, 1945, Hiroshima was the target of a nuclear weapon. In an instant, 92,000 buildings were destroyed, and 140,000 people perished as a result of the bombing. Mayor Awaya Senkichi died at his home, and many other officials were killed in their offices. Transportation, communication systems, and factories were also destroyed. Almost 60 years later, to all appearances, Hiroshima has recovered from the tragedy, although the suffering of the survivors has not abated. Neither has the city's mission of peace. In 2004 Hiroshima hosted the first Japan–U.S. Cities Summit to appeal for the realization of lasting world peace and discover ways in which cities can achieve sustainable development, while addressing global environmental concerns.

Hiroshima is the economic capital of the Chugoku and Shikoku regions. One of the largest industries is the manufacture of cars, with a large Mazda factory. Other industries are wholesale, retail, construction, transport, communication, finance, real estate, agriculture, utilities, fishery, and forestry. With a concentration of advanced technology and a market of 1.1 million people, the city has grand plans to develop a new business, research, and residential complex, called Seifu-Shinto, on the outskirts of the city.

Hiroshima prefecture prides itself on having an excellent educational system. An impressive 52 percent of high school students go on to university, which is significantly higher than the national average of 44 percent. There are 12 universities and nine junior colleges. Hiroshima City University is the newest, established in 1994. Their founding principle is to become "an international university which contributes to world peace and to the prosperity of the community through education and research in science and art."

Hiroshima citizens are inclined to remain in their home prefecture for employment, which is also different from trends in other regions. Many young people who go to other areas for higher education come home to find work, unlike the situation in many other outlying areas, which see a brain drain to Tokyo. Locals are encouraged to stay by organizations such as the Hiroshima Institute for the Study of Medium and Small Business Enterprises, which aims to nurture talent and provide information on small- and mid-size businesses.

A *Daily Life Guidebook for Foreign Residents* of Hiroshima is available in six languages (English, Portuguese, Spanish, Filipino, Korean, and Chinese). This guidebook is distributed for free at city hall, ward offices, Hiroshima Peace Cultural Foundation, and online. To gather information on Hiroshima's universities, visit Hiroshima City International House in Naka-ku. If you have children, they are welcome to attend any of the city's elementary and junior high schools, where Japanese language support is available. There is one international school, Hiroshima International School, which has students from 17 countries. There is good health care in the city. Hiroshima University Hospital and others provide medical consultation in English, as well as emergency care.

THE LAY OF THE LAND

The Chugoku Highlands form the northern border of Hiroshima-ken; to the north is Shimane-ken and the Sea of Japan (or East Sea). The Ota and Ashida Rivers flow south from the mountains to the Inland Sea, while the Gono River flow flows north through Shimane prefecture into the Sea of Japan. Hiroshima-shi is surrounded by mountains on three sides and traversed by six rivers that flow into the sea. The people of Hiroshima have something to enjoy every season: *sakura* (cherry) blossoms in March, followed by planting rice; swimming, sailing, and attending the Peace Memorial service in summer; admiring colorful leaves in the Taishakukyo Valley in the fall; and skiing in winter.

Climate

The Inland Sea provides a relatively mild climate, and due to protection by landmass on both sides, typhoons and earthquakes do not often affect the region. Hiroshima prefecture has an average annual temperature of 15°C/59°F and average humidity of 73 percent. Annual precipitation is 1,555 millimeters (61 inches). In Hiroshima city, the average temperature is 6°C/43°F during January and 27°C/81°F in August.

WHERE TO LIVE

The Hiroshima City International House, a five-minute walk from Hiroshima station, is a place where foreign students can live (up to 20 families and 80 singles) and interact with the community while studying at Hiroshima's universities and language schools. A family apartment for international students is ¥17,500/$220 per month, and for a researcher with a family rent is ¥39,000/$488 per month, plus utilities. There is no security deposit or landlord fee. Tenancy is limited to one year. Applications are taken starting in mid-November, and the move-in date is April 1. Public housing is also available if you meet the requirements. Registered foreign residents who live or work in Hiroshima city can apply for residence in municipal housing if they meet the conditions for household composition and income. Apply at the ward (district) office nearest to the residence.

Rents for apartments are reasonable and depend on the size, building material (wood versus reinforced concrete), age, and location (i.e., distance from transportation). You can find a 1DK (one room plus dine-in kitchen) *manshon* (condominium) in the Minami-ku district for as little as ¥56,000/$700 per month, plus a refundable deposit equivalent to three months' rent. The nearest bus stop is three minutes away. A newer 2DK can be found for ¥70,000/$875 and up, depending on the age and location. A 3LDK unit in a five-year-old 14-story *manshon* rents for ¥140,000/$1,750 plus a security deposit of three months' rent. The closest streetcar is a 10-minute walk. As is true

high-rise apartments in Hiroshima

elsewhere in Japan, you must have a Japanese guarantor to sign your lease—this can be your employer or, if you're studying abroad, your university.

DAILY LIFE

The Hiroshima City Tourist Information Center inside Hiroshima station and also at Peace Memorial Park is a good place to get practical information for living in Hiroshima. In front of Hiroshima station is Fukiya Department Store and Junkudo Books. The main shopping district is around Hatchobori and Kamiya-cho near the Hiroshima Prefectural building (Kencho-mae). Kinokuniya Bookstore has English-language books. The Kamiyacho underground shopping center is considered a fashionable spot. You can find *momiji manju* (a traditional sweet shaped like a maple leaf), a trademark of the city. Other tastes of Hiroshima include *okonomiyaki*, something like a Japanese pizza—the local version consists of a thin crêpe topped with thin soba or thick udon noodles, chopped cabbage, and green onions, with an egg on top. Flip it over and pour on a special sweet sauce. Oysters grown in the Inland Sea are best in winter—batter-dipped and fried, steamed in sake, grilled in the shell, wrapped with bacon, dipped in vinaigrette, or added to *okonomiyaki*. Hiroshima prefecture grows 60 percent of the oysters raised in Japan.

Hiroshima city's museums and gardens, including the Hiroshima Botanical Garden, the Transportation Museum, the Hiroshima City Museum of Contemporary Art, and the Health Sciences Museum, are worth a visit. The Atomic Bomb Dome, formerly the Hiroshima Prefectural Industrial Promotion Hall, was built in 1915. The bombing left only the walls and steel skeleton of the dome standing. It was registered as

PRIME LIVING LOCATIONS

© RUTHY KANAGY

Cenotaph for the A-bomb Victims, designed by Kenzo Tange, at the Hiroshima Peace Memorial Park

a World Heritage Monument in 1996 by UNESCO and has been left standing as a message to the world of the importance of peace. The dome is inside the larger Peace Memorial Park, which houses statues, markers, and an eternal flame on its grounds, along with a Peace Memorial Museum displaying documents and artifacts from the nuclear tragedy. The park has an open, spacious feeling, with trees and greenery. To get to the park from Hiroshima station, ride the city streetcar for 15 minutes, exit at Genbaku Domu Mae (Atomic Bomb Stop), and walk for about a minute.

Hiroshima Castle was built in 1589. Mostly destroyed during the atomic bombing of 1945, it was reconstructed in 1958, with a historical museum inside. From JR Hiroshima station, take the streetcar for 15 minutes, get off at Kamiya-cho Nishi (West Kamiya-cho), and walk for 10 minutes. You'll be rewarded with a memorable view of the castle's reflection in the moat and a bird's-eye perspective on the entire city from the top floor.

Miyajima Island, off the shore of Hiroshima, is best known for historic Itsukushima Shrine, which you approach via a *torii* (shrine gate) that appears to float on the waves at high tide. The shrine was originally built in A.D. 593, then rebuilt in 1168 in its present form. It represents the Shinden Zukuri style, with painted pillars carrying a massive roof thatched with cypress bark. In 1996, it was registered as a World Heritage Site. To visit Miyajima Island, take the JR train from Hiroshima station to Miyajima-guchi station (30 minutes), then walk three minutes down to the pier. The ferry to Miyajima departs about every 15 minutes, and the ride is just 10 minutes. It's a leisurely stroll through the town and past restaurants to Itsukushima Shrine.

GETTING AROUND

Hiroshima is a great walking city with an efficient streetcar (stops are announced in both English and Japanese). You can find out which number streetcar to take to various parts of the city from the information booth. "Green Mover" electric streetcars have low floors and make getting on and off a breeze for baby strollers and wheelchairs. Train travel is convenient, with a JR regional line and a *shinkansen* line. By *shinkansen* you can be in Osaka in 90 minutes and in Tokyo in about four hours. Less expensive intercity highway buses travel from Hiroshima to Tokyo in 12 hours, to Osaka in 7.5 hours, and to Tokuyama in Shikoku in an hour and 45 minutes. Although buses take longer, if you travel at night, you save the cost of a hotel and pay about half the cost of a *shinkansen* ticket.

For motor vehicle travel, Hiroshima is connected to other cities via the Chugoku, Sanyo, and San'in Expressways. Seven bridges connect Onomichi, in Hiroshima prefecture, to Shikoku Island via the Setouchi Shimanami Kaido (Seto Inland Sea Highway).

Hiroshima Airport is 60 minutes from downtown. You can fly to Tokyo in just over an hour and to Sapporo or Hakodate in two hours. Miyazaki in Kyushu is 45 minutes away and you can be in Okinawa in less than two hours. There are also international flights to Seoul, Hong Kong, Singapore, several cities in China, and Honolulu.

Ships and ferries through the Inland Sea depart from many ports, including Hiroshima, Kure, Fukuyama, and Onomichi. International container lines operate regularly from Hiroshima and Fukuyama to Korea, Taiwan, China, and beyond.

Shikoku 四国

Across the Seto Inland Sea from Hiroshima is Shikoku, the smallest of the four main Islands of Japan. Shikoku has four prefectures: Kagawa-ken and Tokushima-ken in the east, Kochi-ken in the south, and Ehime-ken in the northwest. There are 88 famous temples in Shikoku considered to be the sites of a sacred pilgrimage. You may see groups of pilgrims in white garb carrying walking sticks as they visit the 88 temples. Shikoku citizens are often described as being rugged, independent, open-minded, and generous. A number of English-speaking foreigners have made their home in Shikoku and written about it in print or online.

LAY OF THE LAND

Steep mountain ranges running east and west slice across Shikoku. Shikoku is rural and more traditional, and has firm cultural and religious roots. Many families are engaged in agriculture, although it may be part-time and supplemented with other jobs. The land is devoted to rice fields, orchards, and upland dry farming.

Climate

The four prefectures have similar overall temperatures, averaging 6°C/43°F in January and 28°C/82°F in August. The mountainous interior is colder than coastal areas. Kagawa-ken in the northeast is blessed with a moderate Inland Sea climate. It has an average annual precipitation of 1,100 millimeters (43 inches), a little less than neighboring Ehime-ken (1,300 millimeters/51 inches) and Tokushima-ken (1,500 millimeters/59 inches). Kochi-ken, facing the Pacific, has the highest rainfall in Japan—an average of 2,600 millimeters (102 inches) per year. Most of the precipitation arrives during the rainy season of June and July.

Tokushima-ken's southeast coast enjoys a wet and warm Pacific climate, while Mount Tsurugi in the west has cool temperatures. In the winter, there is enough snow on the mountains for skiing, and in the summer, surfers head to the beach. The damp, warm, humid climate is also perfect for raising *awa* (millet), which used to be the region's main crop. Kochi-ken borders the Pacific and has hot, humid summers. Winters are mild along the coast and colder in the mountains. Ehime-ken in northwest Shikoku also has a mild climate, averaging 6°C/43°F in January and 28°C/82°F in August. Nearby is Seto Inland Sea National Park and Mount Ishizuchi—the highest mountain in western Japan, at just under 2,000 meters (6,562 feet).

MATSUYAMA 松山

Ehime-ken is situated at the northwest corner of Shikoku, facing the Inland Sea. The Uwa Sea is to the west and Shikoku Mountains to the south. A population of 1.5 million lives within 5,676 square kilometers (2,192 square miles). Matsuyama, the capital, with a population of 517,000, was the first official city in Ehime prefecture, established in 1889. During World War II, Matsuyama suffered major damage but has made a recovery to become the largest city on Shikoku. Matsuyama Castle, which was built in 1602, is perched on top of Katsuyama Hill in the center of the city. The view of the city and mountains is stunning. Matsuyama has little snowfall and has few typhoons compared to cities facing the Pacific Ocean.

The main industries are shipbuilding and the production of heavy chemicals, paper, and textiles. In addition, agricultural machinery, pottery, and porcelain are made in the region. Ehime-ken is famous for cultured pearls and *mikan* oranges (often called satsuma in the United States), which are harvested in winter. Fishery, forestry, and agriculture are important industries outside the cities.

To promote international economic expansion, the prefectural government created an Ehime Foreign Access Zone (FAZ) to stimulate the importation of foreign goods. These zones are in place at Matsuyama Airport and Matsuyama Port. The Ehime World Trade Center hosts a Pan-Pacific Business Fair to help local companies find business opportunities through direct trade, investment, and technological exchange with foreign companies.

Matsuyama has a Spring Festival and a Ship Dance that takes place on Gogo-shima Island. You can visit eight of the 88 sacred temples of Shikoku here. Dogo spa, the oldest spa in Japan, is known for its natural thermal and curative waters. Famous author Natsume Soseki's novel *Botchan* is set in Matsuyama. You can ride the "Botchan" *densha* (antique streetcar) to Dogo spa, watch baseball at Botchan Stadium, and eat Botchan *dango* (sweets). Matsuyama is active in the international haiku movement. To learn about haiku, visit the Shiki Kinenkan (Shiki Hall), named after haiku poet Shiki Masaoka, who lived in Matsuyama. Matsuyama and its sister city of Sacramento, California, share a love of camellias and cherry trees. The city is home to Ehime University (public) and Matsuyama University (private), which have study-abroad programs and possible teaching opportunities.

© RUTHY KANAGY

Sanuki-udon noodles and shiitake rice are regional specialties in Ehime-ken.

© RUTHY KANAGY

streetcar in Matsuyama

Rents are quite reasonable in Matsuyama. A 2LDK (two rooms plus living/dining/kitchen) in a newer, three-story *manshon* (reinforced concrete building) is available for ¥54,000/$675 a month with no fees. It's close to a supermarket and hospital. A 3LDK apartment can be rented for ¥60,000/$750 to ¥120,000/$1,500 a month, depending on the age and distance from public transportation. You will need a Japanese guarantor's signature on your lease, which can be an employer or university, if you're a student.

Getting Around

Matsuyama maintains a streetcar system, which most other cities have abandoned, as well as buses. JR trains link Matsuyama to Takamatsu, Tokushima, and Kochi, the capitals of the other prefectures on Shikoku. The Shiokaze Limited Express train gets you to Okayama city on Honshu in three hours. Matsuyama Airport is your launching pad to Tokyo (an hour and 10 minutes), Fukuoka, Osaka, Nagoya, as well as Seoul and Shanghai. If you're headed to Tokyo, you can save money by taking the express bus Dream Takamatsu Matsuyama to Tokyo, which takes 12.5 hours and costs ¥9,400 ($1,175). There are daily ferries to Hiroshima and regular night ferries to Kokura, Kobe, and Kitakyushu. Cargo ships and tankers depart for domestic and international ports.

TAKAMATSU 高松

Kagawa-ken, in northeast Shikoku, is proud of its status as Japan's "smallest prefecture with the biggest heart." Facing the Inland Sea, this land area of 1,875 square kilometers (724 square miles) is home to just over one million people. By comparison, Hokkaido is the largest prefecture, with 83,400 square kilometers (32,200 square miles). Kagawa's population density is 545 people per square kilometer, compared to Tokyo's 5,550 people per square kilometer and Hokkaido's 72 people per square kilometer.

Major industries include agriculture, forestry, fisheries, manufacturing, trade, commerce, and traditional industries (lacquer ware, bonsai trees, paper fans, and *somen* noodles). Formerly dominated by petroleum, coal, and metal processing and food and textiles manufacturing, the prefecture is now promoting expansion into microelectronics and other technology.

Takamatsu, the capital city (population 419,000), is well known for its natural serenity. You will understand why when you stroll through 17th-century Ritsurin Park, built by a *daimyo* (feudal lord), and view the ruins of Takamatsu Castle at Tamano Park by the sea. Near city hall in the center of town are the Museum of Art and a shopping mall. Kagawa University and Takamatsu City Library are several blocks west. On the way to the yacht harbor and municipal pool, you will pass Takamatsu Center for the Advancement of Women. The Municipal Hospital and Takamatsu City Health Center are in the south.

For health-related needs, Kagawa Prefecture Hospital (Kagawa Kenritsu Chuo Byoin) and other hospitals provide excellent care. The Takamatsu City Health Center offers counseling on health care and exercise classes for "middle and advanced ages." In 1995 the city built the Takamatsu Center for the Advancement of Women to "promote women's independence and participation in society and equal rights movement." Besides a library with books and videos, there are counselors to help with problems, and a children's room to leave your child while you participate in seminars for men and women. Five public and private universities are located in Kagawa-ken, as are six junior colleges.

To open their city to the world, Takamatsu established sister-city affiliations with St. Petersburg, Florida; Tours, France; and Nanchang, China. The city is committed to interacting with the world: "Understanding the cultural diversity and respect for people with different backgrounds is increasingly important in our community." There are 24,000 foreign residents in Takamatsu, and the Takamatsu International Association (TIA) will make sure you feel at home. They have a Japanese Language Salon and publish *TIA Info,* which lists events, movies, culture, recipes, and practical information for English speakers.

You don't need to spend too much of your income on housing when you're living in Shikoku. A 1DK (one room plus dining room/kitchen) unit in a four-year-old *manshon* rents for ¥57,000/$713 a month, with a deposit equivalent to three months' rent. A 2LDK with two rooms and a spacious kitchen/dining/living room in a newer *manshon* is listed for ¥71,000/$888 a month, plus two months' equivalent deposit and ¥71,000/$888 fee to the landlord. It has 58 square meters (625 square feet) of floor space and is a 10-minute walk from the nearest train station.

Getting Around

The Kotoden (Kotohira electric line) is a convenient way to get around the city and beyond. JR trains and expressways take you to Takamatsu to Tokushima, Matsuyama, and Kochi cities. Until 20 years ago the only way to cross over to Honshu was by air or sea. Now Seto Ohashi (Great Seto Bridge) spans the gap to Okayama-ken across the Inland Sea. The top level is an expressway for cars, and the lower level is for trains.

In Okayama city you can transfer to the *shinkansen,* which takes four hours to Tokyo, an hour to Osaka, and 2.5 hours to Fukuoka in Kyushu. A cheaper alternative is a long-distance bus—Osaka is about four hours away and Tokyo 10.5 hours. You can also ride the waves to Osaka or Kobe (2–4 hours) and many other cities by ferry. Takamatsu airport has daily flights to Sapporo, Tokyo, Osaka, Fukuoka, and other cities, including Seoul, Korea.

TOKUSHIMA 徳島

Tokushima-ken (population 820,000) is located in eastern Shikoku and has a land area of 4,145 square kilometers (1,600 square miles). Approximately 80 percent of the land is mountainous, with deeply carved gorges, rivers, and abundant water. Sometimes called the "Awa Kingdom," this small prefecture is just a jump southwest of Kobe and Osaka across Awaji Island. The ferry was made obsolete by the construction of the Akashi and Onaruto bridges and the Kobe-Awaji-Naruto Highway—now you can get there in 100 minutes.

The prefecture has a mild climate and is rich in agricultural products. The Naruto Straits, just off the coast of Naruto-shi, in Tokushima, are a fascinating natural phenomenon. Giant whirlpools measuring up to 20 meters (66 feet) across are caused by the clash of the difference in sea level of the Pacific Ocean and Seto Inland Sea.

Tokushima's natural features and history have led to some unique cultural features: the Awa Odori dance, Ningyo Joruri puppet theater, Aizome indigo dyeing, *shijira-ori* textiles, natural wood products, and *sudachi* (a type of citrus).

Tokushima-shi (city) is the capital, with a population of 264,000. Its history goes back to 1587, when Hachisuka Iemasa, a feudal lord, built a castle. For 14 generations, the Hachisuka family ruled and the area prospered economically. In 1920, several towns merged to become Tokushima city. Every August, thousands of citizens and millions of visitors dance the Awa Odori, nonstop, for four days. The dance is so famous that it has been transplanted to Koenji in Tokyo (on the Chuo line), where they do their own version of the raucous dance. The Yoshino River and Mount Bizan create a green environment, and you can ride a cable car to the top for a sweeping view of the city. Rice, vegetables, and fruit are primary agricultural products, which, along with woodworking, remain an important part of the local economy.

Tokushima has sister-city relationships with Saginaw, Michigan; Leiria, Portugal; and Dandong, China. The University of Tokushima has faculties of arts and sciences, medicine, dentistry, and engineering. They accept international students whose Japanese language skills are advanced enough to take classes with regular students. As of 2005, foreign residents of Tokushima numbered 5,900, of whom 90 percent were of Asian heritage. There are no international schools in Tokushima, but the public elementary and junior high schools welcome children of all nationalities. Pick up the *Tokushima Pocket Living Guide* from the Prefectural Office.

Here's a unique opportunity for artists: The town of Kamiyama in central Tokushima-ken started an innovative Tokushima International Cultural Village Project in 1999. Each year they invite three artists-in-residence to stay in the village for two months (expenses paid) in exchange for producing artwork and interacting with the children and residents of the town. If you're an artist looking for a short-term stay in Japan and would like to apply, the application deadline is March 1 of each year for

NARUTO STRAITS

One of the most powerful sea currents in the world runs through Naruto Straits, located between eastern Shikoku and Awaji Island to the northeast. The ebb and flow of strong opposing currents traveling at a speed of up to 20 kilometers per hour creates giant whirlpools, which can be viewed from observatories on the Shikoku side overlooking the straits. This phenomenon is caused by the difference in sea level between the Seto Inland Sea and the Pacific Ocean. Another vantage point is from the Onaruto bridge, which connects Tokushima prefecture in Shikoku to Awaji Island in Hyogo prefecture. The whirlpools are most dramatic in spring and fall, when their vortexes reach up to 20 meters (60 feet) across. The best times to view the Naruto whirlpools are at high and low tides.

If you miss the best viewing time, you can see the whirlpools on-screen in the Onaruto Bridge Crossing Memorial Museum. The brave of heart can take a sightseeing boat right to the edge of the *uzumaki* (whirlpools). The Uzushio Line ferry departs Kameura Harbor every 30 minutes for a 20-minute cruise (tel. 088/687-0613, www.uzushio-kisen.com/time/index.html, 8 A.M.-4:30 P.M. daily, ¥1,500/$19 adults, children half-price). Check the local tide chart for the best time to go. You can also follow the Uzunomichi Walkway under the Onaruto bridge and look down through glass panels directly above the whirlpools! Love seafood? The fast currents of the tide in the Naruto channel make it one of the best fishing spots. Sea bream, yellowfish, mackerel, and perch are some of the seasonal delights.

programs in the fall (see www.kamiyama-gvi.jp/kair/index_eng.html). They call their town surrounded by mountains Green Valley, Inc.

Finding housing is easier if you speak Japanese or have someone who can help you. Look at postings outside real estate offices and in real estate magazines. You can find a 2LDK (two rooms plus living/dining/kitchen) to rent for around ¥60,000/$750 and up with a deposit equal to two months' rent, close to the bus line. Public housing is available if you qualify. Contact the Tokushima Prefecture Housing Division (tel. 088/621-2590) or the housing division of Tokushima City Hall.

Getting Around

JR Tokushima station and bus terminal is the hub of transportation in Tokushima. To get to Honshu by land and sea, ride a highway express bus over the Onaruto and Akashi Bridges to Kobe. From there you can transfer to *shinkansen* east to Osaka and Tokyo, or west to Hiroshima and Kyushu. You can fly from Tokushima to Tokyo, Nagoya, or Fukuoka in 90 minutes. If you love the slow life and the sea, pack some good books and sleep on the ferry from Tokushima to Tokyo (about 19 hours).

KOCHI 高知

Kochi-ken, the largest of Shikoku's prefectures and shaped like a lobster, is on the whole southern coast bordering the Pacific Ocean. This area is far enough removed from Tokyo and Osaka to provide a real *inaka* (down-home) lifestyle. The mountains, rivers, and sea are suited for outdoor sports, and the region's long history and local crafts of sword- and paper-making are of interest to many. You can enjoy Katsurahama beach's white sand and green pines and explore a limestone cavern called Ryuga-do, named for a dragon. Kochi Castle, built in 1603, overlooks the city of Kochi from a hill. Kochi city has 343,000 residents. Most of the city is situated on a narrow plain on Urado Bay, with mountains to the north, east, and west. Historically it was a castle town of Tosa Province and was incorporated as a city in 1889. Kochi is known for the Yosakoi dances held in August. Makino Botanical Garden and Chikurinji Temple—on the 88-temple circuit of Shikoku—are located on Mount Godaisan, with a commanding view of the city. The Obiyamachi shopping arcade and Sunday street markets provide daily needs. The city has two universities—Kochi University and University of Kochi (formerly Kochi Women's University)—and four two-year colleges. The Kochi International Association produces *Tosa Wave,* an informational magazine for foreign residents.

Getting Around

In addition to city buses, the Tosa Electric Railway crisscrosses the city north–south from Kochi station to Sanbashi-Dori, and east–west from Gomen to Ino. JR (Japan Railway) trains connect it to other parts of Shikoku as well as Okayama, where you can transfer to the *shinkansen* to east and west Honshu and beyond. You can also take an express bus from Kochi to Hiroshima or Kobe in four hours and to Kyoto in five hours. An overnight bus to Tokyo takes almost 12 hours and costs ¥12,500 ($156), a savings over the *shinkansen* ticket. Japan Airlines and All Nippon Airways have daily flights out of Kochi Airport to Tokyo, Osaka, Nagoya, Fukuoka, and points south.

PRIME LIVING LOCATIONS

KYUSHU 九州

Kyushu is the southernmost of Japan's four main islands. Regarded as the cradle of Japanese civilization, this was the first area to begin rice cultivation in Japan, in the 4th century B.C. Kyushu's distinct international flavor comes from a long history of trade and cultural exchange with its closest neighbors, Korea and China. It has also been the gateway to Western culture and religion, beginning with the arrival of European traders and missionaries in the 16th century.

Kyushu (pronounced "Q-shoe") is divided into seven prefectures. From north to south they are: Fukuoka, Saga, Nagasaki, Oita, Kumamoto, Miyazaki, and Kagoshima. Perhaps the most cosmopolitan city is Fukuoka, a major international port on the northern coast of Kyushu. Nagasaki, on the western flank, was the only entry point for foreign ships during the Tokugawa shogunate, and the second city to suffer the atomic bomb, three days after Hiroshima. In the south are the cities of Kagoshima and Miyazaki. Although there are many attractive areas to live in Kyushu, this chapter introduces Fukuoka as a prime living area.

© RUTHY KANAGY

Fukuoka 福岡

Fukuoka city (capital of Fukuoka-ken), with a population of 1.4 million, is the largest city in Kyushu and among the top 10 in Japan. It was established in 1889 when Hakata, a port city, and the former castle town of Fukuoka were combined. In addition to the port, Fukuoka has an international airport and the JR West *shinkansen* "bullet train," which arrives at Hakata station after passing through an undersea tunnel from Shimonoseki in western Honshu. You can transfer to the Kyushu *shinkansen,* which speeds you south to Kagoshima. Fukuoka is home to IT-related industries and has 22 universities. It is also a magnet for its nonstop nightlife in the Tenjin and Nakasu districts, and draws passionate crowds for the Fukuoka SoftBank Hawks baseball games. According to the city's official website, "120 percent excitement is born in this city every day!"

Fukuoka is known for its modern architecture, along with a few vestiges from the past. The Fukuoka Asian Art Museum is housed in a modern, multi-complex building where you can watch Kabuki performances and musicals and see contemporary art. Two important Meiji era (1868–1912) artifacts are a historic redbrick building from 1909, which now serves as the city's Cultural Center, and a two-story French Renaissance–style house built in 1910 as the Prefectural Hall and guesthouse. The latter is in Tenjin district's Central Park and is worth a visit. In addition there are numerous historic temples, shrines, gardens, and the ruins of Fukuoka Castle.

You can step back in time at the Hakata Machiya Folk Museum, which is a replica of the town during the Meiji and Taisho eras (1868–1926). Among the displays are traditional folk crafts, Hakata weaving, ceramic pottery, and dolls.

As for foreign community, Francis Xavier is reported to be the first Westerner to visit Hakata in 1550 on his way to Kyoto. Today there are about 20,000 foreign residents in the city, of which 43 percent are of Chinese heritage, 34 percent Korean, followed by Filipino, American, British, Indonesian, Canadian, and other nationalities. American, Canadian, and Australian Consulates are located here, and there is an international school. Fukuoka has sister-city ties with Oakland, California, and Atlanta, Georgia.

A city with an international heritage, Fukuoka actively welcomes foreign visitors and issues a Fukuoka Welcome Card to overseas visitors as a mark of hospitality. The card is good for discounts and perks at participating tourist facilities, hotels, stores, and restaurants in Fukuoka and the surrounding region. In addition, a bilingual magazine called *Fukuoka Now* features events, education, and tips on preserving the environment for foreign residents and visitors.

The Fukuoka International Association has an online magazine, *Rainbow Cybernet,* with information on living in Fukuoka, including how to apply for National Health Insurance, the medical expenses assistance program, and the national pension system. Also useful is a hospital guide with an interactive checklist to help residents find medical facilities by neighborhood and by medical specialization. The international association offers free legal consultation on immigration issues as well as personal counseling for foreign residents. The Rainbow Plaza library has foreign magazines and newspapers, such as *USA Today, Japan Times, Time,* and *National Geographic,*

OKINAWA 沖縄

Though not included in this book, Okinawa is also a viable living location.

Far south of Kyushu, halfway between Japan and Taiwan, Okinawa is most accessible by air. If you have time to see—or the chance to live in—"the Hawaii of Japan," you'll find an area with its own distinct history, language, and culture. It was established as the kingdom of Ryukyu at the beginning of the 15th century and traded with both China and Japan. Okinawa was taken in 1609 by a Japanese clan from southern Kyushu. During the Meiji era (1868) it was made a prefecture of Japan and called Okinawa-ken.

The Ryukyu language is distinct from both Japanese and Chinese, and the cuisine, clothing, housing, and religion are unique to the islands. You can feel the splendor of the last Ryukyuan king by visiting ornate Shuri Castle. Sadly, Okinawa was the stage for some of the most horrifying battles during World War II, victimized both by Japan and the United States. The United States controlled Okinawa and took almost half the prime land for U.S. military bases. Okinawa reverted to Japan in 1972, though the U.S. military still has a strong presence.

Like the Ainu (native people) in the far north, Okinawans have faced discrimination in education and employment. Today, there is something of a revival to teach the younger generation their cultural roots. Several popular singers, such as Amuro Namie and Natsukawa Rimi, are of Okinawan heritage.

Lots of information on Okinawa can be found in English online; "Okinawa, Japan's Tropical Side" (www.okinawastory.jp/en) will get you started.

plus many other titles in Chinese and Korean. They also have a message board with help-wanted notices, run a home-stay and home-visit program, and maintain a list of Japanese-language classes taught by volunteers—ask for the *Nihongo Class Map* guide at any ward office.

Fukuoka is known for its quality of education and has 22 universities. The city's public elementary and junior high schools welcome children from other countries. Information on enrolling your child is available at any city ward. The city maintains a Fukuoka City Services hotline to answer questions about the types of services offered at ward offices and other city hall facilities.

THE LAY OF THE LAND

Aside from the small coastal plains, Kyushu is filled with mountains and volcanoes. The largest caldera is at Mount Aso and measures 25 kilometers (15 miles) across. Wherever there are volcanoes, there are abundant hot springs. Beppu city, in the east, is known for its steaming mud pits and spas in the colors of the rainbow. Sakurajima, a volcanic island in the bay, next to the southern city of Kagoshima, regularly erupts and spews ash all over the city. Outdoor opportunities abound, from hiking in the Kirishima-Yaku National Park to skiing and surfing. There are numerous pottery villages such as Arita, known for Arita-yaki, and Karatsu, with superb Korean-influenced pottery.

Fukuoka-ken (prefecture), in the north, is surrounded on three sides by the sea, with mountains to the south. It faces Suho-nada (Suho Sea) to the northeast, Genkai-nada (Genkai Sea) to the northwest, and Ariake-kai (Ariake Sea) in the southwest. The capital city of Fukuoka spreads out over a crescent-shaped plain, an area of about 338

© RUTHY KANAGY

Hakata station

square kilometers (130 square miles). The main business districts are Hakata, Tenjin, and Nakasu, which are connected by subway. Businesses, shops, and restaurants are clustered around Hakata station.

Between Hakata Bay and the Sea of Genkai is a long, narrow spit called Umino-Nakamichi. At the end of the spit is Shikano-shima (island). From the highest spot on the island there is a grand view of the bay and sea, and a fantastic night view of Hakata Bay, the Fukuoka Dome, and Fukuoka Tower. In the summer, the fires lit on scores of squid-fishing boats light up the waves.

Climate

Kyushu has hot, muggy summers and a long growing season. The rainy season during late spring and early summer often brings deluges, and in the fall typhoons brings more rain and wind. Winters can be quite cold, especially in the central mountains. Kagoshima and Miyazaki, in the south, have mild winters. Fukuoka-ken has a mild temperate climate and sufficient rain. Snow falls on the mountains but rarely in the cities. The city of Fukuoka has an annual average temperature of around 17°C/63°F. Because of the warm Tsushima Current, winter temperatures rarely dip below freezing on the plains.

WHERE TO LIVE

Fukuoka city is divided into seven districts: Higashi-ku and Hakata-ku in the eastern port area, Naka-ku (central), Minami-ku (south), and Jonan-ku, Sawara-ku, and Nishi-ku in the west. As in other cities, rental costs depend on the age and construction of the building, size, and location. Older apartments tend to have rooms with

© RUTHY KANAGY

Though the coastal areas are mild, some of Kyushu's majestic mountains have snow year-round.

tatami (woven rush) floors (other than the kitchen), while *manshon* (condominiums) have wood or laminate wood flooring.

In Chuo-ku, or the central district, you can find inexpensive 1K units in in older buildings from ¥35,000/$438 a month (plus one month's rent as deposit) with 21 square meters/225 square feet. Centrally located high-rise *manshon* (condominiums) with two or three rooms plus LDK (living-dining-kitchen) range from ¥80,000/$1,000 to ¥120,000/$1,500 a month. Move-in costs include two months' equivalent deposit and a landlord's fee equal to one month's rent. Bus and train transportation are nearby. In Minami-ku, on the south side of the city, a brand new 1LDK in a two-story apartment with 45 square meters/450 square feet lists for ¥60,000/$750 a month with one parking space (free). Pay the the equivalent of two months' rent as deposit and one month as the landlord fee to move in.

In Sawara-ku, where Fukuoka International School is located, you can find newer 2LDK apartments for ¥65,000/$813 and up, and 3LDK for ¥67,000/$837 a month. Add one month's equivalent deposit and a landlord fee equal to two months' rent. Single-family homes with 80 square meters/1,000 square feet or more floor space are available for ¥100,000/$1,250 to ¥120,000/$1,500 per month. Figure on a landlord fee equivalent to two months' rent and a security deposit equal to one month's rent to move in, plus a small maintenance fee.

If you're single (or a couple) and looking for an inexpensive apartment, Higashi-ku, in the east, has many 1DK apartments catering to university students. The Najima area has slightly larger 2DK units. Walk around the neighborhood and look at housing ads posted outside real estate offices.

Most areas of the city are close to public transportation (subway or bus) and have supermarkets, convenience stores, and parks nearby. Many of the universities have international student housing on campus. City housing is also available if you qualify. The city takes applications four times a year: in May, August, November, and February. Apply at the local ward office.

DAILY LIFE

Tenjin is the business and entertainment center, with offices, department stores, boutiques, and an underground mall. The Hankyu department store and Tokyu Hands (DIY store) are located in the recently opened JR Hakata Station Building. At night head to Nakasu's entertainment district, stretched out along a sandbank. Here you will find numerous *yatai,* or street venders, along the Nakagawa (river), with down-home tastes. Fukuoka is famous for Hakata ramen (noodles), Korean *yakiniku* (grilled meat), *fugu* (blowfish), and *karashi mentaiko* (spicy cod roe). The Kawabata district has an arcade with traditional shops and the Kushida Shrine. Nearby is Canal City Hakata along a moat, with theaters, cinemas, and an amusement park. There are several large shopping centers, including Hakata Riverain.

If you're new to the city, contact the Fukuoka Convention and Visitors Bureau to set up a tour with a volunteer guide. Every May during the Golden Week holidays, visitors descend on the city to see the Hakata Dontaku festival, with a parade of more than 10,000 people in traditional costume on decorated vehicles, playing musical instruments. Two days of festivities culminate in the Dontaku dance and fireworks.

Avid fans cheer at professional baseball and soccer games. Fukuoka hosts an international marathon yearly, and every December, the Grand Sumo tournament comes from Tokyo.

Foreign listeners enjoy LOVE FM, Fukuoka's foreign language radio station.

GETTING AROUND

With efficient land, air, and sea transport, Fukuoka is a major travel hub for Kyushu and southwest Japan. The *chikatetsu,* or subway network, makes it easy to get around the city. There are three lines: the Kuko (airport) orange line from Meinohama in the west to the airport in east Fukuoka; the Hakozaki blue line from Meinohama in the west to Kaizuka station in the northeast, just past Kyushu University; and the green Nanakuma line, which starts at Tenjin-Minami (south Tenjin) in the central city and curves southwest to Hashimoto. The subway is definitely the quickest way to get to Fukuoka International Airport and JR (Japan Railway) Hakata station.

The new JR Hakata Building connects the *shinkansen* to local train lines and promotes tourism to and from other parts Asia as well as within Kyushu. Hakata is the western terminus for the *shinkansen* high-speed trains from Tokyo and Osaka. The train from Hakata to Osaka takes two hours and 40 minutes, and you can get to Tokyo in about six hours. The Kyushu *shinkansen* line was completed in 2011. The train speeds you from Hakata to Kagoshima in the south in just 69 minutes—a third of the time it took before. Both JR and Nishitesu trains connect you to other cities in Kyushu. The Japan Rail Pass can be used on JR trains, buses, and ferries (except on the fastest Nozomi *shinkansen*).

You can fly from Fukuoka International Airport to Tokyo in 90 minutes. Regular

FESTIVALS

© RUTHY KANAGY

Parades often take place during traditional festivities.

Almost every town and city in Japan has its own *matsuri* (festival) celebrating the new year, changing seasons, or a historic event. *Matsuri* often take place at local shrines and are a chance for neighbors and communities to join together; spectators are often welcome to participate.

If you travel to Fukuoka in May or July, plan to take in at least one of their popular festivals. The Hakata Dontaku Festival is held May 3 and 4 during Golden Week. Groups of musicians in unique costumes play traditional or brass instruments and parade through 1.2-kilometer-long "Dontaku square"; others dressed as one of three lucky gods beat *shamoji* or wooden rice spatulas. In addition, thousands of dancers and singers perform on stages set up around the city. The festival has an 800-year history and attracts two million visitors each year. The term *dontaku* comes from the Dutch word *zontag* (Sunday or holiday), revealing Kyushu's history of trade with the Dutch.

The other well-known Fukuoka festival is Hakata Gion Yamagasa, which takes place July 1–15 each year. Elaborate floats called *yamagasa*, adorned with beautiful Hakata dolls, are pulled by men in headbands and loincloths to Kushida shrine. The climax is the Oiyama race on the final day of the festival. Precisely at 4:59 A.M. teams of men race five kilometers carrying the one-ton *yamagasa* floats. There are also performances of traditional Noh dramas at Kushida shrine. This festival was designated as an intangible folk cultural asset by the government in 1979. To get to Kushida shrine, take the Nishitetsu bus to Canal-city from JR Hakata station.

August 12–15 is Obon (festival of the dead) throughout Japan, a time when ancestral spirits return to visit. People go back to their hometowns to meet relatives and visit their family graves. At night there is lively folk dancing, music, and food. After three days the spirits are sent off on lanterns floated on rivers and seas. If you plan to travel during Obon season, be ready for crowds.

One of the most famous Obon festivals is Awa Odori (Awa dance), which takes place in Tokushima city in eastern Shikoku. Dancers in colorful *yukata* (cotton kimono) dance through the streets accompanied by three-stringed *shamisen*, taiko drums, flutes, and gongs. Awa is the old name for Tokushima and the unique "drunken-style dancing" is said to have started when Tokushima Castle was built in the 16th century and peasants celebrated by drinking and dancing. More than one million tourists descend on the city each year to see the Awa Odori.

See www.jnto.go.jp/eng/location/festivals for more festivals.

flights connect you to all other parts of Japan, as well as Seoul, Shanghai, and numerous other international destinations.

If you're feeling adventurous, why not take a leisurely ferry and explore other parts of Asia? Hakata Port International Terminal has overnight ferry service to Pusan, Korea, three times a week, which takes about 14 hours. If you're in a hurry, a jetfoil will launch you from Fukuoka to Pusan in just under three hours. To get to the port, take the Nishitetsu bus to Chuo Futoh bus stop.

RESOURCES

Contacts

EMBASSIES AND CONSULATES
In the United States
EMBASSY OF JAPAN
2520 Massachusetts Avenue N.W.
Washington, DC 20008
tel. 202/238-6700
fax 202/328-2187
www.us.emb-japan.go.jp/english/html/index.html

CONSULATE-GENERAL OF JAPAN IN ANCHORAGE
3601 C Street, Suite 1300
Anchorage, AK 99503
tel. 907/562-8424
fax 907/562-8434
www.anchorage.us.emb-japan.go.jp/anchorage

CONSULATE-GENERAL OF JAPAN IN ATLANTA
One Alliance Center, Suite 1600
3500 Lenox Road
Atlanta, GA 30326
tel. 404/240-4300
fax 404/240-4311
www.atlanta.us.emb-japan.go.jp

CONSULATE-GENERAL OF JAPAN IN BOSTON
600 Atlantic Avenue, 22nd Floor
Boston, MA 02210
tel. 617/973-9772
fax 617/542-1329
www.boston.us.emb-japan.go.jp

CONSULATE-GENERAL OF JAPAN IN CHICAGO
737 North Michigan Avenue, Suite 1100
Chicago, IL 60611
tel. 312/280-0400
fax 312/280-9568
www.chicago.us.emb-japan.go.jp

CONSULATE-GENERAL OF JAPAN IN DENVER
1225 17th Street, Suite 3000
Denver, CO 80202
tel. 303/534-1151
fax 303/534-3393
www.denver.us.emb-japan.go.jp

CONSULATE-GENERAL OF JAPAN IN DETROIT
400 Renaissance Center, Suite 1600
Detroit, MI 48243
tel. 313/567-0120
fax 313/567-0274
www.detroit.us.emb-japan.go.jp

CONSULATE-GENERAL OF JAPAN IN HONOLULU
1742 Nuuanu Avenue
Honolulu, HI 96817
tel. 808/543-3111
fax 808/543-3170
www.honolulu.us.emb-japan.go.jp

CONSULATE-GENERAL OF JAPAN IN HOUSTON
909 Fannin Street, Suite 3000
Houston, Texas 77010
tel. 713/652-2977
fax 713/651-7822
www.houston.us.emb-japan.go.jp

CONSULATE-GENERAL OF JAPAN IN LOS ANGELES

350 South Grand Avenue, Suite 1700
Los Angeles, CA 90071
tel. 213/617-6700
fax 213/617-6725
www.la.us.emb-japan.go.jp

CONSULATE-GENERAL OF JAPAN IN MIAMI

80 S.W. 8th Street, Suite 3200
Miami, FL 33130
tel. 305/530-9090
fax 305/530-0950
www.miami.us.emb-japan.go.jp

CONSULATE-GENERAL OF JAPAN IN NASHVILLE

1801 West End Avenue, Suite 900
Nashville, TN 37203
tel. 615/340-4300
fax 615/340-4311
www.nashville.us.emb-japan.go.jp

CONSULATE-GENERAL OF JAPAN IN NEW YORK

299 Park Avenue, 18th Floor
New York, NY 10171
tel. 212/371-8222
fax 212/755-2851
www.ny.us.emb-japan.go.jp/en/html/index.
html

CONSULATE-GENERAL OF JAPAN IN PORTLAND

Wells Fargo Center, Suite 2700
1300 S.W. 5th Avenue
Portland, OR 97201
tel. 503/221-1811
fax 503/224-8936
www.portland.us.emb-japan.go.jp/en/index.
html

CONSULATE-GENERAL OF JAPAN IN SAN FRANCISCO

50 Fremont Street, Suite 2300
San Francisco, CA 94105
tel. 415/777-3533
fax 415/974-3660
www.sf.us.emb-japan.go.jp/e_top.htm

CONSULATE-GENERAL OF JAPAN IN SEATTLE

601 Union Street, Suite 500
Seattle, WA 98101
tel. 206/682-9107
fax 206/624-9097
www.seattle.us.emb-japan.go.jp

In Canada
EMBASSY OF JAPAN

255 Sussex Drive
Ottawa, ON K1N 9E6
tel. 613/241-8541
fax 613/241-2232
www.ca.emb-japan.go.jp

In Great Britain
EMBASSY OF JAPAN

101-104 Piccadilly
London W1J 7JT
tel. 020/7465-6500
fax 020/7491-9348
www.uk.emb-japan.go.jp

In Australia
EMBASSY OF JAPAN IN CANBERRA

112 Empire Circuit
Yarralumla, ACT 2600
tel. 02/6273-3244
fax 02/6273-1848
www.au.emb-japan.go.jp

RESOURCES

U.S. Embassies and Consulates in Japan
U.S. EMBASSY
1-10-5 Akasaka
Minato-ku, Tokyo 107-8420
tel. 03/3224-5000
fax 03/3505-1862
http://japan.usembassy.gov

AMERICAN CONSULATE FUKUOKA
2-5-26 Ohori, Chuo-ku
Fukuoka 810-0052
tel. 092/751-9331
fax 092/713-9222
http://fukuoka.usconsulate.gov

AMERICAN CONSULATE NAGOYA
Nagoya International Center Bldg. 6F
1-47-1 Nagono, Nakamura-ku
Nagoya 450-0001
tel. 052/581-4501
fax 052/581-3190
http://nagoya.usconsulate.gov

AMERICAN CONSULATE NAHA
2-1-1 Toyama
Urasoe-shi, Okinawa 901-2101
tel. 098/876-4211
fax 098/876-4243
http://naha.usconsulate.gov

AMERICAN CONSULATE OSAKA
2-11-5, Nishitenma
Kita-ku, Osaka 530-8543
tel. 06/6315-5900
fax 06/6315-5914
http://osaka.usconsulate.gov

AMERICAN CONSULATE SAPPORO
Kita 1-jo, Nishi 28-chome
Chuo-ku, Sapporo 064-0821
tel. 011/641-1115
fax 011/643-1283
http://sapporo.usconsulate.gov

Canadian, British, and Australian Embassies in Japan
CANADIAN EMBASSY
7-3-38 Akasaka
Minato-ku, Tokyo 107-8503
tel. 03/5412-6200
fax 03/5412-6247
www.canadainternational.gc.ca/japan-japon

BRITISH EMBASSY
1 Ichiban-cho
Chiyoda-ku, Tokyo 102-8381
tel. 03/5211-1100
fax 03/5275-0346
http://ukinjapan.fco.gov.uk/en

AUSTRALIAN EMBASSY
2-1-14 Mita
Minato-ku, Tokyo 108-8361
tel. 03/5232-4111
fax 03/5232-4149
www.australia.or.jp

IMMIGRATION AND RESIDENCY

Information concerning procedures for entry and stay for foreign nationals is given over the phone or by direct visit in various languages, including English, Korean, Chinese, and Spanish.

IMMIGRATION BUREAU, MINISTRY OF JUSTICE
TOKYO REGIONAL IMMIGRATION BUREAU
5-5-30, Konan
Minato-ku, Tokyo 108-8255
tel. 0570/013904
www.immi-moj.go.jp/english/info

Immigration Information Centers are located in Fukuoka, Hiroshima, Kobe, Naha, Nagoya, Osaka, Sapporo, Sendai, Takamatsu, Tokyo, and Yokohama.

NATURALIZATION
Ministry of Justice, Nationality Division, Tokyo
Legal Affairs Bureau, Kudan Building No. 2,
1-1-15 Kudan Minami
Chiyoda-ku, Tokyo 102-8225
tel. 03/5213-1234

PLANNING YOUR FACT-FINDING TRIP
Guided Tours
CYCLE TOKYO!
http://cycle-tokyo.cycling.jp
One-stop information on biking in
Tokyo, including suggested routes and
volunteer guides on the weekend.

HIROSHIMA CITY FUN WALKS
www.kankou.pref.hiroshima.jp/foreign/
english/guide/hiroshima_city/guide.html
Information desk at Hiroshima station. The
staff will help you send your luggage to your
hotel so you can explore the city hands-free.

IACE TRAVEL ASIA
http://iace-asia.com
Package tours and discount airfares.

JAPANICAN.COM
www.japanican.com/tours
Tour booking and train, bus, and hotel
packages.

JAPAN NATIONAL TOURIST ORGANIZATION (JNTO)
www.jnto.go.jp/eng
One- to five-day detailed model trips
throughout Japan, self-guided.

KYOTO CYCLING PROJECT
www.kctp.net/en
Guided tours of Kyoto on two wheels.

TOKYO FREE WALKING TOURS
http://5.pro.tok2.com/~tcgc/english
Weekend walking tours by Tokyo City
Guide Club.

Information
ABOUT JAPAN
http://gojapan.about.com

ACCESSIBLE TOKYO AND ACCESSIBLE OSAKA
http://accessible.jp.org/tokyo/en/index.html
Tips on arrival and departure from airports; guide to hotels, shopping, museums,
and parks with inclusive accommodations.

GOURMET NAVIGATOR
www.gnavi.co.jp/en
Search restaurants in major cities by location and cuisine.

JAPAN EXTERNAL TRADE ORGANIZATION (JETRO)
www.jetro.go.jp
A government-related organization promoting mutual trade and investment between Japan and the world.

JAPAN GUIDE
www.japan-guide.com

JAPAN HELPLINE
tel. 0120/46-1997
http://jhelp.com
Offers 24-hour multilingual emergency
service and practical information.

JAPAN WITH KIDS
www.tokyowithkids.com/fyi/international_
schools.html
List of international schools.

KYOTO VISITOR'S GUIDE
www.kyotoguide.com

SAPPORO INTERNATIONAL COMMUNICATION PLAZA FOUNDATION
www.plaza-sapporo.or.jp/english/index_e.
html

VISIT JAPAN LINKS
www.mofa.go.jp/link/visit.html

Accommodations
GUESTHOUSE JIYUU-JIN KYOTO
www.0757085177.com/english.html

JAPANESE GUESTHOUSES
www.japaneseguesthouses.com
Free service for booking traditional inns.

SAKURA HOUSE
www.sakura-house.com
Tokyo shared houses, apartments, dormitories.

TOHO YADO
www.toho.net
Bed-and-breakfasts in Hokkaido and elsewhere; in Japanese.

TOKYO APARTMENT
www.tokyoapartments.jp
Short- and long-term furnished/unfurnished apartments, houses, and real estate.

TOKYO COZY HOUSE
www.tokyocozyhouse.com
Furnished, shared rooms.

TOKYU STAY RESIDENCES
www.tokyustay.co.jp/e/index.html
Serviced apartments for extended stay travelers.

WEEKLY MANSION OSAKA
www.wmt-osaka.com

MAKING THE MOVE
Living in Japan
ABOUT MOVING TO JAPAN
http://aboutmovingtojapan.com/preparation.html

AMPONTAN—JAPAN FROM THE INSIDE OUT
http://ampontan.wordpress.com

EXPAT EXCHANGE
www.expatexchange.com
Advice on moving abroad, forums, and classifieds; click on Japan.

FUKUOKA EXPAT GUIDE
http://kyushu.com/fukuoka

GAIJINPOT
www.gaijinpot.com
Jobs, apartments, classifieds, living in Japan info.

GLOBAL COMPASSION
www.globalcompassion.com/moving.htm
Tips for moving and getting settled in Japan.

HANDBOOK FOR NEWCOMERS, MIGRANTS, AND IMMIGRANTS TO JAPAN
www.debito.org/?page_id=582
Information about every aspect of life as a foreigner, co-authored by a legal expert.

METROPOLIS CLASSIFIEDS
http://metropolis.co.jp/classifieds
Apartments, homes, furniture, household items, bicycles, cars for sale.

MOON LIVING ABROAD IN JAPAN
http://livingabroadinjapan.com
Companion site for this book.

MOVING WITH CHILDREN
www.tokyowithkids.com
Helpful information on living in Japan with children.

PETS
www.dog-superguide.com/dog_run
Dog runs, parks, and pet-friendly inns (in Japanese).

VETERINARY SANITATION SECTION
Living Environment Division, Bureau of Public
Health, Tokyo Metropolitan Government
tel. 03/5320-4412

WORLD WIDE ELECTRIC GUIDE
www.kropla.com/electric2.htm

International Moving Companies
Check to see if the company is an FIDI
Member (www.fidi.com) Registered
International Mover Certified, and has been
in business for at least 10 years. Get at least
three estimates (www.movingscam.com).

JAL ABC
www.jalabc.com/english/index2.html
Airport and domestic baggage delivery service.

NIPPON EXPRESS USA
www.nipponexpressusa.com/services/
moving_service/index.php
International moving service, sea/air,
storage, delivery. Offices in major cities
in the United States.

STERLING INTERNATIONAL
tel. 800/989-2198
www.sterlinginternational.com

YAMATO TRANSPORT CO., LTD.
www.kuronekoyamato.co.jp/en/personal/
airport
Airport, domestic, and international baggage delivery service.

When You Leave Japan
NIPPON EXPRESS CO., LTD.
tel. 03/6251-1111
www.nipponexpress.com/global_locator
Offices in Tokyo, Nagoya, Osaka,
Fukuoka, Sapporo.

Entry Procedures
ANIMAL QUARANTINE SERVICE
Ministry of Agriculture, Forestry, and
Fisheries
www.maff.go.jp/aqs/english

CUSTOMS/IMPORT
www.customs.go.jp/english/index.htm

IMMIGRATION INFORMATION CENTER
www.moj.go.jp/ENGLISH/IB/ip.html

U.S. DEPARTMENT OF STATE TIPS FOR TRAVELING ABROAD
http://travel.state.gov/travel/tips/tips_1232.
html#residing

VISAS AND FAQ
www.mofa.go.jp/j_info/visit/visa/index.html

HOUSING CONSIDERATIONS
METRIC TO IMPERIAL CONVERSION
www.onlineconversion.com

TOKYO PRICE GUIDE
www.tokyopriceguide.com/list.htm
Prices of consumer goods.

Rental Apartments and Houses
CLAIR
www.clair.or.jp/tagengo/index.html
Multilingual guide to housing and living
in Japan.

CRAIGSLIST
http://osaka.craigslist.jp
http://tokyo.craigslist.jp

GAIJINPOT
http://apartments.gaijinpot.com
Rentals, guesthouses, serviced apartments, agent list.

JAPAN HOME SEARCH
www.japanhomesearch.com

RESOURCES

LEOPALACE 21
http://en.leopalace21.com
Apartments for international students, business purposes in Tokyo, Osaka, and Fukuoka. English spoken.

RELOJAPAN
www.relojapan.com
Relocation service, information on cost of living, expat areas, international schools.

TOKYO RENT
tel. 03/3265-6363
www.tokyorent.com

TOKYU RELOCATION SUPPORT SPECIALIST
www.tokyu-relocation.co.jp/en/management

WMT HOTELS & APARTMENTS (WEEKLY MANSION TOKYO)
www.wmt.co.jp/en

Buying a House
NEW CITY MORTGAGE K.K.
www.ifg-asia.com/newcitymortgage.html
tel. 03/6822-9911
Housing loans for non-Japanese residents.

REAL ESTATE TOKYO
www.realestate-tokyo.com

LANGUAGE AND EDUCATION
INTERNATIONAL SCHOOLS IN JAPAN
http://japan.english-schools.org

Japanese Language Instruction
ASSOCIATION FOR THE PROMOTION OF JAPANESE LANGUAGE EDUCATION
www.nisshinkyo.org
Check if language schools are authorized by this professional organization.

JAPANESE LANGUAGE PROFICIENCY TEST–JAPAN
Japan Educational Exchanges and Services
http://info.jees-jlpt.jp/?lang=english

JAPANESE LANGUAGE PROFICIENCY TEST–UNITED STATES
Japan Foundation Los Angeles Language Center
tel. 213/621-2267
www.jflalc.org/jlpt.html

Tokyo
ASSOCIATION FOR JAPANESE-LANGUAGE TEACHING
2F Bridgestone Toranomon Bldg.
3-25-2 Toranomon, Minato-ku, Tokyo 105-0001
tel. 03/3459-9620
www.ajalt.org/e

HIROO JAPANESE CENTER
Palacion Hiroo Bldg. 402, 5-19-2 Hiroo, Shibuya-ku, Tokyo 150-0012
tel. 03/3444-3481
www.japaneselanguage.net

KAI JAPANESE LANGUAGE SCHOOL
3F, Miyuki Bldg., 1-15-18 Okubo, Shinjuku-ku, Tokyo 169-0072
tel. 03/3205-1356
www.kaij.jp

SHINJUKU JAPANESE LANGUAGE INSTITUTE
2-9-7 Takadanobaba, Shinjuku-ku, Tokyo 169-0075
tel. 03/5273-0044
www.sng.ac.jp

TOKYO SCHOOL OF THE JAPANESE LANGUAGE
16-26 Nampeidai-cho, Shibuya-ku, Tokyo 150-0036
tel. 03/3463-7261
www.naganuma-school.ac.jp

Sapporo
JAPANESE LANGUAGE INSTITUTE OF SAPPORO
2-7 Nishi-26, Minami-6, Chuo-ku, Sapporo, Hokkaido 064-0806
tel. 011/562-7001
www.jli.co.jp

Gunma
NIPPON LANGUAGE ACADEMY
2-5-10 Otemachi, Maebashi-shi, Gunma 371-0026
tel. 027/243-2222
www.nila.jp

Nagano
MARUNOUCHI COLLEGE OF BUSINESS JAPANESE COURSE
1-3-30 Josei, Matsumoto-shi, Nagano, 390-0875
tel. 0263/32-5589
www.marubi.ac.jp

Kyoto
KYOTO CENTER FOR JAPANESE LINGUISTIC STUDIES
Kyoto Japanese Language School
394-2 Higashihinotono-machi, Higashi-hairu, Ichijodori-shinmachi, Kamigyo-ku, Kyoto 602-0917
tel. 075/414-0449
www.kjls.or.jp

KYOTO UNIVERSITY OF FOREIGN STUDIES
6 Kasamecho, Nishiin, Ukyo-ku, Kyoto 615-8558
tel. 075/322-6043
www.kufs.ac.jp/english_site/index.html

KYOTO VISITOR'S GUIDE
www.kyotoguide.com/ver2/guide/language-.htm
Language schools in Kyoto.

Osaka
OSAKA JAPANESE LANGUAGE EDUCATION CENTER
8-3-13 Uehonmachi, Tennoji-ku, Osaka 543-0001
tel. 06/6774-0033
www.jasso.go.jp/ojlec/index_e.html

Hiroshima
HIROSHIMA YMCA INTERNATIONAL BUSINESS COLLEGE
7-11 Hacchoubori, Naka-ku, Hiroshima 730-8523
tel. 082/223-1292
http://hymca.jp/jp

Shikoku
ANABUKI BUSINESS COLLEGE JAPANESE COURSE TAKAMATSU
1-7-5 Nishikimachi, Takamatsu-shi, Kagawa, 760-0020
tel. 087/823-7700
www.anabuki.ac.jp/college/ajk/en

EHIME PREFECTURAL INTERNATIONAL ASSOCIATION JAPANESE LANGUAGE CLASSES
1-1 Dogo Ichiman, Matsuyama-shi, Ehime-ken 790-0844
tel. 089/917-5678
www.epic.or.jp/english/japanese.html

JAPANESE CLASSES AT TOPIA TOKUSHIMA
Clement Plaza 6F, 1-61 Terashima Honcho Nishi, Tokushima-shi, 770-0831
tel. 088/656-3303
www.topia.ne.jp/e_index.htm

Fukuoka
ASIA JAPANESE ACADEMY
4-2-29 Nagazumi, Minami-ku, Fukuoka-shi 811-1362
tel. 092/557-8667
www.a-j-academy.jp/aja_en/index.htm

RESOURCES

Online Language Tools

ABOUT.COM: JAPANESE LANGUAGE
http://japanese.about.com/library/mmore.htm

ALL ABOUT RADICALS
http://japanese.about.com/library/weekly/aa070101a.htm
Mastering written Japanese.

CHARLES KELLY'S ONLINE JAPANESE LANGUAGE STUDY MATERIALS
www.manythings.org/japanese

KEIKO SCHNEIDER'S BOOKMARKS
www.sabotenweb.com/bookmarks
Links for teachers and students of Japanese.

YOOKOSO
www.yookoso.com/pages/study.php
Japanese language study links.

Studying Abroad

AMERICAN ASSOCIATION OF TEACHERS OF JAPANESE
www.aatj.org/studyabroad/index.html
Database on study in Japan.

AT HOME IN JAPAN: WHAT NO ONE TELLS YOU
http://athome.nealrc.org
Cultural tutorial to help learners cope with homestays.

JAPANESE STUDENT SERVICES ORGANIZATION
www.jasso.go.jp/study_j/index_e.html
Comprehensive information on studying in Japan and scholarships.

STUDENT GUIDE TO JAPAN
www.jasso.go.jp/study_j/sgtj_e.html
Essential information for studying in Japan.

STUDY-ABROAD PROGRAMS OF U.S. UNIVERSITIES
www.studyabroad.com/programs/academic/japan

STUDY IN JAPAN: A COMPREHENSIVE GUIDE
www.studyjapan.go.jp/en/index.html
A government-sponsored guide for foreign students in Japan.

Tokyo

AOYAMA GAKUIN UNIVERSITY
4-4-25 Shibuya, Shibuya-ku, Tokyo 150-8366
tel. 03/3409-8156
http://web.iec.aoyama.ac.jp

COUNCIL ON INTERNATIONAL EDUCATIONAL EXCHANGE (CIEE)
www.ciee.org
Offers a program at Sophia University.

EARLHAM COLLEGE
http://japanstudy.earlham.edu
Study-abroad program at Waseda University.

TEMPLE UNIVERSITY JAPAN
www.temple.edu/studyabroad/programs/semester_year/index.html
Japanese language and degrees in social sciences and humanities.

TOKYO UNIVERSITY OF FOREIGN STUDIES
3-11-1 Asahicho, Fuchu-shi, Tokyo 183-8534
tel. 042/330-5184
www.tufs.ac.jp/english

WASEDA UNIVERSITY–OREGON ABROAD
http://oregonabroad.ous.edu/countries/japan/waseda/waseda.html
One-year program in Japanese language and Japanese studies.

Hokkaido
HOKKAIDO UNIVERSITY SHORT-TERM EXCHANGE PROGRAM
tel. 011/706-2177
www.hokudai.ac.jp/en/index.html
Program in language, society, environmental studies, engineering, medicine.

HOKUSEI GAKUEN UNIVERSITY
2-3-1 Ohyachi-Nishi, Atsubetsu-ku, Sapporo 004-8631
tel. 011/891-2731
www.hokusei.ac.jp/en

Gunma
UNIVERSITY OF CREATION: ART, MUSIC, AND SOCIAL WORK
2-3-6 Yachiyo-machi Takasaki-shi, Gunma-ken 370-0861
tel. 027/388-2301
http://english.souzou.ac.jp/index.htm

Nagano
NAGANO UNIVERSITY
Shimonogo 658-1, Ueda-shi, Nagano 386-1298
tel. 0268/39-001
www.nagano.ac.jp/english/index.html

Kyoto
DOSHISHA UNIVERSITY, KYOTO
www.associatedkyotoprogram.org
www.doshisha.ac.jp/english/education/index.html

KYOTO CONSORTIUM FOR JAPANESE STUDIES
www.kcjs.columbia.edu
One-year program in advanced Japanese language and Japanese studies.

Osaka
KANSAI GAIDAI UNIVERSITY
www.kansaigaidai.ac.jp/asp/03_academics/02/01.html

Hiroshima
HIROSHIMA CITY UNIVERSITY
3-4-1 Ozuka-Higashi, Asa-Minami-Ku, Hiroshima, 731-3194
tel. 082/830-1500, fax 082/830-1656
www.hiroshima-cu.ac.jp/english/index.php

HIROSHIMA UNIVERSITY STUDY ABROAD PROGRAM
www.hiroshima-u.ac.jp/en/husaprogram_incoming
Information for incoming exchange students.

Shikoku
MATSUYAMA UNIVERSITY
4-2 Bunkyo-cho, Matsuyama, Ehime-ken 790-8578
www.matsuyama-u.ac.jp/english/index.htm

Fukuoka
KYUSHU UNIVERSITY INTERNATIONAL STUDENT CENTER, FUKUOKA
www.isc.kyushu-u.ac.jp/center/home.htm

HEALTH
General
ACCESSIBLE TOKYO
http://accessible.jp.org/tokyo/en

HEALTH ISSUES FOR TRAVEL ABROAD
U.S. Department of State
http://travel.state.gov/travel/tips/tips_1232.html#health

JAPAN ACCESSIBLE TOURIST CENTER
www.japan-accessible.com
Accessibility information arranged by city.

JAPAN FOUNDATION FOR AIDS PREVENTION
tel. 03/5940-2127
www.aidsmap.com/org/9556/page/1411896
AIDS support line.

RESOURCES

MEDICAL RESOURCES IN TOKYO
http://japan.usembassy.gov/e/acs/tacs-tokyodoctors.html

MINISTRY OF HEALTH, LABOUR, AND WELFARE
www.mhlw.go.jp/english/index.html
Information on health and medical care, child-rearing, long-term care, and health and welfare services.

NISHI-SHINJUKU PUBLIC HEALTH CENTER
7-5-8 Nishi-Shinjuku, Tokyo
tel. 03/5273-3859
www.city.shinjuku.lg.jp/foreign/english/oshirase/teiki/aids.html
Telephone consultation services in English, Thai, Portuguese, and Spanish.

STEDMAN'S ENGLISH-JAPANESE MEDICAL DICTIONARY (6TH ED.)
www.appannie.com/stedmans-english-japanese-medical-dictionary-6th-ed
Available for iPhone/iPod Touch.

TOKYO ENGLISH LIFE LINE (TELL)
tel. 03/5774-0992
www.telljp.com
Problem-solving assistance, counseling, and referrals.

USEFUL JAPANESE EXPRESSIONS AT A HOSPITAL
www.city.shinjuku.tokyo.jp/foreign/english/guide/byouki/byouki_3.html

Health Insurance
ENROLLMENT IN NATIONAL HEALTH INSURANCE
www.city.shinjuku.lg.jp/foreign/english/guide/tax/tax_4.html
Everyone living in Japan is obliged to enroll in public health insurance.

Hospitals and Clinics
AMDA INTERNATIONAL MEDICAL INFORMATION CENTER
tel. 03/5285-8088
http://amda-imic.com/lng_eng
Referrals, interpreter assistance, and advice on the medical system in Japan.

ENGLISH-SPEAKING MEDICAL FACILITIES IN JAPAN
http://japan.usembassy.gov/e/acs/tacs-7119.html

EMERGENCY TRANSLATION SERVICES
tel. 03/5285-8185
Telephone translation for foreign patients who need help communicating with a doctor.

INTERNATIONAL MENTAL HEALTH PROFESSIONALS JAPAN
www.imhpj.org
A database of professional therapists.

TOKYO METROPOLITAN HEALTH AND MEDICAL INFORMATION CENTER
tel. 03/5285-8181
www.himawari.metro.tokyo.jp/qq/qq13enmnlt.asp
Search hospitals and clinics by location or nearest train station.

Emergency Phone Numbers
EMERGENCY
tel. 119

AMBULANCE
tel. 119

FIRE
tel. 119

POLICE
tel. 110

JAPAN HELPLINE
tel. 0120/46-1997
http://jhelp.com
A 24-hour multilingual service with practical and emergency information.

EMPLOYMENT
ASSOCIATION OF INTERNATIONAL EDUCATION JAPAN (AIEJ)
JLPT Section, Testing Division
tel. 03/5454-5577
www.aiej.or.jp
Japanese Language Proficiency Test.

JAPANESE ARTIST-IN-RESIDENCE PROGRAMS (AIR JAPAN)
http://en.air-j.info

JAPANESE LAW TRANSLATION
www.japaneselawtranslation.go.jp
Know employment laws and your rights.

METROPOLIS
www.metropolis.co.jp
Classified listings.

WWOOF JAPAN
www.wwoofjapan.com
Work on an organic farm in exchange for room and board.

Business
GAIJINPOT
www.gaijinpot.com

JAPAN EXTERNAL TRADE ORGANIZATION (JETRO)
www.jetro.go.jp
A government-related organization promoting mutual trade and investment between Japan and the world.

NIHON KEIZAI SHINBUN (JAPAN ECONOMIC NEWSPAPER)
http://e.nikkei.com/e/fr/freetop.aspx

SMALL BUSINESS PROMOTION AGENCY
www.tokyo-kosha.or.jp
Tokyo Metropolitan Small and Medium Enterprise Support Center.

TEMPSTAFF GROUP
tel. 03/6731-3334
www.tempstaff.co.jp/universal/eng/index.html

WORK IN JAPAN
www.daijob.com/en

Teaching English
DAVE'S ESL CAFE
www.eslcafe.com

ELT NEWS
www.eltnews.com/jobs

HOKKAIDO TEACHING JOBS
www.ne.jp/asahi/hokkaido/kenhartmann/index.html

INTERAC
tel. 03/3234-7857
www.interac.co.jp/recruit
Recruits assistant language teachers for Japanese elementary through high schools.

JAPAN ASSOCIATION OF LANGUAGE TEACHERS
http://jalt.org
Professional organization with chapters in many cities; job listings.

JAPAN EXCHANGE AND TEACHING PROGRAM (JET)
www.jetprogramme.org

JAPANESE UNIVERSITIES
www.debito.org/greenlist.html
List of universities that grant tenure to foreign teachers; see also Black List (www.debito.org/blacklist.html).

Teaching at International Schools
INTERNATIONAL SCHOOLS
www.tokyowithkids.com/fyi/international_schools.html

Volunteering
IT'S NOT JUST MUD
http://itsnotjustmud.com
Nonprofit volunteer organization specializing in disaster relief and grass-roots support and rehabilitation of disaster-affected individuals and small businesses. Based in Ishinomaki, in the Tohoku region.

PEACE BOAT
tel. 03/3362-6307
http://peaceboat.jp/relief/volunteer
Japan-based international nongovernmental and nonprofit organization that works to promote peace, human rights, equal and sustainable development, and respect for the environment. Volunteer at 10 sites in Japan including the Tohoku region.

SECOND HARVEST JAPAN
www.2hj.org/index.php/eng_home
Second Harvest Japan is working to create a food lifeline by providing food resources to low-income households and aid agencies.

SENDAI YMCA VOLUNTEER SUPPORT CENTER
http://sites.sendai-ymca.org/volunteer_support/home_e

TOHOKU WALKER VOLUNTEER YELLOW PAGES
http://sp.walkerplus.com/tohokuwalker/volunteer (in Japanese)
Search by location and type of work you want to do, and read stories of others who have volunteered.

FINANCE
Legal Consulting
JAPAN EXTERNAL TRADE ORGANIZATION (JETRO)
www.jetro.org
Market entry consulting, as well as business and economic trends.

JAPAN MANAGEMENT CONSULTING
www.japanconsult.com/japan-company-guidebook-faq/japan-corporate-law

SHINSHU SERVICES, INC.
www.shinshuservices.com

TOKYO STOCK EXCHANGE, INC.
Information Services Department
tel. 03/3666-0141
www.tse.or.jp/english

International Banks
BANK OF TOKYO-MITSUBISHI UFJ
www.bk.mufg.jp/english

CITIBANK JAPAN
www.citibank.co.jp

JAPAN POST BANK
www.jp-bank.japanpost.jp/en_index.html

MIZUHO BANK
www.mizuhobank.co.jp/english/index.html

SUMITOMO MITSUI BANKING CORPORATION
www.smbc.co.jp/global/index.html

Taxes
GUIDE TO METROPOLITAN TAXES (FOR TOKYO RESIDENTS)
Tokyo Metropolitan Citizens Information Room
3F, Main Bldg. No. 1, Tokyo Metropolitan Government, 2-8-1 Nishi-Shinjuku, Shinjuku-ku, Tokyo
tel. 03/5321-1111

Investing
TOKYO STOCK EXCHANGE, INC.
Information Services Department
tel. 03/3666-0141
www.tse.or.jp/english

NIKKEI INDEXES
http://indexes.nikkei.co.jp/en/nkave/index

NIKKEI INTERACTIVE
http://e.nikkei.com/e/fr/marketlive.aspx

NIKKEI WEEKLY
www.nikkei4946.com/sb/e_index/index.asp

JAFCO CO., LTD.
www.jafco.co.jp/english

JAPAN SECURITIES AGENTS, LTD.
www.jsa-hp.co.jp
Subsidiary of Sumitomo Mitsui Trust Bank, Ltd.

COMMUNICATIONS
Media
ASIA WALL STREET JOURNAL
http://asia.wsj.com/home-page

DAILY YOMIURI
www.yomiuri.co.jp/dy

INTERNATIONAL HERALD TRIBUNE
http://global.nytimes.com/?iht

JAPAN TIMES
www.japantimes.co.jp

MIXI–JAPANESE SOCIAL NETWORK
http://mixi.jp

NHK WORLD
www3.nhk.or.jp/nhkworld

NIKKEI BUSINESS ONLINE
http://e.nikkei.com/e/fr/freetop.aspx

Mobile Phones
KDDI AU
www.au.kddi.com/english/index.html

NTT DOCOMO
www.nttdocomo.co.jp/english

SOFTBANK
http://mb.softbank.jp/en
http://mb.softbank.jp/en/prepaid_service

Mobile Phone Rentals
CELLULARABROAD.COM
www.cellularabroad.com/japan-phone.php

JAL ABC MOBILE PHONE RENTAL
www.jalabc.com/rental/domestic_eng/index.html

PUPURU
www.pupuru.com/en

RENTAFONE JAPAN
www.rentafonejapan.com

SOFTBANK RENTAL
www.softbank-rental.jp/en/index.php

TELECOM SQUARE
www.telecomsquare.co.jp/en

Landline Telephones
KDDI
tel. 0057
www.kddi.com/english/telephone

RESOURCES

NTT COMMUNICATIONS
tel. 0120/532-839
www.ntt.com/index-e.html

Internet Service Providers
ASAHI NET
tel. 0570/013522 (in English)
http://asahi-net.jp/en

J:COM
www.jcom.co.jp/english.html

KDDI AU
www.au.kddi.com/english/internet/index.html

NIFTY
www.nifty.com

SPINNET
www.spinnet.jp/indexe.html

Baggage Delivery Services
NITTSU (NIPPON EXPRESS)
www.nittsu.co.jp

SAGAWA EXPRESS
www.sagawa-exp.co.jp/english/main.html

YAMATO TRANSPORT CO., LTD.
www.kuronekoyamato.co.jp/en

Express Mail Services
DHL JAPAN
www.dhl.co.jp/publish/jp/en.high.html

EMS INTERNATIONAL MAIL SERVICE
www.post.japanpost.jp/int/ems/index_en.html

FEDEX JAPAN
www.fedex.com/jp_english

OVERSEAS COURIER SERVICE (OCS)
www.ocstracking.com

Delivers foreign newspapers, magazines, and books to you in Japan.

Postal Services
JAPAN POST
www.post.japanpost.jp/english

POSTAL INFORMATION SERVICE
tel. 03/5472-5851 or 03/5472-5852 (in English)

TRAVEL AND TRANSPORTATION
JAPAN VISITOR TRAVEL INFORMATION
www.japanvisitor.com/index.php?cID=374&pID=800

JTB (JAPAN TRAVEL BUREAU)
www.jtb.co.jp

Air
AIR DO
www.airdo.jp/ap/index.html (in Japanese)
Flies between Tokyo and Sapporo and other Hokkaido cities.

ALL NIPPON AIRWAYS (ANA)
tel. 0120/029-222
www.ana.co.jp/eng/index.html

JAPAN AIRLINES (JAL)
tel. 0120/25-5971
www.jal.co.jp/en

KANSAI INTERNATIONAL AIRPORT (OSAKA)
www.kansai-airport.or.jp/en/index.asp

NARITA INTERNATIONAL AIRPORT (TOKYO)
www.narita-airport.or.jp/airport_e/index.html

PEACH AVIATION
www.flypeach.com/home.aspx

Low-cost carrier based in Japan.

SKYMARK AIRLINES
www.skymark.co.jp/en/index.html

Train
HYPERDIA TIMETABLE
www.hyperdia.com
Search schedules, routes, and fares for JR and private railways.

JAPAN RAIL PASS
www.japanrailpass.net/eng/en001.html
Where to get and how to use the Japan Rail Pass.

JORUDAN TRAIN ROUTE FINDER
www.jorudan.co.jp/english
Enter departure station and destination to find schedules and fares.

JR EAST
www.jreast.co.jp/e/charge/index.asp
Routes and fares for East Japan Railway Company.

JR WEST
www.westjr.co.jp/english
Routes and fares for West Japan Railway Company.

KEISEI SKYLINER
www.keisei.co.jp/keisei/tetudou/skyliner/us/index.html

Subway
TOEI TRANSPORTATION
www.kotsu.metro.tokyo.jp/english/index.html
Toei metropolitan subway, bus, and street-car information for Tokyo.

TOKYO METRO
www.tokyometro.jp/en/index.html
One of two subway systems in Tokyo.

Car
BUYING A CAR
www.globalcompassion.com/buying-car.htm

BUYING A CAR IN JAPAN
http://uktoyotaestimasite.tripod.com/Buy_Car_Japan.htm

DRIVER'S LICENSE
www.japandriverslicense.com

JAPAN AUTOMOBILE FEDERATION
www.jaf.or.jp/e/index.htm

LEASE JAPAN
www.leasejapan.com

TOCOO CAR RENTAL
www2.tocoo.jp/?file=rentcar_inbound/main

Taxi
INFO TAXI
www.infotaxi.org/city-2175.htm

Bus
HIGHWAY BUSES
www.japan-guide.com/e/e2366.html
How to use long-distance buses.

JAPAN BUS WEB
www.japan-guide.com/e/e2369.html

JR BUS KANTO
www.jrbuskanto.co.jp/bus_route_e
Use your Japan Rail Pass on JR buses.

Boat
JR KYUSHU JET FERRY
www.jrbeetle.co.jp/english
Travel from Fukuoka to Busan, Korea, in three hours.

KANSAI KISEN FERRY LINES
http://ease.com/~randyj/rjjapanf.htm#kksen
Ferry routes in Japan.

Bicycle
CYCLETECH-IKD
Takasaki, Gunma-ken
tel. 027/324-2360
www.ikd21.co.jp/ikd/about/access.html
Ask store manager Mr. Yoshida about cycle-touring Japan. Takasaki is north of Tokyo.

CYCLE TOKYO!
http://cycle-tokyo.cycling.jp
All the information you need to bike in Tokyo, plus free city tours.

EHICLE (BIKE SHOP)
3-4 Sumiyoshi-cho, Shinjuku-ku, Tokyo
tel. 03/6691-6468
www.bikefriday.com/dealers/
bike_friday_dealers/ehicle-_tokyo
Folding bikes.

ITO CYCLES
5-25-24 Toyosato, Higashi Yodogawa-ku, Osaka
tel. 06/329-2395
www.bikefriday.com/dealers/
bike_friday_dealers/ito_cycles_-_osaka
Bike shop with folding bikes.

KYOTO CYCLING PROJECT
www.kctp.net/en
Rental bikes and guided cycle tours of Kyoto.

GAY AND LESBIAN RESOURCES
GAY JAPAN NEWS
www.gayjapannews.com
LGBT-centered news stories in Japanese. Limited English.

JAPAN VISITOR'S GUIDE TO GAY JAPAN
www.japanvisitor.com/index.
php?cID=362&pID=977
Gay and lesbian bars, clubs, and community in Tokyo.

UTOPIA ASIA
www.utopia-asia.com/womjapn.htm
Resources and listings for gays and lesbians.

PRIME LIVING LOCATIONS
Tokyo
CLAIR
www.clair.or.jp/e/index.html
Information on housing, status of residence, alien registration, and medical services in nine languages.

TOKYO INFORMATION NET
http://jin.jcic.or.jp/en/lifeandstyle

TOKYO METROPOLITAN CITIZENS INFORMATION ROOM
3F, Main Bldg. No. 1, Tokyo Metropolitan Government, 2-8-1 Nishi-Shinjuku, Shinjuku-ku, Tokyo
tel. 03/5321-1111

TOKYO METROPOLITAN GOVERNMENT
www.metro.tokyo.jp/ENGLISH/index.htm
Informative guide for foreign residents.

Tokyo's Core Cities
ARAKAWA-KU
www.city.arakawa.tokyo.jp

BUNKYO-KU
www.city.bunkyo.lg.jp

CHIYODA-KU
www.city.chiyoda.tokyo.jp

ITABASHI-KU
www.city.itabashi.tokyo.jp

MEGURO-KU
www.city.meguro.tokyo.jp

MINATO-KU
www.city.minato.tokyo.jp/e/index.html

MITAKA CITY
www.city.mitaka.tokyo.jp/foreign/english/
index.html

NAKANO-KU
www.city.tokyo-nakano.lg.jp/foreign/english/
index.html

NISHI TOKYO CITY
www.city.nishitokyo.lg.jp/english/index.html

SETAGAYA-KU
www.city.setagaya.tokyo.jp/english/index.
html

TOSHIMA-KU
www.city.toshima.lg.jp

Tokyo Resources
TOKYO CRAIGSLIST
http://tokyo.craigslist.jp

TOKYO WITH KIDS
www.tokyowithkids.com

Tokyo Media
ASAHI SHIMBUN
www.asahi.com/english

DAILY YOMIURI
www.yomiuri.co.jp/dy

INTERNATIONAL HERALD TRIBUNE
http://global.nytimes.com/?iht

JAPAN TIMES
www.japantimes.co.jp

MAINICHI DAILY NEWS
http://mdn.mainichi.jp

METROPOLIS
www.metropolis.co.jp

NIKKEI WEEKLY
http://e.nikkei.com/e/fr/freetop.aspx

NHK TELEVISION
www3.nhk.or.jp/nhkworld

RADIO JAPAN ONLINE
www3.nhk.or.jp/nhkworld/english/radio/
program/index.html

TOKYO CLASSIFIEDS
http://classifieds.japantoday.com

TOKYO TOURISM INFO
www.tourism.metro.tokyo.jp/english

Tokyo Housing
CENTURY 21 SKY REALTY
www.century21japan.com

JAPAN HOME SEARCH
www.japanhomesearch.com

SAKURA HOUSE
www.sakura-house.com/index.htm
Tokyo house share, apartments and
dormitories.

TOKYO LIFE GUIDE
www.housingjapan.com/tokyo-guide
Rent or buy in expat areas.

Tokyo Utilities
**TOKYO ELECTRIC POWER
COMPANY (TEPCO)**
www.tepco.co.jp/en/index-e.html
Operates the Fukushima Dai-ichi
Nuclear Power Plant

TOKYO GAS
www.tokyo-gas.co.jp/index_e.html

**TOKYO METROPOLITAN
GOVERNMENT, BUREAU OF
WATERWORKS**
www.waterworks.metro.tokyo.jp/eng/tws/
ws_05.htm

Tokyo Medical
SEIBO INTERNATIONAL CATHOLIC HOSPITAL
Seibo-kai Seibo Byoin, 2-5-1 Naka-Ochiai,
Shinjuku-ku, Tokyo
tel. 03/3951-1111
http://catholic-toshima.web9.jp/english/
seibohospital.html

ST. LUKE'S INTERNATIONAL HOSPITAL
Seiroka Kokusai Byoin, 9-1 Akashi-cho,
Chuo-ku, Tokyo
tel. 03/3541-5151
www.luke.or.jp/eng/index.html

TOKYO ADVENTIST HOSPITAL
Tokyo Eisei Byoin, 3-17-3 Amanuma,
Suginami-ku, Tokyo
tel. 03/3392-6151

TOKYO METROPOLITAN HIROO HOSPITAL
Tokyo Toritsu Hiroo Byoin, 2-34-10 Ebisu,
Shibuya-ku, Tokyo
tel. 03/3444-1181

Tokyo Organizations
AMERICAN CHAMBER OF COMMERCE IN JAPAN
tel. 03/3433-5381
www.accj.or.jp

ASSOCIATION OF FOREIGN WIVES OF JAPANESE
http://afwj.org

GLOBAL YOUTH EXCHANGE (GYE) PROGRAM
www.mofa.go.jp/policy/culture/people/
youth/gye/index.html

Tokyo International Schools
THE AMERICAN SCHOOL IN JAPAN
1-1-1 Nomizu, Chofu-shi, Tokyo
tel. 0422/34-5300
www.asij.ac.jp

BRITISH SCHOOL IN TOKYO
1-21-18 Shibuya, Shibuya-ku, Tokyo 150-0002
tel. 03/5467-4321
www.bst.ac.jp

CANADIAN INTERNATIONAL SCHOOL
5-8-20 Kitashinagawa, Shinagawa-ku, Tokyo
141-0001
tel. 03/5793-1392
www.cisjapan.net

CHRISTIAN ACADEMY IN JAPAN
1-2-14 Shinkawacho, Higashi Kurume, Tokyo
203-0013
tel. 0424/71-0022
www.caj.or.jp

INTERNATIONAL SCHOOL OF THE SACRED HEART
4-3-1 Hiroo, Shibuya-ku, Tokyo 150-0012
tel. 03/3400-3951
www.issh.ac.jp

THE MONTESSORI SCHOOL OF TOKYO
3-5-13 Minami Azabu, Minato-ku, Tokyo
106-0047
tel. 03/5449-7067
www.montessorijapan.com

NISHIMACHI INTERNATIONAL SCHOOL
2-14-7 Moto Azabu, Minato-ku, Tokyo
106-0046
tel. 03/3451-5520
http//:www.nishimachi.ac.jp

ST. MARY'S INTERNATIONAL SCHOOL
1-6-19 Seta, Setagaya-ku, Tokyo 158-8668
tel. 03/3709-3411
www.smis.ac.jp

Tokyo Services

FUCHU DRIVER'S LICENSE TESTING AND ISSUING CENTER
3-1-1 Tama-machi, Fuchu-shi, Tokyo
tel. 042/362-3591 or 042/334-6000 (English)
www.keishicho.metro.tokyo.jp/foreign/organize/people.htm

IMMIGRATION BUREAU, MINISTRY OF JUSTICE
Immigration Information Center
1-1-1 Kasumigaseki, Chiyoda-ku, Tokyo
100-8977
tel. 03/3580-4111
www.immi-moj.go.jp/english
A new residency management system for foreigners with mid- to long-term status began in July 2012. For details, see www.immi-moj.go.jp/newimmiact_1/en/index.html.

KOTO DRIVER'S LICENSE TESTING AND ISSUING CENTER
1-7-24 Shinsuna, Koto-ku, Tokyo
tel. 03/3699-1151

SAMEZU DRIVER'S LICENSE TESTING AND ISSUING CENTER
1-12-5 Higashi-Oi, Shinagawa-ku, Tokyo
tel. 03/3474-1374 or 03/5463-6000 (English)

Hokkaido: Sapporo

CITY OF SAPPORO
www.city.sapporo.jp/city/english/index.html
Information on living in Sapporo for foreign residents.

ELM FUDOSAN (REAL ESTATE)
www.oba-q.com/elmf (in Japanese)

HOKKAIDO GOVERNMENT
www.pref.hokkaido.lg.jp

HOKKAIDO INSIDER NEWS—JOBS
www.ne.jp/asahi/hokkaido/kenhartmann

HOKKAIDO INTERNATIONAL SCHOOL
tel. 011/816-5000
www.his.ac.jp

INSPECTION DIVISION, LABOR STANDARDS DEPARTMENT
tel. 011/709-2311
http://hokkaido-roudoukyoku.jsite.mhlw.go.jp/madoguchi_annai/soudan04.html
Consultation for foreign workers regarding workplace matters.

JALT HOKKAIDO
http://jalthokkaido.org
Local chapter of Japan Association of Language Teachers.

JAPANESE LANGUAGE INSTITUTE OF SAPPORO
tel. 011/562-7001
www.jli.co.jp/english/frame.html

KINOKUNIYA BOOKSTORE
Sapporo 55 5-7 Kita-Gojo Nishi, Chuo-ku, Sapporo 060-0005
tel. 011/231-2131
English books, magazines, and newspapers.

LEGAL SERVICE NETWORK FOR FOREIGNERS IN SAPPORO
tel. 011/204-9535
www.sapporo-lsnet.com/en

MEDICAL RESOURCES IN SAPPORO
http://japan.usembassy.gov/e/acs/tacs-sapporodoctors.html

NORTHERN ROAD NAVI
http://northern-road.jp/navi/eng/guide.htm
Includes temperature, snow depth, winter driving, traffic safety, and barrier-free mobility information.

RESOURCES

SAPPORO INTERNATIONAL COMMUNICATION PLAZA FOUNDATION
Kita 1, Nishi 3, Chuo-ku, Sapporo
tel. 011/221-3670
www.plaza-sapporo.or.jp/english/index_e.html
Japanese language, city events, bilingual TV, concerts, and movies.

SAPPORO MEDICAL UNIVERSITY HOSPITAL
Nishi 16-291, Minami 1-jo, Chuo-ku, Sapporo
tel. 011/611-2111

SAPPORO REGIONAL IMMIGRATION BUREAU
Odori-Nishi 12-chome, Chuo-ku, Sapporo 060-0042
tel. 011/261-7502
www.immi-moj.go.jp/english/soshiki/kikou/sapporo.html

SIL SAPPORO NIHONGO GAKKOU (LANGUAGE SCHOOL)
tel. 011/614-1101
www.silnihongo.com/homeeng.html

Hokkaido: Obihiro
CHIEN, INC. (REAL ESTATE AGENT)
www.chien.co.jp (in Japanese)

CITY OF OBIHIRO
www.city.obihiro.hokkaido.jp/kurashiindex/e010101.jsp

JOY ENGLISH ACADEMY
11-69 Nishi-17 Minami-5, Obihiro
tel. 0155/33-0198
www.joyworld.com

OBIHIRO UNIVERSITY OF AGRICULTURE AND VETERINARY MEDICINE
www.obihiro.ac.jp/english

Hokkaido: Kushiro
CITY OF KUSHIRO
http://international.city.kushiro.hokkaido.jp

HOKKAIDO UNIVERSITY OF EDUCATION KUSHIRO CAMPUS
www.kus.hokkyodai.ac.jp

KUSHIRO CITY GENERAL HOSPITAL (SHIRITSU KUSHIRO SOGO BYOIN)
1-12 Shunkodai, Kushiro
tel. 0154/41-6121

KUSHIRO PUBLIC UNIVERSITY OF ECONOMICS
www.kushiro-pu.ac.jp/e/index.html

Hokkaido: Hakodate
FUTURE UNIVERSITY–HAKODATE
www.fun.ac.jp/en/index.html
Established in 2000, with emphasis on communication technology.

HAKODATE FUDOSAN WEB (REAL ESTATE)
www.hbf.ne.jp/real (in Japanese)

HAKODATE UNIVERSITY
www.hakodate-u.ac.jp/index.php

HOKKAIDO UNIVERSITY OF EDUCATION HAKODATE
www.hak.hokkyodai.ac.jp

LIVING GUIDE HAKODATE
www.city.hakodate.hokkaido.jp/kikaku/english/livingguidehakodate.pdf

SHIRITSU HAKODATE BYOIN (HAKODATE CITY HOSPITAL)
2-33 Yayoi-cho, Hakodate
tel. 0138/23-8651

Central Mountains: Gunma
ERA COSMO CITY (REAL ESTATE)
tel. 0270/40-6655
www.erajapan.co.jp (in Japanese)

GUNMAJET
http://gunmajet.net
News, events, teaching, travel guide.

GUNMA PREFECTURE OFFICE
1-1-1 Otemachi, Maebashi
tel. 027/223-1111
www.pref.gunma.jp/foreign/foreign_English.
html

GUNMA TOURISM INTERNATIONAL ASSOCIATION
3F Gunma Kaikan, 2-1-1 Ote-machi, Maebashi
tel. 027/243-7271
www.gtia.jp/kokusai/english/index.php
Consultation, interpreting, hospitals, Japanese lessons, resources for daily life.

KOBAYASI FUDOSAN (REAL ESTATE)
tel. 0274/42-8213
www.kobayasi-fudosan.jp (in Japanese)

Central Mountains: Takasaki
CYCLETECH-IKD (BICYCLE SHOP)
tel. 027/324-2360
www.ikd21.co.jp/ikd/about/access.html

IMMIGRATION OFFICE
tel. 027/328-1154

INSIDER'S SCOOP ON TAKASAKI
www.gunmajet.net/guides/
insider%E2%80%99s-scoop

KOKURITSU TAKASAKI BYOIN (TAKASAKI NATIONAL HOSPITAL)
36 Takamatsu-cho, Takasaki
tel. 0273/22-5901

TAKASAKI CITY UNIVERSITY OF ECONOMICS
www.tcue.ac.jp/english/index.html

TAKASAKI UNIVERSITY OF COMMERCE
www.tuc.ac.jp

TAKASAKI UNIVERSITY OF HEALTH AND WELFARE
www.takasaki-u.ac.jp/english/index.html

TEZUKA DENTISTRY
86-1 Tamachi, Takasaki
tel. 027/322-3843
English-speaking dentist.

TTA (REAL ESTATE)
www.tta.gr.jp (in Japanese)

Central Mountains: Ota
GUNMA KOKUSAI ACADEMY
www.gka.jp/english/index.html
A 12-year English immersion school in Ota city.

OTA CITY HALL
2-35, Hama-cho, Ota-shi, Gunma-ken
tel. 0276/47-1111
www.city.ota.tokyo.jp/index.html

Central Mountains: Nagano
NAGANO CITY HALL
www.city.nagano.nagano.jp

INTERNATIONAL EXCHANGE CORNER (IEC)
3rd Fl. of Monzen Plaza, 485-1 Shinden-cho, Nagano
tel. 026/223-0053
http://kokusai.sakura.ne.jp/kokusai.html
Internet, library, and Japanese language classes for foreign residents.

NAGANO CITY HEALTH CENTER, HEALTH CARE SECTION
tel. 026/226-9960
Low-cost medical check-ups, cancer screening, and vaccinations.

NAGANO CITY RESIDENTIAL HOUSING SECTION
tel. 026/224-5424

NAGANO LOCAL LEGAL AFFAIRS JOINT GOVERNMENT BLDG.
1108 Asahi-cho, Nagano-shi
tel. 026/232-3317
www.immi-moj.go.jp/english/soshiki/index.html

NAGANO MEDICAL INFORMATION NETWORK
www.qq.pref.nagano.jp/qq/sho/qqtpforisr.aspx
Search for hospitals and clinics using an interactive map.

NAGANO PREFECTURAL GOVERNMENT
692-2 Habashita Minami-Nagano, Nagano-shi
tel. 026/235-7173
www.pref.nagano.lg.jp/gaikokugo/index.htm
Emergency information and citizens' guide.

NAGANO PREFECTURE HOUSING MANAGEMENT PUBLIC CORPORATION
tel. 026/227-1211
tel. 0263/47-0240 (Matsumoto Branch)

NAGANO SEKIJUJI HOSPITAL
1512-1 Wakasato, Nagano-shi
tel. 026/226-4131

NAGANO WOMEN'S CONSULTATION CENTER (NAGANO FUJIN SODANJO)
tel. 026/235-5710
Support center for domestic violence, marriage, divorce, and other challenges.

SHINANO MAINICHI SHIMBUN
www.shinmai.co.jp (in Japanese)
Nagano City news.

TOKYO REGIONAL IMMIGRATION BUREAU
Nagano Branch Office
Nagano Local Legal Affairs Joint Government Bldg.
1108 Asahi-cho, Nagano-shi 380-0846
tel. 026/232-3317

Central Mountains: Karuizawa
KARUIZAWA HEALTH CENTER
tel. 0267/45-8549
Health exams, cancer screening, vaccinations, consultations on health and nutrition

KARUIZAWA HOSPITAL
tel. 0267/45-5111
www.town.karuizawa.nagano.jp/html/English/contents/residents/life/index.html

KARUIZAWA TOWN HALL
2381-1 Oaza Nagakura, Karuizawa-cho, Saku-gun, Nagano-ken
tel. 0267/45-8111
www.town.karuizawa.nagano.jp/html/english/index.html
Information on hospitals, utilities, banking and post, and transportation.

Central Mountains: Matsumoto
ASIA REAL ESTATE CO., LTD.
3040-53 Sasaga, Matsumoto
tel. 0263/86-7822
www.asia-fudosan.co.jp (in Japanese)

MATSUMOTO CITY
www.city.matsumoto.nagano.jp/english/index.html
History, tourism, city guide.

MATSUMOTO CITY HALL
3-7 Marunouchi, Matsumoto-shi
tel. 0263/34-3000
pi_int@city.matsumoto.nagano.jp

MATSUMOTO TRANSPORTATION
http://welcome.city.matsumoto.nagano.jp/
contents02+index.htm

MATSUMOTO WELCOME PROJECT
http://welcome.city.matsumoto.nagano.jp
Sightseeing, events, shopping, gourmet
spots, accommodations, guest blog by
mostly foreign residents.

SHINSHU DAIGAKU IGAKUBU
FUZOKU BYOIN (SHINSHU
UNIVERSITY MEDICAL HOSPITAL)
3-1-1 Asahi, Matsumoto-shi
tel. 0265/82-2121

SHINSHU UNIVERSITY
www.shinshu-u.ac.jp/english

TALENT EDUCATION RESEARCH
INSTITUTE (SUZUKI METHOD)
www.suzukimethod.or.jp/indexE.html

Kansai: Osaka
AB HOUSING OSAKA
www.abhousingosaka.com

ABLE VICTORY HOUSING
www.v-able.jp (in Japanese)

CANADIAN ACADEMY
4-1 Koyo-Cho Naka Higashinada-ku, Kobe
658-0032
tel. 078/857-0100
www.canacad.ac.jp
K–12 on Rokko Island.

CENTURY 21 WILL HOUSE
tel. 072/246-3123
www.century21willhouse.co.jp (in Japanese)

HANKYU RAILWAYS
http://rail.hankyu.co.jp/en

HANSHIN RAILWAYS
www.hanshin.co.jp/global/en

ITO CYCLES
5-25-24 Toyosato, Higashi Yodogawa-ku,
Osaka
tel. 06/329-2395
cubku302@occn.zaq.ne.jp

JAPAN HOME SEARCH
tel. 06/6344-2223
www.japanhomesearch.com

KANSAI CHRISTIAN SCHOOL
951 Tawaraguchi-cho, Ikoma-shi, Nara-ken
tel. 0743/74-1781
www.kansaichristianschool.com
K–12 American curriculum, east of Osaka
in Ikoma city, Nara.

KANSAI SCENE
www.kansaiscene.com

KANSAI UNIVERSITY
www.kansai-u.ac.jp/English/index-e.htm

KOBE KAISEI HOSPITAL
tel. 078/431-8272
www.icckobe.com
International counseling center.

KOKURITSU BYOIN KIKO, OSAKA
IRYO CENTER (OSAKA NATIONAL
HOSPITAL)
2-1-14 Hoenzaka, Chuo-ku, Osaka
tel. 06/6942-1331

OAK CLINIC GROUP
Parks Tower 8F, 2-10-70, Namba-Naka,
Naniwa-ku, Osaka
tel. 06/6646-0150
Gynecology/infertility, IVF, cosmetic sur-
gery, dermatology.

RESOURCES

OSAKA CITY HALL
1-3-20 Nakanoshima, Kita-ku, Osaka
www.city.osaka.lg.jp/contents/wdu020/
english

**OSAKA EMPLOYMENT SERVICE
CENTER FOR FOREIGNERS**
Umeda Center Building 9F 2-4-12
Nakazakinishi
Kita-ku, Osaka
tel. 06/6485-6142
Job consultation, placement, and information for foreign students and workers of Japanese descent.

**OSAKA INFORMATION SERVICE
FOR FOREIGN RESIDENTS**
www.pref.osaka.jp/kokusai/OIS_web/english
Guide to immigration, employment, housing, medical care, education, daily life, and emergencies.

OSAKA INTERNATIONAL SCHOOL
4-16 Onohara Nishi 4-chome, Minoo-shi,
Osaka-fu
tel. 072/727-5050
www.senri.ed.jp/OIS/index.htm
English pre-K–12, north of Osaka.

**OSAKA MUNICIPAL HOUSING
INFORMATION CENTER**
6-4-20 Tenjinbashi, Kita-ku, Osaka
tel. 06/6242-1177

**OSAKA MUNICIPAL
TRANSPORTATION BUREAU**
www.kotsu.city.osaka.jp/foreign/english

OSAKA PREFECTURE GOVERNMENT
www.pref.osaka.jp/en/index.html

**OSAKA REGIONAL IMMIGRATION
BUREAU**
Alien Residency Comprehensive Information
Center
1-29-53 Nankou Kita, Suminoe-ku, Osaka
tel. 06/4703-2150

OSAKA UNIVERSITY
www.osaka-u.ac.jp/en

OSAKA UNIVERSITY OF ARTS
www.osaka-geidai.ac.jp/geidai/english/index.html

OSAKA UNIVERSITY OF ECONOMICS
www.osaka-ue.ac.jp/english

**OSAKA UNIVERSITY OF EDUCATION
(OSAKA KYOIKU UNIVERSITY)**
http://osaka-kyoiku.ac.jp/en/index.html

**TEZUKAYAMA MONTESSORI
INTERNATIONAL SCHOOL**
1-22-17 Tezukayama, Abeno-ku, Osaka-shi
tel. 06/6652-2615 (English)
www.tmis-osaka.com
English instruction for ages 18 months to six years old.

UEROKU WOMEN'S CLINIC
Osaka Subway Tanimachi 9-chome, exit 8
tel. 06/6762-5842
English spoken.

**YODOGAWA CHRISTIAN HOSPITAL
(YODOGAWA KIRISUTOKYO BYOIN)**
2-9-26 Awaji, Higashi-Yodogawa-ku, Osaka
tel. 06/332-2250

Kansai: Kyoto
**ABLE COMPANY FUSHIMI-TEN
(REAL ESTATE)**
tel. 075/601-6251
fax 075/601-6252

DOSHISHA UNIVERSITY
www.doshisha.ac.jp/english

EAST-WEST PSYCHOTHERAPY SERVICE
tel. 075/724-1356
www.reggiepawle.net

ITAMI AIRPORT (OSAKA INTERNATIONAL AIRPORT)
http://osaka-airport.co.jp/en

JAPAN BAPTIST HOSPITAL
Nihon Baputisuto Byoin
47 Kita-Shirakawa Yamanomoto-cho,
Sakyo-ku, Kyoto
tel. 075/781-5191

KEIHAN RAILWAY
www.keihan.co.jp/en

KYOTO APARTMENT
www.kyoto-apartment.com

KYOTO CITY CLINIC FOR EMERGENCY ILLNESS
tel. 075/811-5072

KYOTO CITY HOUSING SERVICE COMPANY (KYOTO-SHI JUTAKU SERVICE KOSHA)
tel. 075/681-0541

KYOTO CITY INTERNATIONAL FOUNDATION
www.kcif.or.jp/en
Information on health, daily life, and emergencies.

KYOTO INSTITUTE OF TECHNOLOGY
www.kit.ac.jp/english

KYOTO INTERNATIONAL COMMUNITY HOUSE
www.kcif.or.jp/en/kaikan

KYOTO INTERNATIONAL SCHOOL
Kitatawara-cho, Nakadachiuri-sagaru
Yoshiyamachi-dori, Kamigyo-ku, Kyoto
tel. 075/451-1022
www.kyotointernationalschool.org
Grades K–8.

KYOTO JOURNAL
www.kyotojournal.org
Quarterly magazine, essays, fiction, reviews, photos.

KYOTO MUNICIPAL TRANSPORTATION BUREAU
www.city.kyoto.jp/koho/eng/access/
transport.html

KYOTO PREFECTURAL OFFICE
Shimodachiuri-dori, Shinmachi Nishi-iru
Kamigyo-ku, Kyoto
tel. 075/451-8111
www.pref.kyoto.jp/en/index.html

THE KYOTO SHIMBUN NEWS
www.kyoto-np.co.jp/kp/english

KYOTO TRAVEL GUIDE
www.kyoto.travel

KYOTO UNIVERSITY
www.kyoto-u.ac.jp/en

RITSUMEIKAN UNIVERSITY
www.ritsumei.ac.jp/eng

Seto Inland Sea: Hiroshima
HIROSHIMA CITY GOVERNMENT
www.city.hiroshima.jp

HIROSHIMA CITY INTERNATIONAL HOUSE (I-HOUSE)
1-1 Nishi-Kojin-machi, Minami-ku, Hiroshima
tel. 082/568-5931
www.i-house-hiroshima.jp (in Japanese)
www.i-house-hiroshima.jp/pdf/englishguide.
pdf

HIROSHIMA CITY TOURIST INFORMATION CENTER
tel. 082/263-6822
www.hiroshima-navi.or.jp/en
JR Hiroshima station and Peace Memorial Park

HIROSHIMA INTERNATIONAL INFORMATION NETWORK
http://hiint.hiroshima-ic.or.jp/english/index.html

HIROSHIMA INTERNATIONAL SCHOOL
3-49-1 Kurakake, Asakita- ku, Hiroshima
tel. 082/843-4111
www.hiroshima-is.ac.jp

HIROSHIMA PEACE CULTURAL FOUNDATION
www.pcf.city.hiroshima.jp/hpcf/english

HIROSHIMA PEACE MEMORIAL MUSEUM VIRTUAL MUSEUM
www.pcf.city.hiroshima.jp/virtual/index.html

HIROSHIMA REGIONAL IMMIGRATION BUREAU
Foreign Residents Information Center
2-31 Kami-Hatchobori, Naka-ku, Hiroshima
tel. 082/221-4411

HIROSHIMA UNIVERSITY HOSPITAL
Hiroshima Daigaku Igakubu Fuzoku Byoin
1-2-3 Kasumi, Minami-ku, Hiroshima
tel. 082/257-5555
www.hiroshima-u.ac.jp/en/hosp

JAPAN HOME SEARCH
www.japanhomesearch.com

JAPAN STUDENT SERVICES ORGANIZATION (JASSO)
Hiroshima International House
9-3 Hirose-Kitamachi, Naka-ku, Hiroshima
730-0803
tel. 082/503-7133, fax 082/503-7134
www.jasso.go.jp/s_chugoku/hiroshimakaikan_e.html

JETRO HIROSHIMA
Hiroshima Chamber of Commerce and Industry Building
4F, 5-44 Motomachi Naka-ku, Hiroshima City
730-0011
tel. 082/228-2563
www.jetro.go.jp/en/invest/region/hiroshima

Seto Inland Sea: Shikoku
ABLE NETWORK TAKAMATSU (REALTOR)
2-2-19 Boncho, Takamatsu-shi Bldg. 4F
tel. 087/837-0123
www.takamatsuchintai.com

EHIME EMERGENCY MEDICAL TREATMENT NETWORK
www.qq.pref.ehime.jp/qqscripts/qq/qq38mnueng.asp
List of health care facilities where foreign languages are spoken.

EHIME PREFECTURAL INTERNATIONAL ASSOCIATION (EPIC)
tel. 089/917-5678
www.epic.or.jp/english/index.html
Support for foreign residents' daily life.

EHIME PREFECTURE GOVERNMENT
www.pref.ehime.jp/index-e.htm

EHIME UNIVERSITY
www.ehime-u.ac.jp/english/index.html

JETRO EHIME
Item Ehime 3F, 2-1-28 Okaga, Matsuyama City,
Ehime Prefecture
tel. 089/952-0015
ehi@jetro.go.jp

**KAGAWA INTERNATIONAL
EXCHANGE CENTER**
tel. 087/837-5908
www.i-pal.or.jp/en

**KAGAWA KENRITSU CHUO BYOIN
(KAGAWA PREFECTURE HOSPITAL)**
5-4-16 Bancho, Takamatsu
tel. 0878/35-2222

KAGAWA PREFECTURE GOVERNMENT
4-1-10 Bancho, Takamatsu-shi
www.pref.kagawa.jp/foreigner.shtml
Living guide, medical information,
natural disasters.

KOCHI INFORMATION CENTER
www.attaka.or.jp/index.html
Attractions, local food, events, travel,
and accommodations.

KOCHI INTERNATIONAL ASSOCIATION
tel. 088/875-0022
www.kochi-kia.or.jp/english/index.htm

KOCHI PREFECTURE GOVERNMENT
International Affairs Division
1-2-20 marunouchi Kochi-shi
tel. 088/823-9605
www.pref.kochi.lg.jp/english

**KOCHI SEKIJUJI BYOIN (KOCHI
RED CROSS HOSPITAL)**
2-13-51 Shinhon-machi, Kochi-shi
tel. 0888/22-1201

KOCHI UNIVERSITY
www.kochi-u.ac.jp

**KOTODEN (KOTOHIRA ELECTRIC
LINE)**
www.kotoden.co.jp

**LEOPALACE 21 MATSUYAMA (REAL
ESTATE)**
1-11-1 Otemachi, Matsuyama City, Ehime
tel. 089/945-1931
http://en.leopalace21.com/center

**MATSUYAMA INTERNATIONAL
CENTER**
tel. 089/943-2025

**MATSUYAMA SEKIJUJI BYOIN
(MATSUYAMA RED CROSS HOSPITAL)**
1 Bunkyo-cho, Matsuyama-shi, Ehime-ken
tel. 0899/24-1111

MATSUYAMA UNIVERSITY
www.matsuyama-u.ac.jp/english/index.htm

**MULTILINGUAL LIVING GUIDE FOR
TAKAMATSU**
www.city.takamatsu.kagawa.jp/ENGLISH/
living-infomation
Housing, medical, consultation, links
for daily living.

NIHON HOUSING CO., LTD.
Matsuyama Branch
4-7-10 Samban-cho, Matsuyama-shi,
Ehime-ken
tel. 089/934-9611

OKA JUTAKU (OKA HOUSING)
2-36 Okinohama-higashi, Tokushima-shi
tel. 088/625-2112
www.oka-jutaku.co.jp (in Japanese)

**TAKAMATSU CENTER FOR THE
ADVANCEMENT OF WOMEN**
www.city.takamatsu.kagawa.jp/ENGLISH1/
women/women.html

RESOU...

TAKAMATSU CITY HEALTH CENTER
9-12 1-Chome, Sakura-machi, Takamatsu
tel. 087/839-2363
www.city.takamatsu.kagawa.jp/english/
living-infomation/health-and-insurance

TAKAMATSU INTERNATIONAL ASSOCIATION (TIA)
tel. 087/837-6003
ww2.enjoy.ne.jp/~tia/index_e.htm
Japanese lessons, events, movies, culture, and practical information for English-speakers.

TAKAMATSU REGIONAL IMMIGRATION BUREAU
1-1 Marunouchi, Takamatsu-shi
tel. 087/822-5852

TOKUSHIMA CITY
www.city.tokushima.tokushima.jp/english/
index.html

TOKUSHIMA DAIGAKU IGAKUBU FUZOKU BYOIN (TOKUSHIMA UNIVERSITY MEDICAL DEPT. HOSPITAL)
2-50-1 Kuramoto-cho, Tokushima-shi
tel. 0886/31-3111

TOKUSHIMA INTERNATIONAL CULTURAL VILLAGE/KAMIYAMA ARTIST IN RESIDENCE (KAIR)
www.in-kamiyama.jp/en/art

KUSHIMA PREFECTURE RNATIONAL ASSOCIATION
)
aza, 6F, 1-61 Terashimahon-cho,
hi
303
e_index.htm
ish books, Internet, infor-
e Language Proficiency
ie Awa Life.

TOKUSHIMA PREFECTURE HOUSING DIVISION
tel. 088/621-2590

TOKUSHIMA PREFECTURE OFFICE
International Strategies Division
1-1 Bandai-cho, Tokushima-shi
tel. 0880/621-2092
www.pref.tokushima.jp/english/information
Tokushima Pocket Living Guide—emergencies, visas, alien registration, daily life.

TOSA ELECTRIC RAILWAY (TOSADEN)
www.tosaden.co.jp

TOURISM SHIKOKU
www.tourismshikoku.org

UNIVERSITY OF KOCHI
www.u-kochi.ac.jp/english/index.htm
Formerly Kochi Women's University.

UNIVERSITY OF TOKUSHIMA
www.tokushima-u.ac.jp/english

WELCOME TO TAKAMATSU CITY
www.city.takamatsu.kagawa.jp/ENGLISH/
index.html

Kyushu: Fukuoka
A DEAL (REAL ESTATE)
7-32 Higuchimachi, Yahatanishi-ku,
Kitakyushu City
tel. 093/631-3099

FUKUOKA CITY GOVERNMENT
www.city.fukuoka.lg.jp/english/index.html

FUKUOKA CITY SUBWAY
http://subway.city.fukuoka.lg.jp/eng/index.
html

FUKUOKA CONVENTION AND VISITORS BUREAU
www.welcome-fukuoka.or.jp/english

FUKUOKA EXPAT GUIDE
http://kyushu.com/fukuoka

FUKUOKA INTERNATIONAL ASSOCIATION
www.rainbowfia.or.jp/english/top/index.htm
Rainbow Cybernet magazine with information on living in Fukuoka, health and legal consultation, and personal counseling for foreign residents.

FUKUOKA INTERNATIONAL EXCHANGE FOUNDATION
www.kokusaihiroba.or.jp/e00top/index.htm

FUKUOKA INTERNATIONAL SCHOOL
3-18-50 Momochi, Sawara-ku, Fukuoka
tel. 092/841-7601
www.fis.ed.jp
Grades 1–12.

FUKUOKA NOW
www.fukuoka-now.com/en
Magazine, restaurant and entertainment directory, and classifieds.

FUKUOKA PREFECTURE GOVERNMENT
www.pref.fukuoka.lg.jp/somu/multilingual/english/top.html

FUKUOKA REGIONAL IMMIGRATION BUREAU
Foreign Residents Information Center
tel. 092/632-2400

HOW TO ENROLL YOUR CHILD IN ELEMENTARY OR JUNIOR HIGH SCHOOL
www.city.fukuoka.lg.jp/kyoiku-iinkai/gakuji/ed/school-move.html (in Japanese)

INTERNATIONAL CLINIC TOJINMACHI
1-4-6 Jigyo, Chuo-ku, Fukuoka 810-0064
tel. 092/717-1000
www.internationalclinic.org
English-speaking European doctor.

JAPAN HOME SEARCH
www.japanhomesearch.com

KYUSHU FIXERS
http://kyushu-fixers.com
Logistical support for foreign companies with short-term projects in Kyushu.

KYUSHU INSTITUTE OF TECHNOLOGY HOUSING
www.kyutech.ac.jp/english/campuslife/settling.html#sub1

MEDICAL INFORMATION
www.kokusaihiroba.or.jp/cgi-bin/info/eng/njb_medicallist.exe
Medical facilities where foreign languages are spoken.

Glossary

awa: millet
bungaku: literature
chintai: rental
denwa: phone line
dori: road
doyobi: Saturday
en: yen (Japanese currency)
gaijin: outsider, foreigner
gaman: bearing it
ganbaru: effort
geijutsu: art
ginko koza: bank account
hashi: chopsticks
heijitsu: weekdays
hibakusha: atomic bomb victims
hogen: regional dialects
inkan: name stamp or seal
joya no kane: temple bell
juuminzei: residential tax
Kabuki: traditional theater
kami: divine
kana: Japanese phonetic characters
kanji: Chinese characters
katakana: phonetic letters
keijidosha-zei: light motor vehicle tax
keitai: cell phone
ken: rural prefectures
koban: police box
konbini: convenience store
koseki: family register system
kotatsu: family hearth
koteishisan-zei: municipal property tax
ku: city ward
manshon: condominium
matcha: powdered green tea
mikan: mandarin oranges
koshi: portable Shinto shrine

minshuku: family-run inns
minyo: folk music
nashi: Asian pears
nichiyobi: Sunday
odori: dance
onsen: hot springs
Oshogatsu: New Year's Day
rakuyaki: Raku firing
risaikuru shoppu: recycle shop, second-hand store
rotenburo: outdoor spa
ryokan: Japanese-style inns
sabi: austere elegance
sakura: cherry blossoms
sasho: visa
shika: deer
shodo: calligraphy
shohosen: prescriptions (pharmaceutical)
shotokuzei: income tax
shukujitsu: holidays
sumi: ink
taifu: typhoons
takkyuubin: baggage delivery service
takushii: taxis
tancho-tsuru: red-crested crane
tanka: short poems
tatami: woven rush mats
teiki-ken: commuter pass
tomodachi: friend
tsuyu: rainy season
ukiyo-e: wood-block prints
undokai: sports day
yakkyoku: pharmacies
yukata: cotton kimono
yukiguni: snow country
zeikin: taxes

COMMON HOUSING TERMS

Note that each Japanese vowel is pronounced separately and always sounds like: a = papa, i = pizza, u = put, e = pet, o = port. An "r" in Japanese is not pronounced like the English "r," but with a Spanish-style flap of the tongue against the palate.

Number of Rooms

wan-rumu: studio/one room

wan: one

tsu: two

surii: three

1K (wan-K): one room and a tiny kitchen

2DK (tsu-DK): two rooms and a dining room-kitchen

2LDK (tsu-LDK): two rooms and a living-dining-kitchen area

3SLDK (surii-SLDK): three rooms, a storage room, and living-dining-kitchen area

Style of Room

yoshitsu: Western room

washitsu: Japanese room

tatami: woven mats; roughly three by six feet, counted in units called *jo*

Type of Unit

chintai: rental

uri: for sale

apato: apartment

manshon: condominium or newer apartment

bunjo-jutaku: house and lot

toei-jutaku: city housing

ikken-ya: single house

konkuriito: concrete

mokuzo: wood frame

Features

intahon: intercom

erebeta: elevator

oto rokku: automatic lock

genkan: entry

kitchin: kitchen

gasu konro: gas stove

denshi renji: microwave

toire: toilet

uoshuretto: bidet

basu: bath

shawa: shower

shunou: storage

beranda: veranda

barukonii: balcony

ea kon: air conditioner

BS antena: TV antenna

terebi: television

katen: curtains

shiitsu: sheets

Negotiable

kodomo: children

petto: pets

piano: piano

Currency

en: yen

man: ¥10,000

Typical Fees

shikikin: security deposit

reikin: gift to landlord

hoshonin: financial guarantor

chukaihi: real estate agent's fee

kokyuhi: monthly common fee paid by each occupant

Miscellaneous

inkan: name stamp/seal

sain: signature

fudosan: real estate agency

Phrasebook

PRONUNCIATION

Japanese has five vowel sounds, and each has only one pronunciation (transcribed into our alphabet):

"a" like papa
"i" like pizza
"u" like put
"e" like pet
"o" like port

In contrast, "a," "e," "i," "o," and "u" in English can be pronounced many different ways. Notice how "a" is pronounced in apple, ate, father, Paul, and beautiful. Five different ways! In Japanese, two or more vowels next to each other keep their distinctive sound: aoi (blue) is "a-o-i."

Just like Spanish, most Japanese words (when transcribed into our alphabet) have consonant-vowel syllables, like the name Ta-ka-ha-shi. Syllables always end with a vowel, except for "n."

Note that the Japanese consonant transcribed with the letter "r" sounds nothing like the American "r"! Instead, it's a flap, almost a soft "d," like the Spanish "r". We unconsciously produce the Japanese "r" when we say karate, party, photo, and butter (tongue flap on the roof of the mouth),

except that we spell it with a "t"! If you see "r" in a transcribed Japanese word, think "t," as in "party."

One more point. English has strong and weak syllables, but Japanese has high and low pitch syllables, like this common name:

Ta-ka**-ha-shi**

The second syllable, "ka," has a higher pitch than the other three syllables.
Take the name "Ha-shi-mo-to":

Ha-shi-mo-to

The first syllable has a lower pitch than the last three syllables.
Note that "n" can be a syllable by itself, as in e-n (yen). This "n" is a nasal sound, like holding your nose shut. Your tongue floats and doesn't touch the inside of your mouth.

Once you know these rules you can pronounce any Japanese word transcribed into romaji (Roman letters). Note that the hyphens in these examples are used to break the words into syllables to aid pronunciation and are not how the words would be represented in English.

NUMBERS

ENGLISH	ROMAJI	JAPANESE
	i-chi	一
	ni	二
	sa-n*	三
	shi / yo-n*	四
	go	五
	ro-ku	六
	shi-chi / na-na	七
	ha-chi	八
	ʼ / kyu-u	九
	ʼ	十

...oats and doesn't touch the inside of your mouth.)

100	hya-ku	百
500	go-hya-ku	五百
1,000	se-n	千
5,000	go-se-n*	五千
10,000	i-chi-ma-n*	一万
100,000	ju-u-ma-n*	十万
500,000	go-ju-u-ma-n*	五十万
1,000,000	hya-ku-ma-n*	百万

DAYS OF THE WEEK

ENGLISH	ROMAJI	JAPANESE
Monday	ge-tsu-yo-o-bi	月曜日
Tuesday	ka-yo-o-bi	火曜日
Wednesday	su-i-yo-o-bi	水曜日
Thursday	mo-ku-yo-o-bi	木曜日
Friday	ki-n*-yo-o-bi	金曜日
Saturday	do-yo-o-bi	土曜日
Sunday	ni-chi-yo-o-bi	日曜日
Is today Tuesday?	Kyo-o wa ka-yo-o-bi de-s ka?	今日は火曜日ですか。
Yes, that's right.	Ha-i, so-o de-s.	はい、そうです。
What day of the week is it?	Na-n*-yo-o-bi de-s ka?	何曜日ですか。
It's Friday.	Ki-n*-yo-o-bi de-s.	金曜日です。

TIME

ENGLISH	ROMAJI	JAPANESE
1 o'clock	i-chi-ji	一時
2 o'clock	ni-ji	二時
3 o'clock	sa-n-ji	三時
4 o'clock	yo-ji	四時
5 o'clock	go-ji	五時
6 o'clock	ro-ku-ji	六時
7 o'clock	shi-chi-ji	七時
8 o'clock	ha-chi-ji	八時
9 o'clock	ku-ji	九時
10 o'clock	ju-u-ji	十時

RESOURCES

11 o'clock	*ju-u-i-chi-ji*	十一時
12 o'clock	*ju-u-ni-ji*	十二時
What time is it?	*Na-n-ji de-s ka?*	何時ですか。
It's 7 o'clock.	*Shi-chi-ji de-s.*	七時です。
today	*kyo-o*	今日
yesterday	*ki-no-o*	昨日
tomorrow	*a-shi-ta*	明日
the day before yesterday	*o-to-to-i*	おととい
the day after tomorrow	*a-sa-t-te*	あさって
this week	*ko-n*-shu-u*	今週
last week	*se-n*-shu-u*	先週
next week	*ra-i-shu-u*	来週
	(say "r" like a soft "d")	
this morning	*ke-sa*	今朝
this afternoon	*kyo-o no go-go*	今日の午後
this evening	*ko-n-ba-n**	今晩
last night	*sa-ku-ba-n**	昨晩
one month	*i-k-ka-ge-tsu*	一ヶ月
six months	*ro-k-ka-ge-tsu*	六ヶ月
late	*o-so-i*	遅い
early	*ha-ya-i*	早い
soon	*mo-o-su-gu*	もうすぐ
later on	*no-chi-ho-do*	後ほど
now	*i-ma*	今
second	*byo-o*	秒
minute	*fu-n**	分
one minute	*i-p-pu-n**	一分
five minutes	*go-fu-n**	五分
quarter of an hour	*ju-u-go-fu-n**	十五分
half an hour	*sa-n-ju-p-pu-n*	三十分
that day	*so-no-hi*	その日
every day	*ma-i-ni-chi*	毎日
all day	*i-chi-ni-chi-ju-u*	一日中

USEFUL WORDS AND PHRASES

ENGLISH	ROMAJI	JAPANESE
good morning (and bow)	*o-ha-yo-o go-za-i-ma-s*	おはよう ございます。
good afternoon	*ko-n-ni-chi-wa*	こんにちは
good evening	*ko-n*-ba-n*-wa*	こんばんは

How are you? (only used with someone you haven't seen for a long time)	o-ge-n-ki de-s-ka	お元気ですか。
fine ("thanks to you")	ha-i, o-ka-ge- sa-ma-de	はい、おかげ さまで。
And you?	[name]-sa-n* wa?	__さんは？
so-so	ma-a-ma-a de-su	まあまあです。
thanks	do-o-mo	どうも
thank you	a-ri-ga-to-o go-za-i-ma-s	ありがとうご ざいます。
Thank you very much.	do-o-mo a-ri-ga-to- o go-za-i-ma-s	どうもありがと うございます
You're welcome.	do-o-i-ta-shi-ma-shi-te	どういたしまして。
It's nothing.	i-i-e	いいえ
yes (correct)	ha-i, so-o de-s.	はい、そうです。
no (incorrect)	i-i-e, chi-ga-i-ma-s.	いいえ、違います。
is __	__de-su.	__です。
isn't __	__de-wa a-ri-ma-se-n*	__ではありません。
I don't know. (I don't have knowledge of __)	shi-ri-ma-se-n*	知りません
please (asking for something)	o-ne-ga-i-shi-ma-su	お願いします。
please (offering something)	do-o-zo	どうぞ。
How do you do? (it's the first time)	ha-me-ma-shi-te	はじめまして。
Nice to meet you. (I hope that our relationship will have good things)	do-o-zo yo-ro-shi-ku	どうぞよろしく。
I'm sorry.	su-mi-ma-se-n*	すみません。
good-bye (Permanent good-bye; not to family members or people you see everyday.)	sa-yo-o-na-ra	さようなら
See you later.	ja-a ma-ta	じゃ、また。
See you tomorrow.	ma-ta a-shi-ta	また明日。
more	mo-t-to	もっと
less		
a little	su-ko-shi	少し
a lot	ta-ku-sa-n*	たくさん
big	o-o-ki-i	大きい

small	chi-i-sa-i	小さい
good	i-i de-s	いいです。
better	mo-t-to i-i de-s	もっと いいです。
best	i-chi-ba-n* i-i de-s	一番いいです。
bad	wa-ru-i de-s	悪いです。
quick, fast	ha-ya-i de-s	速いです。
slow	yu-k-ku-ri	ゆっくり
easy	ya-sa-shi-i de-s	やさしいです。
difficult	mu-zu-ka-shi-i de-s	難しいです。
he	[name]-san*	＿さん
she	[name]-san*	＿さん
it	so-re / a-re	それ・あれ
I don't speak Japanese well. (can't do Japanese)	ni-ho-n*-go ga de-ki-ma-se-n*	日本語ができません。
I don't understand.	wa-ka-ri-ma-se-n*	わかりません。

SHOPPING

ENGLISH	ROMAJI	JAPANESE
Do you have __?	__ a-ri-ma-s-ka	＿ありますか。
I want... (please give me __)	__ ku-da-sa-i.	＿ください。
How much? (quantity)	do-no ku-ra-i de-s-ka	どのくらいですか。
How much? (money)	i-ku-ra de-s-ka	いくらですか。
May I see... (please show me __)	__mi-se-te ku-da-sa-i	＿みせてください。
this one	ko-re	これ
that one	so-re	それ
expensive	ta-ka-i de-s	高いです。
cheap	ya-su-i de-s	安いです。
too much (quantity)	o-o su-gi-ma-s	多すぎます。
too much (money)	ta-ka-su-gi-ma-s	高すぎます。
Can you go cheaper?	mot-to ya-su-ku de-ki-mas ka	もっと安くできますか。

GETTING AROUND

ENGLISH	ROMAJI	JAPANESE
north	ki-ta	北
south	mi-na-mi	南
east	hi-ga-shi	東

English	Romaji	Japanese
west	*ni-shi*	西
central	*chu-u-shi-n**	中心
taxi	*ta-ku-shi-i*	タクシー
go straight/keep going	*ma-s-su-gu*	まっすぐ
the right side	*mi-gi-ga-wa*	右側
turn right	*mi-gi-e ma-ga-t- te ku-da-sa-i*	右へ曲がって ください。
the left side	*hi-da-ri-ga-wa*	左側
turn left	*hi-da-ri-e ma-ga- t-te ku-da-sa-i*	左へ曲がっ てください。
Stop here!	*ko-ko-de to-me- te ku-da-sa-i*	ここで止め てください。
the next street	*tsu-gi no to-o-ri*	次の通り
Please slow down a little.	*mo-t-to yuk-ku-ri o-ne-ga-i-shi-ma-s*	もっとゆっく りお願いします
Hurry up a little.	*mo-t-to ha-ya-ku o- ne-ga-i-shi-ma-s*	もっと速くお 願いします。
here	*ko-ko*	ここ
there	*so-ko*	そこ
where is it	*do-ko de-s-ka*	どこですか。
OK, good (it's here)	*ha-i, ko-ko de-s*	はい、ここです。
How much do I owe you?	*i-ku-ra de-s-ka*	いくらですか。
train station	*e-ki*	駅
subway	*chi-ka-te-tsu*	地下鉄
bus	*ba-su*	バス
bus stop	*ba-su te-i*	バス停
bicycle	*ji-te-n-sha*	自転車
map	*chi-zu*	地図
store	*mi-se*	
department store	*de-pa-a-to*	デパート
supermarket	*su-u-pa-a*	スーパー
Where is the __?	*__wa do-ko de-s ka?*	__はどこですか。

HEALTH

ENGLISH	ROMAJI	JAPANESE
Help me please.	*ta-su-ke-te ku-da-sa-i*	助けてください。
I am sick.	*gu-a-i ga wa-ru-i-de-s*	具合が悪いです。
pain (it hurts)	*i-ta-i de-s*	痛いです。
itch (it's itchy)	*ka-yu-i de-s*	かゆいです。
lump	*shi-ko-ri*	しこり
sore	*ha-re-mo-no*	はれもの

rash	ha-s-shi-n*	発疹
fever	ne-tsu	熱
mucous	ne-n*-e-ki	粘液
pus	u-mi	うみ
blood	chi	血
headache	zu-tsu-u	頭痛
stomachache (my stomach hurts)	o-na-ka ga i-ta-i de-s	おなかが痛いです。
I'm hot	a-tsu-i-de-s	暑いです。
I'm cold	sa-mu-i-de-s	寒いです。
vomiting	ha-ki-ke	吐き気
diarrhea	ge-ri	下痢
constipation	be-n-pi	便秘
feces/to defecate	da-i-be-n*	大便
urine/to urinate	sho-o-be-n*	小便
drugstore	ya-k-kyo-ku	薬局
medicine	ku-su-ri	薬
pill, tablet	jo-o-za-i	錠剤
diarrhea medicine	ge-ri-do-me	下痢止め
antacid	i-gu-su-ri	胃薬
cold medicine	ka-ze-gu-su-ri	風邪薬
pain reliever	i-ta-mi-do-me	痛み止め
anti-nausea medicine	ha-ki-ke-do-me	吐き気止め
antihistamine	ko-o hi-su-ta-mi-n-za-i	抗ヒスタミン剤
cortisone	ko-o-chi-zo-n*	コーチゾン
antibiotic	ko-o-se-i-bu-s-shi-tsu	抗生物質
Viagra	ba-i-a-gu-ra	バイアグラ
birth control pills	pi-ru	ピル
condom	ko-n-do-o-mu	コンドーム
period	se-i-ri (say "r" like a soft "d")	生理
pad	na-pu-ki-n	ナプキン
tampon	ta-n-po-n	タンポン
gynecologist	fu-ji-n-ka-i	婦人科医
doctor	i-sha	医者
hospital	byo-o-i-n	病院

FOOD

ENGLISH	ROMAJI	JAPANESE
Water please.	mi-zu ku-da-sa-i	水ください。
Coffee please.	Ko-o-hi-i ku-da-sa-i	コーヒーくださいす。

| No, thanks. | *mo-o ke-k-ko-o-des.* | 結構です。 |
| Another cup please. | *mo-o ip-pa-i ku-da-sa-i.* | もう一杯ください。 |

HOUSING TERMINOLOGY

ENGLISH	ROMAJI	JAPANESE
real estate office	*fu-do-o-sa-n.*	不動産
rent	*ya-chi-n.*	家賃
studio	*wa-n ru-u-mu.*	ワンルーム
apartment	*a-pa-a-to.*	アパート
condominium	*ma-n*-sho-n*	マンション
Japanese style room	*wa-shi-tsu.*	和室
western style room	*yo-o-shi-tsu*	洋室
tatami floor (woven rush)	*ta-ta-mi*	畳
kitchen	*da-i-do-ko-ro.*	台所
toilet	*to-i-re* (say "r" like a soft "d")	トイレ
bath	*o-fu-ro.*	お風呂
entry	*ge-n-ka-n**	玄関
heat	*da-n-bo-o*	暖房
air conditioner	*e-a-ko-n**	エアコン
deposit	*shi-ki-ki-n**	敷金
landlord fee (key money)	*re-i-ki-n**	礼金
maintenance fee	*ka-n-ri-hi.*	管理費
agent's commision	*chu-u-ka-i te-su-u-ryo-o*	仲介手数料
property insurance	*so-n-ga-i ho-ke-n-ryo-o*	損害保険料
parking fee	*chu-u-sha-ryo-o*	駐車料
renewal fee (renewing lease after 2 years)	*ko-o-shi-n-ryo-o*	更新料
guarantor	*re-n-ta-i ho-sho-o-ni-n*	連帯保証人
neighborhood association	*cho-o-na-i-ka-i*	町内会

Shoe and Clothing Sizes

Women's Clothing

Japan	5	7	9	11	13	15	17	19	21
U.S.	2	4	6	8	10	12	14	16	18

Women's Shoes

Japan	21	21.5	22	22.5	23	23.5	24	24.5	25
U.S.	5	5.5	6	6.5	7	7.5	8	8.5	9

Men's Shirts

Japan	36	37	38	39	40	42	43
U.S.	14	14.5	15	15.5	16	16.5	17

Men's Shoes

Japan	24.5	25	25.5	26	26.5	27.5	28.5
U.S.	6.5	7	7.5	8	8.5	9	10.5

Suggested Reading

HISTORY

Bernstein, Gail Lee. *Isami's House: Three Centuries of a Japanese Family*. Berkeley: University of California Press, 2005.

Chang, Ying-Ying. *The Woman Who Could Not Forget: Iris Chang Before and Beyond the Rape of Nanking—A Memoir*. New York: Pegasus, 2011.

Francks, Penelope. *The Japanese Consumer: An Alternative Economic History of Modern Japan*. New York: Cambridge University Press, 2009.

Hicks, George L. *The Comfort Women: Japan's Brutal Regime of Enforced Prostitution in the Second World War*. New South Wales: Allen and Unwin, 1996.

Honda, Katsuichi. *Harukor: An Ainu Woman's Tale*. Berkeley: University of California Press, 2000.

Kamo-no-Chomei. *Hojoki: Visions of a Torn World*. Berkeley, CA: Stone Bridge Press, 1996. "The flowing river never stops and yet the water never stays the same." So begins the 12th-century poet/ Buddhist priest's passionate literary reflections on the human condition—just as timely today.

Molasky, Michael S. *The American Occupation of Japan and Okinawa: Literature and Memory*. New York: Routledge, 2001.

Our Man in Abiko. *2:46: Aftershocks: Stories from the Japan Earthquake*. Enhanced Editions, 2011.

Partner, Simon. *Toshié: A Story of Village Life in Twentieth-Century Japan*. Berkeley: University of California Press, 2004.

Rosenberger, Nancy. *Gambling with Virtue: Japanese Women and the Search for Self in a Changing Nation*. Honolulu: University of Hawaii Press, 2001.

Swanson, Paul, and Clark Chilson, eds. *Nanzan Guide to Japanese Religions*. Honolulu: University of Hawaii Press, 2005.

NONFICTION

Booth, Alan. *The Roads to Sata: A 2,000-Mile Walk Through Japan*. Tokyo: Kodansha Globe, 1997 (reprint).

Davey, H. E. *The Japanese Way of the Artist: Living the Japanese Arts and Ways, Brush Meditation, The Japanese Way of the Flower*. Berkeley, CA: Stone Bridge Press, 2007.

Friedman, Abigail. *The Haiku Apprentice: Memoirs of Writing Poetry in Japan*. Berkeley, CA: Stone Bridge Press, 2006.

Ishikida, Miki Y. *Japanese Education in the 21st Century*. iUniverse, Inc., 2005.

Maruyama, M. Enman, L. Picon Shimizu, and N. Smith Tsurumaki. *Japan Health Handbook*. Rev. ed. Tokyo: Kodansha International, 1998.

Miller, Laura. *Beauty Up: Exploring Contemporary Japanese Body Aesthetics*. Berkeley: University of California Press, 2006. Japanese women and men pay attention to their bodies in ways that are similar and different from American notions—for example, "androgynous" looking guys are considered manly.

RESOURCES

Miller, Laura, and Jan Bardsley, eds. *Bad Girls of Japan*. Hampshire: Palgrave Macmillan, 2005.

Muller, Karin. *Japanland: A Year in Search of Wa*. Emmaus, PA: Rodale Books, 2006.

Roderick, John. *Minka: My Farmhouse in Japan*. Princeton: Princeton Architectural Press, 2007.

Williamson, Kate T. *A Year in Japan*. Princeton: Princeton Architectural Press, 2006.

POPULAR CULTURE

Garcia, Hector. *A Geek in Japan: Discovering the Land of Manga, Anime, Zen, and the Tea Ceremony*. North Clarendon, VT: Tuttle Publishing, 2011.

Nogami, Teruyo. *Waiting on the Weather: Making Movies with Akira Kurosawa*. Berkeley, CA: Stone Bridge Press, 2006.

Ragone, August. *Eiji Tsuburaya: Master of Monsters Defending the Earth with Ultraman, Godzilla, and Friends in the Golden Age of Japanese Science Fiction Film*. San Francisco: Chronicle Books, 2007.

Schodt, Frederik L. *The Astro Boy Essays: Osamu Tezuka, Mighty Atom, and the Manga/Anime Revolution*. Berkeley, CA: Stone Bridge Press, 2007.

FICTION

Ariyoshi, Sawako. *The Doctor's Wife*. Rev. ed. Tokyo: Kodansha International, 2004. Story of two strong women in the Tokugawa period (19th century) and the first medical operation for breast cancer.

Golden, Arthur. *Memoirs of a Geisha*. New York: Vintage, 1999.

Jones, Susanna. *The Earthquake Bird*. London: Picador, 2007.

Kamata, Suzanne, ed. *The Broken Bridge: Fiction from Expatriates in Literary Japan*. Berkeley, CA: Stone Bridge Press, 1997.

Kawabata, Yasunari. *Snow Country*. New York: Vintage Books, 1996. A haunting novel of wasted love that brought the author the Nobel Prize for Literature in 1968.

Kirino, Natsuo. *Out: A Novel*. Tokyo: Kodansha International, 2003. Crime novel involving four women who work the night shift in a factory fabricating boxed lunches. Winner of Japan's Grand Prix for crime fiction.

Mishima, Yukio. *Spring Snow*. New York: Vintage, 1990.

Miyabe, Miyuki. *All She Was Worth*. New York: Mariner Books, 1999. Tale of identity theft and conspiracy and obsessive consumerism in the search for happiness.

Molasky, Michael S., and Steve Rabson. *Southern Exposure: Modern Japanese Literature from Okinawa*. Honolulu: University of Hawaii Press, 2000.

Murakami, Haruki. *Dance Dance Dance*. New York: Vintage, 1995. Sequel to *A Wild Sheep Chase*.

Murakami, Haruki. *Kafka on the Shore*. New York: Vintage, 2006. Fifteen-year-old runaway schoolboy looking for his long-lost mother encounters mysterious and surreal characters.

Murakami, Haruki. *Norwegian Wood*. New York: Vintage, 1995. Haruki's first novel, which turned him into a cult icon in 1987, is a coming-of-age story of searching for love.

Murakami, Haruki. *A Wild Sheep Chase.* New York: Vintage, 2002. An irreverent view of contemporary Japan through a man's odd quest for sheep; Haruki's first novel translated into English.

Shikibu, Murasaki. *The Tale of Genji.* Translated by Richard Bowring. 2nd ed. New York: Cambridge University Press, 2003. Commonly considered the world's first novel, written by a lady in the Heian court of 11th-century Japan (present Kyoto).

Tanizaki, Jun'ichiro. *The Makioka Sisters.* Epic tale of four sisters from a waning aristocratic family and their struggles between preserving the rituals and manners from the past and letting in the modern world in pre–World War II Japan.

Thompson, Holly, ed. *Tomo: Friendship through Fiction: An Anthology of Japan Teen Stories.* California: Stonebridge Press, 2012. Anthology of short fiction for readers ages 12 and up, to benefit teens affected by the Great East Japan Earthquake of March 2011.

Yoshikawa, Eiji. *Musashi: An Epic Novel of the Samurai Era.* Tokyo: Kodansha International, 1995. Tale of Miyamoto Musashi, famed swordsman of the 17th century, in the best tradition of Japanese storytelling.

Yoshimoto, Banana. *Kitchen.* New York: Washington Square Press, 1993. Two stories about young women who lose someone they love and struggle with loneliness and personal and sexual identity through their experience and the unique characters they meet. A slice of contemporary Japanese life.

Yoshimoto, Banana. *The Lake.* New York: Melville House, 2012. From the book description: "With its echoes of the infamous, real-life Aum Shinrikyo cult (the group that released poison gas in the Tokyo subway system), [the book] unfolds as the most powerful novel Banana Yoshimoto has written.... Two young lovers overcome their troubled past to discover hope in the beautiful solitude of the lake." A portion of the proceeds from this book will go to Japanese disaster relief.

LANGUAGE

Esch-Harding, Edith. *The Bilingual Family: A Handbook for Parents.* UK: Cambridge University Press, 2003. Two languages are better than one—give your children the gift of a bilingual heritage!

Hamiru-agui. *70 Japanese Gestures: No Language Communication.* Berkeley, CA: Stone Bridge Press, 2008.

Japanese I–III, Comprehensive: Learn to Speak and Understand Japanese with Pimsleur Language Programs. New York: Simon and Schuster's Pimsleur, 2005. Quick, convenient, and effective way to understand and speak Japanese, by listening and responding. Better than Rosetta Stone.

Kodansha Essential Kanji Dictionary. Rep Blg ed. Tokyo: Kodansha, 2012. Pronunciation, meaning, and stroke order of the core 1,945 *kanji* characters used in Japanese newspapers and magazines, and thousands of compound words, including business terms, with three indices for looking up *kanji*.

Kushner, Eve. *Crazy for Kanji: A Student's Guide to the Wonderful World of Japanese Characters.* Berkeley, CA: Stone Bridge Press, 2007. One hundred carnivals of *kanji* fun, including puzzles, amazing facts, and *kanji* sudoku.

Lammars, Wayne. *Japanese the Manga Way: An Illustrated Guide to Grammar and Structure.* Berkeley, CA: Stone Bridge Press, 2004. Learn three basic sentence types in spoken Japanese, with manga illustrating how they're used in real life. The author is an insider who grew up in Hokkaido.

Mahony, Judy. *Teach Me Japanese & More Japanese: Book and Audio CD Edition.* Minnetonka, MN: Teach Me Tapes, Inc., 2005. Fun way for kids to learn Japanese words and phrases through songs and stories.

Stout, Timothy. *Tuttle Japanese for Kids Flash Cards Kit.* North Clarendon, VT: Tuttle, 2008.

Takahashi, Peter X. *Jimi's Book of Japanese: A Motivating Method to Learn Japanese (Hiragana).* 2nd ed. Atlanta: Takahashi and Black, 2002. Fun way to learn to read and write 46 *hiragana* rounded letters and learn useful words.

Takahashi, Peter X. *Jimi's Book of Japanese: A Motivating Method to Learn Japanese (Katakana).* Atlanta: Takahashi and Black, 2005. Companion volume to the *Hiragana* book. Learn the block-style letters used to write Western words and menus in Japan.

FOOD

Gauntner, John. *Sake Handbook.* 2nd ed. North Clarendon, VT: Tuttle, 2002.

Hosking, Richard. *At the Japanese Table (Images of Asia).* Oxford University Press, 2000. From the book description: "guide to the Japanese way of eating, providing both social and historical

background for what readers might encounter when visiting Japan."

Kaneko, Amy. *Let's Cook Japanese Food! Everyday Recipes for Home Cooking.* San Francisco: Chronicle Books, 2007.

Krouse, Carolyn. *A Guide to Food Buying in Japan.* Bilingual ed. North Clarendon, VT: Tuttle, 2003.

Shurtleff, William, and Akiko Aoyagi. *The Book of Tofu & Miso.* Berkeley: Ten Speed Press, 2001.

CHILDREN'S BOOKS

Cho, Shinta. *The Gas We Pass.* La Jolla, CA: Kane/Miller Book Publishers, 2001.

Gomi, Taro. *I Lost My Dad.* La Jolla, CA: Kane/Miller Book Publishers, 2001.

Hidaka, Masako. *Girl from the Snow Country.* La Jolla, CA: Kane/Miller Book Publishers, 1999.

Nomura, Takaaki. *Grandpa's Town.* La Jolla, CA: Kane/Miller Book Publishers, 1995. Bilingual text in Japanese and English.

Say, Allen. *Tea with Milk.* New York: Houghton Mifflin, 1999. A story about feeling at home in a place that is not your own, illustrated with Say's beautifully detailed and emotive drawings.

Shigeru, Kayano, Peter Howlett, Richard McNamara, and Iijima Shunichi. *The Ainu: A Story of Japan's Original People.* North Clarendon, VT: Tuttle Publishing, 2003. The story of Japan's indigenous people, their history, culture, and present-day life.

Spivak, Dawnine. *Grass Sandals: The Travels of Basho.* New York: Atheneum

Books for Young Readers, 2009. Follow 17th-century haiku poet Basho on his travels through Japan.

Takabayashi, Mari. *I Live in Tokyo.* New York: Houghton Mifflin, 2001.

Takeshita, Fumiko. *The Park Bench.* La Jolla, CA: Kane/Miller Book Publishers, 1989. Bilingual edition in Japanese and English with wonderful, Manet-like illustrations.

Tsuchiya, Yukio. *Faithful Elephants: A True Story of Animals, People, and War.* New York: Houghton Mifflin, 1997. About what happened to the elephants in Ueno Zoo during World War II.

Tsutsui, Yoriko. *Amy and Ken Visit Grandma.* Balcatta, Western Australia: RIC Publications, Har/Com edition, 2006. Amy and her toy fox Ken go on a train trip in Japan.

TRAVEL AND MAPS

DK Eyewitness Travel Guides: Japan. London: DK Publishing, 2011.

Durston, Diane. *Old Kyoto: The Updated Guide to Traditional Shops, Restaurants, and Inns.* 2nd ed. Tokyo: Kodansha International, 2005.

Harada, Masashi. *A Travel Guide to Queer Japan: Exploring Queer Spirits.* Lulu.com, 2007. From the book description: "Japan has a long history related to love and intimate relations between the same sex.... This book explores queer spirits via historical and religious locations in Japan." Includes travel maps.

Japan Atlas: A Bilingual Guide. 3rd ed. Tokyo: Kodansha International, 2011.

Miwa, Takashi. *Cycling Japan: Ten of the Best Rides.* Tokyo Chizu Publishing Co., Ltd., 2009.

Time Out Tokyo. 6th ed. London: Time Out, 2010.

Tokyo City Atlas: A Bilingual Guide. 3rd ed. Tokyo: Kodansha International, 2004.

Wiltshire, Diane, and Jeanne Huey. *Japan for Kids: The Ultimate Guide for Parents and Their Children.* 2nd ed. New York: Kodansha USA, 2000.

Zarifeh, Ramsey. *Japan by Rail.* 2nd ed. Hindhead, UK: Trailblazer Publications, 2007. Includes rail route guide and 29 city guides.

RESOURCES

Suggested Films

Japanese names are listed surname first.

After Life (Wandafuru Raifu). Directed by Koreeda Hirokazu. 118 min., 1998.

Castle in the Sky. Directed by Miyazaki Hayao. 124 min., 1986.

The Cat Returns (Neko no Ongaeshi). Directed by Morita Hiroyuki. 75 min., 2002. From Studio Ghibli.

Jiro Dreams of Sushi. Directed by David Gelb. 81 min., 2011. Documentary of 85-year-old Jiro Ono, great sushi chef and proprietor of Sukiyabashi Jiro, a 10-seat, sushi-only restaurant inauspiciously located in a Tokyo subway station.

Kagemusha. Directed by Kurosawa Akira. 2 hours, 59 min., 1980.

Kikujiro (Kikujiroo no Natsu). Directed by Kitano Takeshi. 121 min., 1999.

Lost in Translation. Directed by Sofia Coppola. 102 min., 2003.

The Makioka Sisters (Sasameyuki). Directed by Ichikawa Kon. 140 min., 1983. Based on the novel by Tanizaki Junichiro.

My Neighbor Totoro (Tonari no Totoro). Directed by Miyazaki Hayao. 86 min., 1988.

Ran. Directed by Kurosawa Akira. 160 min., 1985. Director's version of King Lear set in medieval Japan.

Rhapsody in August (Hachigatsu no Kyoshikyoku). Directed by Kurosawa Akira.

98 min., 1991. About memories of the Nagasaki atom bomb.

Senbazuru (Thousand Cranes). Directed by Masumura Yasuzo. 97 min., 1969. Based on the novel by Kawabata Yasunari.

Shall We Dance? Directed by Suo Masayuki. 118 min., 1996. A Tokyo salaryman's life is transformed through a growing passion.

Spirited Away (Sen to Chihiro no Kamikakushi). Directed by Miyazaki Hayao. 125 min., 2001.

Tampopo. Directed by Itami Juzo. 114 min., 1985. A woman's quest to create the ultimate bowl of ramen, aided by a cowboy truck driver.

A Taxing Woman (Marusa no Onna). Directed by Itami Juzo. 127 min., 1987.

Tokyo Story. Directed by Ozu Yasujiro. 136 min., 1960. An elderly couple visit their offspring in Tokyo, leading to generational conflict and a realization that traditions are changing.

Wings of Defeat. Directed by Risa Morimoto. 2007. Japanese heritage director's documentary of surviving "tokko-tai" (kamikaze) pilots—including her uncle—60 years after World War II.

Woman in the Dunes (Suna no Onna). Directed by Teshigahara Hiroshi. 123 min., 1964. Based on the novel by Abe Kobo.

Index

A

accidents: 133-134
accommodations: 72-73, 75-76, 77-78, 79; resources 274; *see also* housing
addresses: 166
air travel: 172-173, 284-285
apartments: 100
Arakawa-ku: 204-205
Arakawa River: 205
arrival plans: 97
art: 55-57
arts, the: 52-57
asset-based tax: 157

BC

banking: 152-155, 283
bicycle transportation: 181-183, 286
boat transportation: 178, 285
bowing: 61
Buddhism: 50-51
business cards *(meishi):* 84
bus travel: 177-178, 285
car travel: 179-181; buying/leasing 181; licenses 180; rental cars 180-181; resources 285; traffic laws 180
cell phones: 162-163, 283-284
Central Mountains: 190, 224-235; map 225; resources 291-293
cherry blossoms *(sakura):* 56
Chiba-ken: 205-206
childbirth: 131
children, moving with: 88-91, 273, 274
Chiyoda-ku: 202
chopsticks: 43
Christianity: 51-52
city buses: 177
Clark, William Smith: 214
class and ethnicity: 40-42, 44
climate: 14, 16
communications: 160-169; Internet access 161-162, 284; media 93-94, 168-169, 283; postal service 165-167; resources 283-284; telephone service 162-164
connections, human: 63
consulates and embassies: 270-272
consumer rights: 154-155
consumption tax: 60
cost of living: 151-152
country divisions: 12, 14
crime: 134-135
cultural activities visas: 84
currency: 60

customs and etiquette: 42, 43, 44-45, 120
customs and immigration: *see* visas and immigration

DE

delivery service: 166, 284
dependent visas: 88
dialects: 115, 118
disabilities, travelers with: 135, 273
documents: 59, 96
driver's licenses: 180
earthquakes: 15, 16, 33
economy: 37-38
education: 121-123; curriculum 122; international schools 123, 273, 276; Japanese language 117-121; Japanese schools 123; resources 276-279; student visas 84
electronics and media: 93-94
embassies and consulates: 270-272
emergencies: 273, 280-281
Employee Health Insurance: 127
employment: 136-148; employers 140-141; finding 137-140; health insurance 127; interviews 138-140; labor laws 143-144; resources 282; self-employment 144-148; teaching 141, 142, 281-282; visas 84-86
English language, teaching: 141, 281-282
ethnicity and class: 40-42, 44
etiquette and customs: 42, 43, 44-45, 120
expat contacts: 274
expat profiles: 19, 217, 232

F

family register system: 126
farm work: 141
fauna: 17
festivals: 267
films, suggested: 316
finance: 149-159; banking 152-155; investing 157-159; living expenses 151-152; money 93; resources 282-283; taxes 155-157
financial guarantors: 106-107
flora: 16-17
food/restaurants: 43, 74, 75, 76-77, 78-79
Fukuoka: 193, 262-266, 268; accommodations 79; daily life 266; food/restaurants 79; neighborhoods 264-266; overview 263-264; resources 298-299; transportation 266, 268
furnishings: 111

Acknowledgments

I am grateful to my parents, Lee and Adella Kanagy, for their courage and adventurous spirit in going to Japan in 1951, as Mennonite missionaries. Thank you for a lifetime of love and support. To my daughters, Erin and Elena, and my sister Lois—thank you for your encouragement and love. Thanks to my editor, Kathryn Ettinger, for editing expertise and advice on this third edition. Lastly, to friends who shared the joys and challenges of living abroad in Japan, *arigatoo gozaimasu*.

In memory of my father, Lee Hartzler Kanagy, and for Seven, the next generation.

www.moon.com

DESTINATIONS | ACTIVITIES | BLOGS | MAPS | BOOKS

MOON.COM is ready to help plan your next trip! Filled with fresh trip ideas and strategies, author interviews, informative travel blogs, a detailed map library, and descriptions of all the Moon guidebooks, Moon.com is all you need to get out and explore the world—or even places in your own backyard. While at Moon.com, sign up for our monthly e-newsletter for updates on new releases, travel tips, and expert advice from our on-the-go Moon authors. As always, when you travel with Moon, expect an experience that is uncommon and truly unique.

KEEP UP WITH MOON ON FACEBOOK AND TWITTER
JOIN THE MOON PHOTO GROUP ON FLICKR

MAP SYMBOLS

▦	Expressway	○	City/Town	✈	Airfield	▰	Archaeological Site
▬	Primary Road	◉	State Capital	✈	Airport	▮	Church
▬	Secondary Road	✷	National Capital	▲	Mountain	▯	Gas Station
▪▪▪	Unpaved Road	★	Point of Interest	♣♣	Park	▨	Mangrove
⋯⋯	Ferry	■	Other Location			▨	Reef
▬▬	Railroad			⛷	Skiing Area	▨	Swamp

CONVERSION TABLES

°C = (°F − 32) / 1.8
°F = (°C x 1.8) + 32
1 inch = 2.54 centimeters (cm)
1 foot = 0.304 meters (m)
1 yard = 0.914 meters
1 mile = 1.6093 kilometers (km)
1 km = 0.6214 miles
1 fathom = 1.8288 m
1 chain = 20.1168 m
1 furlong = 201.168 m
1 acre = 0.4047 hectares
1 sq km = 100 hectares
1 sq mile = 2.59 square km
1 ounce = 28.35 grams
1 pound = 0.4536 kilograms
1 short ton = 0.90718 metric ton
1 short ton = 2,000 pounds
1 long ton = 1.016 metric tons
1 long ton = 2,240 pounds
1 metric ton = 1,000 kilograms
1 quart = 0.94635 liters
1 US gallon = 3.7854 liters
1 Imperial gallon = 4.5459 liters
1 nautical mile = 1.852 km

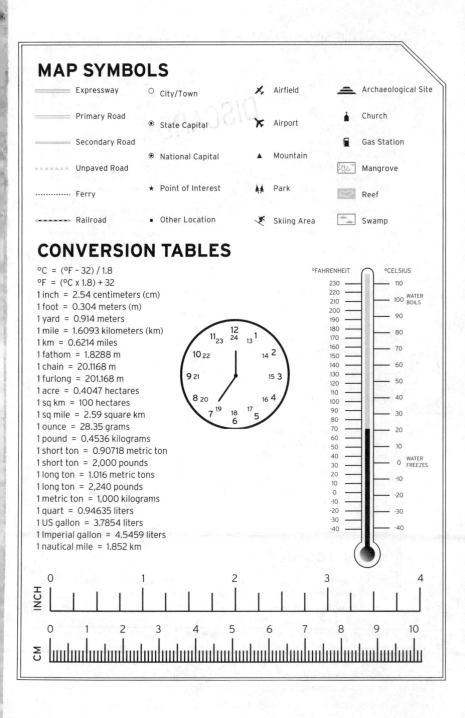

°FAHRENHEIT / °CELSIUS

WATER BOILS (100)
WATER FREEZES (0)

MOON LIVING ABROAD IN JAPAN

Avalon Travel
a member of the Perseus Books Group
1700 Fourth Street
Berkeley, CA 94710, USA
www.moon.com

Editor: Kathryn Ettinger
Series Manager: Elizabeth Hollis Hansen
Copy Editor: Deana Shields
Graphics Coordinator: Tabitha Lahr
Production Coordinator: Tabitha Lahr
Cover Designer: Tabitha Lahr
Map Editor: Kat Bennett
Cartographers: Chris Henrick, Kat Bennett
Indexer: Greg Jewett

ISBN-13: 978-1-61238-297-5
ISSN: 1548-6478

Printing History
1st Edition – 2004
3rd Edition – March 2013
5 4 3 2 1

KEEPING CURRENT

Although we strive to produce the most up-to-date guidebook that we possibly can, change is unavoidable. Between the time this book goes to print and the time you read it, the cost of goods and services may have increased, and a handful of the businesses noted in these pages will undoubtedly move, alter their prices, or close their doors forever. Exchange rates fluctuate—sometimes dramatically—on a daily basis. Federal and local legal requirements and restrictions are also subject to change, so be sure to check with the appropriate authorities before making the move. If you see anything in this book that needs updating, clarification, or correction, please drop us a line. Send your comments via email to feedback@moon.com, or use the address above.